JAMES I AND THE POLITICS OF LITERATURE

D0592060

Frontispiece to James I, *Workes* (1616).

JAMES I
AND THE POLITICS
OF LITERATURE

Jonson, Shakespeare, Donne, and Their

Contemporaries by Jonathan Goldberg

STANFORD UNIVERSITY PRESS   1989

Stanford University Press, Stanford, California
© 1983 by The Johns Hopkins University Press
Originating publisher: The Johns Hopkins University Press, 1983
Reissued by Stanford University Press, 1989
Printed in the United States of America
Cloth ISBN 0-8047-1739-7   Paper ISBN 0-8047-1740-0   LC 89-60357
Last figure below indicates year of this printing:
98   97   96   95   94   93   92   91   90   89

FOR STEPHEN ORGEL

Napoleon's historian Thiers, like other of his historians, tries to justify his hero by saying that Napoleon was drawn on to the walls of Moscow against his will. He is as right as other historians who seek the explanation of historic events in the will of one man; he is as right as the Russian historians who maintain that Napoleon was drawn to Moscow by the skill of the Russian commanders. Here, besides the law of retrospection, which represents the past as a preparation for future events, the law of reciprocity comes in, confusing the whole matter.
—Tolstoy, *War and Peace*

CONTENTS

ILLUSTRATIONS

ILLUSTRATIONS

PREFACE

THIS IS a study of the relationships between authority and its representations in the Jacobean period. As the prime example of the representation of authority, James I is a central figure in this investigation. Representation does not have only a political meaning, however, and in the course of the work I consider the writings of James I, his poetry as well as his political treatises and speeches; literature produced for the court, most notably Ben Jonson's masques; representations that were not necessarily directed to the royal view—plays for the public stage by Chapman, Massinger, Jonson, and Shakespeare, as well as poems and prose by Donne and Jonson. Visual representations that bear on public concerns are crucial, too, and I have taken as an important instance the genre of family portraits in the period.

The underlying thesis of this study is that language and politics —broadly construed—are mutually constitutive, that society shapes and is shaped by the possibilities in its language and discursive practices.[1] I use the terms language and politics in large ways. I intend *language* to subsume such terms as *writing, discourse, literature,* and *representation;* by *politics* I refer to those social processes in which relationships of power are conveyed. Writing represents authority; however, representation is not simply the transcription of power into other terms. The real requires realization; representation, understood in its full complexity—both as restatement and as recasting, replacing presentation—realizes power. This is as true for poets as for kings, and as true in explicitly political writing as in other forms of discourse. Such, at any rate, is the thesis that governs the pages that follow.

As the articulate and visible center of society, James I is my focus. I consider his writings, less to restate his ideas about kingship than to discover his means to articulate power. In the sonnet that opened his most important statement on kingship, the *Basilikon Doron,* James proclaimed himself a king by Divine Right, ruling in "the stile of *Gods*": it is that style that I seek to identify, and my procedure in the first half of this book is to work from that authorized, official, imperial style to the possibilities it offered for representation. I am concerned to show both the power and authority James derived from his mode of representation as well as the limits that were imposed upon him. The style was Roman, and one point I pursue entails the contradictions contained in that precedent. More broadly, I aim at exploring the contradictions inherent in language and the power and limitations conveyed by ruling contradictions; as a telling instance I consider

James's attempt to suppress Spenser for—as he claimed—misrepresenting his mother, Mary Queen of Scots, an episode that displays the king's belief in the power of representation, his attempts to control writing and to control by writing; but as I also suggest, the incident culminates in the king's need for writing, James authorizing for himself representations of the sort he wished to condemn in *The Faerie Queene.* The confrontation with Spenser points to one of the lines of power connecting royal authority and writing; it also serves to demonstrate the complex path that leads back from writing to authority.

Such lines of power are the concern throughout the pages that follow, and they explain why this book has a less familiar shape than might be expected from a study of literature and society. Political realities and literary representations—background and foreground, as they might be designated—are not kept separate here; nor is the division between political and supposedly apolitical literature entirely respected. In unfolding some of the shapes of social discourse in the Jacobean period, I have been led to ignore certain familiar modes of organizing historical knowledge—there is, for example, no chronological survey, either of political events or literary ones, nor have I kept separate the various authors. In the opening chapters, I tend to trace the lines of power by pursuing connections that can be made from the king's language to that of his poets. This is done because it seems easiest to identify the politics of language in explicitly political contexts. I focus on tropes crucial in James's writings. State secrets—*arcana imperii,* as Tacitus would call them—are the mysteries of state, the necessity for secrecy, silence, a declaration of absolute royal prerogative, and a clothing of actions in announcements of inscrutability. In a word, state secrets offer one definition of language—as ideology—and I take that clue as a way of working from the Jonsonian masque, constructed in imitation of the royal mystery, to a number of works at a distance from the court and the centers of power: *Volpone,* Donne's *Songs and Sonnets* and his *Devotions Upon Emergent Occasions,* as well as Stuart family portraits. These, admittedly, extend the territory of the political quite broadly; my justification lies in the trope of state secrets itself. It declares all territory as the king's, and its particular concern is the mystification of the body, the transformation of privacy into public discourse. The language of state secrets leads to the perception that without exactly subverting royal authority, the imitation of it could lend power to representation. Donne's lovers are absolutists as much as the king.

The mere imitation of the royal language, however, begins to suggest that such representations have the potential for subversion built into them, and in order to round out the picture of the contradictions inherent in the discourse of power I explore another trope in James's writing, the metaphor of the king as actor, displayed publicly. Taken in conjunction with the king's assertions of inscrutability and secrecy, the theatrical metaphor points to a contradiction within the king's discourse itself. And it is one, I argue, replicated in the political theory he presented, in the Roman ideas and ideals upon which he depended. In the chapter "The Theater of Conscience," I take James's ruling contradictions as a guide to the complexity of representation, even in court productions, which, in this context, can be seen to capitalize on the king's contradictions or, at the very least, to participate in them. The king who ruled by contradiction was also ruled by contradiction, and this ensured a latitude for the representation of power. From the king's imagined stage, one can move to real ones, and I consider Chapman's Bussy d'Ambois as a mirror of Jacobean absolutism and Shakespeare's Henry V as a realization of the royal trope that declares the inherent theatricality of power and the power of the theater.

The stage of history, the stage as history: the reversibility in the metaphor that declares all the world a stage, taken in conjunction with the official Roman style of the Jacobean period, explains the attention I give to Roman plays. These works might appear to be at some remove from the center of power; however, as hardly needs to be said, the links between the state and the theater were particularly strong in the period, and not only because the theaters had come under direct royal patronage with the accession of James. The theater was the public forum in which the royal style could be most fully displayed. The Roman plays of Jonson and Shakespeare focus, not surprisingly, on the question of power and its representation. With Massinger's *The Roman Actor,* it is finally impossible to separate the stage from the staging of power. Perhaps the most profound summation of the inherent theatricalization of Jacobean culture is offered in Shakespeare's *Measure for Measure,* a play that has been thought to have an especially close relationship to James I. In viewing that text as a representation of representation, I formulate one of the shapes of authority and authoring in the period. A review of the careers of Donne and Jonson provides two other models for this relationship, each grounded in Jacobean absolutism. In concluding with these three patterns, I mean to stress that there is no single way to describe the relationship between power and representation and to underscore that no directly functional bond links authority to literature.

The assumption of such functional relations has often vitiated studies of literature and society in the past. The belief that literature directly reproduces society has led, for instance, to topical identifications of figures in literary works, as if the only reality of literature inhered in such allusions. More sophisticated attempts have nonetheless worked from the assumption that history is inherently more real than its representations. In this study, however, the underlying thesis is that discursivity characterizes the real as fully as the imagined, and in describing the shapes of Jacobean discourse, the tropes of representation have guided my discussion. Although I have proposed some formulas here to cover the cases that follow, I do not offer theory as a substitute for or as separable from practice. The study that I present is not an exercise in theory; in my emphasis on contradiction I wish to register the dynamics of the social text.

This book has been written, in part, to discover more adequate ways of articulating the relationship between society and literature, and it follows from the final chapters of my book on Spenser, *Endlesse Worke: Spenser and the Structures of Discourse.*[2] In this undertaking, I have been guided and encouraged by the examples of others, by none more than Stephen Orgel, whose work on the literature of the Stuart Court, beginning with *The Jonsonian Masque*[3] and continuing through *The Illusion of Power,*[4] has shown the unquestionable power of representation for the representations of power. My understanding of the court has been further enhanced by the collaborative work of Orgel and Roy Strong, *Inigo Jones: The Theatre of the Stuart Court,*[5] as well as by other works of Strong, and by the profound essays of D. J. Gordon.[6] Just as I was completing this book, Graham Parry's *The Golden Age restor'd: The culture of the Stuart Court*[7] appeared, and I applaud it for its application and summary of such work; Parry's book complements my own, offering a survey of texts and events of the period that supports my analyses. I have learned much about the language of politics in the period thanks to J.G.A. Pocock and Kevin Sharpe,[8] two historians whose work, however different in many respects, has drawn attention to the languages in which politics is conducted. Although his formulations of such relationships do not always tally with my own, I have read Arthur Marotti's essays on the bearings of social life on private matters with profit; he sees acutely, as he puts it, that all literature in the Renaissance is the literature of patronage.[9] Louis Adrian Montrose's essays on the Elizabethan court and stage have impressed me in his ability to show the re-creative force of recreations (pastorals and plays).[10] Finally, I have had as a model Stephen Greenblatt's

Renaissance Self-Fashioning: From More to Shakespeare,[11] the most impressive and ambitious recent undertaking in the field. Greenblatt focuses on forces of containment as a means of describing the paradoxical relationship of texts to society; his aim, to reveal "the social presence to the world of the literary text and the social presence of the world in the literary text," I take to be exemplary. My aims are more modest, simply to begin a consideration of the politics of literature under James I in this investigation of some representative instances. If it were not too audacious, I would close by invoking the name of Michel Foucault.

NOTES

1. For a theoretical study that supports this view, see Michael J. Shapiro, *Language and Political Understanding: The Politics of Discursive Practices* (New Haven: Yale University Press, 1981).

2. *Endlesse Worke: Spenser and the Structures of Discourse* (Baltimore: Johns Hopkins University Press, 1981).

3. *The Jonsonian Masque* (Cambridge, Mass.: Harvard University Press, 1965).

4. *The Illusion of Power* (Berkeley and Los Angeles: University of California Press, 1975).

5. *Inigo Jones: The Theatre of the Stuart Court,* 2 vols. (London: Sotheby Parke Bernet and Berkeley and Los Angeles: University of California Press, 1973).

6. Collected and edited by Stephen Orgel as *The Renaissance Imagination* (Berkeley and Los Angeles: University of California Press, 1975).

7. *The Golden Age restor'd: The culture of the Stuart Court, 1603-42* (New York: St. Martin's Press, 1981).

8. For example, Pocock's *Ancient Constitution and the Feudal Law* (New York: W. W. Norton, 1967 [1957]), *Politics, Language and Time* (New York: Atheneum, 1973), and *The Machiavellian Moment: Florentine Political Thought and the Atlantic Republican Tradition* (Princeton: Princeton University Press, 1975); and, for example, Sharpe's introduction to *Faction and Parliament: Essays on Early Stuart History* (Oxford: At the Clarendon Press, 1978), and *Sir Robert Cotton, 1586-1631: History and Politics in Early Modern England* (Oxford: Oxford University Press, 1979).

9. "John Donne and the Rewards of Patronage," in *Patronage in the Renaissance,* ed. Guy F. Lytle and Stephen Orgel (Princeton: Princeton University Press, 1981), pp. 207-34; see also "'Love is not love': Elizabethan Sonnet Sequences and the Social Order," *ELH* 49 (1982): 396-428.

10. For example, "'Eliza, Queene of shepheardes,' and the Pastoral of Power," *English Literary Renaissance* 10 (1980): 153-82; "The Purpose of Playing: Reflections on a Shakespearean Anthropology," *Helios* n.s. 7 (1980): 51-74.

11. *Renaissance Self-Fashioning: From More to Shakespeare* (Chicago: University of Chicago Press, 1980). For a fuller consideration of the work of Greenblatt and Montrose, as well as a recent essay by Orgel, among others, see my review essay, "The Politics of Renaissance Literature," *ELH* 49 (1982): 514-42.

ACKNOWLEDGMENTS

I HAVE HAD the opportunity to present portions of this book to the Dartmouth Renaissance Seminar, thanks to Richard Corum, David Kastan, and Donald Pease; at meetings of the MLA, thanks to Stanley Fish, David Bergeron, and Arthur Marotti; at Berkeley, thanks to Stephen Greenblatt and *Representations;* at UCLA, thanks to Gordon Kipling; at Yale, thanks to Nancy Vickers and a conference on Renaissance Woman/Renaissance Man. Earlier versions of parts of this study have appeared in *ELH, Research Opportunities in Renaissance Drama,* and *Genre.*

The American Council of Learned Societies and the American Philosophical Society made it possible for me to have time to complete the manuscript and to do research abroad. I am grateful to them, and to the courtesy of the staffs at the Folger Shakespeare Library, the Dartmouth College Library, the Newberry Library, the British Library, the Bodleian, the National Library of Scotland, and the Scottish Records Office. I remain grateful to the Johns Hopkins University Press for supporting my work once again. For reading early drafts I thank Elizabeth Frank, Barbara Harman, and Robert Sanoff. Roger Lockyer guided me to manuscripts; Roy Strong helped again with illustrations; Joanna Dodsworth negotiated the Bodleian. Steven Mullaney and Kevin Sharpe have given stimulation and support. I record the pleasures of hospitality extended to me by Leonard Barkan in Chicago and by Nicholas Phillipson in Edinburgh.

In the most literal sense possible, this book would never have been completed without the care of Dr. Robert Hartley and the extraordinary talents of Dr. William H. B. Howard and their colleagues. Dr. Irvin H. Cohen deserves special mention, too. Jane Tompkins and Richard Newton have been remarkable friends. Stephen Greenblatt has been a generous reader, and I am inspired by the model his work provides. For their love, I thank my daughters, Julia and Abigail. In more ways than I could ever say, or than anyone could ever hope or expect, Stephen Orgel has sustained me. This book is rightly his.

JAMES I AND THE POLITICS OF LITERATURE

1. AUTHORITIES

There can be no possible exercise of power without a certain economy of discourses of truth which operates through and on the basis of this association. —Michel Foucault, *Power/Knowledge*

It isn't an easy thing to understand. It isn't that there's no right and wrong here. There's no right. —V. S. Naipaul, *A Bend in the River*

The real is as imagined as the imaginary. —Clifford Geertz, *Negara: The Theatre State in Nineteenth-Century Bali*

IN 1596, THE SECOND HALF OF *THE FAERIE QUEENE,* books IV through VI, appeared for the first time. There is no record of the reaction of the royal reader for whom Spenser's poem was intended, unless a 1598 letter from the queen and privy council urging the appointment of Spenser as Sheriff of Cork represents Elizabeth's recognition of her self-styled poet laureate. However, another monarch responded more directly and immediately to the poem. Robert Bowes, writing to Burghley in November 1596, recorded King James's reaction to the latest installment of *The Faerie Queene.*

> The K[ing] hath conceaved great offence against Edward [sic] Spencer publishing in prynte in the second book p[ar]t of the Fairy Queene and ix^th chapter some dishonorable effects (as the k. demeth therof) against himself and his mother deceassed. He alledged that this booke was passed with priviledge of her mats Commission[er]s for the veiwe and allowance of all wrytinges to be receaved into Printe. But therein I have (I think) satisfyed him that it is not given with such p[ri]viledge: yet he still desyreth that Edward Spencer for his faulte, may be dewly tryed & punished.[1]

James's desire that Spenser be tried and punished is not extraordinary; poets were subject to kings. This Spenser knew, and in the very canto to which James objected, the poet Bonfont is brought before the court and has his name "raced out" (V.ix.26.5), so that he appears named as Malfont instead.[2] The substitute name represents the poet's submission to the truth vested in the authoritative figure of the ruler, Mercilla, and it translates a social reality, that the poet's words are at the sovereign's command. James's desire for justice, we could say, is firmly inscribed in the text he condemns, as is his demand that the poet be subject to royal authority. Trial and punishment are exactly what Mercilla commands, and to be brought to trial

1

is tantamount to condemnation. In the law court of canto ix, first the poet and then Duessa—the figure for Mary Queen of Scots—are "raced out," erased and replanted into the sovereign truths that are the expressions of the royal command.

James's demand that the poet be subject to his ruler is voiced by the poet himself, and the king could as easily have found his position by reading Spenser as by knowing what might be done to a poet in fact. Spenser's scene barely distorts. Perhaps no Elizabethan poet's tongue was nailed to a post, as Bonfont's is in token that what comes from the poet's mouth belongs to the queen, but we might recall that Spenser's first printer, Hugh Singleton, was condemned to lose his hand because he had published a book that offended her majesty.[3] Public dismemberment—including the beheading of Mary Queen of Scots—is congruent with numerous actions that occur in book V of *The Faerie Queene*. It was one way in which the power of the monarch was displayed, inscribing itself on the body of the condemned. Those brought to trial and punishment became emblems of power, and their broken bodies testified to the overwhelming truth represented by the queen.[4]

Spenser's text records such truths. Thereby he is Bonfont—his tongue intact, but sacrificed to the queen nonetheless. James's demand is extraordinary, therefore, not in assuming that the poet's authority depends upon the sovereign, but in believing that the queen would bring Spenser to trial to satisfy James's version of the truth. James's complaint to Elizabeth is extraordinary because the poet's words have become the mediating terms in the struggle for power between the two monarchs—James continually wanting assurances that his mother's treason did not bar his way to the English throne, Elizabeth recalcitrantly withholding her wishes for a successor. Perhaps what is equally remarkable in this situation is James's assumption that the queen lies behind the poet's words and that his poem represents an official position. Again, we can find James's belief in Spenser's text; it is encouraged by the treatment of the poet Bon/Malfont. Yet, if we turn back to Bowes's letter, we might note that he denies this status to Spenser's text, insisting that the publication of the poem does not carry royal privilege. Further, the "dishonorable effects" are "as the k. demeth." Bowes clearly does not agree with the king's judgment. His letter records in its reservations what he takes to be two congruent pieces of misdeeming: James, he implies, has misread the text and has misunderstood the poet's relation to the queen. Yet, we might hasten to add, the misreading of "dishonorable effects" concerning himself and his mother is cer-

2

tainly encouraged by the poem—Duessa's crimes include treason and adultery, two very real hindrances to the succession to the English throne. As Angus Fletcher remarks, Duessa is a supercriminal.[5] The son of such a figure could not easily succeed to the throne of the queen that condemns her. From the opening of book V on, Spenser seems to want his reader to believe that his tongue, like Bon/ Malfont's, is at the royal command, and that his text is "privileged" to speak the truths Elizabeth wanted to hear. The "discourse of so divine a read" (V. pro. 11.7), the text of book V represents—Spenser insists—the reproduction of the queen's justice, her dreadful doom; the hero of the poem, Spenser concludes in the proem to book V, is not his invention but her instrument: "loe here thy *Artegall*," he writes (11.9); her hero, not his.

Thus James's desire that Spenser be tried and condemned represents two beliefs. First, he assumes that the poet stands for the queen, in which case, for Elizabeth to do James's bidding and suppress the poet would be tantamount to a declaration that James would succeed her. Second, he subscribes to Spenser's representation of the relationship of his text (and, through the example of Bon/Malfont, all texts presumably) to the royal word. These two beliefs mirror each other: on the one hand, the assumption that in reality the only authority and power is the sovereign's; on the other hand, the recording of that assumption in the poet's text. The poet thereby authorizes a view of society that denies him authority and makes his text simply a transcription of the social text. In this formulation, however, the poet's subscription is paradoxical, since in voicing it he appears to give the queen the very authority that he claims precedes his ability to write. It is perhaps such a paradox that leads Bowes to record his reservations about James's understanding of the social and poetic situation. These seem to imply that the poet's viewpoint need not be the official one. Yet, Bowes's statement cannot be read without remembering that he was the English ambassador to Scotland sending home a report for Burghley's eyes. The poet's text, the king's response, and the ambassadorial report raise a question. To put it bluntly: did James misread *The Faerie Queene* and misunderstand its relation to the discourse of power, or did Elizabeth, when she sponsored Spenser in Ireland, or did Spenser himself misrepresent? What sovereign truth does the text of *The Faerie Queene* represent? Where is authority to be located?

If we look at the trial and condemnation of Duessa, we may be able to answer these questions. To begin with, it helps to see that her trial follows the poet's, literally and figuratively; they are parallel

3

cases. Bonfont's perversion of language is a version of Duessa's treason and duplicitious sexual behavior: on the one hand, there are
"lewd poems" (ix.25.7); on the other, "lewd *Impietie*" (48.9), the
last of Duessa's crimes, which embrace treason, murder, incontinence,
and adultery. But just as criminality, the opposition to the laws and
norms of society, is an explicit state of contradiction, so, too, is the
response to it. Duessa's crime elicits a double response. Arthegall,
who elsewhere in book V is swayed by the plight of evil women and
finally succumbs to their embodiment in Radigund, is here implacable, and in his "constant firme intent" (49.4) he stands for justice.
Arthur, however, is moved by pity and, aroused by Duessa's beauty,
is "sore empassionate" (46.2). Even the just repudiation of Arthur's
response raises further contradictions. It lies in the advocacy of Zele,
whose charming tongue *procures* a just response (39.9). Hence,
Duessa's contradictions are matched not only by the divided responses of Arthur and Arthegall; there are also duplicitous implications in the appeal of Zele since "procure" suggests Duessa's lewd
crimes. Finally, Mercilla, passing judgment, is an exemplary figure of
contradiction. She ends the canto shedding tears for Duessa; in the
next canto, justice is done, and Duessa is dispatched. The poet imitates the ruthlessness of this decision in his summary treatment of
the criminal; half a stanza reports her death, ambiguously, and the
lines even suggest that Duessa condemns herself:

> When they had seene and heard her doome a rights
> Against *Duessa,* damned by them all;
> But by her tempred without griefe or gall,
> Till strong constraint did her thereto enforce.
> And yet even then ruing her wilfull fall.   (x.4.3–7)

The "strong constraint" upon Mercilla lies, presumably, in Duessa's
actions, which call out for the doom she wishes to reserve. Justice
here, as throughout book V, is an act of imposition. But here, the
sovereign's desire is itself limited by the demands of justice.

This is, of course, a fiction of sovereign power, the ascription of
limits upon the sovereign will that makes the exercise of power seem
authorized by others. As here, Duessa "damned by them all" appears
also self-condemned; or, to take another example, the traitors in
Henry V, who fall on their knees condemning themselves after Henry
has tricked them into confession; or, for one further instance, when
Shylock, standing for justice, gets the justice he demanded and not
the mercy that Portia appeared to offer. So, too, Mercilla weeps; but

we may think hers are crocodile tears, for Duessa is beheaded all the same. Authority is entangled, and enabled, by such fictions.

Looking at the trial of Duessa, we could say that the contradictions that she (or Bon/Malfont, for that matter) represents—the contradictions that are unsayings of the social fabric—are answered by the sustaining contradictions by which power is represented and by which it represents itself. In such a situation it is difficult to find the truth, difficult to unravel or to declare explicitly the differences between one set of contradictions and another. Even to represent this situation in a literary text means to subscribe such contradictions. Indeed, throughout book V it is no easy matter to decide where justice resides or to make judgments. In another court, the tables would be turned, and cases would be decided differently.[6] In the court of Mercilla, the relationship between mercy and justice is the sustaining contradiction. Mercy is the guiding principle. From it the sovereign derives her name and, congruently, the poet is renamed. Yet, although she is mercy, she enacts justice. And when the two values are considered, it is hard to know what their relationship is, or so the opening to canto x affirms:

> For if that Vertue be of so great might,
>   Which from iust verdict will for nothing start,
>   But to preserve inviolated right,
>   Oft spilles the principall, to save the part;
>   So much more then is that of powre and art,
>   That seekes to save the subiect of her skill,
>   Yet never doth from doome of right depart:
>   As it is greater prayse to save, then spill,
> And better to reforme, then to cut off the ill.   (x.2)

Mercy and justice are equally originary, parallel first principles, and although mercy is to be praised beyond justice, it cannot go beyond justice. Thus, although there is "greater prayse to save, then spill,/And better to reforme, then to cut off the ill" (x.2.8-9), nonetheless mercy cannot "from doome of right depart" (x.2.7). Hence, in book V, reformation and cutting off (i.e., decapitation, dismemberment) form a single act. These meet, too, in the pun on "raced": "but *bon* that once had written bin,/Was raced out, and *Mal* was now put in" (ix.26.4-5). Erasure (here, the poet's loss of tongue and name) is also replacement and replanting (elsewhere, the disjointed tongue is put on a pole), for the renamed and silent poet is a fruitful member of the "race" and has rejoined society in his deformed form.

5

He is reformed cut off. So, too, the death of Duessa satisfies justice and yet is done by Mercilla. The contradiction matches one the text wrestles with earlier, the one defining "that part of Iustice, which is Equity" (vii.3.4); equity would appear to be a part of justice from which justice is excluded, a part that is apart. This contradiction has an analogue in the narrative when Arthegall falls to the lures of Radigund, "overcome, not overcome" (v.17.1). Justice, we might conclude, decides contradiction, and decides it by contradiction. Two opponents, each claiming the truth, are answered by a judgment that denies one truth and affirms another. Yet the basis for judgment lies in an appeal elsewhere, to unchanging, ruling principles of law and mercy. For when the sovereign sits "in seate of iudgement" it is "in th'Almighties stead" (V. pro. 11.2), and the ruler occupies "th'Almighties everlasting seat" (x.1.7). (James was to impress this theme upon his Star Chamber audience in 1616, opening his speech to them by declaring that "Kings are properly Iudges, and Iudgement properly belongs to them from God: for Kings sit in the Throne of GOD, and hence all Iudgement is derived.")[7] Hence, power says it submits to a higher power passing judgment. Justice is a discursive power, the power of saying that something is true and, in saying it, making it so by denying that the speaker has this power. In this configuration, all poets have their tongues plucked out, all rulers sit in Jove's judgment seat and not their own.

According to Michel Foucault, sovereign power affirms itself by claiming that what it enacts is outside itself and transcendent.[8] The claim and the appeal to universal principles give language to the fact of power—that power is concomitant with might and that it acts as an imposition. Imposing words give power its strength. In book V of *The Faerie Queene,* the equation of might and right is openly presented in the first part of the poem; then it is obscured in the second half of book V by the concepts of equity and mercy. The obfuscating switch in language brings us closer to real power. And finally the equation reemerges clothed in the grand chivalric rescues of the closing cantos of book V, idealizing the discourse of *Realpolitik.* In these cantos, the events of history—the death of Mary Queen of Scots, English interventions in the Low Countries, the wavering English support for the French—are taken into a discourse which is at once the supreme fiction of the poem and the court. The poem claims an unequivocal univocality giving voice to the language of sovereignty, taking on a sovereign voice of power. But to take it on entirely, or fully to voice the sovereign's voice, is, in either case, to present a masterful, Machiavellian duplicity.[9] To adopt the voice of power is, in Foucault's definition, to speak beyond oneself, ascribing one's powers elsewhere, saying one thing and meaning another. The poet fulfills this paradigm when he says in the proem to book V that his fiction is the queen's. The central paradox here lies in the poet's ascription to the monarch the power to shape the text because it duplicates the monarch's assertion that power itself must be ascribed elsewhere (i.e., to God or to Justice). Power—the ruler's, the poet's—styles itself in denial; the poet points to the ruler, the ruler to abstract principles. Denying itself, contradiction defines the essence of the discourse of power. To voice sovereign power is to enter into duplicities, now twice removed. How, then, can the text be read? How is the truth to be found?

In book V, the answer lies in the concept of submission. Justice is an imposition, and to do justice to the text, one must submit to it. Only by submission are discriminatory differences clear and acts of judgment possible. Since the duplicities of Duessa match those of the queen, to find the truth when both parties can make equally potent claims—when, in the text, they share attributes and seem to mirror each other—one must submit to the power of authority. Here is an example: at the tournament held in honor of the marriage of Florimell and Marinell (canto iii), the bride is confronted with her alter ego and mirror image, the snowy Florimell. The figure of justice, Arthegall, appears disguised, assuming the shape of Braggadocchio, the equally false mate of the false Florimell. In that disguise, Arthegall proves victorious, shows up the false couple, who, thanks to his discriminatory act, disappear, leaving the true pair behind. Yet, this is no instance of clear right defeating falsity, for Arthegall's victory occurs when he is disguised as Braggadocchio. This seems to mean that his act of imposing the truth and making discriminations confirms his power, not his truth (his very form is a lie); it says that power makes truth, might makes right. This crude statement has its complex side, and the disguise points to it. For Arthegall is clothed in the image of falsity and yet affirms his truth. The episode sees through power to its sovereign fictions; yet these are not dismissed. The false *have* been routed. Later in the poem, those who enact justice will represent it clothed in the higher principles of equity and mercy. They, too, will make the false disappear. They, too, will enact the obliterative justice which leaves nothing but the truth—their truth—behind.

The claim then will be that the unjust bring destruction upon themselves, and that the sovereign does nothing but allow them to receive the justice they deserve. This is an argument that Arthegall

7

presents to the egalitarian giant early in book V, when he opposes
the giant's threats of change and stands firm in the unmoving principles that guide the cosmos. The meaning of his argument appears
most clearly at the end of the canto, however, when the giant and his
followers fall to the winnowing scythe of Talus, Arthegall's unmoving
iron man. In his eyes, this is no change at all. Arthegall affirms that
"all change is perillous" (ii.36.7) and insists that the cosmos as
ordered by its "great Maker" (40.8) has all things in place: "He
maketh Kings to sit in soverainty;/He maketh subiects to their powre
obay" (41.5-6). As his example shows, this is a displacement of the
"state of present time" (pro.1.1) to the heavenly state of unmovingness.[10] Arthegall speaks the language of state; in those terms, nothing
happens to the giant at all. The destruction at the end of the canto
fulfills the central symbolic event in the canto, the debate between
Arthegall and the giant crystallized when their words are weighed on
the scales of justice and the giant's prove insubstantial. Talus demonstrates the power of Arthegall's argument, the power to say that
nothing is disturbed, that the single truth ("truth is one, and right is
ever one" [ii.48.6]) triumphs over a contradiction that is no position
at all. There is room for only one truth. In 1609, addressing Parliament, James made the same point: "All novelties are dangerous as
well in a politique as in a naturall Body" (*Political Works,* p. 315).
What Arthegall constellated James naturalized.

Either way, these formulations embody *Realpolitik* and give it
language. Similarly, in another examination of the "state of present
time," Spenser's *View of the Present State of Ireland,*[11] Eudoxius's
Arthegallian precept that "all innovation is perilous" (p. 94) has the
support of Irenius's affirmation of the sword. For, Irenius says, "by
the sword I mean the royal power of the prince" (p. 95), as if thereby
the actual destruction of the Irish could become a metaphor, just as
in book V the metaphors of chivalric rescue, tournament, and the
like shadow real events. The ironies of this iron man's position, the
double-talk inevitable in the figure of Irenius as representative of
Ireland and of peace, meet in a staggering statement: since "we cannot apply laws fit to the people," he says, "we will apply the people
and fit them to the laws" (pp. 141-42). Thus, the laws will remain
unchanged, and the people will be reformed in submission. Heads
must fall if colonies are to be planted; reformation by the sword cuts
off evil. Talus's scythe is the cutting edge of the argument presented
in *A View of the Present State of Ireland.* And, not surprisingly, it
cuts two ways.

Entered in the Stationer's Register in 1596, the book was of-

8

ficially suppressed and did not appear in print until the reign of Charles I. This is surprising, especially when Spenser's *View* is considered, as it usually is, as a statement of the official attitude toward Ireland. Why should the government suppress a work that states its case? The answer can only be that it is a case that cannot be stated. In the *View*, as in book V of *The Faerie Queene*, the premises upon which sovereign power operates are laid bare. There is no shrinking from the implacable Talus, no shunning of the starving Irish. If Ireland is, from the first page of the *View*, a "savage nation," it nonetheless receives savagery in return; the English bring a police state, offering pacification as the path to peace. Genuine power would not admit its savagery, and although the *View* speaks the official language of law and reformation, it does not fail to reveal that decapitation, destruction, and constant surveillance are the facts upon which the language rests. The *View* thus offers a Machiavellian analysis of Ireland, and for that reason alone must be disallowed by a government that has invested itself in the language of eternity and in the myths of chivalry. The telling case here, as in book V, is the career of Lord Grey. He is praised in the *View*, and he is the model for Arthegall in book V; yet the official position on Lord Grey was censorship, recall, humiliation. Spenser clearly never got over that wrong, and twenty years later he was still mulling over the career of Lord Grey. It is an exemplary one, for Lord Grey was punished for doing his country's bidding, for fully unleashing the terrifying powers of England upon the Irish.

The wrong, of course, is the betrayal of the power that unleashes wrong. This is also shown in the *View*, for the work not only reveals what is done in Ireland and the language that represents those acts, but it also judges and exposes what is done. Hence, in examining "the chiefest abuses which are now in that realm," there is no denying that they "are grown from the English" (p. 63). The language of reform—with its accompanying imagery of planting, pruning, and so forth—is here recast, for the Irish have been deformed by what the English plant. The *View* constantly exposes English vices, rapacity, backbiting, envy, license, and the like. Its closing words, Eudoxius's hope that Irenius will soon produce his observations on Irish antiquities, points to a major strand throughout—that Irish origins have been effaced by the English. Repeatedly, he recovers this loss, pausing to record the foundations of manners and customs and, significantly, the etymology of words. Ireland is treated as if it were a foreign tongue that needs to be deciphered, and Irenius is constantly seeking roots. Countering the English desire to reform and replant (that is, to

9

cut off and supplant) is Irenius's desire to return to the "sweet re-
membrances of antiquities" (p. 37). Irenius here is the mouthpiece
for Ireland. Elsewhere he is the spokesman for its pacification. As
the official view, he can always persuade his interlocutor, Eudoxius,
whose name means truth—English truth, that is. Thus the ironies that
run through book V and that are attached to Arthegall's quest to
rescue Irena—the ironies of iron men in an iron age trying to restore
the golden times of just Astraea—are equally present in Spenser's
View. Yet the prose work was not published and, at the same time,
the queen sought to reward Spenser with an Irish commission—as an
arm of the law—for the second half of *The Faerie Queene.*

This suggests the difference between the two texts, for book V
cannot be read as a version of the official language of state. The very
act of reproduction of that language produces ironies and duplicities,
as we saw in the claim that the poem was the queen's. The poet's
voice is inevitably one with Bon/Malfont. In that contradictory voice,
book V is written. Hence, the forces that oppose Arthegall appear
presented as mirror images of what they contradict: if the Soldan is a
sunlike deity (sol = sun), so is the herculean hero; if injustice (Adicia
= A-Dike) is imposition, so is justice (might = right). Love opposes
law, but in a figure like Radigund law and love meet in a fearful
image of the regiment of women, a force which the poem keeps attempting to suppress but cannot, for sovereign power is invested in a
woman, the queen, and fortune and justice are female, too. One state
answers another. Attempting to move out of time and into eternal
principles, Arthegall ends instead by temporizing, lending support to
Sir Burbon in just the manner in which he condemned that false
knight, ends, too, being ruled by a time scheme imposed upon him
by Grantorto, and done in by the defamation of two hags, Envie and
Detraction, who nonetheless manage to sway Gloriana.

Book V closes with those hags screaming and with Arthegall
restraining Talus; for their words, however foul, are the official line,
and it would violate justice to demand justice. Similarly, earlier
Britomart had had to wipe from her mind the thought that Arthegall had betrayed her (a perfectly plausible reading of the Radigund
episode); Talus had imposed this just view upon her. That understanding leads to the even more terrifying vision in Isis Church in
which Britomart sacrifices herself for the sake of Arthegall's destiny.
These are the final moments for her in the poem, for having rescued
Arthegall she submits to him fully, and thereby obliterates herself
and her power. Having assumed the voice of power, book V insists
on the justice of this act; yet, as insistently, a voice of contradiction

is raised screaming at the injustice of such suppression. At the end, that voice belongs to the two hags, who rightly name Arthegall's crimes—yet, when they are heard by the official powers, that voice becomes fully hypocritical, turning a humane response into a monstrosity. The voice of contradiction is absorbed as the official line. Such a transformation is prepared for shortly before the end of book V, in Arthur's last exploit, his defeat of the monster in the church of Gerioneo. The church offers another version of the temple of Isis, and the monster here is modeled on the crocodile there. Both undergo similar transformations. The crocodile goes from being an emblem of fraud to being a sign for equity and a figure for Arthegall. The monster is at first a version of the sphinx, the riddling presenter of the puzzle of humanity; then it presents its "slight" (xi.25.7):

> An hideous monster . . .
> Whose ugly shape none ever saw, nor kend,
> That ever scap'd: for of a man they say
> It has the voice, that speaches forth doth send,
> Even blasphemous words, which she doth bray
> Out of her poysnous entrails, fraught with dire decay.
>
> (xi.20.2,5-9)

A male voice in a female body, the monster is transformed into a hermaphroditic form that figures power throughout *The Faerie Queene*, like the Venus of the fourth book or the sovereign in the proem to the sixth, a queen who is also a prince.[12] The inescapable nature of power is represented by this monstrosity in which the language of mastery is joined to the form of submission.

When we return to James's complaint and possible misreading, the queen's reward, and the poet's position, we can see better why these are such complicated matters. Contradictions govern politics and poetics at once. They are essential to the discourse of power. Commenting on the early years of James's rule in England, a writer viewing James's near escape from treasonous plots, and his furthering of favorites like Somerset, concluded, "Thus may wee see that setled governments doe cherish in themselves their owne destructions, and their own subjects are oftentimes cause of their owne ruine, unlesse God of his mercy prevent it."[13] The voice of the monster—is it the voice of the poet?—inscribes the inevitability of that cherished self-destructiveness as the sustaining condition of power. Yet neither James nor Elizabeth heard power unspeaking itself in book V of *The Faerie Queene*. Both read the text in the light of their sole and sovereign truth, failing to see its supporting contradictions. James's ability

11

to spot treason everywhere except in those he cherished is a cognate phenomenon, as was Elizabeth's insistence on transforming events into the language of romance. Both illuminate the blind spots of power that met when the two sovereigns confronted each other over a text that replicated their power. *The Faerie Queene* speaks the language of power, hedging itself round with disclaimers, denying the poet's voice in order to proclaim the truth, a truth that is not its own.[14]

Although we are hardly in a position to summarize all the complexities of authority that are involved in this meeting of poet and monarch, certain points emerge. There can be no such thing as an unambiguous expression of power, for it is precisely in ambiguity that power resides, making it as capable of direct as of indirect action. This is as true of real power as of represented power, whether such representation lies in the words of monarchs or of poets. And it is precisely because of these inherent contradictions—contradictions that sustain authority—that the meeting of opposing authorities (the king and the poet; the queen and the king) should not resolve the question of authority but complicate it. The relations of power do not flow in a single direction, nor does the circuit easily come to an end. The sustaining of fictions requires continuous readjustments (this cannot be admitted, however, if absolute power is being affirmed). A kind of infinite regress is established in which the affirmation of power is cloaked in denials, and the assumption of authority is effected by erecting one's truth as absolute and submitting to the invention. Kings call such truths God or justice; poets call them kings. Tangled as the knots are in the meeting of Spenser and James, then, the situation points to the elementary conditions behind the assumption of authority and the declaration of absolute truth and power.

WHAT is also extraordinary in the moment when James attempted to impose his truth on the poet is that the truth of that moment had not even always been his truth. Attempting in 1596 to save the memory of his mother, he wished also to rewrite history and his role in her death. Spenser had already rewritten history. In one crucial detail, the trial of Duessa does not replicate Mary's. It presents Mercilla in the seat of judgment, and thereby implicates her. Elizabeth, on the other hand, had absented herself from Mary's trial just as she had avoided meeting Mary during all the years of her English imprisonment. At Mary's trial, an empty chair represented Elizabeth (see fig. 1)—a fitting symbol, for it was a chair of state (it is labeled

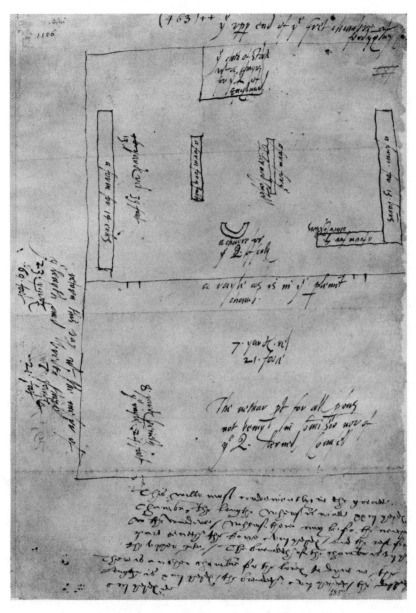

Figure 1. Drawing of the plan of the trial of Mary Queen of Scots.
Copyright British Library.

in the contemporary plan as "a chayr for ye Q of England" placed below "ye cloth of state"), the place where the sovereign sits in place of God. It took justice out of the queen's hands. The empty throne could well stand as an emblem for James's role in the trial, too, for it was on the throne that would be empty after Elizabeth died that he placed his hopes. Mary sat facing the throne as if it were to up-braid her for her treasonous desire for it and to affirm the absent power of the sovereign. Behind her back, her son was angling for that place and was ready to give her up to have it. By the time she came to trial, he had done so. James's protest in 1596 hides his part in the events of ten years past. He continued to act in this way. When he came to the throne of England, one of his first acts was to send a velvet pall to cover his mother's tomb; nine years later, her body was exhumed and placed beneath a monument facing Queen Elizabeth's in Westminster Abbey. In her final resting place, Mary lay next to the kings and queens of England, and her treasonous desires had been suppressed. As James wrote to the Dean of Peterborough on 20 September 1613 ordering the exhumation of Mary's body, his duty to "our dearest mother" compelled him to erect a memorial "in our Churche of Westminster, the place where the kings & Queenes of this Realme are usually interred."[15]

James's filial devotion—once his mother was safely dead—fulfilled the image of mother and son that Mary cherished. Although the king and his mother had been separated when he was ten months old and never saw each other again, Mary preserved the show of a sentimental attachment to her son. A painting from this period seems to represent the relationship as Mary might have hoped it to be, and as James was willing to make it once she was dead, a double portrait dated 1583 (fig. 2). In this fantasy, mother and son meet as alter egos. Between them is a crown and below them a rose. Beside each of them is a rubric; one names her as queen of Scots, the other him as king, in fact a title Mary refused him. Yet it is virtually the only note of discord in a picture that projects a joint rule, the association that James and Mary occasionally envisioned. Although costume does not stress identity, it is the only sign of difference, for the two look like each other (one face served as a model for both), and they are parallel in stance and in hands and eyes. This picture conveys hauntingly the son as mirror of his mother, the king in an essential position of dependence and obligation. At best, he is his mother's equal, but the double portrait suggests that equality is achieved by reproduction, literally and figuratively. This may stanch any suspicions about James's legitimacy. Still she has made him what he is.

14

Figure 2. *Mary Queen of Scots and James VI* (1583).

From the collection of the Duke of Atholl at Blair Castle. Copyright National Galleries of Scotland. Photograph by Tom Scott.

This was Mary's view. During their twenty-year separation she continued writing to him as if the narrow thread that bound them together had not been untied. Yet he was king because she was not queen and the throne of Elizabeth would be his if it were not hers. During her last years, he was corresponding with Elizabeth and had broken off communication with his mother. A letter of 27 June 1585 can stand beside the portrait to suggest how James had replaced Mary. Thanking Elizabeth for a gift of horses that touched him deeply (hunting was always his chief pastime), he writes that they come as if "from sum *alter ego*" rather "than from any strainge and forraine prince." The mirror portrait can be placed beside this statement of identification. An even more startling one follows. In return for this gift, James offers Elizabeth whatever she desires, gifts "to be

15

used and imployed by you as a loving mother would use hir naturall
and devoted chylde." Nor does he stop there; gifts are not the only
child, for James offers himself. Finally he addresses the queen as
"madame and dearest mother" and labels himself her "brother and
sonn"[16]–brother monarch–a fraternal equality and identification
in that–and yet her child. James had replaced his mother with
Elizabeth; angling for her inheritance, he sacrificed his mother for it.

In the letters that follow, Elizabeth writes of the conspiracies
against her and appeals to James to support her, since he knows
from his experience what it is to be the object of treasonous attempts. "By saving of her [Mary's] life the[y] would have had mine,"
she writes, and James goes along with her account. In response to
her letter announcing the death of Mary–and insisting that she had
no part in it–James absolves the queen ("I darr not wronge you so
farre as not to iudge honorablie of youre unspotted pairt thairin"),
expecting that what he hears further from her will be to his "full
satisfaction" and will serve "to strenthin and unite this yle."[17] There
is no difficulty in penetrating these hopes.

In 1596, James leaped to the defense of his mother and spoke
out against the accusations leveled at her; yet his pretext was the
portrait of Duessa and her treatment by Zele, and the object of
James's protest was the poet Edmund Spenser. He deserves trial and
punishment, James claimed, that inevitable sequence. Ten years before, in the face of the real event, not its representation, James had
withheld any comment and acquiesced. Reality was being reconstructed then; one queen for another. And in 1596, reality was once
again being reshaped, and the poet was being called into court to
answer the royal prerogative. James's action in 1596 testifies to the
intimate connection between sovereign power and discourse, and the
need for power to inscribe its truth. Spenser's poem presents a reality
close to that James countenanced in his secret letters to Elizabeth–a
version in which Mary is supercriminal, and in which both Elizabeth
and James have no complicity. Mary condemns herself. But, by
1596, James sought to replace that picture with another, one more
like the portrait of loving mother and son. James wished to extend
his innocence to his mother; having sacrificed her, he now wished to
redeem her–at the poet's expense. Several years later, in a new preface to the *Basilikon Doron,* he assured his English subjects of his love
for them despite those who would blacken his mother's name and
memory. In 1603, the king could safely change his tune–and could
expect others to follow his lead. It was not the mere fact of power
that made this possible. For with the power came a new set of

truths, rewritings of history to accommodate the new sovereign. Yet the sovereign also submitted to discourses that preceded him. We need only recall the divided responses of Arthegall and Arthur at the trial of Duessa for it tells us that at any moment contradiction governs facts and writing. On the one hand there was James's secret correspondence with the queen; on the other were his official statements and ambassadorial missions on his mother's behalf. The portrait of a united mother and son matches hidden alliances. Mary herself offered two possible interpretations: as the image of treason and the image of martyrdom. At her beheading, she managed to transform one into the other.[18] James was subject to these versions of her, too. He capitalized on the first and turned to the second when it served his interest to do so; and when he had power to act as if it were the whole story, he did so. The monument in Westminster Abbey effaces—erases—his part in Mary's death; it represents a royal answer to *The Faerie Queene.* So secure was the king in his sovereign truth that there was not a murmur of protest when *The Faerie Queene* was reprinted at the same time. Spenser's poem had ceased to pose a threat.

The Poet-King

James's protest in 1596 has another dimension as well, for James knew the power of discourse and the connection between power and discourse before he voiced his demand to Elizabeth. The king was a poet. His relationship to language provided a primary identity, one that Ben Jonson, for example, used in his first epigram celebrating the king:

> How, best of Kings, do'st thou a scepter beare!
> How, best of *Poets,* do'st thou laurell weare!
> But two things, rare, the *Fates* had in their store,
> And gave thee both, to shew they could no more.
> For such a *Poet,* while thy dayes were greene,
> Thou wert, as chiefe of them are said t'have beene.
> And such a Prince thou art, wee daily see,
> As chiefe of those still promise they will bee.
> Whom should my *Muse* then flie to, but the best
> Of Kings for grace; of *Poets* for my test?
>
> (*Epigrammes:* 4)[19]

In the economy of Jonson's discourse, the same language celebrates the power of both roles, monarch and poet, just as a single crown

17

marks them. Playing both parts, the king goes beyond limits. Even these are discursive, for his early poetic accomplishments are such as were *said* to be those of supreme poets; his later performance as king makes good what other monarchs *promise*. And the king's inscription into history, a poet first and then a king, is further inscribed. Not only does he fulfill the dictates of others and of the Fates, he is the word found out in Jonson's poem, where his muse ultimately flies. The root of *authority* is *author*.

James's poetic career began in 1584, when the eighteen-year-old monarch published his *Essayes of a Prentise, in the Divine Art of Poesie,* a collection that included translations from DuBartas and others, a poetic treatise, and an allegorical poem, *The Phoenix.* In 1591, a second, similar volume of poems followed, *Poeticall Exercises at Vacant Hours.* In addition, several manuscripts, one in Prince Charles's hand, house more of the king's poems; he continued to write almost to the end of his life, although as king of England he chose to be a coterie poet rather than to put in any appearances before the English public.[20] It is probably fair to say as Jonson does that James replaced one role with another, that once he had the English crown, he could abandon the poet's laurels, at least before the public eye. Yet, in this career, there is also continuity; as Jonson's poem suggests, the powers of poet and king are parallel. James's poems bear this out. They exercise the discourse of power and the power of discourse.

One of James's introductory poems in his *Schort Treatise* on poetics is a "Sonnet Decifring the Perfect Poete." In it, the poet declares his quick-wittedness, his learning that "may be spyit [spied]" (1:69, line 4) and that gives him "everlasting fame" (line 10) in the eyes of his cowed audience. Thirty years later, James railed at Parliament in similar terms. In a poem addressed to the members of the House of Commons, he promises swift revenge—or justice as he recasts his threat—for their impertinence in trespassing on his prerogative; he tells them that he does not need their counsel, that he can rely on his "owne voice" (2:190, line 162), and that if he unleashes his powers they will be devastated: "If I once bend my angrie browe / Your ruyne comes" (lines 167–68). Although the two texts deciphering perfect poethood and royal power are not exactly parallel, they are certainly akin. In both, the forcefulness of the speaker lies in the imposition that his words are expected to make as the expression of his powerful mind. The wonder of his first audience is matched by the obedient silence demanded of the second. Yet there are verbal limits placed on these powers: in the latter text, the royal power re-

18

mains a threat confined to words; in the first, the king's assumption of perfection turns, in the final lines, to a request to the gods that he may come to be the perfect poet he has described. Although "you must submitt" (line 27) is what he tells the commoners, it also marks his own condition when the poet submits to the gods—or the king to God. Hence, in *The Trew Law of Free Monarchies* (1597),[21] the king declares that he is not bound to his people (rather, the opposite), yet hastens to add that this does not mean that "the world . . . [was] ordained for kings" (p. 69); God is the "sharpest schoolemaster" for kings who transgress. So the king must be left to heaven; on earth, however, he declares in the poem to the House of Commons, "by mee you shalbe school'd" (line 65).

James begins his poetic treatise by defining his imagined—and ideal—audience; he seeks neither the ignorant nor the wise nor the inquisitive; all these are ineducable because they either know nothing or think they know all, or think they are capable of such knowledge. Rather, it is "to the docile bairns of knawledge" (1:66) that he directs his work, to those who will submit. Lurking behind these words is the patriarchalism he will unleash in the *Trew Law;* also predicted is the king's behavior with such favorites as Robert Carr. "Carr hath all favours," Lord Thomas Howard wrote to Sir John Harrington in 1611, "the King teacheth him Latin every morning, and I think some one should teach him English too; for, as he is a Scottish lad, he hath much need of better language. The King doth much covet his presence."[22] The boy's presence is enhanced by his docility, being taught to speak. Royal power expresses itself by giving others words. In the *Schort Treatise,* this linkage of discourse to power enforces a view of poetry tied to rules; the ideal of regularity in verse is also a version of social decorum, all things in their place, unmovable, "ever framing zour reasonis, according to the qualitie of zour subiect" (1:76, chap. iii). The poet bound to represent his "subiect" exactly is thereby subjected to a law of decorous representation and to the reproduction of the structure of society. He is in fact restrained from the actual, mimetic representation of politics, since that would involve a transgression of prescribed limits: "Materis of commoun weill . . . are to [sic] grave materis for a Poet to mell in" (1:79, chap. vii), "except Metaphorically," James adds, reinvesting him with powers anew. James returns to the poet those powers of language that allow him to go beyond mere representation. For James, however, even such license carries with it stylistic subjection.

James conforms to these limits; his prescription also describes his practice. His published poems only rarely meddle with political matters, and they are stylistically limited. Hence, despite James's claim in the opening of his treatise to be writing a work suited to the times and to the particular genius of Scots, his treatise in fact is heavily indebted to the plain style poetics of George Gascoigne, whose *Certayne Notes of Instruction* (1575) has a similar emphasis on regularity and invention. And, although James eschews translation in the treatise, he is, in his poetic debut, a translator (mainly, as noted above, of DuBartas); indeed, the decorum he favors is nothing but an art of translation. The treatise proposes subjection and submission to language. James begins his poetic career espousing plain style poetics, and if the poem labeled in manuscripts as his earliest is indeed that, he was at first, at his best, an accomplished plain style poet. But he did not remain in this mode; he also wrote sonnets with a Spenserian rhyme scheme, and soon his matter matched his form, as in so self-consciously Sidneian and golden a poem as the sonnet that opens with these lines:

> Not orientall Indus cristall streames;
> Nor frutfull Nilus, that no bankes can thole;
> Nor golden Tagus; wher bright Titans beam[e]s,
> Ar headlongst hurled, to vew the Antartike Pole;
> Nor Ladon (*which* sweet Sidney dothe extole)
> While it, th'Arcadian Beauties did embrace:
> All thease cannot, thee, nameless thee, controle.　(2:118, #32)

But this was not the final phase in James's career as a poet; as the lines cited above from the poem to the House of Commons might suggest, the last stage of that career was shaped by the model of Ben Jonson. At last his poems speak directly to and of society. Allegory, translation, metrical constriction, and decorous invention are left behind. James's development as a poet reflects the history of poetry from the 1570s to the 1620s. As Jonson's epigram declares, James was in the hands of the Fates, those weavers of the word, when he became, as Jonson says, "chiefe" poet and king. Destiny is what is spoken. The king was subjected, shaped, imposed upon, by the language in which, and with which, he attempted to impose himself on others, to shape their minds to match his.

Spenser's text was not the only one that James wished to rewrite. Discursive imposition became an explicitly political concern. In a poem on a comet seen in 1618, James instructs "you men of Britaine," insisting that they "misinterpret not with vaine Conceit" (2:172, line 7) the heavenly sign; the sign is written in "*letters* such as no man can translate" (line 10). Reality is seen as a text written

20

by a master poet who refuses the interpretations of common understanding. James here is the spokesman for the divine author, and
takes God's authority upon himself. In the *Trew Law of Free Monarchies,* his textual imposition is even more striking. There, in order to
prove that all kings—even the worst—are sent by God, and therefore
cannot be resisted, he takes as his text a passage from Kings in which
Samuel details the abuses of kingship to the Israelites who are
clamoring for monarchical rule.[23] In James's reading, Samuel's anti-
monarchical speech becomes a defense of kings; according to James,
the prophet is testing the Israelites, so that in insisting upon having a
king they have bound themselves to obey even the worst of kings
without murmuring. James's reading of the text demonstrates the
confluence of power and discourse; it makes an interpretive point
that is cognate with his politics. "Kings were the authors and makers
of the Lawes, and not the Lawes of the kings" (p. 62), James argues.
As he was to reiterate often, he was *lex loquens* (*Political Works,* pp.
291, 299, 309, for example), as Bacon said, an animator of the dead
letter (BL, Harl. Ms. 2232, fol. 73). The authority he claims as king
parallels the authoritarian imposition he brings to the text. God's
word becomes the king's word, but it is also the king's support. His
power lies in these authoritative words; he makes these words the
image of his power. Love and obey are the guiding principles for
James; he is to love, his subjects are to obey. Love is shown in the
free gifts of this generous schoolmaster—in giving his understanding
and his words to his people; obedience is shown by the absolute subscription of his audience to his words. "I doe desire noe more of
yow/But to knowe mee as I knowe yow/Soe shall I love, and yow
obey" (2:186, lines 99-101). The mutuality of knowledge in these
lines to the House of Commons is an illusion; the people's knowledge
is what he has given them, imposed upon them. Love and obedience,
the fruits of this supposedly equal love, point to the difference between the king and his subjects.

The poems are throughout exercises in the combined powers of
the poet-king. Characteristic is "A dreame on his Mistris my Ladie
Glammis" (2:82 ff., #9). The poem begins by recounting a dream in
which his mistress appears; when he awakens, a gift presented in the
dream remains behind. So, although the poet confesses "that Idee
oft/My ravish'd minde dois feede" (lines 83-84), in this case, the
idea is a fact, the gift that remains. For the rest of the poem, these
tokens and attributes of the lady are examined and their allegorical
meaning is read. The dream and the gift have licensed the activity of
mind and understanding displayed, and this activity is offered to the

21

reader of the poem as its substantial and real gift. The dream has become reality, ravishing ideas are facts, a conclusion like that of another poem: "This spak Apollo myne,/All that thou seikis, it sall be thyne" (1:82). Fulfillment in love involves possession of the loved object; this is also what love means in the *Trew Law* when James claims ownership of his subjects.

Repeatedly, the poems attempt to impose the royal view and recast the world in the shape of the king's desires. So, in "A Sonet against the could that was in January" (2:116, #31), the king rails against the weather, claiming that it results from a perverse coupling of Saturn and Janus: "Curst bee that love and may't continue short/That kills all creaters and doth spoile our sport" (lines 13-14). Royal pleasures, the final words intimate, are the highest reality. Saturn's union is also a political uprising, and the "cancred Kinge of Creta land" (line 3) has overstepped his boundaries. More overtly political is the sonnet "Upon occasion of some great disorders in Scotland" (2:119, #33); however, the stance remains precisely the same. Rebels are like the bad weather in January, and the curse here is directed at the "cruell constellation" (line 1) under which he was born. "O miserable Mother" (line 3), he begins, and he arrives at the "wise Pierides" (line 7). "In vaine descended I of Royal race/*Which* by succession made a King of me" (lines 11-12). In the course of the poem, his identity as king and his identity as a poet are intertwined in the acts of his "vain" mother and the muses who brought him and his words into the world. The stars and not ourselves make us powerful or limit our powers, James seems to lament. When we remember why he took Spenser to task, we may find that more comprehensible in light of this poem in which he curses his mother and the muse.

A "free" monarch was how he styled himself in his first treatise on kingship, and it was the freedom of the mind that he addressed in his supposed first poem, "Since thought is free, thinke what thou will" (2:132, #36). The invitation to free thought in the poem is self-directed and in fact is severely limited. Thought is free only so long as it remains thought: "Thought unrevealed can doe no evill/Bot wordes past out, cummes not againe" (lines 3-4). The poem allows a free kingdom of the mind, of words held in but not permitted exposure where they may do harm or suffer it. In the world, one must "be cairefull" (line 5). A virtue can be made of this necessity, however; one can "pleas thy selfe with thy concaite/And lett none knowe what thou does meane" (lines 7-8). When James considers the nature of a "free and absolute *Monarche*" (*Trew Law*, p. 54), the coupling of adjectives says it all. The free king is not bound to his subjects, certainly not by any contract. Rather, the king's power derives from Fergus, the Irish monarch who conquered Scotland (pp. 61-62). (Thinking ahead, James adds that the rulers of England owe their powers to the Norman conquest [p. 63].[24]) The king's freedom consists in his ability to please himself (to have the pleasures the cold would deprive him of), to impose the kingdom of the mind upon his subjects. In the Maitland quarto manuscript of the king's earliest poem, it is titled "The Subject," but the king's subjection is not the entire burden of the poem. It ends with the hope that by holding back and by not revealing thoughts, actions in which intentions are fulfilled may become possible. The poem ends, that is, with a piece of Machiavellianism linking free thought, self-pleasing, and the "houpe to vanquise in the end" (line 18), the king, another Fergus, imposing will and making it real. As the subtitle of the *Trew Law* announces, its scope is *The Reciprock and Mutuall Duetie Betwixt a Free King, and His Naturall Subjects.* James's poems are exercises in freedom and subjection.

In James's development as a poet, these processes become increasingly explicit. In *The Phoenix,* for instance, an allegorical poem about the king's relationship with Esmé Stuart, and his eventual downfall, everything is disguised. The poem makes use of the medieval device of the beast (here, bird) fable, although by casting his cousin as a singular bird he is exalted above all mere animals; in the allegory, the phoenix is female, a marvel envied, scorned, and finally forced to flee and die, self-consumed and self-perpetuating. In the poem, the speaker is a kind of onlooker; such disengagement matches the stance in the verses on free thoughts. Here, too, the speaker holds back. It is not difficult to penetrate the allegory, however. The bird's feathers are lovingly described to displace what the king would say; the bird is female to disguise the gender. And since it is both a bird and female, it can be presented at one telling moment running to the speaker for protection:

> When she could find none other save refuge
> From these their bitter straiks, she fled at last
> To me (as if she wolde wishe me to iudge
> The wrong they did her) yet they followed fast
> Till she betuix my leggs her selfe did cast.
>
> (1:50, lines 162-66)

A few lines later the speaker's legs are bleeding (lines 171-72). It is not difficult to imagine the self-pleasing thoughts that move the poem. It becomes clear, too, why the chill in January is due to the coupling of Saturn and Janus that deprives the king of his pleasures. In later poems, the sexual theme is more explicit. In a series of poems about Buckingham, James sings his praises, and the conclusion of one poem leaves little to the imagination: "The Buckes & Stagges in fatt they seeme to smile:/God send a smilinge boy within a while" (2:177, #13).

Free and absolute: this meant that others—Spenser, Elizabeth, the commoners—were seen either as hindrances to be overcome or cursed. Ultimately the transforming powers of discourse absorbed them, erasing all opposition. The phoenix hides between his legs; but in the poems to Buckingham, the royal favorite becomes an extension of the royal self, and prayers for the fertility of Buckingham's land and loins extend the royal progeny and prodigality. More negative processes appear in James's amatory poems—that is, in the poems addressed to women (often to Queen Anne). In the *Treatise*, James had remarked that of all subjects, love is the most hackneyed, and only a *via negativa* and announcements of inability could freshen the tired tropes of courtship (1:78). These remarks may be more revealing than the king meant them to be; at any rate, they fully describe the *Amatoria*. For love poems, they are exceptionally antifeminine, and conventional complaints about the coldness and hardness of the lady's heart often turn into bitter invective (this is more overt and explicit in later poems, for instance the one sending London ladies back to the country where they belong [2:178, #14a]). In one poem, the mistress is implied to be unworthy (2:76, #7, line 42); in another she is likened to "hatefull Juno" (2:68, #1, line 13). At the conclusion of these amorous poems, a confession of sorts is made. "My Muse hath made a willful lye I grante,/I sung of sorrows never felt by me" (2:78, lines 58-60), and the reason for these lies is that he wrote the poems at Anne's request. The palinode lays the blame on the queen for his presentation of an intractable mistress. We have seen this strategy before; it made Mary/Duessa responsible for her own crimes and death. James's confession confesses nothing and leaves him, like Mercilla, absolutely free of fault. Elsewhere, the strategy of absorption is used; in a poem on the absence of his mistress from court (2:80, #8), the speaker dallies with hopes that "presence absence shall amend" (line 58), and then a series of metaphorical exchanges makes it so. The absent mistress becomes the sun; female becomes male; and the sun rises at the close. So, too, the dream poem about Lady Glammis (#9) announces that "in absence are ye present still" (line 265), and that lady, too, becomes the sun. No "Monarch may/Resist a womans might," the

24

poem concludes, especially when her power is imagined as his. Throughout the poems the king of poets takes Apollo, god of the sun, to be his god. It was an identification that James clung to, and when he entered London at the beginning of the new year (in March 1604), he was hailed repeatedly as *roi soleil.*

James's attacks on women explore the strategies of discursive power, the negations and disclaimers and the annihilative erasures that ensure the monarch's freedom and truth. They form a particularly striking episode in James's poetic career, not least because they further illuminate the protest against Spenser. Once again, we may suspect the poet of coming too close to thoughts James harbored and wished to suppress. The ambivalences of the *Amatoria* permit attitudes that James could disclaim. Take, for instance, the identification of the mistress with "hatefull Juno" (2:68, #1, line 13) mentioned a moment ago. It allows James epic fulminations (Aeneas is the model) against incorrect marriages and the mother goddess who sanctifies such unions. As that double portrait of James and Mary had insisted (see fig. 2) it was his mother that made succession possible. His bride ensured the line. Yet these ties made the king that much less absolute and free. "From sacred throne in heaven Empyrick hie/A breathe divine in Poets brest does blowe," the first of the *Amatoria* announces (2:68, line 1); similarly, the divine king claimed he occupied God's throne in the introductory poem to the *Basilikon Doron* and elsewhere. Such claims to absolute power were undercut by the opposing power of Juno. James imposes his power on her. By the third of the *Amatoria,* "hatefull Juno" has become "our earthlie Juno"(line 2)—Queen Anne—and the king styles himself "happie Monarch sprung of Ferguse race" (line 9). He invokes the ideal of political suppression for his conquest in the realm of love. The transformation of opposition into suppression and subjection has occurred here, precisely the same transformation that Mary Queen of Scots underwent: from his opposition to Spenser's portrayal to his revision of the queen; from the queen as menacing force to the queen suppressed by the force of his discourse. Perhaps at this point we might do well to quote a report from M. de Fontenay, Mary's envoy to the Scottish court in 1584: "Of one thing only I am astonished; that he has never asked anything about the Queen [Mary], neither of her health, nor of the way she is treated, nor of her servants, nor of what she eats or drinks, nor of her recreation, nor of any similar matter, and yet, notwithstanding this, I know that he loves and honours her much in his heart."[25] M. de Fontenay ends with some wishful thinking, assuming that he had penetrated the unexpressed "free" thoughts

25

of the king. What he did not say would frequently be important in understanding James's behavior, and James's silences may have been meant to lead the ambassador to these suppositions without compromising himself in Elizabeth's eyes. It is doubtful in this case, however, whether his silence had been rightly read.

The indirections and transformative powers that motivate James's discursive strategies can be seen in the first treatise he published as king of England, *A Counterblaste to Tobacco* (1604).[26] It is a curious work, comprehensible in part once one realizes that here, at least, was a vice that James did not have. Further, it allowed James a chance to parade his knowledge, to construct arguments in which he could—as he does endlessly—show up the limits of the logic of those who promote tobacco. This would seem to be an indifferent matter, yet throughout James affirms that the treatise is serious, that as physician to the commonwealth he must see this diseased habit suppressed. Those who are addicted to tobacco, James avers, are harmful to the land (p. 221). Ralegh may be intended; yet it is difficult to know what exactly James means since his argument is constantly being caught within its own language and rarely seems to move outside of language to actual referents. At one dangerous moment, dangerous because it involves a vice he did indulge, smoking is compared to drink, and drink is called the root of all sins (p. 220). At another, this fierce logician is caught by his own analogy, for example, when he argues that as vapors are "turned into raine and such other watery Meteors," so is smoke trapped in moist brains (p. 217). The logic of language defeats the argument. Indeed, the tone of the work is so excessive that James himself seems willing to give up the project, and he even labels his treatise "smoke" (p. 213), identifying it as the vile weed. But his word play has a serious point: to make great out of small, to use this vice as a way of presenting himself as exemplary, the nation's savior, pure in his life, acute in his wit. James wants here to make analogy the royal road to truth, to marry his powers to speech. The excessiveness of language proclaims his kingdom. Tobacco, he concludes, poisons the breath, God's gift of life to man (p. 222). James restores it, for the king speaks as *verbum dei;* his is the style of gods.

> God gives not Kings the stile of *Gods* in vaine,
> For on his Throne his Scepter doe they swey:
> And as their subiects ought them to obey,
> So Kings should feare and serve their God againe

26

If then ye would enioy a happie raigne,
Observe the Statutes of your heavenly King,
And from his Law, make all your Lawes to spring:
Since his Lieutenant here ye should remain,
Reward the iust, be stedfast, true, and plaine,
Represse the proud, maintayning aye the right,
Walke alwayes so, as ever in his sight,
Who guardes the godly, plaguing the prophane:
   And so ye shall in Princely vertues shine,
   Resembling right your mightie King Divine.

(Basilikon Doron, p. 3)

"The stile of *Gods*" names the discursive power of poets and kings.

THROUGHOUT his career, James invoked the style of gods. In a letter of 1586, he had argued that Elizabeth could not take Mary's life, for sovereigns were those "quhom he [God] hath callid goddis" (BL, Cot. Cal. C.ix, fol. 192v). In the poems, he insistently identifies with Apollo, the god of poetry, medicine, and the sun. Two dedicatory sonnets to *The Essayes of a Prentise* declare James to be "of *Mars* and *Pallas* race" (1:3, line 6), an Alexander and a Caesar in conquest and in writing—Augustus, too, the second dedicatory sonnet adds, concluding that "*Caesars* works, shall iustly *Caesar* crowne." Writing to Queen Elizabeth in 1594, James had drawn upon the *Aeneid* to explain his relationship to Bothwell. The queen had misunderstood the allusion, and James sought to explain his reading of the text and his behavior. "Suppose . . . I am Juno; ye are the rest of the Goddis; Bothwell is Aneas," he begins.[27] The supposition reverses the identification of Elizabeth as his mother, absorbs his identification of his mother as the hated goddess, and reverses gender. James offers a spectacular act of reading to justify his behavior. In it, absolute and free, James indicates what the style of gods meant: the claim to total freedom in the reshaping of discourse to proclaim power. The style James adopted, and which marks his writing, is the key to the symbolics of his power. "*Caesars* works shall iustly *Caesar* crowne." "Works" are opera, writing; discourse reigns supreme, its might is right, the sole truth: the acts of the king are crowned in words. There is an implicit politics in language: the root of author is *auctor*, originator, warrant of the truth, supporter of a law. Spenserian justice had decapitated others to ensure the line and the crown; James's discourse depends upon a parallel force. When

27

James and Elizabeth collided over Spenser's text, also at stake was the symbolics of power, the contrasting discourses in which they affirmed themselves.

The Style of Gods

The contrast between Elizabeth and James is marked in the letter Lord Thomas Howard wrote to Sir John Harington in 1611 cited earlier for its view of Carr as the royal pupil. Here is how he sums up the difference between his king and Harington's queen: "Your Queen did talk of her subjects love and good affections, and in good truth she aimed well; our King talketh of his subjects fear and subjection, and herein I thinke he dothe well too, as long as it holdeth good."[28] The comparison is astute. Neither style is necessarily preferable, and although Howard slightly qualifies his admiration for James's, he makes it clear that both depend upon the ability to make words facts, to affirm discourse in action. For, as Howard sees, both styles begin as words, what the queen "did talk of," what the king "talketh of." Harington is an appropriate audience for these remarks, for his own account of the queen's behavior is, as Stephen Greenblatt has observed, a most cogent description of the operation of power.[29] Harington's analysis occurs in a 1606 letter to Robert Markham.[30] He comments on the queen's ability to draw forth protestations of love. The response to this was, he says, a script provided by her majesty, for she often said that although she was required to command obedience, her people would have given willingly what she demanded. "Who woude wytholde a shewe of love and obedience," Harington concludes, "when their Sovereign said it was their own choice, and not hir compulsion?" (p. 356). What she *says* becomes the warrant for what they do; yet even here there is some recognition of a reserve, for the display of love and obedience is "a shewe," a display that may act in recognition that it is acting. Yet it is also complicit with the queen's show—even as it may recognize its artifice. Harington transforms the dramatic image of play into an image of gambling, another game that Elizabeth played to perfection: "Surely she did plaie well hir tables to gain obedience thus wythout constraint: again, she coude pute forthe such alteracions, when obedience was lackinge, as left no doubtynges whose daughter she was" (p. 356). The queen's legitimacy, the *law* that justifies her power, is the inheritance from Henry VIII of the show of force and the ability to display the actuality of power when the show failed to work. This is a "putting forth" that has also been prescribed. Elizabeth's show of love was not without substance, though what it concealed could hardly be called love. Harington notes this by citing Sir Christopher Hatton's remark that the queen fished for men's souls with "so sweet a baite, that no one coude escape hir network" (p. 358). Or, as Harington continues, "hir speeche was such, as none coude refuse to take delyghte in" (p. 358); the queen's discourse functions to entrap, and Harington describes how Elizabeth's baited words were often, in a moment, reversed; love was a snare. Yet it worked both ways, since it was also the enforced language of the court, where all courtiers were courting the queen; and it could therefore contain subversion (Essex, for instance, never ceased to use the language of love even as he rebelled) in its "shew": "We all did love hir, for she said she loved us" (p. 360).[31]

Elizabeth offered a show of love in her first display before the people in her procession through London in 1558/9. In the description of the day's events, the initial paragraph paints a vivid picture of mutual love, of the people displaying their affection by their prayers and cries, and of the queen returning these, in word and gesture: "And entrying the Citie was of the People received marveylous entirely, as appeared by the assemblie, prayers, wishes, welcommings, cryes, tender woordes, and all other signes, which argue a wonderfull earnest love of most obedient subjectes towarde theyr soveraigne. And on thother side, her Grace, by holding up her handes, and merie countenaunce to such as stode nigh to her Grace, did declare herselfe no lesse thankefullye to receive her Peoples good wyll, than they lovingly offered it unto her."[32] The description uses the language of gifts and their mutual exchange. The queen marvels at the display of love offered to her, and the people are equally "ravished with the loving answers and gestures of theyr Princesse."

It would be naive to take at face value what Clifford Geertz has characterized as the "covenantal" nature of this display, or what David Bergeron describes as an intimate give-and-take, although it would be equally naive to dismiss this display as *mere* display. Bergeron's researches have revealed that Elizabeth paid for parts of this pageant and had a hand in ordering the costumes; she may not have designed the program, but her role in the preparations certainly suggests that the air of spontaneity that she maintained throughout her progress was manufactured at least in part.[33] Elizabeth plays the role in the spectacle of one taking part. The pageants greeting her were thematically unified, as they insistently affirmed.[34] The queen's legitimacy and the nature of good and holy rule were displayed before her and, admonished by these examples, she provided a mirror of the

29

people's hopes and wishes in her attentiveness to the pageants, in pressing the English Bible to her bosom after kissing it, in seemingly spontaneous responses to the words said to her. The queen fit into the frame of the pageants, made herself its mirror and exemplification. She acted out her conformity to the script her citizens presented her with, and although this was a script she had approved of beforehand, and although these were pageants she herself had, in part, paid for, this did not mean that the display failed to correspond to the hopes of the English. "Her Grace's loving behaviour preconceived in the People's heades upon these considerations was then thoroughly confirmed, and indeede emplanted a wonderfull hope in them touchyinge her woorthy Governement in the reste of her Reygne." The people's "preconceptions" are, to some degree, what they have been made to believe; but, equally, the queen, knowing them, has shaped her performance as the fulfillment and the promise of these desires. Giving them what they want, she gets for herself what she wants. There is a mutuality here, but it is not quite the covenant of democratic politics or the naive love feast that the contemporary account seems to describe (and *who* authorized that description?). Rather, the spectacle of state combines deception and display, both the show of participation and genuine participation (after all, the queen *is* involved in what the people desire). The spontaneous show covers the actual interaction. The accord and mutuality, the mirror effects of queen and people bound in love, can be accounted for. Yet to note the queen's presence in the people's pageant means that in another set of terms queen and people are co-partners in this spectacle; it is not, finally, easy to separate their desires, or to judge what is prescribed, what spontaneous, in the show of love in the streets of London.

Elizabeth's progress replayed her brother's, as Sydney Anglo has shown,[35] and James's was also a repeat, the same streets retread, the same locales serving as the stations for scaffolds and, in James's case, elaborate triumphal arches. Yet James's entrance into London was as much a display of his style as was Elizabeth's, a pointed contrast even as continuity by re-creation was affirmed.[36] A drama of love was played out, but not one of mutual love. Rather, as Thomas Dekker's account of the progress insists, London was the bride, James the groom.[37] A hierarchy is thereby suggested, and sexual *domination* is implied in James's ravishing entrance and devastating exit. "Come, therefore, O worthiest of Kings, as a glorious bridegroome through your Royall chamber. But to come neerer, *Adest quem querimus.* Twentie and more are the Soveraignes wee have

30

served since our Conquest; but, conqueror of hearts, it is you and your posteritie, that we have vowed to love and wish to serve whilst London is a Citie" (1:360). "Conqueror of hearts": James's translation of the language of love into the myth of Fergus appears here in its English counterpart, the Norman conquest. The same sentence—whom we have desired has arrived—covers Elizabeth's entrance and James's, but the meaning has changed. Hence, at the end of the king's progress, when "her bridegroome is but stept from her" London becomes "a widdow" (1:374–75).

Whereas Elizabeth played at being part of the pageants, James played at being apart, separate. The pageants presented for Elizabeth form a coherent, mutually reflective whole, and Elizabeth acted within the limits of its design (limits she may have helped design). James's pageants are not connected; each has its own symbolic center, its inherent design. The pageants do not build on each other or lead to each other, as Elizabeth's do. Yet they are connected: each exists only in and for the king. His presence gives them life; his absence robs them. Their existence depends upon him. In Elizabeth's entrance, she is an actor in a total script. In James's, as Dekker notes, the city is the actor, given the part of bride to meet the entering groom, made for the moment into a royal chamber to receive the king, who passes through untouched and unchanged: "And thus have we (lowe and aloofe) followed our Soveraigne through the Seven Triumphall Gates of this his Court Royall, which name, as London received at the rysing of the Sunne, so now at his going from her (even in a moment) she lost that honour; and being, like an actor on stage, stript of her borrowed Majestie, she resumes her former shape and title of Citie; nor is it quite lost, considering it went along with Him to whom it is due" (1:374). The king's presence confers meaning.

Unlike Elizabeth, James said nothing throughout his entrance, displayed no response to the pageants. Rather, the pageants responded to him. As he arrived, like the sun giving life, like the groom entering the bride, like a king in court, the city sprang alive, acting in word and deed to show what the royal presence contains in itself and gives merely by being present and being seen. Dekker's account of the king's progress is told from the king's point of view, for it is only from his eyes that the display takes on life, only when he is seen that the spectators come to see. Whereas Elizabeth kept hushing the crowd, attempting to make the progress totally a theatrical event involving the queen, her people, and their pageants, James stood aloof; for him to see was enough (not necessary for him, but for his viewers). James displayed their subjection to his subjects, showed them

31

their need for him and his aloofness from them. What James displayed, passing by the triumphal arches, was a Roman style, imperial; this was the style of gods. Or, perhaps, it is fair to say that Clifford Geertz's comparison of Elizabeth's allegorical style with the analogical style of fourteenth-century kings of Java in fact applies as well to the difference between Elizabeth and James:

> In sixteenth-century England, the political center of society
> was the point at which the tension between the passions that
> power excited and the ideals it was supposed to serve was
> screwed to its highest pitch; and the symbolism of the progress
> was, consequently, admonitory and covenantal: the subjects
> warned, and the queen promised. In fourteenth-century Java, the
> center was the point at which such tension disappeared in a
> blaze of cosmic symmetry; and the symbolism was, consequently,
> exemplary and mimetic: the king displayed, and the subjects
> copied.[38]

The parallel is not exact, but James did display an unmovingness even as he moved through London; indeed, his responses, insofar as he registered any, were negative, drawing back from his people, pointing to the difference, displaying boredom and fatigue, rather than Elizabeth's rapt attention. Yet, for all that, we know that James regarded himself as exemplary (we might recall the *Counterblaste*), and the pageants performed for him are said to have taken their life from him. Unmoved, he is yet the animating force, the model of an unattainable power and unapproachable virtues to be copied but never achieved. In James's entrance, he is the spectacle although hardly seen, and when seen, hardly offering himself to his viewers.

To understand the nature of this spectacle we might draw on Clifford Geertz again, this time his study, *Negara: The Theatre State in Nineteenth-Century Bali*,[39] in which he examines another culture built upon a series of analogies, which are at the same time identities, representations in two senses of the word: "The state ceremonials of classical Bali were metaphysical theatre: theatre designed to express a view of the ultimate nature of reality and, at the same time, to shape the existing conditions of life to be consonant with that reality; that is, theatre to present an ontology and, by presenting it, to make it happen—make it actual" (p. 104). The entirety of Balinese society aimed at such representations of ultimate designs and realized itself in these aims. From his ethnography, Geertz proceeds to pose some theoretical consequences that may well apply to the ritual played out in the king's progress through the streets of London. Geertz sug-

gests that any view of the state that disregards the symbolic functions and treats them as displacements of something else—something
which is conceived of as being more real—may err. The "symbolic
dimensions of state power" (p. 121), he argues, are real forces. The
Balinese ruler *owned* (p. 127) his land, his servants, and his people in
part because they strove to replicate him, just as he strove to be
divine, and was divine in his striving and in the image he presented of
having achieved that status. "The king owned the country as he ruled
it—mimetically; composing and constructing the very thing he imitated" (p. 128). And, conversely, the king was created by the rituals
and forms of the culture to which he himself gave life and form.
Power, Geertz concludes, is not brute force (p. 135); that view of
power is just that—a conception of power, not a natural fact nor inherent to it. Power can be as truly in display, in the theatrical condition that bound Bali together, making its life a series of repeated
representations of a condition best exemplified in the unmoving
drama that the king presented. For the king of Bali, Geertz remarks,
represented himself, theatricalized himself. And so, too, did James,
in the spectacle he presented in his progress through London. What
he offered was not simply an image of his power, but the power of
himself as image. And such power extended from his exemplary
form to embrace the entire state. "The real is as imagined as the
imaginary" (p. 136), Geertz profoundly concludes.

JAMES's entrance into London bore his mature stamp upon it, in
contrast with Elizabeth's. For all that Elizabeth contributed to her
coronation pageant, her later style was not fully in evidence, and
such figures as Diana or Venus virgo were absent. In the entrance,
Elizabeth was a biblical heroine, a second Deborah. Her legitimacy
and her faith were celebrated, and a biblical typology underlay the
various pageants presented on the scaffolds she passed by. James's
entrace virtually eschews such a matrix, although William Hubbocke,
greeting him at the Tower of London, compared his entrance to the
arrival of Israel in the promised land (1:325) and compared the king
to David. Yet, again and again, classical allusions dominated. James's
entrance was a triumph in the high Roman style; hence Gilbert Dugdale described James's entire course from Edinburgh to London as
The Time Triumphant (1604). Stephen Harrison's arches must be
compared to the ad hoc stages constructed for Elizabeth,[40] for the
arches are not only more elaborate, but bear a strong meaning, since
they announce the basic architectural element of classical style and
situate James's entrance in the context of the absolutist revival of

classicism.[41] Mantegna had painted a series of panels depicting Caesar's triumph, and these, as Andrew Martindale suggests, may have owed their inspiration to—or have inspired—court theatricals.[42] James's entrance was theatrical in this sense—a self-conscious recreation of classical art, adapting classical style to current meaning. It proclaimed his absolute kingship. Lining the streets of London with these arches filled with statuary—and living statues as well, since some of the supposed statues were actors standing in niches about to come to life (see fig. 3)—the spectacle recreated Rome in terms parallel to Sir Henry Wotton's description of the city. Art and Nature, he says, met in the abundance of statues lining the streets, another race of men preserved in marble, representative images: "And true it is indeed that the Marble *Monuments & Memories* of well deserving Men, wherewith the very high wayes were *strewed* on each side was not a bare and transitory entertainement of the *Eye*, or onely a gentle deception of *Time*, to the *Travailer:* But had also a secret and strong *Influence*, even into the advancement of the *Monarchie*, by continuall representation of vertuous examples; so as in that point ART became a piece of *State*."[43]

For James's entrance, what statuary and the exemplary king could not do, the recounting in prose aimed at. Harrison's arches become "perpetuall monuments" (1:331) preserved in print.[44] Or, as Ben Jonson says, after he has described and analyzed the arch erected at Fenchurch, in it was "labored the expression of state and magnificence (as proper to a triumphall Arch)" (7:90),[45] a labor in which figurative unity and lifelike representation meet. Such meetings are the very stuff of the dramatic form developed under James, the masque, in which art and life meet continually in complex acts of representation. The meeting of the momentary show and the enduring word is achieved within a classical vocabulary; architectural frontispieces become the title pages of books as, for example, in John Speed's *Theatre of the Empire of Great Britaine* (1614) (fig. 4), where a triumphal arch serves as the format for presenting an entrance into a work of state. The same format is used in the title page of James's 1616 *Workes* (fig. 5).[46] Not surprisingly, then, when George Marcelline wrote to praise James, he titled his book *The Triumphs of King James* (London, 1610). Awarding his monarch a crown of laurels (sig. B$_3$v) and hailing Prince Henry as "*my young Caesar*" (sig. A$_2$v) following in his father's footsteps, Marcelline found in James's "heroick actions" glory surpassing "all the pompous Triumphes of *Pompey, Aemilius, Scipio,* or *Vespasian*" (p. 1). James's heroism lay in intellectual might, detecting the Gunpowder

Figure 3. Stephen Harrison, *The Archs of Triumph* (1603–4): detail, Edward Alleyn as Genius.

Plot and assaulting Cardinal Bellarmine, and for Marcelline, James was a Mercurial hero (p. 16)—and Solomon, Orpheus, Amphion, and Arion as well. Speed's *Historie of Great Britaine* (1614, 1623) is adorned with Roman medallions and filled with arguments linking English greatness to Roman models. Hence James arrived, he claims, like a second Constantine, "whose person every man prayed for," bringing peace like "another *Octavius*" (1623 ed., p. 1241).

A similar combination of classical form and political content can be seen in the Old Schools Quadrangle of the Bodleian (fig. 6).[47] There a tower illustrating the five classical orders of architecture was erected, probably at Bodley's instigation, and as part of remodeling

Figure 4. John Speed, *Theatre of the Empire of Great Britaine* (1614), title page.

36

Figure 5. James I, *Workes* (1616), title page.

Figure 6a. The Tower of the Five Orders (1619), Old Schools Quadrangle, Bodleian.

Figure 6b. The Tower of the
Five Orders: detail,
James I presenting
his works.

of the courtyard that he undertook. The tower was finished in 1619, and although there is no accurate or reliable account of James's part in its building, the tower celebrates not only the classical revival but the king as well. The addition of Gothic spires and windows and the failed symmetry of the tower make it look less classical to our eyes than it probably did to Jacobeans. It flanks an arched entranceway and, no doubt, its prototype, however distant, is the triumphal arch. On the penultimate story, between Corinthian columns, James is represented enthroned beneath a canopy (fig. 6). On either side of him stands a female figure, representing the University and Fame. James presents his works. His action is appropriate for a library; it also translates James's royal power into verbal power (the inscription below praises him as "most learned, munificent and best of Kings"). And the style in which this is celebrated is unmistakably Roman.

Such mixtures and such meanings dominated the court style of James. His chief architect, Inigo Jones, imported European Palladianism with its attendant absolutist meanings. Jones's architectural fantasies, spun out in the decor of Jacobean and Caroline masques, express imagined power, just as the Banqueting House at Whitehall, which he designed, served as the place where masques were performed and ambassadors and royal guests met and were received.[48] It was the center of state and the center of court display. The two

39

are inseparable and inseparably mixed in the Roman style where, in Wotton's telling phrase, "Art became a piece of *State*." Paul van Somer's 1620 portrait of the king (fig. 7) catches the style accurately. James stands, holding ball and scepter, in crown and robes and jewels. In the window behind him, Inigo Jones's Banqueting House is clearly visible. The building reinforces the monarch's absolutist stance.

Visual and verbal meet and reinforce each other in the court masques. Despite the rivalry of Jones and Jonson, their collaboration offers the best vantage point for this stylistic meeting. In *Prince Henry's Barriers*,[49] to take one example, the visual event of the masque, the rebuilding of the Temple of Chivalry, allows Jones to enact visually what the words also aim at, the celebration of James as a revived hero and of his son as his image. Jones's St. George Portico (fig. 8) offers a mixed classicism congruent with the Oxford tower (it is even more Gothic, however). Again, the triumphal arch is the basic element, although the entire set depends, with its perspective lines, on Italian antecedents, particularly Serlian classicism. In the masque, James is said to reveal "the style of majesty, that knows /No rival but itself" (lines 30-31). This self-referential and absolute style is the verbal equivalent of the visual classicism. In both instances, the masque offers a translation of the Roman style, quite literally in its text, for James is celebrated for restoring a Roman name to his kingdom. Brutus is behind Britain, and through an elaborate and no doubt Pythagorean anagram, Arthur is also found in James's name (line 21). Ancient history and antique style are recreated; in the main masque, new life is breathed into Merlin, and he delivers a prophecy, perhaps most remarkable in its declaration that James knows the date of his own death (lines 353-58). This gives the monarch godlike powers, fitting one who sat on God's judgment seat; even as it admits James's mortality, it allows him to triumph over time. His second life matches the trope of revival that dominates the masque. He is man and statue at once, and his son and successor mirrors him. Ushered onto "another stage/And scene" (lines 164-65), the prince, in fact, is invited to reoccupy his father's place and to regain the Roman stage and scene as yet another instance of the monarch's ability to live beyond himself.

The trope of second life, revival and representation, is even more explicit, although a biblical matrix is also added, in the funeral sermon that John Williams preached at James's death. The dead king is said to have been "a *lively Statue* of King *Salomon*," representing him. Williams continues: "As *Spartianus* ... reports of *Traian*, that after his Death, he triumphed openly in the Citie of *Rome, In Imag-*

40

Figure 7. Paul van Somer, *King James* (1620).

By the gracious permission of Her Majesty Queen Elizabeth II. Copyright reserved.

41

Figure 8. Inigo Jones, design for St. George's Portico, *Prince Henry's Barriers* (1610).

Courtesy, the Duke of Devonshire.

ine, in a Lively *Statue,* or Repraesentation invented by *Adrian* for that purpose: So shall this *Salomon* of *Israel* doe at this time in the Statue, and Repraesentation of our *Brittish Salomon.*"[50] The life of kings, as this passage suggests, is, like Merlin's in the masque, a second life, living again in the imagined form of the "lively statue," a form that lives eternally, unchanging and exemplary. "A Kinge is a Mortall god on earth" (BL, Harl. Ms. 2232, fol. 73). This is the form occupied by kings in life and in death; and its style is triumphal and triumphantly Roman. In Williams's sermon, the biblical matrix is subordinated to Roman art. Second life, as in *Prince Henry's Barriers,* means continual translation, textual transformations into enduring Roman images. This is the style of gods and of royal representation. As John Florio told James in the preface to his 1603 translation of the *Basilikon Doron* into Italian (BL, Royal Ms. 14, A.v), the king

42

was "Cesare," and his writing had the precedent of such works as the *Cyropaedia* or Caesar's *Commentaries,* writings that were so full of prudence that they would last forever, "ogni seculo."

It is thus no surprise, to return to James's London entrance, to find the king ushered into "the triumphs of peace" by William Hubbocke (1:329); at Temple Bar, James saw Peace at the gates of the Temple of Janus, "signifying," Jonson explains, "that Peace alone was better, and more to be coveted then innumerable triumphs" (H&S 7:97), precisely because, as "her word" displayed, *Una triumphis innumeris potior,* peace is more powerful than innumerable triumphs, for it is a triumph itself. Thus Peace stands with Mars at her feet. Such imagery also appears in the allegorical paintings Rubens designed for Charles I, and these concerns also meet in the depiction of James with which he crowned the ceiling of the Banqueting House (see fig. 9). There the program that began James's reign was brought to culmination in a set of images meant to serve as well for his successor. As D. J. Gordon and Roy Strong have shown conclusively, a Roman program lies behind Rubens's design.[51]

It is marked out at the first in Hubbocke's hailing of "you our Caesar" (1:325) or in Henry Petowe's panegyrique, *England's Caesar.* James, for Petowe, is "King of Peace and Plentie" (1:237) as he is on the Whitehall ceiling; he is *"England's Caesar"* come to fetch "Great Caesar's Crowne . . .won,/By true succession."[52] And, finally, for Jonson, James is wished the "lasting glory" of "Augustus state" (H&S 7:109, line 763). Augustus, Prince of Peace, is James's identity in *Hymenaei* as well, and the Roman emperor served as the model for James enthroned in Rubens's apotheosis (see fig. 9). Insistently, in his entrance, James is seen as a Roman emperor. Thus, at the end of the first spectacle, cut to save James from tedium but preserved in print, James is heralded as the founder of Troynovant (1:341), and verses by Martial name him Caesar anew; as Dekker says, the citizens flocked "like so many Roman Ædiles" (1:342) to take part in the "Tryumphes" of peace. When James began his progress from the Tower, he started at "the Hall of the Romane Caesar" (1:327), as Hubbocke calls it, a symbolic locale proclaiming his "soveraigne authority." One reason that the Tower bears this meaning is that "here is mony coyned, the joynts and sinewes of warre, which now a good while since hath borne the image and superscription of you our Caesar" (1:326).

In typical coins (see fig. 10), James is enthroned, and the arms of his chair form classical columns, an imperial allusion to the pillars of Hercules, the device of Charles V adopted by Elizabeth after the

Figure 9. The Apotheosis of James I, from the ceiling of the Banqueting
House, Whitehall (1635). Engraving by Gribelin, after Rubens.

By the gracious permission of Her Majesty Queen Elizabeth II.
Copyright reserved.

Crown, James on
horseback.

Rose royal, with James
enthroned.

Crown, with marriage
motto: "Quae Deus
Coniunxit Nemo Separet."

Medal commemorating
1590 marriage to Anne of
Denmark; laureate bust.

Medal commemorating
1603 accession to the
throne; laureate bust.

Medal commemorating
1604 peace with Spain;
laureate bust.

Coins, with laureate bust.

Figure 10. Coins and medals of the reign of James VI and I.

Courtesy, Trustees of the British Museum.

Armada had been defeated (see fig. 11). Typically, too, James appears on horseback; this has a classical antecedent as well, the famous statue of Marcus Aurelius, the model for many Renaissance statues and for such paintings as Van Dyck's of Charles I on horseback.[53] But Hubbocke's invitation to find the king's imperial style on his coins goes further than these Roman allusions, for in the last set of coins issued in his reign, James appears in imperial costume and crowned in laurel as in Jonson's poem—or in a 1613 engraving by Crispin van de Passe (fig. 12). These all present the image of the king in the poems, the conquering hero and triumphant poet. This is a significant moment in the history of coins, "the first instance of the laureate bust on the English coinage."[54] They are not, however, the first time James was represented in this fashion. In the medals commemorating his accession and his coronation, James appears similarly in Roman dress, wreathed in laurel; but the first instance is the marriage medal of 1590 (see fig. 10).

From the start, then, the king who declared his marriage to his nation, proclaiming himself the peacemaker and uniter of Scotland and England into Great Britain, restorer of pristine unity to the realm, presented himself in the Roman image, stamped with the Roman stamp. In speeches to Parliament at the beginning of his reign, he reiterated the point, declaring in 1607 that England and Scotland would be united as man and wife: "You are to be the husband, they the wife: you conquerours, they as conquered, though not by the sword, but by the sweet and sure bond" (*Political Works,* p. 294). The conquest of Anne was the first triumph of peace and unity. Whom God hath joined, let no man separate: that is inscribed on the coinage of the realm. "Observe . . ./. . . the Kings reall, or his stamped face" (lines 6–7), Donne writes in *The Canonization.*[55] But the king's real face *is* the one stamped on his coins. Real and royal, the image of the king carries currency and value. (Sovereigns are also coins.) The coins and medals preserve, commemorate, and memorialize the style of power and translate it into the vital economy of real life. The images on coins declare the principles of state that operate to give life—and life beyond life, eternal life—to state. Donne's "or" ("reall, or . . . stamped") would appear to juxtapose the living with the dead, the experientially true with the false image. But the real is the royal, and the stamped form lives on and is the very stuff with which real life is lived. This is no antithesis but an explanatory "or," two ways of seeing the royal style stamped in Roman form.

In a Roman matrix, James generated his "style of gods," claiming deity as the emperors had done before him. In Jonson's welcoming entertainment, London is told by its Genius that it can now see "that sight, for which thou didst begin to be."

> When BRUTUS plough first gave thee infant bounds,
> And I, thy GENIUS walk't auspicious rounds
> In every furrow; then did I forelooke,
> And saw this day mark't white in CLOTHO's booke.
>
> (H&S 7:92, lines 285-89)

An original and Roman destiny is fulfilled in James's entrance. "Redeunt Saturnia Regna" is the apt citation that follows (H&S 7:100), "those golden times were returned againe." Fittingly, Jonson offers James a Roman ceremony at the reconstructed Temple of Janus, the gateway through which he passes; so, too, in masques such as *Hymenaei,* Jonson recreates Roman celebrations to fit the court. As Leah Sinanoglou Marcus notes, this is no empty gesture, for James favored Roman law against the pretensions of the common law tradition that supported Parliament, and Roman law underlay the civil law, church law—and Scottish law.[56] In his Star Chamber speech of 1616, he was at pains to distinguish civil and canon law from the common law, and to insist that it keep its place and not encroach on the royal prerogative. It is no accident, no mere excrescence, that the marriage masque performed at court should also celebrate James's married kingdom, and do so in the style favored by the king.

Style here, as in Geertz's Java, is content. When the gates of Janus close they reveal the inscription

> IMP. Jacobus Max.
> CAESAR AUG. P. P.
> Pace Populo Britannico
>   Terra Marique Parta
>   Ianum Clusit. S.C.   (H&S 7:105)

Throughout, James is addressed in Latin, regaled with Latin inscriptions and mottoes deciphered at length by Jonson.[57] These comprise a florilegium of quotations from Virgil, Ovid, Martial, Tacitus, et al. They contextualize James's entrance and give it words. And indeed, it was as the giver of words that James was so often celebrated. Even silent here, his entrance bore his impression. Kings are a *"Kinde* of *Speaker,"* John Williams declared in his funeral sermon for James, on the authority of Alexander the Great (p. 5). Augustus was the model he had in mind for a king whose words and deeds proclaimed his power (p. 6); Solomon's writing, like that of this second Solomon, had imperial precedents (p. 18). "In the *Romane Empire*

47

ELIZABETA D.G. ANGLIÆ. FRANCIÆ. HIBERNIÆ .ET VERGINIÆ
REGINA CHRISTIANAE FIDEI VNICVM PROPVGNACVLVM.
Immortalis honos Regum, cui non tulit ætas   *Queis ipsa tantum superant reliqua omnia regna,*
Ulla prior, veniens nec feret ulla parem,   *Quantum tu maior Regibus es reliquis.*

Figure 11. Elizabeth I between the columns of Hercules (1596).

Courtesy, Trustees of the British Museum.

HBZ IACOBUS D.G. MAGNÆ BRITANNIÆ / FRANCIÆ / SCOTIÆ / ET HYBERNIÆ REX. ANNO MDCXIII

Qui regis imperio divisos orbe Britannos,   Qui pace ecclesiam, jus hiis qui legibus ornas
    Rex tot virorum fortium;   Forum, scholas doctoribus;
Qui terrore tui solius nominis hostes   Atq, inter vates pangis pia carmina, sceptro
    Premis, quietis appetens;   Jungis decenter lauream.

A°. 16 13.   Crisp. Passæus figur. sculp. et exc.

Figure 12. Crispin van de Passe, *King James* (1613).
Courtesy, Trustees of the British Museum.

it is observ'd by *Tacitus,* that the Princes of the first line, *Iulius, Augustus, Tiberius, Claudius,* yea and *Caius* himselfe (as blunt as he was) never borrowed a *tongue* to speake to the people" (p. 9), never borrowed one because they had their own. Under the new Augustus, writing flourished, not always to James's advantage, as Arthur Wilson reports: "Peace was maintained by him as in the Time of *Augustus:* And Peace begot Plenty, and Plenty begot Ease and Wantonness, and Ease and Wantonness begot Poetry, and Poetry swelled to that Bulk in his time, that it begot strange Monstrous Satyrs against the King's own Person, that haunted both Court and Country." James himself may have been their only begetter. For he ruled by the pen, not by the sword. So Bacon celebrated James as Augustus Caesar, using Tacitus's words, "Augusto profluens," or, as Bacon translated it for the king, "your Majesties manner of Speech is indeed Prince-like, flowing as from a Fountain, and yet streameth and brancheth it self into Natures order," issuing into a fountain of learning.[58]

Ben Jonson's entertainment for James's entrance into London encapsulates James's imperial style. Jonson's were the first and last devices that greeted the king. First, the arch at Fenchurch (see fig. 13), where the city of London spread out above a triumphal arch that housed (in descending order) the figures of Monarchia Britannica, Theosophia, Genius Urbis and, finally, the Thames. The city's name is in Latin; metaphorically it is called the "camera regis," properly, Jonson explains, ever since the Norman conquest (H&S 7:83). In a letter of 28 March 1603, James had claimed "our Cittie of London, being the Chamber of our Imperiall Crowne" (BL, Harl. MS. 7021, fol. 236). The names of the city mark the king's triumphal entry. Jonson's discourse turns such impositions into a triumph of peace. Interpreting the architectural setting as an allegory, Jonson descends from the city to the river, discovering a descent and a generation. The Genius Urbis, the guiding spirit in his presentation and its informing principle, serves as an alter ego for James, to whom his words are directed. From this Genius a proper welcome is generated. It involves reading the arch through a running set of textual glosses — Virgil, Ovid, Seneca, and Horace are among the authors most frequently cited. The arch is made to speak — inscriptions are given voice: "In the Freeze over the gate, it seemeth to speake this verse" (H&S 7:83, lines 15-16), and other "dumbe complements" (line 211), "the dumbe argument of the frame" (lines 528-29) preceded the spoken parts. Viewed, Jonson says, they are speaking pictures, declaring themselves (lines 263-65), and the meanings carried by things visible: "Not my fishes heere,/Though they be dumbe, but

Figure 13. Stephen Harrison, *The Archs of Triumph* (1603–4): the Fenchurch Arch.

doe expresse the cheere/Of these bright streames" (lines 315–17). The arches compliment and complement the king, for he is, primarily, what is viewed—the windows are filled with eyes bent to see "the day so much desir'd" (line 271) and the king it has *produced* (line 274). James is what is produced, an image come to life, a dream made true, a hope fulfilled; he is produced by the *genius loci* (a *deus generationis,* as Dekker notes [1:339]) and its maker. For, repeatedly, James is the sun shedding light who gives life to the occasion. "He now was really obiected to their eyes, who before had beene onely, but still, present in their minds" (lines 241–42). James is the image come to life and has the power to make images come to life in the frame that Jonson erects. He need not speak, for even silent he declares his meaning, and Jonson's text echoes him.

James comes as the fulfillment of time. "Time, Fate, and Fortune" (line 270) meet in him, and he makes time, too, bringing to this "point of Time" (line 276) "present happinesse" (line 293).

51

This is the same "present" that opens book V of *The Faerie Queene,*
the "state of present time" (pro. 1.1). "'Now is not every tyde'"
(line 307), the Genius declares; James's time is extraordinary, time
fulfilled, a time out of time; a present state unmoving. It was, James
told his first Parliament, "in the fulnesse of time provided for me"
(p. 269) that he came. In book V, as Angus Fletcher has so admirably
demonstrated, time is of the essence. Talus with his scythe is time
the reaper and generator; Arthegall is the maker of time, the restorer
of the golden age, the hero on a tight timetable.[59] Time and tide wait
for no man; in Jonson's entertainment, the tide speaks. The Thames
echoes the generative words of the Genius Urbis, and seas of pomp,
floods of joy, answer the "nectar" (line 331) of James's sight:

> To what vaine end should I contend to show
> My weaker powers, when seas of pompe o'reflow
> The cities face: and cover all the shore
> With sands more rich than TAGUS wealthy ore?
> When in the flood of ioy, that comes with him,
> He drownes the world; yet makes it live and swimme,
> And spring with gladnesse. (Lines 309–15)

The Thames expresses his inadequacy in the face of the overwhelming
flood that James commands, the flood of history that he controls.
"He drownes the world; yet makes it live and swimme,/And spring"
(lines 314–15). Like Talus, James reaps and sows. The root of *authority* is *augere,* to make grow.

Floods function as a controlling image, a central device in
Jonson's welcome. It is the base of the arch, the undifferentiated
source from which differences are made. So, too, the sea functions in
book V of *The Faerie Queene.* Into it, Arthegall deposits the beheaded
Munera (canto i), the defeated egalitarian giant (canto ii); from it he
plucks the treasure of the sea and passes judgment (canto iv). These
impositions of meaning upon a matrix of meaninglessness are defini-
tive acts in planting justice. But they are equally potent in defining
time, for it, too, depends upon the definition of limits. Hence, James
passes from the greeting of the Thames, the boundary of his city and
another alter ego for him, to the Temple of Janus, beginning and end
of the year. James comes to close the gates, to impress his seal on
time. When the gates are closed, they will reveal the inscription that
proclaims James as emperor. The temple houses a set of characters
familiar from *The Faerie Queene*—or soon to be familiar from the
Whitehall ceiling (see fig. 9): Peace (Irene) and Plenty, the former
treading upon Mars, and her handmaids, Quiet, Liberty, Safety, and

52

Felicity, standing upon their opposites. James fulfills time, taking it on himself, imposing. To make the time his, to make his words powerful, to enact justice: these are congruent acts.

To explicate this, Genius confronts the spirit of the Temple, the misguided Flamen Martialis. His flames need to be replaced, his fire put out by an eternal fire, phoenixlike in its glow. In book V of *The Faerie Queene,* the flames of love needed taming, their force had to be reunderstood and Britomart submitted to the vision in the Temple of Isis. Here, the Flamen Martialis exchanges his "streame/of phantasie" (lines 578-79) for true knowledge. Then he must replace the Temple dedicated to the goddess Anna Perenna with the only Anne that counts, the king's. Although the flamen recognized the "tides,/ Titles, and place" (lines 586-87), awakening to the sun's return on the Ides of March, all has changed. Rome has become England; what was fatal to one Caesar is propitious to another. The lecture of the Genius to the flamen provides an elementary lesson in the meaning of the adaptation of the Roman style. All is the same, and yet all is different, befitting a king who drowns and reinvigorates, remaking the time to suit himself, renaming everything so that it echoes him. "New power" (line 588) changes everything; peace banishes war as in book V of *The Faerie Queene,* where justice as mighty suppression outflanks images of oppression. The triumph of peace is, nonetheless, a triumph. The restoration of Rome is also obliterative and presumptive. Reversals, not repetition, dominate this recreation. To restore the age of gold to this "translated temple" (line 614) is to fix time forever in eternal flames (line 620). The Genius accomplishes a revolution.

It is, in fact, to borrow from Spenser (V. pro. 4.6), "the heavens revolution," and in token of this, the final speaker in Jonson's welcome is Electra, a rare flame. The stars speak, the sun stands still, and James is presented with a day without night—encompassing night, the timeless time of the golden age. It is, as at the opening of book V, a second beginning, after the flood (see pro. 2). So, with the coming of peace, and the closing of the gates, Astraea returns, and James is placed in Jove's "iudging chayre":

> thou wilt powre those ioyes
> Upon this place, which claimes to be the seate
> Of all thy kingly race: the cabinet
> To all thy counsels; and the iudging chayre
> To this thy speciall kingdome. Who[se] so faire
> And wholsome lawes, in every court, shall strive

53

> By Æquitie, and their first innocence to thrive;
> The base and guiltie bribes of guiltier men
> Shall be throwne backe, and iustice looke, as when
> She lov'd the earth, and feard not to be sold
> For that, which worketh all things to it, gold.   (Lines 733-43)

The city the king enters becomes a little room dominated by his words, a place generated by his race; in that little room, which is everywhere, the king sits on a universal throne, restoring, remaking, the golden age. In "lasting glory" the king achieves "AUGUSTUS state" (line 763). In it, the "pure consent of mind" (line 755) flows as a single stream "in every brest" (line 756). Under James, what is, is right; his is the time and the power, and in his state all time is one, all words are one. "Truth is one," Arthegall had claimed (ii.48.6), sending the democratic giant to his doom. Jonson fits his discourse to the time, delivering the just king to view. And his language draws on the imposing terms of book V of *The Faerie Queene*. Spenser had finally been answered; the king had the poet's language at his command. The king entered into authority. The powers—and the limits—of this necessarily contradictory involvement is the subject of the following chapters of this study.

2. STATE SECRETS

His tongue too large for his mouth, which ever made him speak full in the mouth, and made him drink very uncomely, as if eating his drink . . . ; his skin was as soft as taffeta sarsnet, which felt so, because hee never washt his hands . . . ; his legs were very weake, having had (as was thought) some foul play in his youth, or rather before he was born, that he was not able to stand at seven years of age, that weaknesse made him ever leaning on other mens shoulders; his walke was ever circular, his fingers ever in that walke fidling about his cod-piece. —Sir Anthony Weldon, *The Character of King James*

"THE REAL IS AS IMAGINED AS THE IMAGINARY," AND the actuality of politics requires the fiction of poets. Indeed, as we have seen, politics and discourse are inseparably bound, knotted in contradictions. If we attempt now to loosen the threads a bit, it is easiest to start by seeing the shared impulses of writer and ruler. In the pages that follow, the central topic is the ideological function of writing as an instrument of royal power, and the argument is straight-forward, locating an area of presumed univocality. The net cast here is rather wide and, in fact, the chapter ends considering images—family portraits—rather than literary production, for these realize images of state. James had declared his "fatherly authoritie,"[1] and family groups answer this rhetoric. It is, in fact, with such echoes that this chapter is concerned, with patterns of replication that extend the political domain until we arrive at the private bedchamber. The course of this chapter begins with the form that mirrors the royal mind, the masque, and then passes through its reflecting surface to find that on the other side—in antimasques, but also in works not written for court consumption, lyrics by Donne, or Jonson's *Volpone*—privacy is pervaded by the public language of politics. Donne's lovers in bed alone; Donne himself in bed in illness; Stuart families in the intimacy of marriage, procreation, and death: the net of political discourse encompasses this territory. To negotiate it, I pursue here but one thread in political speech, the trope of state secrets, for it declares a domain of surface conformity to absolutist aims sufficiently complex to weave these various strands of argument.

The line can be traced to the king, and to his language, for even before James arrived in England to begin his reign, he had been pre-ceded by his words. The recent English publication of the *Basilikon Doron* had made his treatise on kingship easily available, and Lon-doners were busily reading it for clues about the new king. In the course of his rule, and in conformity with his announced role as "Praeceptour" (p. 4), schoolmaster to the nation, James displayed his "fatherly authoritie" through his writings. In 1607, he told Parliament: "This I must say for Scotland, and I may trewly vaunt it; Here I sit and governe it with my Pen, I write and it is done, and by a Clearke of the Councell I governe Scotland now, which others could not doe by the sword" (p. 301).[2] James ruled by the word. His boast extends beyond himself; in 1616, not only did the king publish his *Workes* (see fig. 5), but Ben Jonson also had the audacity to publish a wholly unprecedented folio. These folios are connected emblematically and in fact. Jonson articulates one way of conceiving the relationship of king and poet during the reign of James I, and having ended the first chapter with the poet in the king's service, we can continue our exploration here. State secrets is our topic.

In his writings, James returned again and again to proclaiming his theory of kingship, making announcements about the divinity that hedged the sovereign round. His theme, as it was in his first appearance before the Star Chamber in 1616, was, repeatedly, "the mysterie of the Kings power" (p. 333). The meaning of that phrase was remarkably straightforward: "Incroach not upon the Prerogative of the Crowne:" James said, "If there fall out a question that concernes my Prerogative or mystery of State, deale not with it" (p. 332).[3] The mysteries, or as James called them in the *Basilikon Doron,* his "secretest drifts" (p. 5), were the center of the royal sphere of power, an inner sanctum from which all subjects were excluded—or almost all. The language of mysteries, the secrets of power, were not only the king's; poets, too, used these words. How closely they touched the king, the example of book V of *The Faerie Queene* has already suggested. And in the Jonsonian masque, we can hear a royal echo. As Ben Jonson explains in his introductory remarks to the text of *Hymenaei,* the princely voices that sound in royal entertainments wrap themselves around "more removed mysteries" (lines 16-17).[4] These, however, are not the king's but the poet's mysteries; his "solid learnings" (line 14), "nourishing and sound meats" (line 24), are purveyed, Jonson says, for those whose palates are sufficiently discriminating to receive them. In such arcana, a meeting of minds, king's and poet's, is made possible; in writing, authority is established.

The Royal Masque: Ideology and Writing

Although the learned apparatus to the text of *Hymenaei* represents Jonson's attempt to extend the mystery, or, as he also termed it, the soul or inner life of the masque, to all readers, he provided his notes knowing full well that the pleasure of the masque as performed at court lay in its presentation of the mysteries without explanations. "Elitist, abstruse, exclusive"; D. J. Gordon's adjectives for court mystification cogently summarize the qualities of the style.[5] The masque presents its "more removed mysteries" for the king, holding up a mirror of his mind.[6] In its form, the masque provides a mirror, too, for it elucidates the spectacle that the king presents sitting in state. The mysteries of the masque reflect the monarch's silent state: the masque represents the king. The king observes and is observed; as much as the masquers themselves, he is onstage. The two shows bear a single meaning, and although the masquers speak, the mysteries of state remain unspoken. Such monarchs as Henry VIII and Charles I did perform in the masques that mirrored them, but James's position and conception of himself excluded him from the images that represented him before his eyes. The reflecting mirror of the masque managed to catch the king in his excluded state, and nonetheless to represent the poet as well, one mystery answering another. When we examine the Jonsonian masque, we can discover how that form came to serve those functions.

Jonson's decision to include the masques in his *Workes,* to transform scripts for performance into the permanence of print, provides one place of meeting between the monarch and the poet.[7] The king's unmoved state is reflected in the transformation of a script into a text. From the introductory paragraph of *The Masque of Blackness* (1605) on, the need for the textual preservation of the short bravery of a night is one of Jonson's themes; text and performance are likened to soul and body, and there is no doubt—as in the quarrel with Inigo Jones—that Jonson believes that the written text matters, and not the performance with its sceneographic and choreographic accompaniments. Although the written masque could merely represent and record the performance, Jonson insists that the text is closer to the informing spirit of the masque; it lays bare the invention and the moving conceit. The words may report a performance, but they do not aim at one. Their silence—the fact that they are not meant to be spoken—is more eloquent than speech; as texts, masques come closer to their inherent principles, their deep mysteries.

Indeed, the text realizes what performance only approximates. This can be seen, for instance, when Jonson halts his description of the witches in *The Masque of Queens* (1609). He seems at first to acknowledge the centrality of the performance when he notes that "the device of their attire was Master Jones his, with the invention and architecture of the whole scene and machine" (lines 30-32). Yet he immediately adds that on the best authorities, ancient and modern, he "prescribed them [the witches] their properties" (line 32), and in that statement at least the privileged term *invention* is replaced by the even more potent *prescription*. It is not the witches onstage but the textual nature of the invention that counts for Jonson. The poet asserts authority and claims authorship; Jones merely invented the witches as a visible spectacle, Jonson created them as a legible text. It is the source—in texts—that Jonson's notes emphasize. The witches are made intelligible; they become bearers of meaning. Hence, even their visible attributes are, he says, "ensigns" (line 33), badges to be read and deciphered. In performance, they are meant to be read, and the ideal performance of the masque would have it a text.

Jonson's sense of the masque—even in performance—as an elitist text caused contention not only with Jones but with Samuel Daniel as well. The entrance of the witches in *Queens* is self-consciously reminiscent of another masque of twelve ladies, Daniel's *Vision of the Twelve Goddesses* (1604), and when the queen of the witches arrives, Jonson launches a lecture that seems aimed at Daniel: "For to have made themselves their own decipherers, and each one to have told upon their entrance what they were and whether they would, had been a most piteous hearing, and utterly unworthy any quality of a poem, wherein a writer should always trust somewhat to the capacity of the spectator, especially at these spectacles, where men, beside inquiring eyes, are understood to bring quick ears" (lines 92–97). Although Jonson seems here to be minimizing the importance of the words spoken, that is not his point. Daniel's masque, in which characters announce their identities, lacks the proper encouragement to decipherment that Jonson favors. For him, as this passage suggests, the entire performance becomes a text— he calls it a *poem*—and the spectator is primarily an auditor and, as in the first of the *Epigrammes,* an understander, a reader. Jonson wishes to make the performance of the masque a text with the same qualities that shape a proper poem. His spectacle aims at "inquiring eyes" that read beyond the show to its meanings, at "quick ears" that find the spirit beneath the flesh.

For Jonson, then, the performed masque aimed at the condition of writing. This was an implicitly royal and royalist aim. Text and monarch stood in the same relationship to the performance onstage; at the masque, there was another silent text, the king himself. As much as Jonson's invention, he was the soul of the masque. Silent, uncostumed, offstage, no part of the visible design, yet there would be no design without him. All the words, all the spectacle aim at

58

him. He embodies the mystery of the masque. His is the permanent form of the masque, its life beyond words, a living image, represented. Jonson's text, as he insists in his prefatory remarks, points beyond—beyond its body to an informing spirit, beyond itself to the monarch, points to the poet's mysteries and royal secrets. The invention of the masque is translated into the flesh of the king. Printed, the masque gains an everlastingness, a royal imprimatur. The king is dead, long live the king: the king, too, has the permanence of a text. The masque as text, the masque that reproduces and represents the performance in an unchanging form, assumes the ideal form of the king, the "lively statue" of Bishop Williams's funeral sermon, standing eternally. In Jonson's masques, to celebrate the king means to reveal their shared status as writing. In the headnote to *Blackness* Jonson characteristically stresses the permanence of such representation. After presentation and performance comes re-presentation, "a life of posterity" (line 4), nothing less than the eternal life of the text.

Jonson's prefatory remarks about the textual form of the masque not only suggest how the masque is a royal form; they also point to the design and content of *Blackness;* form is content. The plot of the masque involves the journey of a group of African nymphs to the sun that will give them a second life like the "life of posterity" achieved in the written form of the masque, and transform them, "a sun to this height doth grace it,/Whose beams shine day and night, and are of force/To blanch an Ethiop, and revive a corse" (lines 223-25); such meanings are read in the movement of court ladies to state. In the invention of the masque the *roi soleil* promises what the printed text accomplishes: preservation; life beyond death; permanent transformation; the defeat of time. This sun makes day and night one eternal day and transforms black into endless white. The king's powers are analogous to the poet's and are signaled in language. Thus, the Ethiops know they have arrived at the promised light when it is renamed, no longer called Albion but Britannia. This "new name" (line 221), the king's doing, matches the reviving transformation; new life and new names are both in the king's textual powers. Thus, the masque moves to the beyond glimpsed in its preface, the place where royal powers are textual ones. First, the queens arrive at the king who sits observing and yet informing the masque, the moving power of its invention; second, Jonson's text records that the promised transformation occurred—the printed sequel, *The Masque of Beauty,* presents the transformed, bleached nymphs. The poem takes a fact of nature (for the next masque no one wore blackface) and

59

makes it a royal event (the king transformed them—or, the king ordered them to appear without makeup) that is equally a poetic one (the conceit came to life). In quarto and folio, royal power and poetic power echo each other, and the condition of performance represents a textual situation.

In a number of masques, Jonson figures the relationship between the poet and the king, between the form of the masque and the idealization of the monarch, through Mercury, the god of eloquence. In these masques, Mercury is simultaneously a surrogate for the king and for the poet, and presents their matching powers. In *Mercury Vindicated from the Alchemists at Court* (1616), the plot traces Mercury's path, from his refusal to serve tyrant Vulcan and his false arts to his submission to the true fire of the *roi soleil*. First, Vulcan's false arts manifest themselves in an antimasque dance of "imperfect" creatures (line 161), men with limbecks for heads. Then, the king's arts are brought forth in his, the "maker's sight" (line 178), and the masque concludes with the dances of his own creatures, the members of the court. Whereas Vulcan's trumpery represents court corruption, James's courtiers embody the meeting of nature and art.

The poet is intimately involved in this plot, and this is suggested by the importance of language to the transformation in the masque; Mercury first complains that the cozeners at court, upstairs and down, take his name in vain, and justify themselves "under the specious names" (line 40) of famous alchemists, false creators. Mercury offers a list of "what they list to style me" (line 48), and shows that he has become their "bill of credit" (line 60), the word upon which they make their insubstantial pledges and false promises. The creatures of Vulcan always talk business: "That's the word of tincture, the business. Let me alone with the business, I will carry the business. I do understand the business. I do find an affront i'the business" (lines 137-39); in short, it is all "a huge deal of talk" (line 149), lacking in substance. Like the members of a Dickensian Circumlocution Office, they talk of nothing; theirs is a creation *ex nihilo* that comes to nothing, too. What they call *business* and activity is merely motion, juggling, deception, wordplay. Mercury, the name taken in vain, is worn out, effaced, rendered insubstantial in their talk; "It is I that am corroded and exalted and sublimed and reduced and fetched over and filtered and washed and wiped" (lines 48-50).

At the moment of transformation in the masque, the falsely used god, and the abuses of language, are finally effaced; Mercury disappears, withdrawing before the true power of the king. Yet this moment serves, too, as his vindication, for he now submits to genuine

60

creativity, providing the motion and life, the real activity and business of the final dances. The masquers' "absolute features" (line 171) replace the "imperfect creatures" of Vulcan; "they are the creatures of the sun" (line 180). Whereas the antimasque had revealed a world where men were made, whole cloth, out of monstrous lies that lead to self-promotion and self-aggrandizement, the main masque reveals the life created when the king sheds his countenance on the court. The king's arts make nature, generative motions. The king creates, yet stays removed from what he makes. This is also the position of Mercury—he is present in the new life of the masque although nowhere visible in it. What James's arts create is life, or is said to be life. True assertions: James is indeed the life of the court—and of the masque.

The shared position of Mercury and the monarch is not theirs alone, for the powers of the king are poetic ones. His life-shedding beams create, the word becomes flesh. In the final part of the masque, Nature and Prometheus represent the king's creativity, the wedding of nature and art. His ability to make life is, like the masque itself, both a metaphor and the truth, mercurial power. At the end of the masque natural procreation serves as a metaphor for royal power and its reflection in the poet's creation—the text that gives back to the king what he authorizes. The vindication of Mercury is a triumph of language in which real and imaginary meet.

Although Mercury is not literally present in a masque that Jonson provided for the court the next year, *The Vision of Delight* (1617), a suppressed myth involving the god of eloquence underlies its action.[8] This is quite fitting, for like several other Jonsonian masques, this one is highly self-reflexive. As its title indicates, the masque presents a vision. This masque is about the nature of spectacles, how they are to be seen, and about the royal spectator, how he sees and is to be seen. It instructs its viewers in the coincidence of the aims of poet and king. At the crucial moment in the masque when its wonder—the scene of transformation—is to be explained, Fant'sy points to the king: "Behold a king/Whose presence maketh this perpetual spring" (lines 189-90). As in *Mercury Vindicated,* the king's presence matches the poet's making,[9] and the trope of "perpetual spring" is the masque's truth. To attain proper vision, the choir voices the "wish" that "their bodies all were eyes" (line 210). Mercury lurks in that wish, for in a mythological precedent, hundred-eyed Argus, lulled by the charms of Mercury, was murdered to be metamorphosed into the hundred-eyed spectacle, the peacock. This is how one becomes all eye and attains the vision of delight that the

61

masque provides and the monarch affords. Once again, Mercury is behind the moment of transformation when the masque's trope finds a royal truth, the assertion of power in language.

The Argus story involves a transformation in which the instruments of sight become the object of sight. That transformation also underlies *The Vision*. "How better than they are are all things made/ By Wonder!" (lines 157-58), Fant'sy comments. The lines read two ways, making it difficult to know whether seeing works wonders or whether the wonder lies in what is seen. Such slippery transformations are essential to Fant'sy, the figure who presides over the entire masque; they are crucial, too, as we have already noticed, to the monarch's power. Fant'sy's role moves from the wonders of language to the wonders of state.

The masque offers a vision, a way of seeing what is shown, that lights on the royal beholder as the model for this meeting of matched wonders. The masque means to educate its viewers into this complex view. Seen properly, it gives to the monarch the creative powers it claims for itself. Thanks to the monarch, what might have been merely a metaphor becomes a fact. The masque erects the king's Arcadia, his self-proclaimed state. Absolutist claims to permanent power, to achieved stability, to transcendent glory, are embodied in the scene of transformation that reflects what art can achieve and what the sovereign makes possible. The tropes of masques are vitally informed by the king. Yet, as we have seen, these equations between absolutist ideology and poetic power are presented elusively, mysteriously, refigured by Jonson in the role of Mercury, surrogate for the poet and monarch, the spirit of writing as the permanent embodiment of ideology, container of the secrets of state. Thus, in *Mercury Vindicated,* the king and the god of eloquence had presided over the transformation although both had been absent, not literally present onstage as the creatures of the king came forth. In *The Vision of Delight,* the moment of transformation is a view of a view; it literalizes and embodies the mysteries that lie in the king's eyes, the mysteries that can be read from his view, and from viewing him. The masque aims at giving form and words and, thereby, everlastingness, to this absolutist prospect. In the masque of the following year, *Pleasure Reconciled to Virtue* (1618), power and vision are once again of concern. Here they are embodied in the figure of Hercules, whose career in the masque represents his transformation into an emblem for the king; heroic potency becomes royal passivity; observer and observed again serve as mirrors. Hercules' transformation is, not surprisingly, managed by Mercury. Although this masque is so central in coming to understand the secrets of state that we will have occasion to return to it several times in this chapter; for the moment, the relation of Hercules and Mercury must be our concern, and the education of Hercules our theme. He learns the royal view.

When the masque begins, Hercules responds heatedly—that is, in heated words—to the spectacle presented in the antimasque, a dance of men transformed into tuns of wine, turned into the instruments of their pleasure. To Hercules, this is a vision of vice. Immediately, he wishes the antimasquers away; his wish is at once fulfilled. Then, invited by the choir to rest, and "from thy mighty labor cease" (line 112), Hercules accepts and obligingly falls asleep onstage. Having been asked, Hercules succumbs—to ease, inactivity, passivity, almost, that is, to a reward for virtue that looks like vice because it is so pleasurable. This is the first way in which the stance of the heroic figure is transformed and begins to suggest the reconciliation of the title. But the redefinition of virtue itself is even more compelling in advancing the masque's perspective that Hercules comes to learn and represent. Hercules' "mighty labor" has been to think strenuously virtuous thoughts; the muscular hero immediately serves as an image of active opposition to fleshly excesses. His seductive sleep almost does him in; pygmies surround him and are about to brain him. But to save himself from this danger, all he need do is wake up; the chorus obligingly rouses him. Thus Hercules overcomes the waking assault of the senses by wishing them away, and the attack of sleep by being awakened. Heroic activity has been transformed thereby into acts of the imagination. Onstage, these have become images. The masque presents in the figure of Hercules reconciliation, not opposition to pleasure.

In Hercules' sleep, the masque offers a most potent image for the passive heroism that Hercules comes to embody. When he awakens, the chorus tells him, "'Tis only asked from thee to look" (line 141). This completes his imaginative transformation: he has become —in the masque—an observer of the masque, a spectator. Virtually silent for the remainder of the performance, he speaks only when the dances occur, to ask their meaning. The questions he asks then are those a spectator might raise. So doing, he maintains his role in the masque as an image of one viewing the masque. His instructor at the end, as well as when he awakens, is, not surprisingly, Mercury, mouthpiece for the meaning of the masque, explaining its tropes, presenting the king. Mercury tells Hercules the meaning of the image he himself presents, what spectator he is privileged to represent.

"Rest still, thou active friend of Virtue" (line 147), Mercury

63

says, and he draws those eyes "only asked . . . to look" (line 141) to the complementary gaze, the royal gaze, that defines his stance. In Hercules' new role he is "Virtue looking on" (line 192), a role modeled in the king, that privileged spectator who embodies and exemplifies the hero's new-found passivity. Mercury directs Hercules to Hesperus (Hesperus is the king's name in this masque): for "in the sight/Of Hesperus, the glory of the west" (lines 170-71), pleasure and virtue are reconciled. Mercury invites Hercules to see the king and to see with his eyes; "the sight of Hesperus" carries both meanings. Once again, a vision of delight is offered, overcoming differences, shedding steady beams that countenance activity in inactivity. To be a hero, Hercules must assume the king's stance, and he has done so when he becomes "Virtue looking on." From that vantage point, oppositions melt, are contained, reconciled. He observes but fails to participate; barred from acting he reenacts the potent role of passive witness. He embodies a dazzling transformation. "In the sight" of the monarch—in royal vision, exclusive sight—the masque is resolved. Hercules represents the solution; in him the poet's image has a royal sanction.

Jonson thus writes into the masque the king's role as nonparticipating spectator. By the time of *Pleasure Reconciled to Virtue,* this role is onstage and before the king's eyes. In each of the masques we have thus far considered, the king's role as maker of the masque has been figured. Hesperus in *Pleasure Reconciled to Virtue,* the king is always a *roi soleil,* "the majesty of this light" (*Mercury Vindicated,* lines 167-68), "a king/Whose presence maketh this perpetual spring" (*The Vision of Delight,* lines 189-90). His presence casts its light; the scene reflects upon him. Even in the earliest masques, this central role had been marked out. Boreas, for instance, opens *The Masque of Beauty* (1608) by asking, "Which among these is Albion, Neptune's son" (line 20), and January points to the king. The printed masque uses this opening device, too; its first words often "set" the king in place to make the masque begin. For example, *The Masque of Queens* (1609) opens with this dramatic flourish: "His majesty, then, being set, and the whole company in full expectation . . ." (line 20).[10] Jonson makes the masque an inclusive structure. The king's arrival, his "setting," his observation, even his occasional interruptions, are recorded in the text to become part of the poet's device. Written into the text, all is said to be the king's devising. Even the king's exclusive stance is thereby included.

What Jonson claimed for his text, his text claims for the king. Thus, to take one further example, in *News from the New World*

(1620), the king again has the poet's part. At first, these appear to be contradictory roles; for the antimasque presents the poet's fancy, his trip to the moon to bring back the lunatic conceits of a world of idiots, whereas the main masque, entirely the king's, offers, as the herald tells him, "a race of your own, formed, animated, lightened and heightened by you" (lines 274-75). Here the king becomes a genuine poet, and his tropes are true since the chief dancer in the masque is Prince Charles, "the Truth" in the masque, and an "excellent likeness" (line 283) of the king as well. James's productive and reproductive powers are those of representation. Once again, his light quickens and refines, a "light sciential" that gives knowledge to the spectators once they accustom their eyes to "behold/The body whence they shine" (lines 300-301), the very form of "favor" (line 285). So constituted, James is the poet's king, a poet-king, the one "that did this motion give" (line 320), and the king of poets, a true masquemaker, making the masque true, including all "so full you cannot add" (line 330). James appears in the essential configuration of poetic transformation, as "a mirror" (line 308) offering "the sun's reflected light" (line 309). "Read him as you would do the book/Of all perfection" (lines 310-11). The maker of the text is a text. James is written, a book with a full name: "Say but James" (line 345), and all is said. Having inscribed the king's name in the text, as a text, the masque is over. Its echo in the texts James wrote can readily be seen. Rubens, in the Whitehall ceiling (fig. 10), depicts the figure of Mercury and, as Roy Strong says, "Mercury surely represents James in his spoken and written pronouncements, the learned monarch who is able to instruct his subjects in the mysteries of his office by speeches to Parliament or the Court of Star Chamber."[11] Jonson's Mercury carries these meanings, too, the revealer of the mysteries of state that became works of art, to reverse Sir Henry Wotton's description of Roman images of state. As Jonson practices it, the masque is an inherently royal form.

Arcana Imperii

Royalist mysteries of state are not confined to texts intended for royal ears or eyes, however. James's elitist hedge, the "removed mysteries" of the Jonsonian masque, can lead us to broader and more pervasive considerations. The king's command to respect royal territory—"incroach not"—and the exclusive view replicated in the masque can be seen in apparently apolitical contexts, too. "For God-sake hold your tongue," Donne's audacious lover demands at the opening of *The Canonization*.[12] The "you" addressed is sent hurtling from the lovers' domain and out into a public world that emphatically includes the world of politics: "Take you a course, get you a place / Observe his honour, or his grace, / And the Kings reall, or his stamped face" (lines 5-7). The authority of these commands comes from an act of usurpation and from a reversal of political power. The intimate sphere of love has been elevated to a divine mystery, "Wee dye and rise the same, and prove / Mysterious by this love" (lines 26-27); this divine mystery draws upon the language of state secrets. The lovers' divinity at first excludes the inhabitants of the profane world; finally, however, it becomes an object of veneration. The worldly implore some participation in the "mysterious . . . love" from which they have been excluded, and rightly so, since it is the "patterne" (line 45) for "Countries, Townes, [and] Courts" (line 44). The reversal accomplished at the end of the poem resituates the text's trope and makes apparent the political model that at first seemed repudiated.

In this pattern, *The Canonization* is like other poems in the *Songs and Sonnets* that begin as if they were rebelling against political values. In *The Anniversarie,* for instance, the speaker distinguishes his transcendent love from worldly lovers. The poem opens by rejecting "All Kings, and all their favorites" (line 1). Yet, in the second stanza, the lovers are allowed a metaphorical foray into the royal construct that seemed at first to have been specifically repudiated; they are "Prince enough in one another" (line 14). And by the final stanza they are kings indeed; indeed, the only kings: "Here upon earth, we'are Kings, and none but wee / Can be such Kings" (lines 23-24). The last line of the poem celebrates the second year of their "raigne" (line 30), firmly situating them in the political and temporal contexts initially apparently denied. To establish their exclusiveness and to maintain their intimate and frail union the lovers need in the end to become genuine absolutists. Love and politics are not exclusive spheres; private life bears on public life. As we shall see later in this chapter, the realm of state secrets embraces these distinctions. In *The Anniversarie,* we may note for now that the lovers are not only absolutists at the end of the poem; even the initial gesture of repudiation makes claims on the royal rhetoric of exclusion.

This was true, too, of *The Canonization,* and the transformed lovers of that poem take on royal prerogatives even more explicitly. They manifest how fully the ideal that they represent draws upon the language of political idealization, absolutist ideology. The lovers in Donne's poem contain a mystery that the world requires; moreover, they are themselves contained in a mysterious form that renders them divine. That locale is the poet's sphere, too, the space of "sonnets pretty roomes" (line 32), an ideal realm, for the text condenses the "whole worlds soule" (line 40) into a place of private retreat, a hermitage (line 38) where pleasure and virtue are reconciled to each other and share a single mysterious form. Donne's lovers, as much as the king in the masque, represent an ideal construct, an artifice of eternity poetically inscribed, politically potent. United, they join flesh and spirit, yet remain mysteriously disembodied, phoenix-like; their substance is no more—and no less—than the words that fill the sonnet. The power of language can be seen in the fact that like the king they are mirrors, spies, and epitomes to be invoked, hymned, and petitioned. They give language to the world's desires, shape to their aspirations. Yet as ideal forms they remain beyond these invocations as surpassing images, spectacular mirrors. At the end they are still mysterious, offering no revelation beyond what can barely be seen, seeing them. Observable, they remain inscrutable, occupying the royal position in which the king was first located, the place of observation: "Observe his honour, or his grace,/And the Kings reall, or his stamped face" (lines 6-7). As we know from *The Vision of Delight,* the king occupies a place where the act of observation becomes the object to be seen. This is the mysterious wonder glimpsed by Jonson in masque after masque, when the poet's trope realizes itself in the movement to state. In Donne's poems, the celebrations of the mysteries of the flesh and the joys of intimacy take on this royal shape. The lovers enter the realm of the observed.

If we look again at *Pleasure Reconciled to Virtue,* we can find a model for the transformation of Donne's lovers, for masques, too, celebrate love, the king's love to be sure. The concluding section of *Pleasure Reconciled to Virtue* reveals the mysterious state shared by the lovers and the monarch. Here is the opening of the song that accompanies the first of the three revelatory dances in *Pleasure Reconciled to Virtue:* "Come on, come on; and where you go,/So interweave the curious knot,/As ev'n th'observer scarce may know/Which lines are Pleasure's and which not" (lines 224-27). Although elsewhere Jonson, unlike James, wanted "to make the Spectatours Understanders,"[13] observation here is properly royal, leading to mystification, obscuring boundaries, absorbing differences. So doing, Jonson's text follows a royal injunction expressed in the only poem of his own included in James's 1616 *Workes,* the prefatory sonnet to the *Basilikon Doron* (p. 3). The burden of its vision is summed up in a single line: "Observe the Statutes of your heavenly King" (line 6).

The "heavenly King" in this line is the divine monarch and *his* divine monarch. To be observed, then, the king must observe. He must shine "in Princely vertues," which, the sonnet says, are those of "your mightie King Divine" (lines 13-14). The king must be and must offer himself as an image and a reflection of the "heavenly King." That is what is to be observed. Just as poets derived their style of the scarcely observable by observing the king, shining in state, the king, too, derived his style from observation. "God gives not Kings the stile of *Gods* in vaine"; the style is based on the mystery of observation. This is also the mystery housed in Donne's lovers.

This mystery in the style of gods, not surprisingly, has a Roman precedent. *Arcana imperii* is the phrase to cover the phenomena we have been observing in the royal rhetoric and the language of Donne and Jonson, and its use in the *Annals* of Tacitus provides the model for absolutist language. Tacitus describes how Gallus, attempting to fathom Tiberius's depths, thereby meddled in the *arcana imperii,* or "the unspoken premises of autocracy," as Michael Grant translates the phrase.[14] To Gallus, Tiberius responded disarmingly; pretending to misunderstand his challenge to authority, he dissimulated receptiveness, conciliation, participation. Offering to observation a show of openness, he nonetheless masked himself. Pretended republicanism covered absolutism. Observable, he nonetheless remained obscure. This, as we shall see, was a model performance, and it lurks behind the examples we have been considering, not surprisingly, for Tiberius was seen in James's show. Thus, Arthur Wilson reported the commonplace that "Some Parallel'd him to *Tiberius* for Dissimulation," while Anthony Weldon claimed that the king's familiar motto, *Beati pacifici,* Blessed are the peacemakers (see frontispiece), was joined to another, *Qui nescit dissimulare, nescit regnare,* He who does not know how to dissimulate, does not know how to rule.[15] Bacon found that he could make use of the Roman emperor's strategies in approaching his monarch. Writing to James on 25 April 1615, he cited Tacitus's account of Tiberius as a precedent for disturbing the king in his country pleasures: "I may remember what Tacitus saith, by occasion that *Tiberius* was often, and long absent from *Rome: In Urbe, & parva, & Magna Negotia, Imperatorem simul premunt:* But saith he, *In recessu, dismissis rebus minoris momenti, summae rerum magnarum magis agitantur.*" A monarch pressed at court has leisure in the country; so, Bacon concludes, "this maketh me think it shall be no Incivility, to trouble your Majesty with Business, during your abode from *London.*" This imperial motto of dissembled rule had poetic consequences; it serves as a paradigm for courtly representation, as Puttenham's discussion of "the Courtly figure *Allegoria*" makes clear: in that context, he mentions "the great Emperour who had it usually in his mouth to say, *Qui nescit dissimulare nescit regnare.*" Puttenham invokes an imperial precedent for the style of mystification.[16] *Cabinet-Council Containing the Chief Arts of Empire and Mysteries of State; Discabineted* (once thought to be by Sir Walter Ralegh) recommends Tacitean stratagems for maintaining authority, bolstering them, too, with Machiavellian *sententiae.* The recurring sentence we have seen returns again: "Dissimulation is as it were begotten by diffidence, a quality in princes of so great necessity, as moved the emperor Tiberius to say, *Nescit regnare, qui nescit dissimulare.*"[17] Both the allegorical images of the masque and the conceits of metaphysical poetry find support in this imperial matrix. The Roman style found a home in Jacobean England, in court production and in lovers' laments. And not there alone.

BEN JONSON exhibits the latitude possible in the trope of *arcana imperii,* for its usage—even in masques—is not always as straightforward as we have been seeing. The ironic reserve possible in the mystery of state was not entirely in the king's disposal. In Jonson, political talk is rarely far from the mysteries of state; but these also can become tools for parody, revelations of insubstantiality beneath the dazzling show. *Arcana imperii* are central in Jonson's political vision, and they animate antimasques as well as main masque, court theatricals, but also, as we shall see, his major work for the public stage, *Volpone.* For one turn he gives the trope, we can instance "The New Crie" (*Epigrammes:* 92).[18] There, Jonson offers "Ripe statesmen" for sale:

> Ere cherries ripe, and straw-berries be gone,
>> Unto the cryes of *London* Ile adde one;
> Ripe statesmen, ripe: They grow in every street.
>> At sixe and twentie, ripe.   (Lines 1-4)

The ripe politicians he hawks are in fact rotten food. Jonson reverses the discriminating diet promised before *Hymenaei.* Yet these overripe offerings also have "no savour, but of state" (line 5). State secrets, which are the substance of these politicians, are here parodic, a mask covering insubstantiality; these statesmen are all show: clothes, not men; intelligencers without intelligence. They are like the false creatures of *Mercury Vindicated,* royal language without substance, words used in vain. They assume that politics is a sham, that the mysteries are merely matters of deception and illusion. As a consequence, their minds are consumed by plots, they speak only in whispers, write in code or cipher or, better yet, in disappearing ink: "They'have found the sleight/With juyce of limons, onions, pisse, to write" (lines 27–28). The authority for these hollow statists can be found just beneath their surface, beneath their cloaks: "They carry in their pockets *Tacitus*/And the *Gazetti,* or *Gallo-Belgicus:*/And talke reserv'd, lock'd up, and full of feare" (lines 15–17). Tacitus or gossip sheets are equally viable hermeneutic guides for these parodically paranoid politicians.

Jonson fleshes out these statists in the tawdry newsmen of *News from the New World Discovered in the Moon,* where the "matter of state" (line 19) mixes the obvious (a head count of the audience) with lies manufactured for the occasion. These parodies come dangerously close to his own performance as spectacle maker. But the parodic edge to the trope could have been found in the king himself had Jonson been aware, for instance, of the correspondence of King James with Cecil and other English magnates before his succession to the throne; these letters offer a most telling instance of the chicanery of Jonson's false statists, newsmen, and time-serving poets. In the king's correspondence with Cecil, an elaborate code is used in which numbers rather than names figure. James is 30, Cecil 10, Lord Henry Howard 3, the queen 24.[19] Occasionally, these numerical references do indeed mystify. A sentence beginning "We did wonder greatly at your newes and no less at the curiositie and diligence of 7" (from a letter written by 8 [Edward Bruce] to 3; p. 38) leaves the identity of 7 very much up in the air (only a piece of marginalia identifies the cipher with Cobham). But, in large measure, the correspondence is absolutely transparent. 24 is always clearly a queen, 30 as evidently the king of Scotland, 10 at pains to address 30 in terms that echo public declarations. Hence 10 repeatedly accords James the style of gods, comparing him to God, in fact, as the "lively image" (pp. 27, 35) of the deity in thinking so well of Cecil and in so generously agreeing to accept money from him. The correspondence is filled with intrigues at court and, as one might expect, fears about Elizabeth's attitude were she to discover the letters. Cecil assures James that his letters are so innocent that were they to fall into the queen's hands, they would not disturb her. Cecil makes sure that this is so by urging James to keep his "secretts" and "deepest misteryes" (p. 18) to himself, and although it was presumably to keep the queen in the dark that the cryptic correspondence was started in the first place, the entire exchange is written from her presumed vantage point and under the possibility that the letters might come to her eyes. Allaying James's fears, Cecil safeguards himself in the queen's sight. The secrecy meant to assure their safety rather affirms her power. James and Cecil are like two bad boys plotting behind their mother's back; no one—except perhaps the king—is taken in by this show. Any secrets here could as easily be said aloud.

In the main masque and antimasque Jonson serves up a "metaphorical dish" of secrets of state worthy of King James in *Neptune's Triumph* (1624), written to celebrate the return of Charles and Buckingham from their mission to woo the Spanish infanta. The masque is a complex mix of state secrets, poetic mysteries and their parodies. There is a genuine statist in the masque, Proteus, "father of disguise" (line 95), played by Sir Francis Cottington, an accomplished secret agent, as Stephen Orgel notes. The masque rewrites history to serve the state, and the fiasco of the negotiations becomes the triumphant return. Similarly, it glosses another failure, that the masque was never performed because of a diplomatic squabble. On the contrary, it appears to record a performance, beginning like other masques by "setting" the king in state; and in the masque of the next year, *The Fortunate Isles, and Their Union* (1625), Jonson refers to *Neptune's Triumph* as if it had been performed. On the page, it is as if the production took place, and in the masque, it is as if the return of Charles was indeed a triumph. So is state discourse manufactured.

The ironies extend to the parodic antimasque, a debate between Poet and Cook, the latter claiming to be a genuine poet as the inventor of the antimasque. Grudgingly, the Poet assents to at least some of the Cook's claims, and after first recoiling at being called "brother poet" (line 82), he seems unperturbed when the Cook repeats the phrase (line 221). Finally, he stops protesting the vulgarity of the antimasque and consents to it, attempting to preserve some of his dignity by agreeing in Martial's Latin: "*Nam lusus ipse triumphus amat*" (line 223), even a triumph likes a good time. The Poet in the masque is not entirely the poet of the masque, just as the Cook is not entirely his rival and co-provider of masques, Inigo Jones. For Jonson's masque does include those tasteless antics that the Poet wanted to exclude; to "please the palates" (line 28) of the audience, the Cook's notion of the function of art, the masque presents an antimasque of men who have become food for a stew. Not surprisingly, they "do relish nothing but *di stato*" (line 176); Italianate mysteries of state comprise their sole talk and savor. But this is as true of the masque itself; that is what makes it a single "metaphorical dish" (line 169). The catalog of ingredients in the Cook's stew is familiar

71

from "The New Crie": it is composed of those who "know all things the wrong way, talk of the affairs,/The clouds, the curtains and the mysteries/That are afoot" (lines 178–80). Not surprisingly, too, these are the suppliers of gossip for St. Paul's, newsmongers. Their chief is the epicoene Archy (in fact, the king's dwarf), and their company does not shirk sexual perversion and abuses of the body. Once more, the private realm intimates the public sphere. And parodic secrets of state echo against real ones.

In *Neptune's Triumph,* as in *News from the New World,* Jonson operates with extreme tact in perilous waters. In the next chapter, the possibility that these parodies have a political point will be entertained, and the full duplicity of the language of power will be explored. Here, it is enough to indicate how widely the absolutist trope of state secrets was used; in *Volpone* the full dramatic potential in the trope emerges, allowing us to consider further the language of politics as well as the politics of language. State secrets in all their trappings were on Jonson's mind when the public theater was his concern as much as when a royal masque was called for, and the fearful parody of absolutist arcana that "The New Crie" offers comes to life outrageously in Sir Politic Would-Be, the Englishman let loose in Volpone's Venice. Sir Pol has rightly been understood as an imitator of that magnifico of intrigue and duplicity;[20] in him, we will see further into the ways in which the body is subverted for the sake of the state, ways in which absolutist rhetoric undermines republican values, ways in which parodic state secrets come close to the real thing. What Jonson presents in the public theater extends from the locus of state power. The arcana housed in Sir Pol image more profoundly disturbing acts. Like Volpone, Sir Pol is full of plots and stratagems, and his are quite explicitly aimed at overthrowing the state; like the ripe statesmen of "The New Crie" he sees plots everywhere and adds to those he sees. Sir Pol is, however, not merely an imitation of Volpone and a parody of a politician. He carries a world of meaning with him, as perhaps his discovery creeping beneath a tortoise shell, that archetypal pillar of the world, implies. *Arcana imperii* is the supporting idea in his world, and this reflects upon his model in the play. For he is, however unwittingly, a guide to a genuine menace. The parody has a point.

Sir Pol assumes that there are secrets behind all events, that nothing that happens is simply natural. Everything is prodigious and monstrous; there is always a conspiracy. Commenting on the death of Stone the fool, Sir Pol reveals that he was "a conceal'd states-man" (2:1, line 78) who received and dispensed his secrets "in oranges, musk-melons, apricotes,/Limons, pome-citrons, and such like" (lines 72-73). Sir Pol explains to the amazed Peregrine the essential knowledge of "the ebbes,/And flowes of state" that governs his "private use" (lines 104-5). No wonder that mysteries lurk in melons; to him all of private life masks public purposes. In this belief, Sir Pol is an ironic and troubling figure in *Volpone,* for although absolutely blind to the world he moves in, and easily caught in its machinations— nothing he observes does in fact advance his "private use" or his public posture—he is, nonetheless, perfectly correct in principle. The world of *Volpone* is fully conspiratorial, and its inhabitants are monstrous. Private life is repeatedly suborned. In the second act of the play, when Volpone leaves his bedroom and moves into the public square, Sir Pol provides a running commentary on Volpone's performance as Scoto, the mountebank with his regenerative oil; Sir Pol fails to penetrate the disguise, of course; although absurdly wide of the mark in praising the speech—how could he know what the "rarest secrets" (2:2, line 161) offered by the mountebank amount to?—his observations of Scoto's "state" (2:2, line 32), however awry, lead him to affirm, quite rightly, that "some trick of state" (2:3, line 10) would explain what he has viewed. There is more to Scoto than meets the eye. Indeed, even our dismissal of Sir Pol's presumably ridiculous admiration for Scoto's rhetorical skills should not blind us to our own admiration for Volpone's arts. Sir Pol is not alone in responding to his words. We should not forget that Celia drops her handkerchief in tribute to his powers. We might pause, too, over Sir Pol's most bizarre fantasies before we dismiss them entirely; like the Cook in *Neptune's Triumph,* he is obsessed with secrets buried in food.[21] Such fantasies cannot be dismissed easily since they are matched by Volpone's most seductive appeal to Celia:

> See, behold,
> What thou art queene of; not in expectation,
> As I feed others: but possess'd, and crown'd.
> See, here, a rope of pearle; and each, more orient
> Then that the brave *Ægyptian* queene carous'd:
> Dissolve, and drink'hem. See, a carbuncle,
> May put out both the eyes of our *St. Marke;*
> A diamant, would have bought *Lollia Paulina,*
> When she came in, like star-light, hid with jewels,
> That were the spoiles of provinces; take these,
> And weare, and loose'hem: yet remaines an eare-ring
> To purchase them againe, and this whole state.

> A gem, but worth a private patrimony,
> Is nothing: we will eate such at a meale.
> The heads of parrats, tongues of nightingales,
> The braines of peacoks, and of estriches
> Shall be our food: and, could we get the phoenix,
> (Though nature lost her kind) shee were our dish.
>
> (3:7, lines 188-205)

Volpone offers the spoils of state to Celia as part of a meal fitting a queen, the glitter of the world, its rarest productions, to be conspicuously consumed. As we know from *Hymenaei*, this consummation recasts a central Jonsonian trope.

Sir Pol's knowledge of plots, his observations, his professed reading in Bodin and Machiavelli, do then have private consequences, and do point to the main plot, which appears to be about greed, pride, and lust, those private vices. Sir Pol instructs Peregrine on table manners, "When you must eat your melons, and your figges" (4:1, line 31), and Peregrine asks, "Is that a point of state, too?" (line 32). It is the right question to ask, for in *Volpone* private desires followed to their ends would undermine the state; there is no separation of private and public. Sir Pol finally reveals his plots to Peregrine, even allowing him a perusal of his private writings, his diary. The plots, as Sir Pol proudly acknowledges, when known are nothing (4:1, line 126), as insubstantial as the food of "The New Crie," the notes "'bout *ragion del stato*" (line 141) amount to a catalog of purchases —food and clothing—that conclude in another bodily necessity: "And at *St. Markes,* I urin'd" (line 144). Sir Pol's language of state here mystifies the natural body and its needs. His role suggests that the natural body is always a function of state. What Sir Pol brings to Venice is an English mind schooled in absolutist subversion, a mind like the ripe statesmen's of "The New Crie" or the parodic statists in Jonson's masques, glutted on foreign intrigue. That this occurs in Venice conveys a political point.

THE Venice in which Sir Pol moves is as a political configuration the home of republicanism.[22] No better intimation of its use for *arcana imperii* can be found than the masquerade Tiberius indulged when he pretended to invite consultation and open discussion of his absolutist behavior. Despite the atmosphere of Italian vice that hangs over *Volpone,* it is not the world of the corrupt Italian court that we find, not the lubricity of incest, adultery, murder, madness, and bestiality of the plays of a Webster or a Tourneur. Rather, Venetian traits are

74

in full evidence, not merely in the locale and customs casually alluded to—with a security, however, that suggests knowledge of the city—but especially in the central themes of the play, greed, the vice of a commercial city, and justice, the pride of Venice.[23] There is a point in considering the play's setting in some detail, for Venice—especially what historians call the myth of Venice—was richly appreciated in England, and Venice could be appropriate for absolutist dissimulation. In 1603, after a forty-four-year lapse, regular ambassadorial relations between the two states had been resumed. Sir Henry Wotton sent back letters from Venice (he was ambassador during 1603-10, 1616-19, and 1621-23) filled with political intrigue, machinations involving the republic's defiance of the pope, and hopes of its conversion to Protestantism; Wotton sounds the depths of Venetian vice, however, at least for our purposes, when he reports them great "swallowers of news" (1:112).[24] This vice stands as the opposite side of republican virtue as manifested in consultation, deliberation, endless discussion, the openness that Tiberius pretended for Gallus. As Wotton wrote to Sir George Calvert in 1622, "Abundance of counsel, and curious deliberation, by which they subsist in time of peace, is as great a disadvantage in time of action" (2:228). The myth of Venice enshrined their counsels; it was the pressure of history, however, that created this timeless myth.

The history of Venice is tied to the revival of republicanism in the Renaissance, first in Florence, in the reunderstanding of Roman history and the exaltation of Brutus as hero and with him a new definition of the relation of antiquity to active participation in political life. In *The Crisis of the Early Italian Renaissance*,[25] Hans Baron calls this "civic humanism." At first, around 1400, a Florentine phenomenon, bred of the threat of Milanese invasion, the notion soon attached itself to Venice, as in a *Discussion on the Preferable Way of Life* of Giovanni Conversino da Ravenna, a Paduan humanist, a dialogue measuring life under a prince against the Venetian republic and coming out in favor of Venice (pp. 134-35). Venice was subsumed by Florentine rhetoric, and for about thirty years during the fifteenth century (ca. 1420-50), facts answered rhetoric—a republican alliance was formed of city-states facing down the princely tyrannies. Venice soon withdrew from the alliance, however, preferring power politics to philosophy. This withdrawal marked the political triumph of Venice, and by 1500, when Florence was tottering, as Machiavelli reminds us, between the need for restoration of strong rule and the return to republicanism, Venice appeared to be a republic not merely preserved but politically and economically supreme. The triumph

75

was short-lived, and after defeat in 1509 at the hands of the League of Cambrai, the republic began to decline. Just at that moment, the myth of Venice began to emerge. Against the actuality of historical defeat and of political decay and decline, a group of humanists proclaimed Venice preserved, the myth of timeless Venice.

The Venice known to Englishmen at the opening of the seventeenth century was a compound of the facts and the myth. Jonson's Venice derives from Contarini's account of the republic, which had been translated by Lewes Lewkenor in 1599 as *The Commonwealth and Government of Venice*.[26] According to J.G.A. Pocock, this is the most "mythical" of accounts of Venice: "The *mito di Venezia* consists in the assertion that Venice possesses a set of regulations for decision-making which ensure the complete rationality of every decision and the complete virtue of every decision-maker. Venetians are not inherently more virtuous than other men, but they possess institutions which make them so." And he adds, "To an Elizabethan mind, Venice could appear a phenomenon of political science fiction."[27] Could indeed; not, of course, to those like Wotton, "*il volpone vecchio*" (1:39), famous for his definition of an ambassador as one sent to lie abroad (1:49); he said to the Earl of Salisbury in a letter of 1606, "I call that honest which tendeth to the discovery of such as are not so, by what means soever, while I am upon the present occupation" (1:351), and a month later, explained his need of cash — "I find knaves dearer than honest men, and in this country fully as necessary" (1:367). Wotton was not above invoking "reason of state" (2:237) to justify his activity, which he did not hesitate to define as a form of spying. Yet Wotton also was entranced by the myth. His public declarations to the doge are full of it;[28] but so, too, are the opening pages of a history of Venice he began to write in the 1620s. In a letter sent in all probability to Buckingham, Wotton included the preface to this history. There he describes Venice as "timely instructed with temperance and penury (the nurses of moderation)"; these founding principles, he declares, remain with the republic to this day (2:255). He might be quoting Contarini.

Venice, Contarini writes, is a paragon of "institution and lawes" (p. 5), founded "in a consenting desire to establish, honour, and amplifie their country, without having in a manner any the least regarde of their owne private glorie or commodity" (p. 6). Man as a naturally political animal finds his fulfillment in Venice, where law is the product of consultation, rationality overcomes private desire, and the state, in its complex interlocking of princely rule in the doge, aristocracy in the senate, and democracy in the council of citizens, presents the perfect order of the Polybian mixed state, replete with checks and balances, opportunities and limits, self-regulating and self-controlling in its totally rational disposition. Temperance and moderation are the key words in Contarini's praise for Venice (for example, pp. 146 ff.) as they are in Wotton's preface. These virtues have maintained it and preserved it. It was this lesson that Lewkenor expected his readers to derive from the book: a mirror of perfect government, uncorrupted justice (see "To the Reader," esp. sig. A2).

The dedicatory sonnets to the *Commonwealth and Government of Venice* tell a more complicated story, however, and reveal how complexly Venice could be perceived, the range of meanings inherent in the place. The poem contributed by Spenser praises Venice since it "farre exceeds in policie of right"—far exceeds Babel and Rome, however; as the "flower of the last worlds delight," Spenser sees its decay as well as its flourishing. The ambiguity of "policie" conveys this: politics and policing—spying—meet in that word. Lewkenor's language, he concludes, surpasses the architecture of Venice; Venice decayed meets Venice preserved. They meet, too, in the pairing of the following sonnets, one by I. Ashley, who sees Venice as Narcissus looking into the sea, a fatal glass, another by M. Kissen, who proclaims the myth full-blown. H. Elmes closes the sequence, paying tribute to Lewkenor, and avoiding the mixtures that Venice provoked for the other sonneteers, the double Venice behind *Volpone*.

It was just such a mixed Venice that Thomas Coryat reported when he visited in 1608 (*Coryat's Crudities* appeared in 1611).[29] Like Jonson's, Coryat's Venice includes "muske melons" and tortoises (1:396), courtesans and mountebanks (1:401 ff.; "these fellowes doe act their part upon a stage" [1:410]; "the principall things they sell are oyles, soveraigne waters, amorous songs printed, Apothecary drugs, and a Commonweale of other trifles"—his hucksters also meddle with matters of state). Coryat has read Contarini (1:3) and regards his own book as the supplement to that account. Not that he would meddle in affairs of state: "It is dangerous to prie very curiously into State matters," he confesses, and "policie" is hence avoided (1:12). In one of the numerous dedicatory poems to the *Crudities,* Donne ironically hails him: "Mount now to Gallo-belgicus; Appeare / As deepe a States-man, as a Gazettier" (1:37). In large measure Coryat fulfills Donne's vision of his newsmongering. Yet there is an implicit politics in this tombstone traveler. Copying inscriptions, recording customs, monuments, works of art, Coryat enshrines Venice as "the fairest Lady, yea the richest Paragon and Queene of Christendome" (1:302), a "mayden Citie ... never conquered" (1:301). He

praises Venice first for sponsorship of the arts, specifically of literature (Sannazaro is the example); "I would to God my Poeticall
friend Mr. Benjamin Johnson were so well rewarded" (1:301).
Venice, republic of letters, is here enshrined as well. And, in his final
pages on Venice, Coryat repeats Contarini; it is a divine state, he
says, "ever preserved" (1:416), a state "as well governed as any City
upon the face of the whole earth ever was" (1:417), a compound of
the best of democrary, oligarchy, and monarchy, "contayning in it
an Idea of the three principall governements of the auncient Athe-
nians and Romans" (1:418).

The myth of Venice was peculiarly suited to the English political
mind. Although nominally Venice was a republic, and although
famed for its consultative, rational institutions, the myth took Venice
out of time, placing it in an eternal present like the time of book V
of *The Faerie Queene* or a Jonsonian masque. As Pocock remarks, it
is timelessness that is normally associated with the *imperium;* the
principle behind the *arcana imperii* is eternal and justifies action
without consequence, action taken without the consultations for
which Venice was extolled. The proliferation of Venetian institutions, as detailed in Contarini, also points, finally, to ultimate secrecy, just as, finally, it was no secret that the official rhetoric of mixed
government cloaked a government dominated by its aristocrats (even
Coryat had no trouble discerning that; see 1:414). In Venice, contradictions cohere, and the republican myth masks an oligarchic state.
This is an ideological point worth emphasizing.

What might be regarded as completely opposite systems of
politics—absolute imperialism on the one hand, participative republicanism on the other—divine right and imperial Rome versus the
councils of Venice—may not have been. The two meet in classical
Rome, and the debate on Rome initiated by the early quattrocento
revaluation of Brutus was still going on in James's time; Shakespeare's
Julius Caesar is evidence enough for that. Renaissance treatises on
government tend toward absolutism, but they also tend to espouse
the Polybian model of mixed government. The most profound political mind of the period, Machiavelli's, embraces both views, and not
merely separately in the *Prince* and the *Discourses*. Both treatises
arise out of the same sense of the nature of political life. Machiavelli
believes in the republic as the best form of government, but given the
precarious nature of government, subject to decline and decay because of the natural depravity of men, the intervention of strong rule
is inevitable. Ultimately, it should lead to the foundation of the republic, but when the republic fails, strong rule is preferable to no

rule at all. Given the choice, Machiavelli takes Rome before Venice, prefers a republic like Rome, expanding to become the empire, rather than a republic like Venice, contracting into a myth of eternity that hides the fact of powerlessness and decay (see *Discourses,* 1:6). Machiavelli praises mixed government as a provisional form more likely to be able to handle the fact that political life is a mass of contingencies facing an abyss of decay. He is not a democrat despite his republicanism; liberty arises only out of a state of conflict. Committing oneself to a single form means handing oneself over to fortune, which does not stand still for such decisions.

Jacobean ideology tends to reverse the Machiavellian moment, focusing on the shared language of eternity rather than on the contingencies. Machiavelli had failed to realize the power of Venice as myth—the actuality housed in the fiction—just as he had been blind to the fact that his own realism was as much a piece of ideology; his commitment to the contingent as the only way to stay afloat in the running waters of politics enshrines contingency as an idea with mythic force, capable of binding opposites and staving off decay by giving form to the ongoing restructuration necessary to ensure the life of the state. Under James, the mythology of empire serves as a preserving image, erecting stability against the contingent, achieving form against the chaos of consultation. One cloaked the other. The king withdrew into mysteries of state and into the rhetoric of atemporality, and declared in himself the mysteries from which he excluded all others. There is, to twist the phrase, something Machiavellian in this, too, the construction of the self as an icon of perfection in a world that lacks perfection. Stand the republican mixed state on its head, and we can find James in a sustaining illusion, the riddle of the phoenix once again.

Hence, the significance of locating *Volpone* in Venice. Volpone, sly wolf, penetrates the myth of Venice and aims at the subversion of the republic, the unmasking of the vice beneath the show, absolutist aims that he exemplifies and which his suitors and servants imitate; Sir Pol is his most unknowing parodist. Sir Pol's plots are bare imitations of Volpone's more thoroughgoing attempts to overthrow family and state; Sir Pol can barely see into these mysteries. Yet it is the success at suborning justice that Volpone labels Mosca's "master-peece" (5:2, line 13), and Voltore's address to the "fathers" of the state that Volpone repeats with relish (lines 33 ff.). "Fathers" of the state: even Venice reveals an absolutist and patriarchal organization and the fathers of the law court are the final working out of the undoing of the family bonds linking husband and wife, father and son. Against the intricacies of the legal system and the laws of inheritance, Volpone works his own "crotchets" and "*conundrums*" (5:11, lines 16, 17), only revealing himself when he has no further recourse. Yet, as a lawyer exclaims at that moment, "the knot is now undone, by miracle!" (5:12, line 95), and Volpone's art is Jonson's. Volpone is assigned to the hospital of the *Incurabili* precisely because, absolute as he is, he is responsible both for his own undoing and his eternal, unchanged preservation. Not surprisingly, he closes the play requesting the "seasoning" of applause; for although Venetian law may condemn him, the absolute claims of the play and its protagonist are a law unto themselves. Throughout the play, Volpone's politics seem casual, virtually nonexistent, yet his private and secret desires would undo the state, his plots work against republican principles. In Volpone, Jonson reveals that the myth of Venice preserved was attached to a dying body.

IN "The New Crie," Jonson had seen the subversiveness of statesmen with their secrets from an opposite but, in the context of English society, equally threatening vantage point, not the absolutist undoing of the republic but the threat of the overthrow of monarchy. The secrets of his statists are allied to puritanical revolutionaries, opponents of bishops and kings:

> All forbidden bookes they get.
> And of the poulder-plot, they will talke yet.
> At naming the *French* King, their heads they shake,
> And at the *Pope,* and *Spaine* slight faces make.
> Or 'gainst the Bishops, for the Brethen, raile,
> Much like those Brethren; thinking to prevaile
> With ignorance on us, as they have done
> On them. (Lines 31–38)

In Jacobean England, religion is politics, and *arcana imperii* have religious implications as well; the phrase also covers the mysteries of God's state, which must not be looked into too closely.[30] In the *Basilikon Doron,* James writes: "The Scripture is ever the best interpreter of it selfe; but preasse not curiously to seeke out farther then is contained therein; for that were over unmannerly a presumption, to strive to bee further upon Gods secrets, then he hath will ye be" (p. 14). *Hymenaei* adopts a similar injunction: "Bid all profane away; /None here may stay/To view our mysteries" (lines 56–58), and it presents to observation the unobservable: "This same is he,/The king, and priest of peace" (lines 80–81), a combined image of empire

80

and divinity. "Wee dye and rise the same, and prove/Mysterious by this love" (*The Canonization*, lines 26-27): Donne's lovers fully appropriate the king's appropriated divinity. They, too, embody a mystical union, joining the imperial eagle and the Christian dove. Their "ridle" of the phoenix, that exclusive and singular creature, is a standard item in the lexicon of the mystical body politic, the body that cannot die. Donne makes it the focus of idealization in another poem, the epithalamium written for the marriage of Princess Elizabeth to the County Palatine; in their coupling, two phoenixes become one. The lovers in *The Canonization* raise the state on their desires. Volpone, on the other hand, undoes it with his. It is a clear measure of his politics that he would eat the phoenix, incorporate it for his private pleasures. This suborns a spiritual and political emblem. The mystical bird has served a similar function for James before, we might recall; *The Phoenix* is his poem about his first love, Esmé Stuart. The secrets of state—mystical and sublime—invariably end in the flesh.

Sir Pol was therefore right; the inscrutable mystery of state is to be read in the body. In his *Devotions Upon Emergent Occasions*, Donne's exploration of the course of a near-fatal illness, the arrival of the king's physician occasions political meditations.[31] The body, rebelling, yet keeping its secrets to itself, represents a challenge to the physician, and Donne reads this as an analogy for rebellion in the state, the danger of whispering plotters to the royal physician. The physicians consult and prescribe, and Donne finds in their behavior a hopeful sign that his body's state is not entirely desperate: "They *consult;* so there is nothing *rashly, inconsideratly* done; and then they *prescribe,* they *write,* so there is nothing *covertly, disguisedly, unavowedly* done" (9 Med., p. 47). The king's physician joins his fellow doctors in forming a society in which deliberation, rational and prudential consideration, and consultation are the chief characteristics. The society these colleagues form is an ideal Venice, the republic governed by the precepts of civic humanism. Later in the *Devotions,* in fact, Donne allows himself a republican fantasy when he takes a stab at defining the original state of society; it is "no *Superioritie,* no *Magistracie*" (11 Med., p. 57), "no *Propertie,* no *Meum & Tuum,* but an universall *Communitie* over all" (ibid.) that he proposes in his founding myth. Or, to bring politics home, it is a parliamentary action that is taken over Donne's body. And Donne is thankful that his condition does not require the extraordinary measures regularly claimed as the prerogative of ruling by *arcana imperii.* He notes that his treatment, in its deliberation and consultation, is not like the speedy seizure of the moment that would signify that his state was desperate. Yet, in being thankful for this, he records a tacit opposition to the principle of absolutist statecraft. Had his case been more serious, it would have required something that Donne appears to regard as politically perilous—sudden action. Here is the analogy as he presents it: "In States & matter of government it is so too; they are sometimes surprizd with such *accidents,* as that the *Magistrat* asks not what may be done by *law,* but does that, which must necessarily be don in that case" (9 Med., p. 47). As Donne's editor remarks, there is something remarkable in the implicit reversal of James's rhetoric of mystery and prerogative here. [32]

As Donne proceeds, *lentè & Serpenti* (10 Med., p. 51), he enters more fully into royal territory. For, resistant to the physicians' prescriptions, the body sets itself up as a counterstate, enclosed in its own arcana: "The *pulse,* the *urine,* the *sweat,* all have sworn to say *nothing,* to give no *Indication* of any dangerous *sicknesse* . . . and yet . . . [the doctors] see that invisibly, & I feele, that insensibly the *disease* prevails. The *disease* hath established a *Kingdome,* an *Empire* in mee, and will have certaine *Arcana Imperii, secrets of State,* by which it will proceed, & not be bound to *declare* them" (10 Med., p. 52). The symptoms that have been read as the secrets of plotters bent on overthrowing the state, signs of desperate civil disorder, are now reconceived. The serpentine hiss of secret whispers, the Sir Pol-like perceptions of conspiracy—"In his curse, I am cursed too; his *creeping* undoes mee" (10 Exp., p. 53)—lead Donne to God's secrets, and to raise the *"brazen Serpent* . . . against a *Serpent,* the *Wisedome of the Serpent,* against the *Malice of the Serpent"* (10 Prayer, p. 55).

This transformation reflects significantly on the poets' appropriation of the royal arcana; one mystery could answer another, parodic images could imitate state. Serpent against serpent; thus the king constructed a hedge of divinity around his own rebellious desires. Regularly, James asserted himself in his mystical body and justified his behavior in such assertions. They gave him the latitude he desired for his physical self. To justify such abuses as his frequent absences from court, his pleasure jaunts to the countryside, his general disinclination to take seriously the business of state or to appear in public, the king called for the rhetoric of the royal arcana and its exclusions. The behavior started early, and the two themes of pleasure-seeking and secretiveness recur in reports of him throughout his career. In 1584, a visitor to Scotland had noted that the young king was "too lazy and indifferent about affairs, too given to pleasure, allowing all business to be conducted by others." [33] Unlike later commentators, this reporter was, presumably, disposed to be favorable; his report was written for Mary Queen of Scots, and, striking a prophetic note, he worries that these habits may become habitual. Sir Henry Wotton, paying a surprise visit to the king in Scotland in 1601 on an ambassadorial mission from the Duke of Tuscany, arrived disguised as Ottavio Baldi. Whispering in James's ears that he was an Englishman, he immediately won the king's love. Wotton wrote to Belisaria Vinta the next year that James could be considered one of the most secretive princes in the world ("e tenuto per un di piu secreti Principi del mondo" [1:314]) despite his habits of taking counsel and the familiarity and favoritism he displayed. The king had, it should be noted, assured de Fontenay in 1584 that a network of spies kept him informed of all activity. With less kindness than Wotton, Nicolo Molin, the Venetian ambassador, sent back in his *relazione* of 1607 an account of a king disinclined to rule, disposed only to the chase, and leaving all in the hands of his council: "Ma molto piu dispiace l'aver Sua Maesta abbondonato in tutto e per tutto il governo dei suoi regni, rimettendo il tutto al suo Consiglio, non volendo egli nè trettar nè pensar ad altro che all caccia."[34] In the following years, when James extended promises to Venice in its opposition to the pope, he came to earn the scorn of Paolo Sarpi, who repeatedly wrote to various correspondents that he could wish that England had a more active and less verbal king.[35] Indeed, it was only in verbal strategies that James joined pleasure and business. A most telling instance is the correspondence with Salisbury in which the harried secretary is addressed as a little beagle, sniffing out business at court while the king hunts with his hounds in the country. To Cecil, James made sanctimonious statements defending his pleasures, telling him, for example, in a letter of 5 February 1604, to assure the council "that I shall never take longer vacancy from them for the necessary maintenance of my health then other kings will consume upon their physical diets and going to their whores." The letters repeatedly defend the king's desire for pleasure and are most animated and least hostile to Salisbury's pressure to attend to business after a successful day of hunting.

The king's retired mysteries clothe royal pleasures; beneath his assertions of the inscrutability of the royal will are secret desires and delights. The arcana provide a rhetoric of virtue—and virtue is power—a rhetoric of power that covers the secret pleasures and shrouds the body in the image of the state.

Hence the secret measures danced out in the closing spectacle of *Pleasure Reconciled to Virtue* inexorably arrive at love. The "curious knot" (line 225) twisted in the first of the three revelatory dances of the masque exposes the pattern of virtue to those observers who can "read each act you do" (line 237). The second dance initiates the observer into the sphere of beauty. This is an elucidating gesture, for thereby the platonizing of virtue—the secret design of the first dance—is replaced by beauty as the image of the secret design itself. The second dance thereby presents the formal principle of the imagery and style of the masque and eroticizes it, calling it *beauty*. Beauty appeals to heightened sense; this second dance is an epitome of the "silent arts" (line 253). Beauty is an image which, silent and labyrinthine, reflects the royal arcana—and beauty leads to the ultimate maze, "the subtlest maze of all, that's love" (line 271). In the same way, Donne's lover pleads, "Hold your tongue, and let me love," and "love" begins and ends every stanza of *The Canonization*. This is the language of state; what it masked is suggested by James's outburst at the performance of *Pleasure Reconciled to Virtue*. Tired of the tediousness of the masque and its elaborate measures, he demanded immediate pleasure: "Why don't they dance? What did you make me come here for? Devil take all of you, dance," he blurted out, and Buckingham leaped into action. Similarly, Sir Simonds D'Ewes reports, while the king was taking out Buckingham's wife, Kate, at *Augurs*, he cried out, "Becote George I love thee dearly" and later "fell upon his necke." D'Ewes records a similar outburst some time later, on 20 July 1622: "And a little before, hugging him one time very seriouslye, hee burst foorth, 'Begott man, never one loved another more then I doe thee and let God leave mee when I leave thee.'"[36] Such directness was rare, however. Only for a moment might the holy pretense be dropped.

The arcana meant to take the measure of the royal mind; revelatory and obfuscatory at once, they masked pleasures of the body. They kept James in state. Typically, James invoked the mystical body as if it were his only one. In the first speech of his reign preserved in his *Workes* he declared: "I am the Husband, and all the whole Isle is my lawfull Wife; I am the Head, and it is my Body" (p. 272). Twenty years later, privately, in a letter to Buckingham, we can hear the same language, and we catch his "secretest drifts": "For God so love me, as I desire only to live in this world for your sake, and that I had rather live banished in any part of the earth with you than live a sorrowful widow's life without you. And so God bless you, my sweet child and wife, and grant that you may ever be a comfort to your dear dad and husband. James R."[37] Head, husband, father: the body mystified. According to G. R. Elton, James's real contribution to Divine Right theory lay in identifying his prerogative with the production of a legitimate male successor.[38] Unlike his Tudor predecessor, James located his power in a royal line that proceeded from him; for him, as for many European absolutists, legitimacy was asserted in genealogy. The kingdom was, quite literally, in his body, the arcana made flesh. The secrets of state are the language of eternity erected against the ravages of the flesh and time, the ideal forms celebrated in masques and plays, love poems and political treatises. A single language binds all these together.

Fatherly Authority: Politics of the Family

The mystification of the body that can be found in James's public and private rhetoric becomes explicitly attached to the *arcana imperii* in the only full defense of the political theory of absolutism written in the Stuart period, Robert Filmer's *Patriarcha*.[39] The title of his book immediately reveals its thesis, that the organization of the ideal state imitates the patriarchalism of the family. Filmer, in fact, goes beyond merely making an analogy. For him, the king is quite literally the father of his country, for parents are "natural magistrates" and children "natural subjects" (p. 72), and kings simply act within the "natural law of a Father" (p. 103) in making their absolute claims to obedience. Society is an extended family. Filmer's historical support for this belief takes him back to Adam as the first father. Not merely a model for kings and a model parent, Adam is, literally, the ancestor of kings. And the Adamic model of the "subordination of children is the fountain of all royal authority" (p. 57). Closer to home, Filmer cites James's most explicitly patriarchal treatise, *The Trew Law of Free Monarchies,* in his support. Knowing that in his "natural" role as subject he has no business talking of the mysteries of state, Filmer opens the *Patriarcha* with a disclaimer. He does not "meddle with mysteries of the present state. Such arcana imperii, or cabinet councils, the vulgar may not pry into" (p. 54). Filmer thus prefaces his essay on absolutism by heeding James's command to "incroach not" upon royal territory, and his patriarchal justification represents the development of the principles of state secrets into a political theory of "the profound secrets of government" (ibid.).

These are secrets that are naturalized, familiarized, supported by hierarchies of head and body, husband and wife, father and child. It is sometimes argued that ideology is never more apparent than when it is treated as a transparency, when the political system is allowed to be an extension of natural laws and processes.[40] The mystification of the body, like the masque's transformation of natural procreativity into royal fiat, is an ideological notion. It reflects and is reflected in the images of the conjugal unit, the family, in the period. Pointing to what he calls the "restricted Patriarchal Nuclear Family" as one flourishing family system in the Jacobean period, Lawrence Stone has argued that "the growth of patriarchy was deliberately encouraged by the new Renaissance State on the traditional grounds that the subordination of the family to its head is analogous to, and also a direct contributory cause of, subordination of subjects to the sovereign."[41] Stone's treatment, of course, is part of an ongoing revaluation of the idea of the family that owes its impetus to the pioneering work of Philippe Ariès, whose *Centuries of Childhood: A Social History of Family Life* first studied the family as a social institution with a history.[42] In the past twenty years, the history of the family has developed as a field of inquiry, and although many matters remain in dispute, the institution of the family is indisputably a historical and cultural phenomenon. Stone's work represents a recent trend, recognizing that a number of family structures exist at any time; discontinuities, disagreements, and multiplicity are the norm.[43] Nonetheless, certain features of family life remain circumscribed in any historical period, and it is within these limits that the ideological function served by the domestic unit emerges, whatever its actual composition from locale to locale or from class to class may have been.

The ideology of the Renaissance family is opposed to modern, liberal views.[44] The family in the Renaissance is inevitably a public unit. Marriages occurred between families; diplomacy was carried on through marriage; kings more and more stressed their legitimacy by pointing to their lineage and invented ancestries tracing their descent from gods and heroes to further the sense that genealogy was destiny. Privacy was neither a value for itself, nor a descriptor of family life — the poor lived in one room, the rich in public rooms. The modern belief in the family as a retreat, as the place of comfort in an uncomfortable world, would scarcely have been recognized in the Renaissance, at least officially. Rather, the individual derived a sense of self largely from external matrices, among which the family and its place in society was paramount. The family was understood as part of the larger world, the smallest social unit, the building block of society, not somehow antisocial or a retreat. This idea goes back at least as far as the eighth book of Aristotle's *Ethics* and to the opening chapters of the *Politics,* where a proclaimed *natural* political economy encompasses household and domestic relations.

86

The ideology of the family does not mirror the actuality of family life. It is related to lived realities as images of the state are to those realities. These images function as part of the apparatus and discourse of power, and they embody such power. Hence, although we know that erotic relations were officially subordinated to larger social concerns, we know, too, that love matches were made. John Donne's is a famous case; and the disastrous social consequences that followed his marriage to Ann More suggest how strong the sanctions against it were. Even Donne's rebellion subscribes to a cultural image; *Romeo and Juliet* might serve as a precedent for his behavior. A great frequenter of plays, Donne may have tried to live out a role he found there; some of the elegies, and *The Canonization,* for instance, seem to have been written with texts like *Romeo and Juliet* in mind. The point may be, as Bacon said, that "the stage is more beholding to love than the life of man" (Essay 10), and that the cultural images that contained rebellion left little room in real life to act outside them. Of course, Donne's life did not end with his marriage, and it proved possible to find ways of acting in his society. The system of patronage was not locked into family ideology. Still, his ten years of discontent suggest how closely the family and society functioned in the period, how powerful the ideology was.

The family functioned in the Renaissance to reproduce society.[45] This is not so simple as it sounds. On the one hand, the family is a mirror, alike in structure to the larger structures of society. But its aim, procreation, is reproductive in a social sense as well. Biology is transformed, and the family serves society. The body is inscribed in a social system. We have seen some literary examples of this already; it is part of the very vocabulary of the culture. The family/state analogy is part of that Renaissance habit of mind to think analogically and to explain events by understanding their origins. There is a family structure in thought, and to seek out the causes of things is to find their genealogical principles (or *logoi spermatikoi*). In his *Fowre Hymnes,* Spenser, drawing upon Plato, and especially upon neoplatonic readings of Plato, makes the creation of the world the manifestation of eros; the Christian mystery declared the word made flesh. The pun with which *King Lear* opens—"*Kent.* I cannot conceive you./*Gloucester.* Sir, this young fellow's mother could."—can serve as an emblem of this habit of thinking, the connection between the generation of issues and of issue.

This idea had a political function, too. In Jonson's *Masque of Queens* (1609) the scene of transformation—the routing of the witches and the arrival of Queen Anne as Bel-Anna—is accomplished by Perseus, the embodiment of Heroic Virtue. His virtue or power is specifically described as the power of giving birth. Heroic Virtue banishes terror to bring forth fame; birth and death meet in the language of conception: "When Virtue cut off Terror, he gat Fame" (line 351) and Terror becomes impotent. "When Fame was gotten Terror died" (line 352), Perseus reiterates, concluding, "I was her parent, and I am her strength" (line 356). Parenting, Perseus acts as a kind of male mother. The full appropriation of generative powers to the father makes him father and mother at once. This conceptual power is extended royally; although the masque ultimately brings Bel-Anna forth, she is presented then to her source, the king, for he makes the queen possible; and she is presented, too, by her source, the poet who creates the masque. Hence, at that moment, Perseus points to the House of Fame, newly arisen, "whose columns be/Men-making poets" (lines 361-62), and finally to what Bel-Anna has newly "brought forth" (line 403), the poet's conception, which appears before the sovereign light that makes her visible, that makes her existence palpable, before whom she humbles "all her worth/To him that gave it" (lines 402-3), paying tribute to the father/creator. Bel-Anna's creativity and activity are continually subordinated to the poetic conceit and political situation. These create her. Hence, when Fame appears, she, too, begins by acknowledging "Virtue, my father and my honor" (line 431), before proceeding to confer her attribute on the twelve queens. At the masque's close, the penultimate song celebrates "this famous birth" (line 500) and the last couples virtue and power. "Who, Virtue, can thy power forget" (line 516). Here, as in *Mercury Vindicated* or *The Vision of Delight,* the king's power makes nature.

The masque links the generative powers of virtue, ideas, poetry, and monarchy. Perseus, the poet, and James mirror each other, appropriating conceptual powers that might seem biological. The masque suggests a notion that we have seen at the heart of the secrets of state, that the body is consumed for the sake of ideology. One further ideological point needs to be made—the relation of modern ideas of the family to Renaissance conceptions.

As the title of a recent book by Christopher Lasch suggests, *Haven in a Heartless World,* the modern liberal view of the family as a retreat from the state is an ideological construct, a point argued even more strongly by Jacques Donzelot in *The Policing of Families.* [46] Even as it withdrew from public life, cutting itself off from the world it once replicated, the modern family opened itself to a continual surveillance from the outside world. Modern parents worry endlessly about childrearing; a whole structure of society is brought into the home in manuals and in a pervasive support system that includes doctors, psychiatrists, social scientists, therapists of all sorts, judges when children prove delinquent, teachers. The modern family is the insecure family; no longer part of the world, it is attached by what Donzelot characterizes as a system of relays, extensions of society into the family far from easy to recognize because of the myth of privacy, but all-pervasive nonetheless. The modern family is the family of the death of the family, the family in crisis, in need of help—and intervention. This locates the modern family historically and explains the laments of sociologists, feminists, marxists; in this ideological structure lies the crucial difference between the modern, post-Freudian family, and the family in the seventeenth century. The family of the past did not regard its relationship to society as problematic; the modern family does. The modern family does not reproduce society; rather, it represents the problematic of relationship which is part of the dividedness of modern life. R. D. Laing powerfully sees through modern ideology, and his family bound up in double-binds replicates a society that pretends to have secured a locale free from society's constraints, and then to have placed that locale under a continuous but invisible gaze.[47] I do not mean to sentimentalize the Renaissance family. Valued areas of feeling, as Ariès showed, do not exist in the family as public institution, in a world where children become real persons only when they become adult; however, as David Hunt argues,[48] precisely because children were not seen as different, they were included in the adult world. We have a myth of privacy that needs to be demystified; Renaissance images of the family require demystifying, too. Unlike modern families, Renaissance families need to be read from the outside in: from the state to the family; from the spiritual to the material. In these processes, the family is inscribed, reproduced, mirrored. So read, state secrets can be fathomed.

If we look at some typical instances of family representation in the period, it is not difficult to make out their sexual politics, or to connect them with James's rhetoric, its reflection in the masque, or the poet's language of love. In English painting, representations of the family increase as a genre in the seventeenth century. These group portraits, posed, planned, and inescapably conceptualized, are cultural artifacts, official statements about family functions and relationships. Inevitably, they mirror the language of domestic life converted to state use; inevitably, like Donne's poems, they draw upon the metaphors of state power to express the bonds of intimacy.

A most dramatic instance of the ideological functions of the family may be seen in two pieces of official portraiture, engravings by Willem van de Passe. The first (fig. 14) dates from the last years of James's reign (1622–24), the second (fig. 15) from the early years of Charles's (1625–30). In both engravings, James sits on the throne he proclaimed his in his divine lieutenancy. The scene, labeled the triumph of James as King of Peace, joins the imperial formula of Augustan triumph to its Christian counterpart. The representational model for the king enthroned and serenaded by minstrel angels (a transformation of James's dead daughters) is familiar from countless Flemish paintings, as well as Masaccio's Pisa polyptych. It is founded on representations of the Virgin, a familiar source, too, for portraits of Queen Elizabeth. As D. J. Gordon reminds us, the central panel on the ceiling of the Banqueting House has a similar precedent, for there imperial mythology meets its Christian model, and the Assumption of the Virgin stands behind the apotheosis of James as Prince of Peace.[49] Republican Venice again serves the ideology of imperial Britain, for Rubens's Assumption rests upon the model provided by numerous Venetian ceilings; the minstrel angels adapted by van de Passe find their source in Venetian painting, too. A soulful angel plays before the *sacra conversazione* of Bellini in San Zaccaria; three cherubs play stringed instruments in a panel that now hangs in the Accademia; on a more playful note, two putti serenade the virgin on flute and strings in the central panel of the triptych in the Frari. Carpaccio, too, has his minstrel angels, as does Cima. One transformation of the motif should be noted, for it points the way toward van de Passe's usage; the angels can accompany enthroned male saints. Cima's martyred St. Peter Martyr (Brera) shows an angel with stringed instrument below the pediment upon which the saint stands; Vivarini, in triptychs in the Frari twice represents saints—Ambrosius and Mark— enthroned, serenaded by angels with lutes and viols below. Van de Passe most likely drew directly upon Flemish originals, but his models were nonetheless Venetian, for, as Terisio Pignatti has argued, the motif of the minstrel angels came to Flanders by way of Venice.[50]

The iconographical mixture in this portrait of the royal family, of imperial *rex pacificus* and Christian saint or virgin, makes a political point. The image of James draws upon two languages at once, the imperium and its Venetian antithesis. The image conveys double meanings, hints at reconciliations. Borrowing Venetian formulas for this image of empire, the picture of James produces that mixed form so dear to the English, a visual version of the king-in-parliament, the king-under-law. James often officially repudiated his own Divine

90

Right positions when he found them mouthed by others—the condemnation of John Cowell's *Interpreter* for articulating principles of prerogative is one instance. So, on the other hand, he was presented in forms that carried meanings that might win wide support. We have seen Venice subverted already, in *Volpone.* In this official portrait, absolutism means again to absorb the republic; reasons of state clothe the body and make it politic. The image offers an ideal of state, a preserving ideology, representing the king.

We can see this ideal when we consider where van de Passe locates this family scene. James's court is the court of heaven, where the dead and living are mingled, and not only in the angelic daughters. In both plates, the deceased Prince Henry and Queen Anne stand beside the throne; in the second state, James holds a skull. Although the representation has not changed, his status has: he, too, is dead. Replaced as monarch, he has not been deposed; he remains as a memorial image, dead and yet eternally alive. The king has two bodies. The transformations of the masque are here reenacted, played for keeps. James is a "lively statue," in Bishop Williams's phrase. Still the father of his family and of the kingdom, in the latter engraving he plays the role of spiritual father, the dead father living beyond himself. It was a role he had assumed before, in Jonson's masques, when he lived a second life. And in the preface to the *Basilikon Doron* he wrote as if from the grave, declaring that his book was his last will and testament; his "fatherly authoritie" (p. 4) there rested in his divinity. His disembodied words carried spiritual weight; they were meant to impress his son, to make him an imitation of his word. The principle can be seen in an anonymous portrait of another father and son, Sir Walter Ralegh and his son, Walter (fig. 16). It is not only their names that echo. In stance and expression, and despite differences in costume—mere variations upon a theme—this picture proclaims that sons are the images of their fathers. James had been seen in this matrix, too, his mother's son (see fig. 2).

Only a few years separate the two van de Passe engravings, and one could easily assume that the differences between them are simply accommodations to some natural facts—that James died and Charles became king, married, and that his sister Elizabeth added to her enormous number of progeny. Yet the changes have their political point and affect, as we have seen, even constant elements. Charles's relationship to his father is refigured. In the first engraving, he stands with his hands placed on the Bible; the King's *Workes,* dignified with the Latin title *Opera Regis,* lies beside it. Charles is shown as the heir to James, and in the first state this means that he is the

91

Figure 14. Willem van de Passe, *The Family of James I*, first state (1622–24).

Figure 15. Willem van de Passe, *The Family of James I*, second state (1625–30).
Courtesy, Trustees of the British Museum.

inheritor of the royal word. The literal and spiritual heir is balanced iconographically by the teeming family of Elizabeth and Frederick, the Elector Palatine, on the right side of the picture. The background of the picture reinforces the deployment of its figures. Behind Charles a deer park can be seen; behind Elizabeth there are church spires. The pleasures of the body and the demands of the spirit complement each other, books and deer, children and churches. Elizabeth's womb serves Protestant propaganda, Charles's study does not keep him from being cast fully in his father's image. The background to the first state of the engraving offers a *paysage moralisé*, pleasure and virtue flanking the throne of the king of peace. Once again, pleasure is reconciled to virtue.

The most fundamental difference between the two engravings heightens the ideological function of the image of the family. First, Elizabeth's brood has increased and is more emphatic, although the labels naming the children are simply reassigned; these are not, in other words, representations of individuals. Second, although a spiritual father presides over the second engraving, other spiritual signs have been removed—the divine word and the books are gone, as are the backgrounds with their emblematic meanings. The additional continental progeny and Charles's wife, Henrietta Maria, have obscured them. They are, perhaps, a subtext, hidden from view. In short, the spirit of James, the royal word, has, quite insistently, become flesh. The legitimacy of his rule has been translated into the bodies that fill the engraving. James's contribution to Divine Right theory has been fulfilled. Domesticity, sexuality, family life: this is the sphere in which the arcana are enacted, Volpone's field of action.

The transformation of state is equally notable in an engraving, *James I and His Family,* by Gerrit Mountin (ca. 1634) (fig. 17) that is clearly based on the van de Passe plates. John Webster's verses printed below it provide an interpretive guide. The inexpressibility of James is Webster's rubric for the dead monarch: "Could Art his quistes [silences] of mind express as well,/no Picture in the World should this excell." That silent expression is imaged, however, in the "Happy Coniunction" that Webster reads in the marriage of Charles and Henrietta Maria; they shed heavenly influence.[51] As Roy Strong cogently remarks, not only does the neoplatonic love that Henrietta Maria fostered as a court style have a political meaning, but "the blissful royal marriage and her ever fruitful womb are exalted almost to the level of a state philosophy. Charles and Henrietta are the first English royal couple to be glorified as husband and wife in the domestic sense."[52] Not surprisingly, the two masques that

94

Figure 16. *Sir Walter Ralegh and his son* (1602).
National Portrait Gallery, London.

Figure 17. Gerrit Mountin, *James I and His Family* (ca. 1634).
Courtesy, Trustees of the British Museum.

Jonson wrote for Charles celebrate the love uniting the royal couple. In *Love's Triumph through Callipolis* (1631), Charles, impersonating Heroic Love, leads the masquers to the queen in state; in *Chloridia* (1631), the action is reversed. Love is "a special deity in court" (line 18), the note prefacing *Love's Triumph* declares, and the masque concludes celebrating the imperial meanings in "Beauty and Love, whose story is mysterial" (line 184).

Mysterial, Strong's "domestic sense," the private sphere, is mystified, politicized, made into an ideological construct. This is intimated in the betrothal picture of the royal pair (fig. 18). Nothing less than an angel sanctifies their marriage. A similar meaning hovers in the background of a van de Passe engraving of Frederick and Elizabeth (fig. 19); God's name and a biblical text fill the sky, while, directly beneath, are the children produced by the unfortunate and ever more prolific winter monarchs. The conjunction of heaven and earth is, however, the familiar theme in representations of Charles and his bride, and they normally domesticated the mythological energies of Mars and Venus by exchanging their attributes of laurel and olive, as they do in a Van Dyck portrait (fig. 20). This is a piece of royal mythology endlessly elaborated in Caroline masques. The politicization of their marriage and their private pleasures is beautifully captured in a painting by Daniel Mytens (fig. 21). The couple stands ready to go hunting; only the dogs strain toward the countryside. The royal pair stands firm, hands clasped, an angelic putto showering them with roses. The Mytens painting poses the king before his palace, the queen before the landscape, and then unites them in their pleasures and virtue. A portrait of the couple with the first of their children by Henrick Gerritsz. Pot (fig. 22) conveys further the politics of family life. The king stands haloed and independently erect on the extreme right of the painting. On the left, Henrietta Maria sits and supports her seated and slightly tottering child. The long table is strewn with symbols, among them the olive and laurels. Charles's domestic hat rests beside him. Yet, at the center of the table, and at the center of the picture as well, is the crown, and the curtains so dramatically drawn on this family group and the vast space between its members open upon the symbol of power which is imaged as well in domestic relations—and not only in the royal family.

Patriarchalism is a regular feature of family life in which the natural event of procreation becomes an extension of male prerogative and male power. The family of Sir Richard Saltonstall as painted by David des Granges (ca. 1635) (fig. 23) nicely illustrates this concept. The husband draws the curtain on a dramatic event, the birth

97

Figure 18. Francis Delaram, *Engagement of Charles I and Henrietta Maria* (ca. 1624).

Courtesy, Trustees of the British Museum.

Figure 19. Willem van de Passe, *Frederick and Elizabeth of Bohemia* (ca. 1620).

Copyright Rijksmuseum-Stichting, Amsterdam.

of a male child. Yet his wife is in the background, depicted in a way that was equally appropriate iconographically for the representation of a woman who died in childbirth, as a painting by John Souch reveals (fig. 24). This is not the case in the Saltonstall family, but it is a sign of the place of natural reproduction in the patriarchal family. The family line is symbolized by the joined hands that describe a line rising to the top hat of the *paterfamilias*. The connection of hands is broken, however. The space between the extended hand of Elizabeth Saltonstall and the glove of Sir Richard is like the space in Pot's painting of the royal family. It is the gap between nature and power that political rhetoric transforms. It is the space in which patriarchal rhetoric is constructed, the space of the mystification of power. As in the *Masque of Queens,* the patriarch absorbs female creativity.

The living and the dead are strikingly and disturbingly present as well in William Dobson's picture of the Streatfeild family (fig. 25); mortality again divides the sexes. The mother, on the right, points to her dead child; behind her a column topped with skulls testifies to

99

Figure 20. Anthony Van Dyck, *Charles I and Henrietta Maria* (ca. 1634).
Courtesy, the Archbishop's Palace, Kroměříž, Czechoslovakia.

the mortality of infants and the connection to the mother's as the
body of death. Although the father gazes in the direction of the
dead, he is tied to the earth. His hand rests on his son and heir's
head, and the son embraces a younger child who grabs hold of his
father's clothes. A curtain behind these children answers the funeral
monument behind the dead, angelic child. This disturbing picture
makes no final balance in the claims of the living and the dead; both
the dead child and the heir engage the viewer's eyes, as does the gaze
of the mother. The father looks away, and is yet attached to his children; but the circle of hands does not extend to his wife; hers encompass the dead child.

Patriarchal formulas are fully in place in Cornelius Johnson's
portrait of the royalist family of Arthur, Lord Capel (ca. 1639) (fig.
26). The picture again divides men and women (the younger sons are
dressed in girls' clothing as was typical for boys in their early years).
Males face forward, females look left. The youngest daughter pays
homage to her latest brother. The flower is fittingly presented as a
sign of natural obeisance—she is, Filmer would say, a "natural subject"—to the patriarch. The daughters, indeed, connect with the land-

100

scape behind them. Nature has already been ordered in the elaborate garden seen in the vista. Here, it is further subordinated to the civilized architecture that frames the family group of husband, wife, and sons. The old principle of echo is still there, too. Eldest son and father share the same tilt of the head, and Lord Capel's hat is above his son's head. The boy, too, displays his own similar piece of headgear. Nature and its genealogical order are subordinated to the patriarchal line. In these pictures, the facts of life serve the powers of state.[53] There is no doubt who is the head, who the body.

The facts of life are what art makes, representing. The conditions of production have their place in the representation of reproduction. Hence, in family pictures in which self-portraiture is involved, the matrix of family images serves as an image of artistic authority, too, for instance, in a late painting of Rubens and his second wife, Helena Fourment (fig. 27). Many familiar elements are transformed: although the couple is set outdoors, the landscape is nonetheless divided; flowers behind the woman, stone and statuary behind the man. The movement of eye-glances from husband to wife and child seems more intimate, less patriarchal than in other family groups. Nonetheless, the eyes move hierarchically. The family seems self-involved, and the viewer's eye is engaged directly only by the statue behind the artist's head. Yet that fixed gaze introduces an element in the painting that enforces meanings that drive away from apparent intimacy. The gaze signifies the relationship of artistic production to natural reproduction.

The statue is a storehouse of contradictions, female, yet a herm. A fixed gaze and a maker of limits, the statue is nonetheless a thing made and an object without hands; this wholly artificial female garden god virtually circumscribes the figure of the artist, save for his hand, which extends beyond its boundary. Elsewhere, the presence of deities or ghosts spiritualizes the family; here, in the statue, we see what an artist might make, a phantom wife to replace the flesh and blood one engaged by his eye: a lively statue. And just as the stone female, a limit transcended by the artist's hand that makes it, points to male powers of making, so, too, that extended hand is raised almost in benediction over the couple's child, no doubt a son. The figure of Rubens, his sculpted wife, and blessed child, form a family group that divides the picture in half. On the left side of the canvas, his heir and his art, as the products of his hand, as things made, meet. Nature and art split this picture, and art joins creation and procreation.

These meanings are enforced by what is only at first glance a bit

Figure 21. Daniel Mytens, *Charles I and Henrietta Maria Depart for the Chase* (ca. 1630).

Figure 22. Henrick Gerritsz. Pot, *Charles I and His Family* (1632).

By the gracious permission of Her Majesty Queen Elizabeth II. Copyright reserved.

of realistic rendering, the lead that supports the child who has only begun to walk, a device commonly used in the period. Here, it defines a transitional moment, the child moving out of natural bestiality into humanity by standing up and walking. The rope connects him to his family, tied, the heir in the female line. The lead extends from the hands. For, although the artist's right hand hovers above the child's head, his other hand supports his wife's; she in turn holds the rope. The intimate pressure of his touch is undeniable; it echoes in his gaze and suggests the affection between the pair. Yet the hands also tell another story, of subordination, support, hierarchy, and ultimate separation. The child born of woman is handed over to the man, let loose from his mother. The umbilical cord becomes a rope, nature replaced again by art. The child, coming into his own, is coming into his father's sphere. Of the mother's sphere, the painting makes one

103

Figure 23. David des Granges, *The Family of Sir Richard Saltonstall* (ca. 1635).

The Tate Gallery, London.

more emblematic point. Flourishing amid the flowers behind Helena is the parrot, that imitative creature, the true Sir Pol, that mocker in nature of human speech. The parrot's head and the wife's face in parallel directions, as do the father and son's. And the parrot's eye gazes out like the herm's. What nature can do is reserved for the right side of the painting. The realm of art, artifice, creation, and pro-creation is on the left.

We can find similar meanings in a quite different picture, one painted during Van Dyck's first visit to England, in 1620, or shortly thereafter. It may serve to summarize much that we have been seeing, not only in terms of representation of the family, but of the relationship of art to society. The painting shows Daedalus and Icarus (fig. 28), father and son. Icarus, however, is a self-portrait, done in the Venetian manner that Van Dyck came to master in part by viewing

Figure 24. John Souch, *Sir Thomas Aston at the Deathbed of His Wife*
(1635).

City of Manchester Art Galleries.

the paintings in the collections of the Earl or Arundel and the Duke
of Buckingham.[54] The earl had probably been responsible for James's
invitation to the young artist, and Van Dyck painted Arundel's
portrait during his stay. For Buckingham, he painted the canvas of
The Continence of Scipio (fig. 29), a celebration of generosity and
abstinence in a high Roman mode. Van Dyck was taught—or learned
quickly—the style of gods, and those paintings reflect the values of
his patrons. But so, too, does his self-portrait as Icarus. For, much as
our eyes may be captivated by the display of flesh and the drapery,
both handled in the manner of Veronese, this nude boy is nonetheless clothed in a recognizable style, masking *all'antica*. No actual
masquer would be so undressed; but as in masques, disguise serves as
self-revelation. This is a court style on more than one count, antique,
Venetian; artistic self-assertion meets subservience to the prevailing

105

Figure 25. William Dobson, *The Streatfeild Family* (ca. 1640).

Yale Center for British Art, Paul Mellon Collection. Photograph by Joseph Szaszfai.

winds of taste and style. The artist as Icarus may seem a strange choice, heavily loaded with tragic implication. But it has a wonderful ambiguity. As Carlo Ginzburg has shown, Icarus was undergoing a transformation in the early seventeenth century, turning into an emblem of intellectual daring.[55] Icarus, who failed to be daunted by the limits of knowledge, stood for the opening of the intellectual community, the daring in natural science which ultimately was to challenge the hierarchies of power. The artist here takes that emblem for himself, and a challenge to the *arcana imperii* is offered in this assertion. Not blatantly, of course. For, his father, Daedalus, the mazemaker, gives instructions to the boy to keep him aloft, and his

106

upward-pointing finger (a gesture from Leonardo) is answered by the child's declining and horizontal gesture, keeping him on earth. Whether the figure of Daedalus is also a portrait is unclear—it might be Van Dyck's father, or his spiritual father, Rubens, though there is no reason to make either of those specific identifications. Rather, Daedalus is the transcendent father, the master artist. Placing himself in this family matrix, the artist alludes to his dependency upon his forebears, qualifies his self-assertion with subscription to higher powers. And his extended hand links him with those powers that be. The master artist here, old Daedalus with his hermetic powers, stands for the sovereign power that would keep the boy aloft. Daring as his self-assertion is, it is clothed in the understanding that the artist is produced and produces for those who stand behind him and who survive his end.[56] A mythology of artistic production is rendered here under the mask of the antique, in a Venetian style, in a family grouping. In short, private life points to public life, as Sir Pol knew. And no matter how gentle or domestic some of these depictions of family life are, they carry a meaning revealed more graphically in a typical piece of sexual crudity on James's part. For, the morning after the wedding of Elizabeth and the County Palatine, James appeared in their bedroom and, as D. H. Willson puts it, "with shocking pruriency . . . questioned Frederick minutely about what had happened during the night."[57] Such knowledge is a prerogative of state.

Perhaps there is a somewhat similar shock in recognizing the common rhetoric shared by James's arcana, representations of the patriarchal family, and the driving, domineering, urgent voice that sounds throughout Donne's love poems. The mystification of love, the disguise of sexuality in platonized spirituality, the parade of learning to cover ribaldry, these are characteristics of the *Songs and Sonnets,* rebellious and atheistical in their manipulation of the *arcana imperii.* Long before he considered his own rebellious body silently murmuring the secrets of state, Donne had appropriated royal absolutism for his own private sphere. No text shows this better than *The Sunne Rising,* and we can end this investigation of the shared state secrets of artists and monarch by looking briefly at it.[58]

At the opening of the final stanza of the poem, the speaker makes the absolutist declaration toward which the entire poem tends: "She'is all States, and all Princes, I,/Nothing else is" (lines 21–22). The absorption of the lovers in each other, their replication of the power of the world, constitutes an appropriation of and a reversal of the language of state secrets. "Princes doe but play us," the poem continues, and with that reversal the world of *Realpolitik* is reduced

Figure 26. Cornelius Johnson, *The Family of Arthur, Lord Capel* (ca.1639).
National Portrait Gallery, London.

Figure 27. Rubens, *Rubens, His Wife Helena Fourment and Their Child* (1632–34?).

All rights reserved, The Metropolitan Museum of Art, Gift of Mr. and Mrs. Charles Wrightsman, 1981.

Figure 28. Anthony Van Dyck, *Daedalus and Icarus* (ca. 1620).

Art Gallery of Ontario, Toronto, Gift of Mr. and Mrs. Frank P. Wood, 1940.

Figure 29. Anthony Van Dyck, *The Continence of Scipio* (1620-21).
Courtesy, the Governing Body, Christ Church, Oxford.

to a spectral play of images, illusions of power. The real sphere of power lies in the body, in the absolute privacy of lovemaking from which others are excluded. But that secret moment is clothed in state, for that is the only language available to Donne to proclaim the mystery, to assert power, to create a sphere of privacy. The appropriation of the language of state reverses and fulfills the direction of the poem. It began by castigating the "unruly Sunne," and it ends by establishing rule and ordering the sun's presence. It began by sending the sun to the usual places of pleasure and power: "Goe tell Court-huntsmen, that the King will ride,/Call countrey ants to harvest offices" (lines 7-8); and it began by hedging the lovers round with eternity. It ends by redefining the sun's offices, relocating its sphere. The real world, all the world, is replayed in the flesh. And the reversal occurs in the twinkling of an eye. Observe: "Thy beames, so rever-

111

end, and strong/Why shouldst thou thinke?/I could eclipse and cloud them with a winke" (lines 11–13). The unruly sun, like some lord of misrule, apes the true *roi soleil;* the speaker's observations are dazzling. The epistemological reversal replaces the antic sun with his true image. At the end, his calling upon the lovers becomes his being called to witness a royal levée, an invitation to find his sphere in that reflected light.

That light surrounds the image of the king, dazzling in obscurity, dark with excessive brights. The king is *deus absconditus,* hidden beneath the mask. In the final line of the prefatory sonnet to the *Basilikon Doron* James observes the king shining in "Princely vertues." "Vertues" are powers, the royal prerogative, the blaze of majesty: "And so ye shall in Princely vertues shine,/Resembling right your mightie King Divine" (lines 13–14). Resembling . . . a spectral mask, borrowed robes: that is the secret behind the secrets of state.[59]

3. THE THEATER OF CONSCIENCE

Two truths are told, / As happy prologues to the swelling act / Of the imperial theme. —*Macbeth*, 1:3

A country is the things it wants to see. —Robert Pinsky, *An Explanation of America*

THE MAINTENANCE OF THE MYSTERIES OF STATE occupied both the king and poets and, as we have seen, even in that shared language, there was room for a wide range of possibilities. Yet, the language of absolutist politics is more complex, and the range of possibilities includes contradictions of the sort we glanced at in James's encounter with Spenser. These are now our concern in the pages that follow. The threads we wish to untie once again can be found in the king's language; this time, we catch him contradicting himself. The crucial figure of speech that trips him up is the familiar metaphor of the king as actor,[1] a commonplace of Jacobean culture, and a trope Queen Elizabeth had used as well. The king's double view of the royal performance leads us to see the doubleness in performances in the royal view and, indeed, finally, once again, leads to the public stage. The course of this chapter thus mirrors the one that came before, but with a crucial difference. This time, as we survey Jonson's masques, or poems written for the court by Chapman or Donne, we can see radical strategies of contradiction at work—contradictions which nonetheless do not fall outside the scope of the king's language. This time, when we move from the body politic to the body itself, we focus on the language of marriage that covered the king's relationship to his favorites. This time, when we move to the public stage, the subversiveness in absolutist rhetoric is our concern. The trope of performance—the king onstage—is central to this chapter; its conjunction with the secrets of the last chapter begins to define the complex area in which we now mean to move.

James invokes the figure of the player king twice in the *Basilikon Doron*, first in a 1603 prefatory letter to the English reader, and again at the beginning of the final section of the treatise. In the first instance, public performance is potentially transparent and revelatory; the person offered to public sight is an index to the private, undisplayed self. Inner and outer man are one, and time reveals their coincidence:

> Kings being publike persons, by reason of their office and authority, are as it were set (as it was said of old) upon a publike stage, in the sight of all the people; where all the

113

> beholders eyes are attentively bent to looke and pry in the least
> circumstance of their secretest drifts: Which should make Kings
> the more carefull not to harbour the secretest thought in their
> minde, but such as in the [sic] owne time they shall not be
> ashamed openly to avouch; assuring themselves that Time
> the mother of Veritie, will in the due season bring her owne
> daughter to perfection. (P. 5)[2]

James had frequent recourse to this notion of transparency, offering
himself as a mirror of majesty. In a favorite metaphor, the king's
breast was a "Christall window" (p. 285), "Not such a Mirror wherein you may see your owne faces, or shadowes; but such a Mirror, or
Christall, as through the transparantnesse thereof, you may see the
heart of your King" (p. 306).

But in the *Basilikon Doron,* James also saw public show as obfuscating and opaque; although time would eventually heal the
breach between appearance and reality, he thought, until that happened, the king's public person would be misread by his audience:

> It is a trew old saying, That a King is as one set on a stage,
> whose smallest actions and gestures, all the people gazingly doe
> behold: and therefore although a King be never so præcise
> in the discharging of his Office, the people, who seeth but
> the outward part, will ever iudge of the substance, by the
> circumstances; and according to the outward appearance, if his
> behaviour bee light or dissolute, will conceive præ-occupied
> conceits of the Kings inward intention: which although with
> time, (the trier of all trewth,) it will evanish, by the evidence of
> the contrary effects, yet *interim patitur iustus;* and præiudged
> conceits will, in the meane time, breed contempt, the mother
> of rebellion and disorder. (P. 43)

James assigns two causes to this interpretive dilemma: the king's outward behavior may be at variance with the inner man; his audience's
perceptual and conceptual tools may cause them to misinterpret the
king's behavior. The king had declared, after all, that his transparency
was that of a mirror.

James's two uses of the metaphor of the player king point in a
number of directions. First, he reveals a divided king, convinced on
the one hand of his integrity, on the other of a disparity between
"outward appearance" and "inward intention." Second, he reveals
conflicting beliefs about "outward appearance": in the first instance,

114

"secretest drifts" inevitably surface; in the latter, "inward intention" cannot be read rightly. The source of these conflicts lies in the king (who both believes and disbelieves in the transparency of his show) and in his audience. In the first passage, perception arrives at true knowledge, immediately and in time. In the second, only time may unify the division between the king's self-understanding and the "præ-occupied conceits" of his misperceiving audience, who look at the mirror only to find their own minds. At issue here seems to be the question of whether the royal mind and the secrets of state can ever be accessible to the populace; or, viewed from another perspective, whether James believes that he is being misunderstood or is afraid that he is being understood all too well and wishes a philosophical means to invalidate correct but potentially seditious perception.

The questions raised by James's language thus bifurcate into a complex set of relationships between self-perception and other-perception. In the Jacobean period the area in which these conflicts occur was conveniently housed in a single word, "conscience," a word that contains both the idea of the knowledge of self and the knowledge of others ("consciousness" in a modern vocabulary). The unity between conscience and consciousness that the word *conscience* declares is in James's thinking divided—both in himself and in his audience.

The history of the word *conscience* would require a separate study; in the following pages I aim first at sketching some of the backgrounds in political thought that led to James's bifurcating use, for James's metaphor of the player king, I will argue, points to two strands of political thought that meet uncomfortably in the *Basilikon Doron*. The image of a transparent, knowable king—an image that endorses the unitive meaning of conscience—is rooted in the egalitarian implications of stoic political theory. The image of the misread king—and of cloven conscience—finds its source in a theory of kingship derived from Roman law.[3] James's self-division required his half-hearted subscription to both of these conflicting political theories, and in his hands these theories themselves bifurcate just as the metaphor does.

Language, especially figurative language, reveals James's situation; the way the king spoke serves as a guide to the politics of language, for, as we have seen, language cannot escape being political. At the very least, as J.G.A. Pocock suggests, "any formalized language is a political phenomenon in the sense that it serves to constitute an authority structure."[4] Language constitutes the reality of politics and history; the articulation of events is itself a historical event; words themselves participate in the life of society.[5] As the example of *The Faerie Queene* shows, even supposedly official language carries the contradictions of society. The sovereign attempts to impose a truth on the multivalency of language, to rule out its subversiveness. The sovereign's efforts, however, are not themselves monolithic because the epistemic limits of language include at any point a range of multiple meanings. Elizabeth's claim that she had no responsibility for the death of Mary Queen of Scots was technically true. She had signed the death warrant, but gave no orders for its execution. Playing on the multiplicity of language, she nonetheless was not immune to poetic representations of her power play. The same might be said for James's use of the trope of the player king, in which he offered and withdrew himself at once. In the pages that follow his interpretation serves as a key to a range of multiple meanings, some of which the king wished to control—and did—some of which inevitably controlled and limited him. In the last chapter, we saw James imposing upon the poets, saw Jonson offering the king a looking glass, holding up his own reflection. Now we can see further, for the double language surrounding the player king suggests that the mirror might as easily insulate the king as reflect him, and that royal language—transparent and opaque—was supported by contradictions. Poets could follow the king there, too.

Conscience is the crucial term here, affecting the king and the poets who wrote for the court. For poets the question was which king they saw of the two James offered to view, and how they meant the language of the *arcana imperii*[6] they were expected to speak. Yet, whether opaque or open, approving entirely or holding back, the language they spoke was mirrored in royal discourse, in the double language James spoke. Using James's own strategy of equivocation to represent the king, poets could rely on his self-division and self-contradiction to keep him from understanding implications in their language impossible to express directly. Employing royal language, poets turned the tables on the monarch, appropriating power against power by engaging the most radical potential that resides in language, its own multivalent, self-contradictory nature.[7] This does not make the king's poets subversives or revolutionaries; on the contrary, royalists all, they followed the king's prescriptions, pursuing his sustaining contradictions.

Roman Thoughts in a Crystal Glass

We have seen already that the Jacobean "style of gods" frequently drew upon an imperial Roman vocabulary. Rome, however, could not be drawn upon so selectively, and there was the republic to contend with as well as the empire to emulate. The play of the two Romes defines the first of the sustaining contradictions in James's political thought, for to define his rule, he required the language of Rome in all its complexity, both the stoic affirmation of individual conscience, and theories of the ownership of consciousness rooted in Roman law.

James applied the stoic theory of conscience to himself, justifying his inner impulses; but he also expected his subjects to display similarly upright consciences. The equality of all souls before God, proclaimed in the *Basilikon Doron* (p. 3), is the Christian version of the stoic affirmation of equity. James depends upon it, too, in inviting the "loving Reader, charitably to conceive of . . . [his] honest intention in this Booke" (p. 9). Charity begins at home, and James assumes that he and his readers share upright consciences. James invites his loving reader to view his intentions; the king's conscience is as available to his subjects as his subjects' consciences are to him. For James, however, this ideal of transparency and availability is problematic, for stoic politics permits an individual to rebel against social law (which the king creates, ideally on the basis of natural law) when conscience tells him that natural law demands rebellion. As a partial safeguard against this consequence James adds patriarchal assertions to his rhetoric of charity. The king aims "to win all mens hearts to a loving and willing obedience" (p. 20), the kind a son owes to a father. Yet insofar as stoic egalitarianism sanctions disobedience on the basis of the dictates of individual conscience, James depends upon another set of precepts to make sure his subjects do not have the right to rebel.

To do this, James claims Divine Right, and the language of paternal love and willing obedience becomes the language of "fatherly authoritie" on which absolutism rests. James depends upon Roman law in which the power of rule derives from ownership of the ruled.[8] This belief ensures that the royal will is absolute law and that subjects have no justification in rebelling; we have already seen that James had a justifying myth of originary kingship to support this view, the conquest by Fergus.[9] This tale represents an absolutist gesture, since it roots law in the will and *summum imperium* of the monarch, and places the royal prerogative outside the domain of law; further, it serves to break the notion of the king's place in immemorial time, time out of mind. Instead, kingship is an originary gesture, a moment in time, absolute unto itself.

Although James clearly needs the paternalistic argument in order to justify his will, he also views it as a burden; it is a double-edged concept, and its limits upon the king are a frequent subject in the *Basilikon Doron*. Placed above all men, occupying God's place as his lieutenant, the king stands in relation to God as the populace does to him, in a position of obligation because possessed; owned, and therefore owing. Outwardly, the king stands in God's place. Beneath the trappings of show, he is still a man. Patriarchy represents a double bind; subjecting the king's subjects, it also subjects the king to God and, as we shall see further, to his genealogy. Knowing his own burden, James also knows that although he can command his subjects' obedience, he cannot own their consciences.

James attempts to combine the two theories so that he can be both father to his people and yet assure himself that the dictates of his conscience are always right. These two beliefs imply mutually contradictory consequences, however; if he owns his subjects, then their consciences are irrelevant; if he has right conscience, then so, too, do his subjects. The strain in his theory is particularly evident in two issues he raises in the introduction to the English edition of the *Basilikon Doron,* his attitude toward Puritans, and to those who vilify his mother.

James finds Puritans his worst audience, precisely because their beliefs are so close to stoic theories of conscience. He rails at their egalitarianism, unleashing absolutist, patriarchal rhetoric against those "rash-headie Preachers, that thinke it their honour to contend with Kings, and perturbe whole kingdomes" (p. 6), "not for any evill or vice in me," James claims, "but because I was a King, which they thought the highest evill" (p. 23). Even as he invokes patriarchal and juridical language—the king heads a body politic that is attempting to turn the world upside down by being "rash-headie," attempting to dismember the "whole" kingdom and, thereby, the integrity of the king—he depends upon the principle he disclaims; for James also appeals to the reader to believe in the uprightness of the king's individual conscience. He clings to the stoic theory of conscience for his own sake, dreads its extension to his audience yet needs his audience somehow to sympathize with him. Kings stand upon the stage as exemplars to their people, yet can only exemplify what they deny their people, the right to individual conscience.[10] And the audience becomes, appropriately enough, a *"Hydra* of diversly-enclined spectatours" (p. 9).

James founders on the contradictions in the juridical theory of ownership when he attempts to make peace with his mother's revilers. Although he wants to separate attacks on her from attacks on him, he cannot because she is the source of his claims to the throne, the founding stone in his arguments about Divine Right. Genealogy is destiny, and having Mary as his mother is, as we have seen, a mixed blessing, the consequences of which are not entirely in the king's control. Much as he would wish to be free from the past, he nonetheless wants to control the future. This is equally clear in his addresses to Prince Henry, the immediate audience of the *Basilikon Doron.* James offers his book as his "Testament, and latter will" (p. 4), binding the prince to him, even as he assures him of his unaccountability to the populace. His indebtedness to his father is James's constant theme, both in the *Basilikon Doron* and in a letter he wrote to Prince Henry on 24 March 1603, just before leaving Scotland to begin his reign in England (BL, Harl. Ms. 6986, fol. 65). James delivers a series of moral saws worthy of Polonius (for example, "be thairfor merrie but not insolent, keepe a greatness but *sine fastu"*), urging the prince to realize that his new inheritance is an "augmentation . . . but in caires" and that the prince's prime duty remains to be his father's echo and mirror. Hence James sends Prince Henry "my booke latelie prented" for him "to studdie & profite in it as ye wolde deserve my blessing & as thaire can na thing happen unto you quhair of ye will not finde the generall grounde thairin, if not the verrie particulaire pointe touched." Thus Henry is to "be diligent & earnist in youre studdies, that at youre meeting with me I may praise you for youre progresse in learning." Henry inherits the king's double language.

The *Basilikon Doron* is caught in the contradictions of conscience. Addressed to Prince Henry and to the populace, it attempts to speak two ways at once. Appeals to the reader's conscience turn into assertions of ownership, demands for an outward conformity (p. 8) that leave inner territory inscrutable. Similarly, the prince is allowed free reign, and then made accountable to his father. These divisions and double entendres in conscience describe the king's situation, too. Punningly calling kingship an *onus,* not *honos* (p. 3), James reported the burden of his office, trammeled by divine and human audiences in his every act. "Clothed with two callings" (p. 18), the king suffered division.[11]

The counterdirectives of the *Basilikon Doron* issue in opposing possibilities. By treating half of the king's thought as if it were all of it, a poet could, in effect, contradict the king and yet echo him. This was Ben Jonson's strategy in "A Panegyre, on the Happie Entrance of James" (1603),[12] a poem written on the occasion of the king's first appearance before Parliament. Jonson depends upon the king's proclamation of his own transparency and the stoic politics that lies behind it. Ostensibly a poem of outright praise, Jonson's verse carefully uses James's own vision of himself trapped between two audiences to glance at a mode of mediative reconciliation that James could not entirely sanction. Jonson's protection, in speaking in ways that carry half of James's thought beyond the point that he would have allowed, lies in presenting the king in the position of the double calling that he had used to describe himself. Further, Jonson seems to be speaking from direct exposure to the language of the *Basilikon Doron*. As we shall see, the poem often effectively turns the king's words against himself, not through blatant assertions, but through a familiar device, the poet's appropriation to himself of kingly functions. Jonson's royalist egalitarianism depends upon the idea of the transparent king that James proposed and then withdrew in the *Basilikon Doron*. Jonson pursues the first understanding of the player king to its logical conclusion.

Jonson's main point in the poem is a theme of conscience, that the king's proper existence is the product of his right seeing and being rightly seen. In the body of the poem, the poet locates the king as a rhetorical "object" (line 64) situated between the divine Themis, goddess of justice, and the populace. A similar placement introduces the poem: the king stands between the sun and the dark caverns of human depravity and misprision. We can easily see what this location means by looking closely at the lines, for they provide a condensed version of the entire poem:

> Heav'n now not strives, alone, our brests to fill
> With joyes: but urgeth his full favors still.
> Againe, the glory of our Westerne world
> Unfolds himself: & from his eyes are hoorl'd
> (To day) a thousand radiant lights, that stream
> To every nooke and angle of his realme.
> His former rayes did onely cleare the skie;
> But these his searching beams are cast, to prie
> Into those darke and deepe concealed vaults,
> Where men commit blacke incest with their faults;
> And snore supinely in the stall of sin:

120

Where *Murder, Rapine, Lust,* doe sit within,
Carowsing humane bloud in yron bowles,
And make their denne the slaughter-house of soules:
From whose foule reeking cavernes first arise
Those dampes, that so offend all good mens eyes;
And would (if not dispers'd) infect the Crowne,
And in their vapor her bright mettall drowne.

(H&S 7:113, lines 1–18)

Absolutist metaphorics could have led Jonson as he does in masques to identify James as *roi soleil;* yet the enlightened heavens of the opening couplet do not quite carry this meaning. The resplendent return of the sun translates a seasonal rebeginning into a metaphor for a new kind of perceptual clarity. As the instrument of such perception, the sun stands above and outside of any king that might embody its symbolic divinity. In a similar fashion, what the sun illuminates is treated in a general fashion; the vaults of depravity are not confined to a misguided populace; they "offend all good mens eyes" presumably because all men are capable of harboring such black faults. The sun represents in these lines a faculty of continuous vigilance and ongoing perception, a means of bringing to conscience and consciousness (the unitive mediating position occupied, presumably, by the king, who is present by implication in these lines, as standing between the contrasting images of sun and vaults) the dark within and below. That such an act is expected of the king the final lines imply, for the king is conceived as the chief agent in removing the fog of misperception and thereby the potential infection of the crown.

Indeed, the structure of the "Panegyre" follows the movement suggested by the opening pair of antithetical images. The poem articulates a progress from proper perception (lines 19–56), to proper understanding (lines 57–150; James literally stands under Themis here), to final, corrected language. The poem is at once panegyric and pedagogic, constructing an object worthy of praise by refusing to countenance either the flaccid adulation of the populace as proper response to the king (see, for example, lines 34–35): "Upon his face all threw their covetous eyes,/As on a wonder . . .") or to permit the descent of Themis to signify the king's deification. Rather, she descends with the burdensome demand that James labors under in the *Basilikon Doron,* to conform to the requirements of history and to the needs of the time; in short, to be exemplary upon the public stage:[13]

121

> She tells him first, that Kings
> Are here on earth the most conspicuous things:
> That they, by Heaven, are plac'd upon his throne,
> To rule like Heaven; and have no more, their owne,
> As they are men, then men. (Lines 77–81)

The goddess of justice's speech ties the unitive thread of the poem; Themis's words "began in him [the king]/And ceas'd in them" [the populace] (lines 134–35). And the poet has access to these words because the goddess is what poets see (lines 19–20); as Jonson affirms in the final Latin tag to the poem, poet and king share an equality in their access to such discourse. Jonson's stance depends upon the unity of conscience and consciousness affirmed by stoic theories of equity.

James, receiving this poem of welcome, must have read it differently. What James may have thought is speculation, of course, but it is necessary speculation. Perhaps, hearing the echo of his own words, he did not see that Jonson had pursued them to their egalitarian (not, it should be noted, democratic) consequences. Or, flattered by Jonson's recognition of his poetic talents, he did not notice that Jonson had used the recognition to affirm himself. Or, seeing the populace depicted praising him and a goddess at his ear, he may have failed to see Jonson's sober response, as spectator and spokesman, to the responsibilities implied by the king's conspicuous placement. For, as the "Panegyre" shows, Jonson, the poet who came to be a favored spokesman for the court, hardly subscribed fully to James's absolutism. Transcribing half the king's argument, Jonson pursued a strategy that at once allowed his conscience and was sure to be acceptable to the king, not only because he appeared to echo the royal rhetoric, but because the very contradictions in the *Basilikon Doron* boxed James in. To safeguard his right to act improperly and to exercise his prerogative, the king needed to see in Jonson's verse the version of himself he wished his audience to see, transparent, a mirror of virtue before their eyes.

James's rhetoric assured his blindness. There was no controlling the consequences of his contradictions. It was, we know, the king's mystery he wished to preserve, and it was most characteristic of Jonson to echo those state secrets in the masques he wrote for the court. At first, Jonson's masques were dualistic structures in which the power of royal goodness dispelled the forces of evil. But, as the form developed, main masque and antimasque came to share a single invention, to elaborate a central figurative device. It is in that development that one can see the masque veering away from a simple replication of the king to a more complex representation. Both secrets and what lies behind them could be presented at once, and again, Jonson could count on the king to read only so far. The masque so entirely echoes the king as to catch his conscience unawares; more penetrating gazes might perceive how fully the contradictions of discourse and the multivalencies of power were revealed.

By unifying main masque and antimasque through a thread of figuration, Jonson set up a situation in which there was the potential for his figures to speak two ways at once. This is perhaps clearest in *Oberon* (1611), one of the first of the unified masques, precisely because the masque does not quite manage to bring off what it is attempting and thus reveals the strain in Jonson's design. Convincingly, Stephen Orgel has argued that in this masque Jonson struggles with the conflicting requirements of metaphorically unifying a masque from which the king must nonetheless be excluded since he was not a masquer.[14] As Orgel demonstrates, the hinge of the masque—carried in its name—is the figure of Oberon, Prince Henry in disguise, and the masque's language leads naturally to him, and not to the king enthroned in state; although the requirements of the form must bow in that direction, the language and the internal design of the masque do not. This is the most palpable fissure in the masque, the most clear-cut point where the masque seems to divide from itself. But the entire design, in fact, presents a series of geological faults. Through the breaks, double meanings can be read.

Oberon is virtually the first masque of Jonson's in which the antimasquers bear a relationship to the court. Earlier, witches and cupids had supplied the errant troops and, although in truth the putti of *The Haddington Masque* (1608) have a glancing relationship with James's pleasure-loving court, the parallels are not emphasized, nor would it have suited the decorum of the masque's occasion, the wedding of Lord Haddington, to have done so. But, in *Oberon,* the antimasquers are satyrs, fierce pleasure-seekers, and to suit the integrity of the design, unlike earlier threats to order and stability, they are not banished from the final revelation and transformation offered by the masque. Rather, they partake of it. Thus, from the first, Silenus, their leader, encourages them to believe that their lives will only be better when Oberon comes:

> *4th Satyr.* Will he give us pretty toys
> To beguile the girls withal?
> *3rd Satyr.* And to make 'em quickly fall?

123

> *Silenus.* Peace, my wantons; he will do
>   More than you can aim unto.
> *4th Satyr.* Will he build us larger caves?
> *Silenus.* Yes, and give you ivory staves
>   When you hunt, and better wine—   (Lines 62–69)

If, for a moment, it appears that Silenus puts the eager satyrs in their place—"more than you can aim unto"—it is rapidly made clear that "more" here is simply quantitative, not qualitative. The pleasures of the reign of Oberon will be surpassing, but they will still be pleasures, indeed the very pleasures that characterized James's court—wine, hunting, sexual promiscuity. If at first it seemed that the satyrs were expected to reform to be suitably incorporated into Oberon's reign ("we shall leave to play/With Lyæus now, and serve/Only Ob'ron" [lines 58–60], they assure Silenus), it is because Oberon can outdo even the pleasures of Bacchus. He surpasses all the gods, Silenus assures the satyrs, Pan, Bacchus, Phoebus, and Mars (lines 49 ff.) in his bounty. And they prepare to welcome his arrival with bells that will jangle more loudly than "the stripes/Of the tabor when we carry/Bacchus up" (lines 90–92). "He's the height of all our race" (line 48), Silenus seductively intimates. The promise of Prince Henry is an endless bacchanale, outdoing his father.

For the masque to have denied these meanings, it would have needed to repudiate the satyrs, or to undermine the authority of Silenus. Yet precisely the opposite occurs. The masque is not structured like earlier, dualistic masques, as a series of exclusions rising to a final truth. Rather, it is constructed by layerings and deepenings, a study in mediation and dissolution. The action moves deeper onstage; first the rock that is the backdrop opens: "See, the rock begins to ope!/Now shall you enjoy your hope;/'Tis about the hour, I know" (lines 94–96). Here, Silenus's promise to the satyrs is interrupted by the sylvans who sleep before the palace revealed by the opening of the rock. Their eyes need to be opened before the masque can proceed. It is the satyrs who waken them, and Silenus makes several ironic stabs at them, culminating in his question as they start up amazed, "How, now, sylvans! can you wake?" (line 153). The ironies proliferate when we view these peaceful gatekeepers of the pastoral realm in the context of James's most prized accomplishment, his maintenance of peace. (As Arthur Wilson suggested, such security was the fruit of peace.) The masque continues when "the whole palace opened" (line 213) to reveal Oberon "afar off in perspective" (line 215). He then moves forward through the openings in depth that have supplied the space of the masque. "Melt earth to sea, sea flow to air,/And air fly into fire" (lines 220–21): dissolution attends his arrival. His chariot moves to "the face of the scene" (line 234) where the satyrs welcome him with leaps of joy.

At this moment the masque reveals its most visible fissure. The chief Sylvan silences the celebration and draws the satyrs' attention to the one toward whom Oberon has been moving as he comes forward—not to them, but to the king who sits in state and occupies in the space of the hall the complementary position to the perspective space where Oberon was first discovered. The Sylvan speaks here as a spokesman for James and wrenches the entire design of the masque; the decorum of the trope of the masque that knows no higher ruler than Oberon is violated to maintain the decorum of the court. The sylvans who, before, could be taunted by the satyrs and their leader have now acquired a new dignity. Even more striking, however, is the role that Silenus plays at this moment. Until now he has functioned as a spokesman for the pleasures of a licentious and acquisitive court epitomized by his "wantons," the satyrs; at the moment when the masque turns to James, Silenus becomes his eulogist:

> This indeed is he,
> My boys, whom you must quake at when you see.
> He is above your reach, and neither doth
> Nor can he think within a satyr's tooth.
> Before his presence you must fall or fly. (Lines 253–57)

The words appear to preserve James in all his virtue. But having Silenus speak them makes them ambivalent, for no repudiation of his earlier role in the masque has occurred. Nor does he quite maintain his exalted tone all the way through the speech. Although the satyrs have been given the choice to "fall or fly," the praise of James as it continues seems to allow another course of action. Silenus stresses his "sweetness" (line 263), that although divine, James "stoops" (line 262) to govern, and that he is a king after every man's desire, giving peace, liberty, and prosperity:

> He's such a king as they
> Who're tyrans' subjects, or ne'er tasted peace,
> Would, in their wishes, form for their release.
> 'Tis he that stays the time from turning old,
> And keeps the age up in a head of gold. (Lines 264–68)

These promised virtues might well suit the taste of Silenus's "boys." When Oberon's chariot came forward to James's throne, the song celebrated this movement to state as the expression of "Oberon's desire" (line 223) leading to James, "the wonder . . . of tongues, of ears, of eyes" (line 226). Thus, even the break in the masque is figured as a moment of sensual fulfillment. And the break in the masque—when its unity is violated, moving outward to praise its royal spectator, and ultimately having Silenus speak his praise—is, in fact, Jonson's safeguard, a break that can serve to separate the poet from the double meanings that might be read in his designs. From *Oberon* on, however, the seamier side of court life entered the masque, usually through some side door that allowed the king to look aside and the poet to claim impunity. The masque then mirrored the royal mind in its self-division;[15] poet and king found such division self-protective.

These designs were, on occasion, the subject of masques. Their self-referentiality points us to the kind of double entendres we find in *Oberon*. In *Love Restored* (1612), the highly self-conscious production that followed, the propensity of figures in masques to speak two ways is a central subject revealed at first in the person of a Masquerado who tells the king that no masque can be performed, and affirms his truth by affirming his lie. "I can speak truth under a vizard" (lines 4-5) is his assurance, and unmasking is the very action of the masque, in which Plutus, disguised as Cupid, needs to be unmasked so that true cupidity can be restored. The presiding figure in the masque is Robin Goodfellow, who arrives to tell how hard it has been for him to get onstage, and how many costumes he tried on at the door before he gained admission to the hall. Robin is nothing but a shapeshifter,[16] and when he arrives "in this shape you see me in" his affirmation that it is "of mine own" is immediately coupled with the assurance that it is at the same time "part o' the device" (lines 127-29). Robin is the spokesman for the masque, and his message is clear: appearances are not to be trusted. This might be an apt message for a monarch who declared that there was more to him than met the eye; it might also suggest that there was less. In the words of Robin, "we are all masquers sometimes" (lines 95-96); such is the duplicitous norm for the language of the Jonsonian masque.

Hence, when the bowlbearer in *Pleasure Reconciled to Virtue* (1618) turned to the king and asked him to "pardon me for my two senses" (line 60) he pointed to the potential for double entendre in the masque. The opening bacchanale might well have the hard-drinking sovereign in mind, and might explain the need for royal assurances—"if it please our new god" (lines 73-74)—before an anti-masque of men become bottles danced before the king.[17] Nor can it

126

be beside the point that the king's heroic counterpart in the masque, Hercules, whom the bowlbearer serves, was as famed for drunken rampages as for his martial virtues. Jonson was hardly someone who considered drinking a vice, and these double entendres seem broad and good-natured. Yet we cannot fail to recall that James was palpably disturbed by the masque, and interrupted its performance to demand more dances and fewer words. When Jonson recast *Pleasure Reconciled to Virtue* as *For the Honor of Wales* (1618), the bowlbearer disappeared, along with the bellygod he hailed, and the part of Hercules was severely curtailed. The antimasquers are in the new version Welsh bumpkins, not, as it might have appeared, courtly roués. The revised masque is full of burlesque learning, but equally full of assurances that such parody does not affect the learned monarch. All faults are placed on the poet, who is said to have been drunk when he presented such monstrous antimasques in *Pleasure Reconciled to Virtue,* so unsuitable for the Prince of Wales. The assurances are so insistent that at the end Welsh dialect disappears entirely, and in solemn tones James is told of the loyalty he had perhaps momentarily suspected. This most unusual end for the masque suggests the perils of the path Jonson negotiated.

He did not, however, shift his tactics, and we can see protective disclaimers in *News from the New World* (1620) erected to repudiate meanings that are nonetheless there. The antimasque presents the poet's fancy, fetched from the moon; the main masque, the sovereign's creation. And although these are said to be utterly different worlds, the first impinges on the second. For the crowd of lunatics, composed of lawyers, Puritans, Rosicrucians, religious fanatics, women, lovers, narcissists, and idiots, is swelled with the addition of knights and squires (line 219), and soon the topography of the moon includes a Hyde Park for promenades (line 226) and "their new Wells too" (line 237). Court creations and fashions are being satirized in this lunatic utopia, and court prodigality, too; the herald reveals those on the moon plagued by debts (lines 245 ff.). Finally, the moon offers "the Isle of Epicoenes" (lines 249-50). This may be the poet's fancy (he had a play to prove it), but it also mirrors court debauchery. No wonder that when Charles and the dancers are ushered in the herald needed to make loud disclaimers dismissing objects of delight for "a more noble discovery" (line 273). He dispels the possibility that what an earlier figure in the masque had revealed about the news he pandered might also be true of the news brought from the moon: "Why should not they ha' their pleasure in believing of lies are made for them" (lines 49-50). A similar design informs an earlier masque, *Mercury Vindicated from the Alchemists at Court* (1616), in which the king's true creations come to replace the false creations of tyrant Vulcan. Yet these, as much as the poet's lunatics, are court creatures, and Mercury indicts the court for its bartering of honors (line 84). He does this before the king's face, indeed, encouraged by his "favor" (line 98), launching an attack on the court explicitly countenanced by the king. James's presence is his safeguard. For to parade before him the buying of titles, the actions of intelligencers, the corruptions of the law, the debasement of manners, was the only way to get away with it. James is dissociated from the debaucheries of court, sealed off in the space of idealistic praise with which the masque ends, appealed to throughout as the benign monarch who disapproves of Vulcan's reign. James is shown a mirror of his court but is invited not to identify it as his; new creations are presented in the finale as in *News from the New World* who are not the debased creatures of Vulcan's reign. They are the new men made by James's "favor" and warmth. Not only is the king invited to see himself in that flattering glass; it is, as well, an accurate representation of how the court looked to James. For it was a world made by him in his own image. He did not see it as Vulcan's realm. And Mercury, that juggler of words, falls silent, playing into the king's power. For, as he acutely expresses, such dissociation is the only means to acquire royal favor. His words to Vulcan reflect upon his own fate in the masque: "Vanish with thy insolence, thou and thy impostors, and all mention of you melt before the majesty of this light, whose Mercury henceforth I profess to be, and never again the philosophers'. Vanish, I say . . ." (lines 166-69). And, just before *he* vanishes, he makes it clear that James, replacing the philosophers, is the chief alchemist at court, capable of transforming the dross of the antimasque into the pure gold of the main masque.

Mercury's strategy is nowhere better seen than in *The Gypsies Metamorphosed* (1621). This was James's favorite masque, and it was performed an unusual number of times. What is surprising here is what Dale Randall has so fully revealed about the masque, its undoubted satiric thrust.[18] In *Gypsies* we have then an epitome of the doubleness of the Jonsonian masque, for it managed to delight the sovereign and yet did not shirk criticism. In *Gypsies,* we can see fully the consequences of making the masque an entirely figurative form. Jonson presents in the actions of the masque a metaphor that cuts at least two ways precisely because main masque and antimasque are virtually one and the same; it is the courtiers who are disguised as the reprobates, the gypsies—and they interact with the townspeople—

128

who are the antimasquers, as well as with the royal entourage. The masque considers the fortune that the gypsies read in James's hand and the fortunes that they pocket; fortune serves as the conceit of *Gypsies,* its metaphoric hinge. Although the town puppy asserts that the gypsies "have other manner of gifts than picking of pockets or telling fortunes" (lines 1072-73), those two activities define the laying on of hands in the masque. In truth, these activities are all one, for the king is fortune, as the Captain of the gypsies (a role played by Buckingham) acknowledges:

> But why do I presume, though true,
> To tell a fortune, sir, to you,
>   Who are the maker here of all;
> Where none do stand or sit in view,
> But owe their fortune unto you,
>   At least what they good fortune call?   (Lines 323-28)

The action of the masque is simple: first the gypsies read the fortunes in the hands of the king and his company, then they proceed to pick the pockets of the townsmen. The duplicitous meeting of hands in these actions of giving and taking fortunes is wittily registered in the reading of the Countess of Buckingham's palm:

> Your pardon, lady, here you stand,
> If some should judge you by your hand,
> The greatest felon in the land
>   Detected.
> I cannot tell you by what arts,
> But you have stol'n so many hearts,
> As they would make you at all parts
>   Suspected.   (Lines 473-80)

Claims are made in the masque that its version of giving and taking is as benign as this lady's stealing of hearts.

After the townsmen are robbed, the masque presents the claim that the transformation of courtiers into robber gypsies is a mere "*deceptio visus*" (line 888). Although robbers, they have given everything back. Returning what they have taken amounts to not having taken it; hence, returning the money means that no money was taken. The townsmen, not uncannily, realize that the gypsies have a good thing going, robbing and then claiming that they have not, and they ask to be made "one of your company" (lines 1054-55) so that they, too, can pick pockets "like a gentleman" (line 1061). The gypsies refuse, of course, and soon throw off their disguises to reveal

129

their identities. It was one thing for the court to claim that its devastations of the countryside were no crime, that the king in depleting game reserves was, for instance, merely taking his own, and thus committing no robbery (this argument is offered in the masque at lines 81 ff.); it would be something else if townsmen made similar claims. In the masque, only a gypsy can "play loose with his hands" (line 1158) and stay clear of "the trap of authority" (line 1153), for those actions are royally countenanced. When the gypsies are metamorphosed, Buckingham, the king is assured, "is no Gowrie" (line 1183). Robbing the countryside is not treason against the king, even if the country thinks so. Jonson's masque reveals a predatory court and its all-allowing, all-giving, bountiful sovereign. James authorizes the masque. And Jonson? His art, like that of the gypsies, is "true legerdemain" (line 196). He, too, makes the robbery good:

> *Townshead.* Excellent, i'faith, a most restorative gypsy. All's
> here again; and yet by his learning of legerdemain he
> would make us believe we had robbed ourselves.
> *Cockerel.* A gypsy of quality, believe it, and one of the king's
> gypsies this . . .   (Lines 933–37)

Here is, in their Patrico's words, the gypsies' art revealed: "If your hand be light,/I'll show ye the slight/Of our Ptolemy's knot;/It is, and 'tis not" (lines 1116–19). It is, and it is not. Jonson reveals the illusion of the royal spectacle while seeming to support it.

However good-humored, however unthreatening, Jonson's presentation of the court as the country's pickpocket and of the royal favorites as a band of stylish thieves is a revelation that expresses a widely shared contemporary sentiment, which was often less obliquely expressed. Jonson could always claim that his identification of courtiers and gypsies was all in play, that no analogy was really being affirmed. An impartial eye would see that antimasques are as much a version of the court as apotheoses are, but Jonson could count on James's partial reading.

Gypsies is perhaps the most wonderful example of Jonson's art of turning the king's self-perception against himself, but it is not a singular case, and the masques for the last years of James's reign, when his absolutist assertions tended to be increasingly vehement, invariably are couched within the divisions of the king's language. Thus, in *Pan's Anniversary, or the Shepherd's Holiday* (1620), a birthday celebration for the aging monarch, the ideological trope that made all of nature the king's creation entirely informs the masque. "Pan is our all, by him we breathe, we live,/We move, we

130

are" (lines 170–71) is its central declaration. But this figure runs amiss when a bumptious shepherd takes it literally and appears before the king aping his court. "Beware of presuming, or how you offer comparison with persons so near deities" (lines 132–33), he is told, but once again the saving grace of Mercury is invoked. "Behold where they are that have now forgiven you, whom you should provoke again with the like, they will justly punish that with anger which they now dismiss with contempt" (lines 133–36). The king is allowed to be all, as long as he allows what he would dismiss. And in the final masque, *The Fortunate Isles* (1625), Jonson recasts *Neptune's Triumph,* a masque that had played on the duplicities of state secrets. In the new version, the antimasque figure is named Merefool, and what he desires is a vision, what masques provide. He is satisfied in ways that point to the court, for, at the end of the masque, when Merefool has been banished, James is asked to forgive the masque for trespassing (line 290). No actual crime is named, but the masque certainly suggests that the court does not always know a real poet from a false one and prefers mindless revels to full-bodied ones. To allow the masque, James must forgive that trespass upon the king's intelligence.

In the *Basilikon Doron,* the king had demanded that he be unaccountable. That meant that he must take no account when the masque offered an unflattering mirror of the monarch. Nor was it only in masques that this echo of the royal rhetoric managed to fathom more secrets than the king would have wished to acknowledge. For a further example, we might turn to some texts provided for a particularly scandalous event at court, the marriage of the king's favorite, Sir Robert Carr, the Earl of Somerset, to Frances Howard. The king had taken an active part in securing the bride's divorce from the Earl of Essex and in furthering his favorite's desire. For the wedding, celebrations were offered, Jonson's *Irish Masque* and poems by Donne and Chapman, among others. For the masque, Jonson blanketed courtiers beneath unseemly Irish apparel, perhaps a reflection upon the scandalous surface that needed to be ignored. Donne and Chapman found protective devices, too; they wrapped themselves in the royal rhetoric of mystery.

In his *Ecclogue* and *Epithalamium* (1613)[19] for the occasion, Donne makes a bid for royal largesse in terms that echo the king's language. He at one and the same time celebrates the marriage as entirely the king's doing and stands aside from it, adopting a royal stance. James's claim that surface events could not indicate internal motives becomes Donne's license to present a world of false surfaces, like the creatures of Vulcan in *Mercury Vindicated.* But in this instance, true to the king's claims to be all, Donne makes the king the creator of these false creatures. For himself, he chooses to appear as nothing (he calls himself Idios); the representative courtier he encounters, he names Allophanes. His name means that he is someone else. Donne plays upon a historical accident, that his best friend and the king's favorite both were named Carr; but the play has a point. As Margaret Maurer remarks about another poem to a patron, the reader must be "either frivolous enough to have indulged his conceits or wise enough to have seen through them."[20] Here, in the play of names, Donne intimates that not to be at court is to be no one, but to be there means to lose identity. The court is a world of duplicates—a duplicitious world—where to have life one must become the king's creature.

Donne reveals his meaning progressively; an initial court-country debate in the *Ecclogue* establishes the artificiality of a court that owes its eternal spring to James, "that early light, which did appeare/ Before the Sunne and Moone created were" (lines 21–22), all-maker in the diffusion of favors ("From which all Fortunes, Names, and Natures fall" [line 24]), all-receiver of zeal and love. Light becomes heat when the king couples with the "wombes of starres" (line 25), the eyes of the bride, to enflame the court with a warmth that Allophanes vainly attempts to distinguish from lust (lines 33 ff.). The consuming flame that moves through the poem destroys all vestiges of individuality, including the attempt of Idios to treat the trope as metaphysical (and to stay comfortably absent), and at the end he sacrifices his peculiar poem to the court; the paper, Allophanes says, is "not/His only that presents it, but of all" (lines 229–30). This fact underlies the central conceit of the *Epithalamium,* since the couple not only consume each other in the flames of their heart and eyes (the refrain), but destroy as well the capacity of any witness of the event to make any distinctions in perception or language. The allophanic couple merely extends from the king ("A Court, where all affections do assent/Unto the Kings" [lines 76–77]), Somerset wearing the livery of Cupid only from James's largesse:

> Our little Cupid hath sued Livery,
> And is no more in his minority,
> He is admitted now into the brest
> Where the Kings Counsells and his secrets rest.   (Lines 87–90)

Granted that, it is no wonder to find that Somerset, although made one for the time with his bride, will return to his maker:

> . . . having laid downe in thy Soveraignes brest
> All businesses, from thence to reinvest
> Them, when these triumphs cease. (Lines 133–35)

When Idios attempts finally to separate himself from this consuming court, his gesture—to burn the poem, or, earlier, to bury himself—turns out to be self-defeating; to be consumed is to be a courtier.

In the same situation, Chapman even more fully appropriated to himself royal inscrutability. In his poems occasioned by the wedding, *Andromeda Liberata* and its *Free . . . Justification,* Chapman denies validity to popular readings of the event. In the prefatory letter Chapman calls his readers "prejudicate and peremptory" (the phrase is reminiscent of James's description of his worst audience as those who judge the king through "præ-occupied conceits" [*BD,* p. 43]), accusing them of seeing themselves when they find the Somerset affair licentious: "All the faults you can finde are first in your selves" (p. 303).[21] The answer to their misperceptions (satirized by Chapman throughout the poem) lies in seeing the event through the poet's eyes. For him, Somerset and Lady Frances occupy the heroic world of the poetic allegory of Perseus and Andromeda. Chapman, in his initial verses addressed to the couple, claims, as he regularly does, that his perceptions have the sanction of *divinus furor.* These grant him *"Integritie"* (line 22), and the same quality is said to reside in Somerset, whose sexuality is praised as temperate (line 70) and who is said to be "even absolute now" (line 106), containing, like the sun, all virtue "still (in himselfe) alike" (line 114). *"Joyes plac't without you, never are your owne"* (line 193), he concludes. The absolute integrity of an interiority seen only by the poet's divine eye counters the false perceptions of the world. Throughout *Andromeda Liberata,* Chapman presents the false opinions of the "monster vulgar thought" (line 351) and then reconstructs the truth on the basis of his higher, interior knowledge.

For Chapman, as for James, misunderstanding and misperception signify upright conscience, for "Acts that are too hie/For Fames crackt voice, resound all Infamie" (lines 357–58). Perseus's task, like the poet's, is to alter perception through revitalization of conscience, and his argument to Andromeda at the conclusion of the poem (lines 457 ff.) turns their marriage into a metaphor for this creative act: "All mortall good, defective is, and fraile;/Unlesse in place of things, on point to faile,/We daily new beget" (lines 499–501). When Chapman suffered the same scorn that met his heroes, he showed their heroism, affirming himself against the populace—"*One may be worth all*" (*Free . . . Justification,* line 53)—and joying in his condemnation. This has some interesting consequences when Chapman appeals to patrons for support. Unlike Jonson, who will demonstrate the mutual need of patron and poet, Chapman denies that he has any need of patronage; rather, his patrons need him. Thus, in the epistle dedicatory to the *Iliads,* Chapman lectures Prince Henry on the power poets have to make princes. Chapman aims at making Henry a proper recipient of what the poet can give. No wonder Chapman's career was marked by poverty and an inability to find support. Some of this was certainly willfull, Chapman, for instance, standing by Somerset long after he had any largesse to bestow. The reason, not far to seek, he makes explicit in the dedicatory poem accompanying the *Hymns of Homer* (1624). Chapman claims there that Somerset's disgrace is his grace, and that retirement signifies heroic retreat from the false values of the world. In this position, Somerset must apply to the poet for patronage and counsel: "Retire to him then for advice, and skill/To know, things call'd worst, Best; and Best most ill;/Which knowne; truths best chuse; and retire to still" (lines 81–83).

Calling best worst and worst best, Chapman's counterdirectives echo a king who had declared his inscrutability and opacity. It was the king who could not be read from his performance that Chapman imitated or that Donne appropriated in his part of Idios or that Jonson claimed as his safeguard for the double entendres of his masques. That the king was incomparable, and therefore incapable of being touched by such comparisons, James himself had declared in the *Basilikon Doron:* "A moate in anothers eye, is a beame into yours: a blemish in another, is a leprouse byle into you: and a veniall sinne (as the Papists call it) in another, is a great crime into you" (p. 12). Differences in degree become differences in kind. To secure his absolute position, the king cannot be touched at all.

Thus, James's pose was that he gave but could not receive. He gave himself to the public eye, and was only half-convinced that he would be seen properly. To guard against misperceptions, he declared that he was unseeable, even when onstage. And to save himself from misperceptions, he shut his eye to them. The performance he gave was couched largely in words, for, as we know, he was loath to make actual appearances. His book on kingship, the *Basilikon Doron,* means the royal gift, and he gave himself giving his words. We cannot be surprised to find that the metaphor of the gift caused James as much hesitation as the metaphor of the player king: both point to the troubled territory of conscience and consciousness, the place where what is given and what is received meet, and where the intentions of the giver and receiver color the gift. In the metaphor of the gift or of the player king, James imagines the elementary situation of language with its residues of contradictions that cannot be controlled.

James gives his book to Prince Henry as his gift to him, but also as a mirror for the prince, for he, too, has his life only thanks to his father, and is himself a royal gift. James makes the analogy explicit, calling both "this birth of mine" (*BD,* p.11). The ownership of book and prince is in question in this declaration: it is an absolutist assertion. And so, too, are James's prescriptions for reading. Just as the prince must be read as if he were his father, so the book must be read, not for itself, but for its author. To "interprete favourably" this second birth, James demands that it be viewed "according to the integritie of the author, . . . not looking for perfection in the worke it selfe" (ibid.). Rather than the surface, the reader is invited to view what cannot be seen, the "vive Idees of the authours minde" (p. 9). The disparity between surface and depth in this formulation is like the two versions of the player king, transparent and opaque; this is a formulation in textual terms that define the practice of the king's poets. The king declared that surface appearances were false; so did Donne, or Jonson with his masquerado. And certainly Chapman's mythological figures occupy a world of "vive Idees." With them, he made things worst seem best.

The division between surface and depth was meant to safeguard the king; but it could, as easily, be the source for complaint about misinterpretation and misappropriation of the royal gift. And it could also divide the king against himself. Just as he wished to appropriate his reader's response for himself—and, thus, just as he wished entirely to own his gift, whether it was his book or his child that he had in mind, so, too, he could view himself as owned. This was the source of his Divine Right, that he sat on God's throne as his lieutenant and that he was the legitimate heir to that position because of his mother's lawful claims. But this meant that what was true of his gift—that it was not what it appeared to be—was also true of himself. James invites the reader of the *Basilikon Doron* to enter his mind; yet the text itself does not serve as a way of getting there, and the reader must take the king on faith. The gift is in the mind of the giver. And, similarly, the king announces that he must be taken on faith and despite appearances. No viewed, embodied self can be the true secret self; the king is an opaque text, not to be seen in word or fact. This defense has a price. It means, as James says, that he must endure his time onstage and be misconstrued. But the misconstruc-

135

tion lies in what he gives. For the royal gift, the *Basilikon Doron,* the "trew image of my very minde, and forme of the rule, which I have prescribed to my selfe and mine" (p. 11) is also a false image and itself prescribed. James is subject to the dictates of the past, cast in a part not of his making. His conscience is occupied territory. "How can they be trew to the Sonne, that were false to the Father" (p. 32), he asks, attempting to own the future. But the patriarchal assertion has its own hidden terror, for it binds James to his past. James attempts to implant himself in his son; he writes to him on 24 March 1603, "Above all things give neue goode countenance to any but according as ye shall be informed that they are in estimation with me" (BL, Harl, Ms. 6986, fol. 65). Attempting to own his son, he cast him in the part of a player king, acting his father's part.

James's script comes from God—and his mother; this is both a justification and a liability. He is bound to observation. As he puts it in the prefatory sonnet to the *Basilikon Doron,* this is the ruling command: "Observe the Statutes of your heavenly King." The observed of all observers, the king himself must also observe his "heavenly King." To observe is both to see and to obey, and "Statutes" as their derivation from *stare,* to stand, suggests, stand in-the-place-of the king, for the king is a lieutenant, taking the place of heavenly commands. He stands as a representation, a lively statue, to recall the phrase from Bishop Williams's funeral sermon. He stands in a place of obligation, giving only because he has received. "God gives not Kings the stile of *Gods* in vaine," that prefatory sonnet begins. But, now, we can see its double bind. The style might not be the man; what God gave was not his to give. His conscience was burdened by an unpayable debt. "The Throne ye sit on is Gods" (p. 22), he writes, and thus not his own. Whatever is given can never be received properly: this is the burden on the royal actor, giver of the royal gift.

Characteristically, James projected his burden, complaining that his "overdeare bought experience" (p. 20) had taught him one lesson, "the losse of my thankes." James's assertions that he gave, but never received, were a common poetic trope for his poets. Donne as Idios, with nothing to give, makes a bid for royal largesse by claiming that the king gives all; this is Donne's way of praising the king and keeping clear of the corrupt event. Jonson praises a golden age restored by James; but his use of the royal gift cannot fail to suggest that it is an age where all is bought and sold.[22] And, indeed, the central trope of *Gypsies,* the play on fortune, is nothing but a turning of the royal trope. Donne's court of duplicates stamped with the royal seal, minted as a series of identical coins, conveys the same point. Whether we look to court productions as extensions of royal favor, or look to the royal favorites themselves, we find this theme of "overdeare bought experience" so central to James's presentation of himself.

We can see this best with Buckingham, who received most from his master. *Gypsies* offers an argument on his behalf when the Porter explains that there is no way to pay the king back for his largesse. Unpayable debts are—simply—unpayable; excessive gifts create excessive obligations. Buckingham responds by doing nothing, for his existence is the king's gift, and, simply by being, he pays the king back. This is as much a sleight of hand as the gypsies' robbery, and the king is assured that his pockets are as full as the townsmen's are. The masque's attempt to convince the king that his favor was repaid in this manner was also Buckingham's. Repeatedly, in letters to the king, Buckingham recorded his inability to return the king's gifts or, indeed, to use them at the rate that James offered them. Showered with gifts of food, Buckingham characteristically remarked (in a letter of December, 1624) that "your presents are so greate wee can not eate them so fast as the [sic] come" (Bodl. Ms. Tanner 73/2, fol. 501). It was "that ould custome of yours of ever giving a way the best," the king was told (Adv. Ms. 33.1.7, vol. 22, fol. 75), and Buckingham and his wife, Kate, record gifts—"your excellent mellons, payres, sugard beenes" (fol. 77), "boxex of drid ploms and graps and the box of viallat caks and chickens" (fol. 82). In these gifts, Sir Pol's secrets of state hidden in melons come true.

To these gifts, and more (as James told Buckingham, he was "borne in a happie howre for all thy kinne" [BL, Harl. Ms. 6987, fol. 69]), Buckingham confessed inadequacy. "If I should give you dewe thankes for all you have done for me, I should spend my time in nothinge els" (fol. 128). James was his "maker" and to his redeemer alone could thanks be given (Adv. Ms. 33.1.7, vol. 22, fol. 85). When he failed to thank the king, it was not because his thoughts were elsewhere, he claimed (see, for example, fol. 73), but because "all I can say must bee short of what I should say" (fol. 87; this from a letter in which the favorite responds to a royal command to write *shortly*). In such "a verie unequall returne" (fol. 94), Buckingham claimed, as Jonson's Porter does, his very being was all he could give the king, thoughts without deeds, self-advancement as a mirror of majesty: "What I ame hath bine your act" (fol. 94). The king is all-bountiful, all his parts "are more then ever one man had" (fol. 88), and hence, the duke exists in his reflected glory and to reflect it.

In a staggering letter (fol. 79), written, it appears, when his failures to repay the king and his rapacity and self-serving broke the veneer of humble servitude, Buckingham attempts to reverse appearances and to fill silence, inactivity, and acquisitiveness and turn them into thanks and self-sacrifice. The letter opens with a justifying confession: "Though I have reseved three or foure letters from you since that I writt last to you yett . . . I have made a hundred answeres to them in my minde yett none that could satisfie my minde." This is an exercise in *deceptio visus* like Jonson's masque. It seems to have been as successful at pleasing the king, who took Buckingham's thoughts of response for real responses, what was on his mind for what might have been written. As Buckingham went on to explain, the reason for the disparity between thought and deed was not far to seek: the disparity between servant and monarch made it impossible for Buckingham to do anything in return:

> For kinder letters never servant reseved from master, and for so
> great a kinge to desend so loe as to his humblest slave & servant
> to communicate himselfe in a stile of such goodfellowship,
> with expressions of more care then servants have of masters
> then fesitions have of there patients which hath largelie appered
> to me in sickness and in helth of more tendernes then fathers
> have of children of more frendship then betweene equalls of
> more affection then betweene lovers in the best kinde man and
> wife, but what can I returne nothinge but silence.

He goes on to explain why "nothinge but silence" is the only possible response in this excessive, supplementary situation in which there is no proportion between giver and receiver: "If I speake I must be sausie, and say thus, or short of what is due, my pourvier, my goodfellow, my phesition, my maker my frend my father my all, I hartelie & humblie thanke you for all you doe and all I have, iudge what unequall langage this is it selfe, but espetiallie consideringe the thinge that must speake it, and the person to whome it must be spoken." Hence, this "thinge" concludes, "tell me whether I have not done discreetlie to be silent," and Buckingham promises that when James appears in person a fuller account will be forthcoming. The letter is the other side of a relationship in which neither king nor favorite pulled any punches. In a postscript to a letter, Buckingham urges James to make Sir Francis Lake a baron because there is £8000 in it for him ("I pray you burne this letter," he ends [fol. 70]), and James acted in Buckingham's "bussienesis . . . [taking] the chairge of thame upon me" (fol. 16), acting as "thy best Stewarde" (fol. 135).

Yet another version of Buckingham's excuses is offered in

138

Gypsies with the Jackman's song of Cock Lorel's feast for the devil. The devil comes and eats up everything in sight—including a fair portion of society—and ends the meal "with a fart" (line 1037). And that, the Jackman explains, is why Buckingham's home came to be called the Devil's Arse. Jonson plays here, not very kindly perhaps, with something central to James's sense of himself and closely tied to his most characteristic actions. James felt that what he gave was never returned, and he felt that way because he believed that what he gave was not his own to give. The giving, and the grieving, were joined in an endlessly repeated cycle of self-destruction and frustration. Emptying the royal coffers faster than they could possibly be filled, James acted out a drama of conscience and guilt. If, like God, he gave "not . . . in vaine," it was only because he felt he had nothing to give; and when he gave he took it all back again to assuage his own emptiness. Around him he attempted to assemble a group of young lovers who would reflect upon the king; he stamped them with the royal coin, or so Sir Henry Wotton writes in *The Life and Death of George Villiers:* "The King had taken by certain Glances, (whereof the first was at *Apthorpe,* in a Progresse) such liking of his person, that he resolved to make him a Master-piece, and to mould him as it were Platonically to his own *Idea.*"[23] David Mathew puts it this way:

> He liked to form those who were nearest to him as in the case
> of the two favorites of his later life, Robert Carr and George
> Villiers. From the time he grew up, he had one salient quality,
> pleasure in giving. A strain of meanness is often allied to
> majesty; but King James loved to give and go on giving. This
> went side by side with an absence of a money sense. He was
> extravagant in his gifts to his subjects. In this respect he was
> very royal.[24]

Suffering to maintain an illusion of divine personhood, James created a spectral kingdom.

Although he arrived there by way of absolutist avowals of ownership and opacity, the other side of his thought could have brought him to similar perceptions about his role on stage. For although stoic thought encouraged a belief in individual will, it also called for the submission of the will to large and inapprehensible concepts, like natural law. All individuals might be equal, but this was because they were all the same, informed by a single guiding spirit. James wanted his style to be divine and imperial. Here, however, is a Roman emperor speaking, testifying to the spectral nature of politics; history offers a script that no actor can claim to own:

Reflect often how all the life of today is a repetition of the past; and observe that it also presages what is to come. Review the many complete dramas and their settings, all so similar, which you have known in your own experience, or from bygone history: the whole court-circle of Hadrian, for example, or the court of Antoninus, or the courts of Philip, Alexander, and Croesus. The performance is always the same; it is only the actors who change.[25]

As head of his kingdom, as a king whose conscience imposed obligations to God and to the past, James projected repressive pressures. Aware that to appearance he was dissolute, the king could only disallow appearance; but if his revolting body was not to be countenanced, how could the king speak to the commons, his *body politic*? He could do so only, as in "The Answere to the Libell Called the Comons teares,"[26] by attempting to disallow and discountenance them, deflecting and projecting his burden onto them as a means of alleviating himself. This is a typical pattern of denial. In that extraordinary poem, James removes himself to the position that his theatrical trope ensures and surrounds himself with protective metaphors. The commons "shall never peirce" (line 24) the king, he says, for they have no right to expression or perception. The king gives all.

Placed under the pressure to perform, aware that all he gave would never be read or received rightly, the king retreated within himself, and attempted, by reduplicating himself, to form a court of mirroring self-images. Receiving a role that robbed him of his ability to be himself (a feeling we have seen in his supposed earliest and certainly finest poem, "Since thought is free, thinke what thou will"), James clung to the fiction that inwardly the king was always right no matter how he appeared, rather than construct himself in a manner pleasing to the public eye:

> O what A calling weere A King
> If hee might give, or take no thing
> But such as yow should to him bring
> Such were A king but in A play.
>
> ("The Answere to the Libell," lines 41–44)

James's inability to heed the demands of his times, his refusal to pay attention to details of his administration, his loathing of public appearances, and his retirement to the country, "th'Arcadian state," are parts of this pattern.[27] Forced inevitably to play one role or

140

another, James chose the illusionary idealization that he hoped would give him most comfort. The official ideology of secrecy and prerogative resulted. Yet, as his rhetoric shows, James knew that the part he had chosen to play could never be understood. His attempts to communicate with his people turn from early desires to mold all his subjects into images of himself (his poetic treatise, we might recall, appeals repeatedly to a "docile" reader; he surrounded the throne with 934 new knights on his entrance into England), or to expect charity from them (as in the *Basilikon Doron*), to the threats of the late "Answere to the Libell," which are also held over Prince Henry in the *Basilikon Doron,* of the removal of paternal love. In his anger God becomes Momus; the "satyricke voice," James explains in *Basilikon Doron,* is an expression of "fatherly love" (p. 27):

> If I once bend my angrie browe
> Your ruyne comes though not as nowe
> ffor slowe I am revenge to take;
> And your Amendments wroth will slake
> Then hold your pratling spare your penn
> Bee honest and obedient men
> Urge not my Justice I am sloe
> To give yow your deserved woe.
> If proclamations will not serve
> I must do more, Peace to preserve
> To keepe all in obedience
> And drive such busie bodies hence.
> ("The Answere to the Libell," lines 167–78)

The Married State

Ownership was central to James's absolutist claims, fundamental to the patriarchal rights he declared on the basis of Roman law. The language of the royal performance and the royal gift is entwined in these claims, and in its broadest extension James declared that all that was belonged to him. As we have seen, this attitude toward his kingdom was perhaps most strikingly embodied in his first speech to Parliament in 1603, when he declared: "I am the Husband, all the whole Isle is my lawfull Wife; I am the Head, and it is my Body" (*Political Works,* p. 272). The metaphor explains his concern about Prince Henry's marriage articulated in the *Basilikon Doron:* "Ye are the head, shee is your body" (p. 36), he reiterates. But it also lies behind the king's claims to own himself and to be right no matter how he appeared. Incorporation of the kingdom is a sign of the

141

king's singularity; the king is beyond comparison because that which is other—other people—or sexually other, whether it is his wife or his kingdom, are nonetheless his. A "loving nourish-father" (p. 24) he terms himself, father and maternal nurse at once, giving his kingdom "their very nourish-milke," which they greedily engorge, depleting the royal gift. As father and mother, the king is *sui generis,* self-contained as a hermaphrodite,[28] an ideal form. But such terms for self-ownership were also appropriate to a king who married for reasons of state but who courted male favorites.[29] The language of marriage could also point to those relationships, and James's interest in marriage choices and connubial behavior, whether of his children or his favorites, reflects upon himself. The king's relationship with Buckingham's family was particularly incestuous, and James seems to have indulged fantasies in which his favorite's children were his own. He offered Kate, Buckingham's wife, advice during pregnancies and weaning, and yearned for the fruit of their lovemaking: "I may have sweete bedchamber boyes to play me with" (BL, Harl. Ms. 6987, fol. 180), he wrote, and versified his desire, as we have seen: "God send a smilinge boy within a while" (*Poems,* 2:177).

Jacobean dramatists glance at this marriage to his kingdom in the homosexuality of Tiberius or in Sejanus's rise to power, or in the strong terms of identification of Aufidius and Coriolanus:

> Know thou first,
> I loved the maid I married; never man
> Sighed truer breath. But that I see thee here,
> Thou noble thing, more dances my rapt heart
> Than when I first my wedded mistress saw
> Bestride my threshold. Why, thou Mars, I tell thee,
> We have a power on foot; and I had purpose
> Once more to hew thy target from thy brawn,
> Or lose mine arm for't. Thou has beat me out
> Twelve several times, and I have nightly since
> Dreamt of encounters 'twixt thyself and me.
> We have been down together in my sleep,
> Unbuckling helms, fisting each other's throat,
> And waked half dead with nothing.   (4:5, lines 114–27)[30]

"Our general himself makes a mistress of him" (4:5, line 198), one of Aufidius's servants comments. He might be referring to James's behavior with his favorites. Although the king had declared his virtue, he had also declared his impenetrable secrets. And, although the king had announced his all-embracing marriage to his kingdom, to Buck-

ingham he wrote that his favorite was his "sweet child and wife."
Perhaps here we reach James's "secretest drifts," the private utterance
that matched the dissolute performance he wished to disown. In the
Basilikon Doron (p. 20), sodomy is sedition. James's marriage to his
kingdom, like his royal gift or royal performance, bore with it traces
of his own undoing, latitude for contradictions.

SIR SIMONDS D'Ewes regaled a guest with modern license, "of
things I discoursed with him that weere secrett as of the sinne of
sodomye, how frequente it was in this wicked cittye . . . ," adding, "I
tolde him that boyes weere growen to the height of wickednes to
paint." These revelations of 29 August 1622 were modeled on behavior at court, if Anthony Weldon's description of the king hanging
on his favorites, playing with his codpiece, is accurate. It is a picture
supported by Francis Osborne's *Traditionall Memoyres* with their
claim that the king chose his favorites solely on the basis of their
looks, and that "the love the king shewed was as amorously conveyed,
as if he had mistaken their sex, and thought them ladies; which I
have seene Sommerset and Buckingham labour to resemble, in the
effeminateness of their dressings." And not in that alone, for James
was seen, Osborne continues, "kissing them after so lascivious mode
in publick, and upon the theatre, as it were, of the world" that it
"prompted many to imagine some things done in the tyring-house,
that exceed my expressions."[31] The king's private life was played out
on the public stage, and this is nowhere more evident than in his
private correspondence with Buckingham, especially voluminous
during the trip Buckingham made to Spain with Prince Charles in
1623 to negotiate for a marriage with the infanta, and during a subsequent illness upon the duke's return. The letters were read aloud in
court, particularly when the king had trouble making out Buckingham's hand, and one way or another their contents were known at
large almost as soon as they came to James's ears, as can be seen
from the contents of letters of court chroniclers like Chamberlain
or Thomas, Viscount Fenton (he wrote almost daily to the Earl of
Mar in Edinburgh), for they are filled with the latest news. James remarks in a letter to Buckingham that he could not find time to read
his favorite's latest epistle without someone reading over his shoulder.
This was not an extraordinary event in the life of a man who was
entirely a public person.

Nonetheless, the letters have their revelations. The letters James
addressed to Buckingham and Charles, his "sweete boyes," are
answered by the duke's invariable close in letters to their "dere dad

and gossope"; he is always "your humble slave and doge [sic] Steenie." The language of the letters to Spain is that of romance ("deare ventrouse knights, worthie to be putte in a new romanse," James addresses them in February 1622/3, BL, Harl. Ms. 6987, fol. 13). The language, like the disguises of the adventurers, is a mask which, however obfuscatory its intentions, is nonetheless simultaneously revelatory. After his return to England, Buckingham was to tell James of what he regarded as the outrageous assumption that met his behavior, "this unfavorable interpretation I find made of a thankefull and loyall hart in cauling my words crewed catomite words" (fol. 196). The outrage lay in the saying, for it is a reading that the letters support. The mask of romance carries with it the language of love. Fairly shortly into the correspondence with Buckingham in Spain, James is numbering the letters he sends; thus on 11 March 1623, he records that epistle as "being the sixte letre I have written to you two, fyve to Kaite, two to Su & one to thy mother, Steenie, and all with my owin hande" (fol. 28v). And just as soon, the delays in correspondence, the failure of the knights to keep pace with their master, are the subject of the king's complaints.

These are the letters of lovers separated, chafing at the time it takes for letters to arrive, lamenting absence, longing for reunion. Thus, on 24 March, Buckingham writes that his sojourn teaches him "never to lous sight of that I love so pretiouslie againe" (fol. 37v). When, at first, it seemed that the Spanish visit would be brief, Buckingham told James (in a letter of 28 March) that he would be in his master's arms as soon as Charles had embraced his love: "Your babie shall no soner have her in his armes but Steenie shall make hast to throw him selfe at your feete" (fol. 48). As he confessed even before that, "Never none longed more to be in the armes of his mistris" (fol. 23), making clear the parallel between the prince and himself. The abasement longed for by this slave and dog has a strong erotic component. At one point, Buckingham refers to the king's "well shaped legs" (fol. 37), and when return was actually in sight, on 1 September 1623, the favorite wrote in exaltation at the thought of once more embracing those well-shaped objects: "My hart and verie sole dances for ioy for the change will be no less then to leape from trouble to ese from sadnes to merth nay from hell to heven, I can not now thinke of given thankes for frend wife or child my thoughts and onlie bent of haveing my dere dad and master [here something is crossed out] legs sone in my armes" (fol. 164v). All relationships—master and servant, father and son, husband and wife—are replicated in the intensity of feeling, "the best father maister and I may with sausines put in frend" (fol. 157v). And, of course, James's rhetoric was, if anything, even more excessive.

He had, from the first, derived all his pleasure in the absence of his sweet boys, he wrote them, from their letters (fol. 50; although the letters were nominally joint productions, they were, except when Buckingham was briefly ill, always written by him). But when they were delayed in the Spanish "laborinth" (fol. 88) of new conditions and delays, James expressed most insistently his feelings for this man upon whom he heaped favors and whose picture he wore on a ribbon over his heart. When, on 14 June, he wrote in response to the delay of his boys, he said that their "letre ... hath strukken me deade" (fol. 100). "I nowe repente me sore," he continues, "that ever I suf-ferd you to goe awaye, I care for matche nor nothing, so I maye once have you in my armes againe, god grawnte it, god grawnte it, god grawnte it, amen, amen, amen." And although the king could change his tone, for instance in a letter of 31 July urging them to engage in Palatine diplomacy in Holland en route to England, "that the worlde maye see, ye have thoght as well upon the businesse of christendome, as upon the codpeece pointe" (Bodl. Tanner Ms. 73/2, fol. 344v), more to the point—and closer to his heart—was his urgency at their delay. In a letter of August 1623, Sir Tobie Matthew wrote begging the king not to make himself sick over Buckingham's ab-sence (fol. 352). At the same time, the king was writing with fer-vency that "my extreame longing will kill me" (Harl. 6987, fol. 137v), and five days later, on 10 August, "I proteste to god I have written myne eyes almost drye" (fol. 139). When Buckingham re-turned, the flow of letters did not cease. Letters to his "onlie sweete & deare chylde" heap "blessing blessing blessing on thy hairte rootes" (fol. 182). To his "sweete hairte" (fol. 186) he asks that he "love me still & still & so" (fol. 184). And, presumably, Buckingham did. At the end of a letter that patches a lovers' quarrel, the duke moons about "the time, wch I shall never forgett at Narneham where ye Beds hed c^d not be found betwene y^r Master & his Doge" (fol. 214). It seems to fulfill the promise made before leaving Spain, in a letter of 20 August 1623, that "when he once getts hould of your bedpost againe never to quitt it" (fol. 149v). When, in James's final years, Buckingham was absent, he repeatedly assured his sovereign that he was always with him, for it was the king's business he went about. "Alace sweete hairte I fynde by this," James replied, "how precise thow are to keepe thy worde to me, quhen thow præferris it to thy owin greatest confort in comming to me" (fol. 188). At least once, the sharing of a bedchamber was celebrated publicly. At Wroxton, stained

145

glass windows of James and Buckingham were mounted. Beneath the monarch are these words: "Icy dans cete chambre coucha nostre Roy Jacques premier du nom le 25me aoust 1619." They might celebrate a marriage.

THE celebration of marriage in a high Roman mode, and the assertions of state rhetoric in this form, was Jonson's accomplishment in *Hymenaei* (1606). The masque managed also to glance at the duplicities inherent in the metaphor of union. In this masque, Jonson raises a looking glass for King James that catches both the public show and the private concerns that underlay it. "Union, mistress of these rites/ Will be observed with eyes/As simple as her nights" (lines 63-65) is the guiding conceit. To observe in this unitive manner, one must see as the king sees, and one must see the king. Observation of this sort is hardly simple, for it means the sacrifice of one's own view for the royal prospect. The masque makes this point by regarding union also as a sacrifice, "two noble maids/Of different sex to Union sacrificed" (lines 94-95). It is difference that must be sacrificed to the king's vision; and it is difference that is registered by the masque's sacrificial union.

Hymenaei celebrates the marriage of true minds, the "one strong knot that binds ... all married minds" (lines 175-76). To achieve this simple feat binding conscience and consciousness, refiguration must occur. Thus, the affections and humors, which offer opposition in the antimasque, must see that they are versions of the spiritual union of the couple. The trick of this lies in the saying, to call the body spirit. To become a wife means to acquire "a name of dignity" and not one of pleasure (line 374). "Soft embraces bind/To each the other's mind" (lines 468-69). The marriage of minds rereads physical desire and calls it spirit. Such a retranslation catches perfectly the royal rewriting of homosexual desire as marriage, of public dissoluteness as an obfuscation of spiritual integrity.[32]

The doubleness of the masque, playing on the union and difference of mind and body, is clearest in its coda, the barriers performed the next night. There, Truth and Opinion, dressed identically, debate. Opinion claims, "My name is Truth" (line 630), showing one way to overcome difference. Her argument throughout is in favor of the single life, and she ends praising "One god, one nature, and but one world framed,/One sun, one moon, one element of fire,/So, of the rest; one king ..." (lines 722-24). To this, Truth, who stands for marriage, can only argue that one is the product of two, the body

146

married to the soul, the king to the kingdom. James's double stance, as transparent and opaque, is replayed in this debate, and it is a draw.

To resolve the debate, an angel announces that "Truth is descended in a second thunder" (line 795). This Truth is not the same as the first Truth, however. Refiguration, reinterpretation, rereading occur: a politics of knowledge is implied, for this new Truth comes in "state" (line 796). Uniting all opposites, she offers a model of transparency, simulates egalitarian openness because she has absorbed difference in her absoluteness. She is the answer to James, and his mirror in the masque. In token of this, she wears a mirror upon her transparent breasts, "by which men's consciences are searched and dressed" (line 814). She gives form to interiority, shaping men's consciences to match her own, invading and imposing upon them. Her crystal is James's, that "window in my breast" (*Political Works*, p. 285) that he offered, offering himself to view, the gift of his presence, "a great and a rare Present, which is a faire and a Christall Mirror" (p. 306). "*It is a conquest to submit to right*" (line 844) is the fittingly paradoxical conclusion to the masque. The masque ends exhibiting that marriage to duplicity that constituted James's contradictory truth. In the marriage of true minds that closed the masque, the theater of conscience had been erected.

The Royal Gaze: Bussy d'Ambois *and the Public Stage*

The married state that the mirror of conscience displays at the end of *Hymenaei* defines the Jacobean state and its conditions of representation. To summarize: poets found their way in court by duplicating the royal language, approaching James by the very indirections that he marked out. His duplicities paved the way, and Jonson, Donne, and Chapman followed, each seizing the royal road, that doubly crossed path. Each author found authority in the royal prerogative of double speech. This linguistic domain James called a theater; he saw himself onstage. The theater pervaded the king's sense of self and role, and provides a defining term for the bifurcations that mark his language. The pages that follow explore further the implications of this conjunction by inquiring into the theatricality of James's representations and looking at the theater James imagines; finally, this chapter closes—in preparation for the next—by viewing the Jacobean theater as another stage where the theater of conscience was replayed.

147

"SPECULATION turns not to itself/Till it hath travelled and is married [or mirror'd?] there/Where it may see itself." These are Achilles' words to Ulysses in *Troilus and Cressida* (3:3, lines 109-11).[33] The theater is by definition (theater derives from theatron, Greek; to see, to view) a place of speculation, of spectators, and what they "gazingly . . . behold" is, in James's eyes, the royal spectacle. When the king turned his eyes upon himself, Achilles' words define his condition. That moment of self-consciousness remains a theatrical scene, for the king sees himself being seen—by the audience without, and by one within, the eye of God, observing him as he is observed. Conscience/consciousness, which treads the boundary between interiority and exteriority, and which makes interiority exteriorized and imposes an outward gaze upon the inner self, leads to an all-pervasive theatricality and to the effacement of other normative distinctions.[34] The theater of conscience makes the line between inside and outside difficult to define or to maintain as an absolute boundary—and, so doing, seems to open an ever-receding horizon of duplications; it also makes the boundary between the spectator and the spectacle elusive. Everyone is onstage, and there is no offstage if even the innermost recesses, the "secretest drifts" of the monarch, are available to view. The crucial terms that are affected by this boundary crossing are "public" and "private," a distinction we have already seen blurred in family representations. The terms could be theatrical, too, defining two kinds of theaters in James's time. But, first, let us consider the terms themselves.

Today, public and private function as essentially opposing categories and, according to one recent political scientist and social observer, we tend to devalue the public and to elevate the private.[35] *Individual* is a value-laden term for us, and notions of privacy and of innate internal differences which make for individuality serve as founding principles in modern definitions of the human. The public sphere, on the other hand, seems depersonalized, empty, and, more and more, simply false. This view has colored modern notions about the Renaissance, perhaps ever since Burckhardt projected modern man back on to the Renaissance. Granting this, then, what did the private/public distinction mean in the Jacobean period? When James declared himself a "publike" person on a "publike" stage, what was the opposing category? What did privacy mean?

The answer to these questions restores to privacy its privative meaning of unavailability, invisibility. Privacy is a negative category, for what is not seen does not exist; there is always an audience. Hence the transparent king has no inner life that is not somehow dis-

148

played, or to be displayed, and even the opaque king has an audience, God, and he stands beneath his searching and observing eye. The king attempts to appropriate for himself that view; he makes his gaze a duplication of the divine glance. And, by so doing, the king established himself as ultimately different from all other persons. He was *sui generis*. It is that unmarked privileged and private difference which is the king's special individuality. It does not make him a private person, but it means that in public he also bears another body, his invisible body, the body of his power. In the theater that James imagines, although all "gazingly . . . behold" the king, they cannot see him completely; his gaze is of a different nature, bent on all, seeing as God sees. Sovereignty is a matter of sight.

This is admittedly a difficult point, and it can perhaps be illuminated by a set of distinctions that Michel Foucault draws in *Discipline and Punishment*,[36] a study of the birth of the prison. Foucault shows that punishment was an entirely different phenomenon in the sixteenth century from what it has become in modern times. Then criminals were displayed, tortured publicly, and made to confess. Now they are incarcerated, hidden away; although under constant institutional surveillance, they no longer provide a public spectacle. (Most modern institutions have this structure.) What were the terms of the public spectacle, why display the criminal? We can find an answer when we recall that in the Elizabethan and Jacobean period among the favored public activities of the populace were theatergoing, bearbaiting, sermon attendance, and witnessing public executions and tortures. These are cognate activities; all are moral mirrors and displays of power. To stay with Foucault's point: the criminal presents, literally, a spectacle, a mirror of majesty. His crime represents a direct assault upon the sovereign, his confession, a direct admission; what is done to his body is a manifestation of the power of the sovereign because his body belongs to the sovereign: "The crime attacks the sovereign: it attacks him personally, since the law represents the will of the sovereign" (p. 47); "the body of the condemned man became the king's property, on which the sovereign left his mark and brought down the effects of his power" (p. 109). We have already seen numerous Spenserian illustrations of this fact and the Roman law that made life the king's gift. Foucault argues that the techniques of power have changed radically. For the period we are concerned with, power is manifested in the spectacle, the mirror of the king. Most radically, this means that the king's public person includes, quite literally owns, the public; they are all included in his gaze, an important term in Foucault's discussion. For when the audience views the body of the condemned man it is seeing a palpable sign of the power that extends from the king, beyond the sovereign. "The surplus power possessed by the king gives rise to the duplication of his body" (p. 29). It is duplicated, reproduced, in the body politic. But this also means—and this is crucial—that whereas the sovereign sees all, since all he sees he is—the spectators of the sovereign cannot see the king; they see the mirrors of his power, but in himself, the sovereign's visibility is "scarcely sustainable" (p. 189) because he has another body, the body of his power. [37]

This is what the sovereign displays in public, his own unobservability, observed in his spectacles: the divine word preached, ferocious powers unleashed; and these meet in the theater, where the audience saw kings treading the stage, where the public assembled to see itself. The theater, that tragic scaffold, was a place for self-knowledge precisely because it mirrored state, because its re-presentations duplicated public life. It is there that Renaissance man went to know himself. [38]

Privacy opposes this pervasive public sphere, but we could say, only as absence is opposed to presence. In the seventeenth century, privacy all but merged into the public. Today we demand the opposite, that our public figures display personal authenticity, revealing genuine selves behind official masks. [39] Private displays make public figures real ("authentic") for us. Renaissance "publike persons" were not measured that way; privacy was the unreal category. When persons are in private they are unobserved, withdrawn, invisible. Such a situation is almost unimaginable. The king, so fully a public person, scarcely even had such a moment to himself; his most intimate bodily functions, his dressing, undressing, and going to bed, were attended, public events. Those with less power lived even more openly; but the advantage of power in the period was not the advantage of privacy. We therefore need to get over the shock of James asking Frederick about his wedding night, or the *frisson* that Anthony Weldon's portrait of the king, playing with his codpiece, leaning on his favorites, inevitably produces. We assume that private matters should be hidden—especially sexual matters, the most intimate and, to us, most valuable because most intimate. But in Jacobean society, for these matters to exist, it would seem that they needed to be made public. Shakespeare's Jacobean heroines—Helena, Cressida, Cleopatra, or Marina, to name a few—are remarkably straightforward in handling sexual matters. Achilles tells Ulysses that the self needs to display itself in others' eyes in order for it to see itself. And even private individuals, as opposed to "publike persons," in James's formula-

150

tion, have "præ-occupied conceits": that is, their minds are not their own, they do not own their inner selves. They are watching themselves, too, under observing eyes. The public sphere, the realm of the gaze, constitutes reality as a theatrical space.

To understand this better, we might consider the argument against Husserl that Jacques Derrida offers in *Speech and Phenomena*.[40] Derrida opposes the phenomenological definition of the self, the idea that the self is present to itself, and that such presentness is the very basis of authenticity, an unquestionable first point in being-in-the-world. The premodern discussion of privacy would not accept this phenomenological argument; hence, in opposing Husserl, it may be that Derrida raises terms that more resemble those of Renaissance thought than Husserl's do. Countering the phenomenological view of meaning as soliloquy, Derrida offers the image of the interior theater: "Hearing onself speak is not the inwardness of an inside that is closed in upon itself; it is the irreducible openness in the inside; it is the eye and the world within speech. *Phenomenological reduction is a scene, a theater stage*" (p. 86; his italics). To clarify this, we need to add that Derrida defines speech as "*the* representation of itself" (p. 57), taking representation in all of its meanings, including repetition (*re-presentation*) and substitution. The phenomenological reduction, its supposedly originary point, Derrida says, must be seen as a moment of duplication, not internality itself, but a moment in which the outside is brought inside. This argument denies the private except in its privative meaning, for as soon as there is consciousness, self-duplication is inevitable, inevitable the crossing of the boundary between inside and out; the theater of re-presentation is inevitable, and the phenomenological definition of the self as private to itself falls before it. Derrida's theater offers instead a hall of mirrors, spectacles. He ends his examination of Husserl by quoting from a passage in *Ideas* and offering *it* as a beginning principle: "A name on being mentioned reminds us of the Dresden gallery. . . . We wander through the rooms. . . . A painting by Teniers . . . represents a gallery of paintings. . . . The paintings of this gallery would represent in their turn paintings, which on their part exhibited inscriptions and so forth" (p. 104).

This privative privacy carries over to the distinction between public and private theaters. Private theaters were public places. The difference between the two theaters was a matter of privilege, power, prestige, and class. Public and private as kinds of theaters distinguish public categories of power. The court theater established itself as the crown of these differences and as the pinnacle of the observable.

Writing of German baroque drama, Walter Benjamin describes the role of the monarch: "The sovereign represents history. He holds historical events in his hand like a scepter."[41] The sovereign, onstage or off, is the bearer of history, and it lies in his power. Yet, although he is manifest in history and directs its course, he also represents it (Benjamin's term is *repräsentiert,* the term that catches the spectacular nature of re-presentation), is its representative, playing on that spectral stage that Marcus Aurelius describes, and which is, at once, James's private stage of conscience and the theater in which his power—his invisibility—is displayed, so that viewers are invited to observe the unobservable.

This totalization of theatricality, as we have already seen, has its own queasiness. "A King but in A play" ("The Answere to the Libell," line 44) is the object of James's horror in part because it is the horrible truth that his power on the public stage marks his puppetry on God's stage. And, of course, in the period, the observation that all the world's a stage can lead both Jacques and Macbeth to see life as essentially unreal. The theater, the public place par excellence, which includes the private, is at once most real (external, verifiable, objective) and most unreal (founded in illusion: behind the play lies the hidden playwright; behind the character, the actor). This violates a boundary again: at the end of all these halls of mirrors, for us there is the individual; for the Renaissance, we had better substitute the word *person,* comprehending the full force of its root, persona, mask. The contrast of public/private persons shatters on the notion of person as much as it does on the supposed opposing categories. All the world is a stage, and offstage is, simply, no place, Utopia. Offstage, costumes are changed; and the private man is forever returning onstage. Offstage or on, he never ceases to be an actor. And even offstage exists only when it is on: as when the texts that establish pastoral retreats and utopian visions impose themselves upon our views, if only by their announcements, by being texts; or when the actor playing Rosalind reminds us in the epilogue of *As You Like It* that we can never know whether to take as true his feigned sex:

> It is not the fashion to see the lady the epilogue, but it is no more unhandsome than to see the lord the prologue. . . . What a case am I in then. . . . My way is to conjure you, and I'll begin with the women. I charge you, O women, for the love you bear to men, to like as much of this play as please you; and I charge you, O men, for the love you bear to women (as I perceive by your simp'ring none of you hates them), that between you and

152

the women the play may please. If I were a woman, I would kiss
as many of you as had beards . . . and I am sure, as many as
have good beards . . . , will, for my kind offer, when I make
curtsy, bid me farewell. [42]

Rosalind's epilogue displays power, for it reminds us of a reserve—the actor behind the character—and crosses a boundary that
only the speaker can cross. The "kind offer" of this epilogue con-
fuses all questions of kind. As the actor addresses us, taking us in ("I
perceive . . .": the audience's response is written into the speaker's
words), the actor leaves undecided how we are to take the words we
hear. We "see the lady the epilogue" who says "if I were a woman"
and who invites us to take the play as we would take the speaker; so
"the play may please." We do not know where these words end,
what final reality they point to, which of the referents that pleasant
"if" makes most real. Most real, most royal. What Rosalind does at
the end of *As You Like It* is a model for royal power. Not that
the monarch learned it there specifically; probably, the opposite is
the case, that the theater learned its power from the sovereign. But
the sovereign's power is, in any case, theatrical. "Publike persons"
have power in reserve, the undisplayed body of power that their
words allude to without determining, without defining within the
limits of the visible. As audience, we credit Rosalind with similar
powers. In modern terms we call her the most individual of the characters of that play, the one who most fully displays a person. What
this means, in Renaissance terms, is that she is the most powerful
public figure of the play. Her sovereignty derives from the power of
kings. It is the public figure that creates the private as that which is
displayed but cannot be seen; it is the public figure who says out
loud that there is more to him than meets the eye, who says that
there is more to be said than he is saying, or who speaks and unspeaks himself at once as Rosalind does.

It is, to put it briefly, in language that the king represents himself; it is in language that power is displayed. And the language of
power, the soverign's speech/writing, is, like the sovereign himself,
sui generis. It, like himself, points beyond itself, but does not establish a final referent. The sovereign depends upon sustaining contradictions, and the stage is his place of re-presentation where he is
doubled. Its doubleness is an essential quality of language and of
power, of language insofar as what language does is represent itself.
Modern definitions of representation are related to ideas of realism
(mimesis) compatible with the politics of representative government.

153

The theatrical/political situation in the time of James I was virtually the opposite. James was God's lieutenant; he stood in his place; re-placed him, represented him, and doubled his power. His second body—the body of power—came from this doubling of himself. And the stage, too, has its double.

Again, a modern analogy may prove helpful, Antonin Artaud's notion of the theater and its double.[43] Artaud wrote in opposition to the tradition of mimesis, proposing a theater that violated representation in the nineteenth-century sense of the word. At times, he thought that the theater he wanted had been seen last in Jacobean times; although he may err in his reading of those texts, what he says has a point, just as Derrida's answer to Husserl seemed to return us to Renaissance terms by disabusing us of romantic ones. No more than Sidney in *The Defence of Poetry* does Artaud want mimesis; he does not want the psychology of individual characters. Rather, the stage is to represent a force, providing "the exteriorization of a depth of latent cruelty" (p. 92) that attacks complacent notions of individuality and ordinary reality to reveal powerful universal forces; to represent this, the stage must go beyond ordinary language, since ordinary language seems merely to point to things (that meaning of representation). But the *mise en scène* aims at this latency, this non-visibility; hence it must either speak another language (Artaud proposes hieroglyphics, speaking pictures in Sidney's phrase, "precise and immediately readable symbols" [p. 94] that do not speak ordinary language).[44] Artaud proposes a theater at once destructive—it is not a picture of life as we ordinarily think it—yet meaning to give us the language in which we reach the essence of re-presentation, "solid, materialized language" (p. 38). Space speaks, Artaud says, in this theater; because it is the space of re-placement, re-presentation. What Artaud proposes is theater as spectacle; and to this, we might add the theater of language that Roland Barthes describes in *Sade, Fourier, Loyola.*[45] For Barthes, those three figures share, outrageously, the same role, as "founders of language" (p. 3) characterized by isolation, articulation, ordering, and spectacular theatricalization. All three construct theaters of re-presentation which define their own terms, which speak themselves, mirrors in which the audience is included by the very terms and prescriptions which describe the scene.

This is like James I, demanding that he be seen as *sui generis,* self-generating, as the only one who is two, and the only eye that sees and takes in all in its seeing; as the object of sight that takes the spectator in. The *sui generis* is the unobservable, for it is like nothing else, it is self-referential, for it is like itself; and it speaks a language that crosses this boundary between private and public, inside and outside, a language which is also unspoken, uncommunicative—the privative that is the mark of power, of reserve—or a language that speaks and does not speak at once.[46] This defines the language of the theater and its double, or of James's double theater of conscience, transparent and opaque at once.

To see what this means for writing, let us look to the Jacobean stage, to a hero of absolutism, Chapman's Bussy d'Ambois.[47] Chapman's figure can allow us a concrete glimpse of the appropriation of sovereignty. He begins, before our eyes, a private man, a man without a place; he proceeds through court and courting; he ends, standing dead before our eyes, shot with invisible bullets. All the while he speaks a language so peculiarly uncommunicative that we scarcely know what he is saying beyond the fact that it seems to overthrow language and yet to work. Chapman's fantasies of appropriating royal power, which we have seen already, are given a body in his hero, and the mirror of state is represented before our eyes.

We meet Bussy soliloquizing in a "green retreat" (1:1, line 45); characteristically, the pastoral place serves as a reflection, and for the hero to reflect upon the world at large. This private moment, of the hero alone and displaced, is a moment onstage, before our eyes, and this talking to himself, which represents internal dialogue, is theatrical, and not merely because it is on a stage. For it addresses the world at large, and speaks in a manner that will come to characterize the language of Bussy throughout the play:

> Fortune, not Reason, rules the state of things,
> Reward goes backwards, Honour on his head;
> Who is not poor, is monstrous; only Need
> Gives form and worth to every human seed.   (1:1, lines 1-4)

Within his first breath, Bussy mentions the "state of things": "state" here is political as well as cosmic, like Spenser's "state of present time" (FQ: V. pro. 1.1). Bussy begins in a characteristic manner. Abstractions dominate; what his words have to do with the "poor" (s.d.) figure we see before us is not explained; nor how he came to be where he is, whether by "Fortune" he means simply a lack of cash or a reversal, whether "Reason" refers to what Bussy thinks should be or to some larger cosmic principle (and if so, the stoic natural law or Machiavelli's *ragion di stato*), whether "need" here affirms that "form and worth" are arrived at only by being needed and received, or whether "form and worth" are privative values, had by not being

155

had. These questions the abstractness of the language, the free float-ing of the vocabulary, establishes. Bussy is talking here, talking it seems to himself, yet to us, too—the syntax here is perfectly recog-nizable and ordinary. The incoherence of the relationship between the speaker and his words and the world to which they refer is baf-fling; how we get from one recognizable grammatical unit to another makes the speech puzzling. We overhear someone speaking who speaks our language but who does not communicate his meaning.

Or, rather, out of these words, we piece a meaning; we assume that the figure speaking here is speaking in opposition to a world that has gone so topsy-turvy as to put him where he is. We might well be-lieve that these words mean that the speaker has done with the world; the "green retreat" is not where he belongs, but the world cannot possibly put him anywhere else. If the abstractions, with their universal implications, are true in some broad way, there would seem to be no world for Bussy but the one in which he speaks alone of the world he cannot have. Of course, what follows is precisely not what we might suppose would follow from these words so understood. Monsieur arrives, buys Bussy, and the hero moves to the court. And this raises the central dilemma that Bussy's career continues to repre-sent, for the paradigm established in this opening scene is repeated throughout the play. Bussy says something which we attempt to understand; but then, just when we think we do, he acts just oppo-site to what we might have supposed. Thus, in the first scene, he ac-cepts Monsieur's offer. Yet, typically, he accepts it as if he were rejecting it. Nor is his action unique or unusual in this play. For we might note that Monsieur also has not explained why he wants to bring Bussy to court except self-reflexively by saying it will make his "bounties shine" (line 51). Bussy, too, insists that what he does refers only to himself. He does not directly accept Monsieur's offer, and left alone, insists that he will not tread the path of "policy" (1:1, line 124); rather, he is "for honest actions" and it is "virtue" he means to bring to court (lines 128, 130). The "virtue" he brings turns out to be a mixture of murder and adultery; these are his "honest actions." Chapman's readers have long been puzzled about Bussy's career and what to make of the discrepancy between the program announced in the opening scene of the play and the acts that follow. Is Bussy showing up the corruptions of court by turn-ing them back on the court? Or is he an ignorant braggart headed for an inevitable fall? These are the kinds of questions most Jacobean heroes raise in their combinations of villainy and virtue, white devils all. However, there are terms for what Bussy does, and they are royal ones.

If we stay with the language of the play and its relation to the actions, we will find contradictions rampant. Bussy opens speaking against policy; he will come to embrace it (4:2) at the behest of a demon—raised, as we might expect, by a holy friar. "Policy shall be flank'd with policy" (4:2, line 181) is Bussy's resolve. He begins, when he moves beyond his initial abstractions, to speak of statesmen as hollow men; another typical use of language is here. Bussy strains for a simile. It is not only that his language lacks immediate referents; it is also typical for him to want to compare so that we are offered a reflection *in language* of what he means to describe in the world.

> As cedars beaten with continual storms,
> So great men flourish; and do imitate
> Unskilful statuaries, who suppose,
> In forming a Colossus, if they make him
> Straddle enough, strut, and look big, and gape,
> Their work is goodly. (1:1, lines 5-10)

But, he concludes, such "colossic statues" (line 15) are hollow. Within this simile, we have the typical problem of connective: how do we get from cedars to "statuaries"; how is a great tree that bears out a storm like a hollow statue? How is a natural object, enduring, like an artificial construct doomed to collapse? How is nature comparable to artifice? It is not only that those questions remain unanswered; nor is it, once again, that through the haze, we think we still catch the drift—that Bussy would not be one of these hollow men. For, in his final moments, he is just what he has described here. Monsieur likens him to a "tree solid" (5:2, line 39), and Bussy, in his last speech, affirms himself this way: "Here like a Roman statue I will stand" (5:4, line 97), a representative image. How are such contradictions to be explained?

Bussy has the answer. It lies in the "deep invisible paths" (1:1, line 21) that he sees in elemental processes, and to which his actions become attached in the play. He is forever being compared to the movements of water and air and fire, the least palpable of the elements. What we see, physically, visibly before our eyes, what we observe, is not all that is there. And beyond the contradictions lies the affirmation of an absolutism that is not violated by such discrepancies. Policy, when Bussy embraces it, becomes a principle of invisibility: "A politician must like lightning melt/The very marrow, and not taint the skin:/His ways must not be seen; the superficies/Of the green centre must not taste his feet" (4:2, lines 188–191). What would it mean if we were to say that the Bussy we see onstage is just this sort of politician, that although he appears to tread the green earth he does not, that what moves him is not visible in the form in which he moves, that what connects him with others is a principle of penetrative destruction that leaves the surfaces of things seemingly intact? It would mean that we could not see what was going on, even when it was before our eyes, and that what we could see was likely not to be what was really happening. Thus, Bussy arrives at court in a new suit of clothes; do clothes make the man, is this a change? No, Bussy says:

> *Mons.* Come, mine own sweetheart, I will enter thee.
> [*To the King*] Sir, I have brought a gentleman to Court,
> And pray you would vouchsafe to do him grace.
> *Hen.* D'Ambois, I think?
> *Bus.* That's still my name, my lord,
> Though I be something alter'd in attire.
>
> (1:2, lines 57–61)

This is Bussy's constant affirmation; it keeps him even from death: "Murther'd? I know not what that Hebrew means" (5:4, line 24), and his stand as a statue seems to suggest a triumph comparable to the earlier moment in the play when he kills three courtiers in a duel and emerges himself "untouch'd" (2:1, line 132). A gun is fired offstage; the bullets enter behind, and Bussy remains standing before our eyes. He is as untouched by death, whether he receives or delivers it, as he says that Tamyra is when he courts her.

Entering the court, Bussy becomes a murderer and an adulterer, or so it seems, public and private crimes are inextricably intertwined. Bussy offends courtiers with his self-proclamations, ladies with his scurrility: "I can sing prick-song, lady, at first sight" (1:2, line 88). Yet, it is just such sight we are invited not to see with. At the end, Bussy proclaims Tamyra as his reflection; she, too, has a "spotless name" (5:4, line 59) and his "pure" defense of her renders her "untainted" (lines 58, 62). Tamyra, whose conscience at times needs rallying in the play, enters into "a vault . . . that was never/Known" (2:2, lines 126–27) in which the usual categories by which experiences are judged simply disappear. Ordinary "conscience," as Bussy tells her, "is too nice" (3:1, line 1) when applied to their situation, for "Sin is a coward, madam" (line 20). It is simply not a term that applies to them. Bussy demands that his language refer only to himself and to those who are included in his movement into the court. Or, as Monsieur says, once he has seen Bussy at court, "his great heart will not down . . . /Till he be crown'd with his own quiet foam" (1:2, lines 157, 165). A sea to himself, Bussy's absolutism makes him a royal man, self-crowned and self-contained.

This does not mean that a private self in opposition to the court is the meaning of Bussy's actions.[48] Precisely the opposite. Monsieur and Montsurry turn on Bussy when, in the latter's words, "The King and D'Ambois now are grown all one" (4:1, line 119). It is at killing the king that Bussy draws the line with Monsieur (3:2). Once again, this scene is obscure because we do not know whether Monsieur really intends to kill the king. Bussy's inscrutability is extreme, but, as we have already remarked, it is not aberrant. Absolutism is everyone's goal—it is how to be a person, to reflect the royal self. Because Bussy identifies with the king, he will not kill him. He re-presents him. The king, we are first told, is reflected in his court. King Henry praises Queen Elizabeth and her court in significant terms. Her courtiers are "all observance" (1:2, line 11; actually, this is the Guise speaking contemptuously of what Henry goes on to praise), "demigods" whereas she is an "immortal goddess" (lines 11, 13). The court is "by her inform'd" (line 23). Or, as Monsieur puts it, as the play opens: "in a king/ All places are contain'd" (1:1, lines 35–36). This is the royal rule by which Bussy measures himself and with which he becomes the royal reflection. Thus, when he has murdered, he argues Henry into forgiving him on the very principle that defines Henry's power:

> If my wrong pass the power of single valour
> To right and expiate; then be you my king.
> And do a right, exceeding law and nature:
> Who to himself is law, no law doth need,
> Offends no law, and is a king indeed.   (2:1. lines 200–204)

Wrong becomes right in this argument, and Bussy and the king are made one. This is not a principle of individuality, but the very principle upon which absolutism is based.

And so, not surprisingly, the king sees himself in Bussy, and sees that Bussy is not to be seen as others are (this reflects upon himself as well). Nor does he occupy the same time as others; rather, he is pristine man, the absolute beginning. In the reverse mirror in which Henry reads himself in Bussy, he sees Bussy as his founding stone, as his beginning; his beginning here is established in a repetition, that

159

absolute hall of mirrors of re-presentation. Here is what Henry thinks
Bussy "comprehends" (3:2, line 94):

> kings had never borne
> Such boundless empire over other men,
> Had all maintain'd the spirit and state of D'Ambois;
> Nor had the full impartial hand of Nature
> That all things gave in her original,
> Without these definite terms of Mine and Thine,
> Been turn'd unjustly to the hand of Fortune,
> Had all preserv'd her in her prime, like D'Ambois;
> No envy, no disjunction had dissolv'd,
> Or pluck'd one stick out of the golden faggot
> In which the world of Saturn bound our lives,
> Had all been held together with the nerves,
> The genius, and th'ingenuous soul of D'Ambois.
>
> (3:2, lines 95–107)

Henry sees the golden age when he sees Bussy; he apprehends a
founding myth for the imperium in him, a state which is also a spirit
and a genius, out of time and eternal, before nature and justice were
separated, an originary principle that transcends opposites. This
makes Bussy, in the final paradox of the play, at once virtually inapprehensible and invisible—there is no way to see or to say what he
is—and yet the principle of power, totality, form, and substance in
the play. In Monsieur's final view of Bussy, he apprehends a "whole
man" (5:2, line 41)[49] who will nonetheless fall as "empty men"
(line 45) do; his fall would be their life. And, conversely, his life
seems to be assured by his fall; the parting shade of the friar hails a
fellow spirit, another Hercules, burned and become a star; for him,
Bussy, in death, is "a complete man" (5:4, line 147), and his heavenly
influence sheds "new sparks of old humanity" (line 153). This complete and full man makes a royal end:

> And if Vespasian thought in majesty
> An emperor might die standing, why not I?
> *She offers to help him.*
> Nay, without help, in which I will exceed him;
> For he died splinted with his chamber grooms.
> Prop me, true sword, as thou hast ever done!
> The equal thought I bear of life and death
> Shall make me faint on no side; I am up;
> Here like a Roman statue I will stand
> Till death hath made me marble.
>
> (5:4, lines 90–98)

Alone and unsupported, an emblem of *æqualitas,* this equivocal figure stands, supported not only by his Roman ideal, but by the text that this speech draws upon, the one Seneca wrote for Hercules flaming into immortality. Standing in place, Bussy stands in-place-of, representing, becoming a statue—a "lively statue"—the embodiment of *nunc stans,* timeless as a law, a statute. A law unto himself, Bussy ends as an imperial image.

"THE KING is not bound to answer" (4:1, line 146);[50] these are the words of Henry V, the monarch who comes at the end of Shakespeare's second tetralogy and who must have seemed to Shakespeare the last English king he would show onstage. Rome lay ahead. In 1599, in his own theater, his own world, Shakespeare had achieved his ascendancy, and his crowning gesture was to end his concern with English history and to shift his sights. In the same year, James first published his treatise on kingship for his son. Shakespeare's last English king is a mirror of princes, but one, as he says, not bound to answer. To different eyes, he appears to be different things, and whether he is most Machiavellian or most pious has divided critical response to him. The trouble is that he is very hard to see. Betraying three traitors, he proclaims himself in his purity; they witness, spectacularly, his freedom from their betrayal (2:2). Ruminating on questions of conscience—"I will speak my conscience of the king" (4:1, line 112), he speaks for and in-place-of the king; he wears a disguise, the cloak of another man. The king's humanity, in this scene, is a disguise; but so, he tell us, in his one extended soliloquy, is his body politic, empty ceremony, an idol (4:1, lines 216 ff.). Here the king allows himself another idyll, the dream of common repose, what "private men enjoy" (line 223), "a body filled, and vacant mind" (line 255). But Henry, who forever charges into breaches, occupies an empty space. The soliloquy begins "Upon the king" but it is precisely that there is nothing upon the king, that all reflects—but not on him—that makes his centrality coincide with a radical privation. When the king's cloaked challenge is answered, Fluellen stands in place of him, representing him, and receiving the blow.

Fluellen is also Henry's representative in another sense, as his chronicler, a latter-day Plutarch seeking parallels in ancient history for this modern hero. Alexander is most often in his mouth, just as others give Henry his place by reminding him of history; for Henry, there is "no remembrance" unless history "with full mouth/Speak freely of our acts" (1:2, lines 230, 231–32). The place he fills in time gives him the body of power in which he is clothed, a body neither coincident with ceremonial show nor the cloak of humanity, mere flesh. He is clothed in words, and out of the babel of speech in the play—dialects, foreign tongues, double entendres that keep finding out the sexual imperatives behind imperial pursuits—he emerges as a master of discourse: "Hear him but reason . . . /Hear him debate . . . /List his discourse . . . ; when he speaks,/The air, a chartered libertine, is still,/And the mute wonder lurketh in men's ears" (1:1, lines 38, 41, 43, 47-49). This is the way the untouched king gives "a little touch of Harry in the night" (4 Chor., line 47), in those words that rap the hearer into wonder, and claim him for the king; so the gordian knot is cut, when the king represents himself. And thus is the king represented—by "ciphers to this great accompt" (1 Chor., line 17) "within this wooden O" (line 13). Circle within circle, vacuity within vacuity, the world filled with representation. In an ideal world, the stage would be the world: "A kingdom for a stage, princes to act/And monarchs to behold the swelling scene" (lines 3-4). The ideal theater would be no public theater, but a private one, a masque where power clothes itself in theatrical forms, where Harry, "like himself" (line 5) would be a god, or like a god. The ideal stage would be a Roman theater: there, according to Thomas Heywood, emperors "thought none worthy to present themselves/Save Emperours" $(B2_r)$.[51]

The "acts" of Henry to be told "with full mouth" occur on the empty stage that represents history where emperors play themselves; this is how Henry is apprehended. The French wonder whether "his vanities forespent/Were but the outside of the Roman Brutus,/Covering discretion with a coat of folly" (2:4, lines 36-38). It is not only that they seek a secret within, beneath the surface, or that they imagine that secret form to take the shape of a re-membering of history in Henry, but that they wonder whether it is not the Roman prototype of egalitarianism, the hero who saved Rome from tyranny, whom Henry re-presents. This is how he represents himself to his troops at Agincourt, cloaked in their humility, appealing to their brotherhood: "We few, we happy few, we band of brothers;/For he to-day that sheds his blood with me/Shall be my brother" (4:3, lines 60-62). But after victory, in triumph, another Roman form emerges, the very opposite to the show of republican participation. Returning home, Londoners are said to pour forth "Like to the senators of th'antique Rome,/With the plebeians swarming at their heels,/Go forth and fetch their conqu'ring Caesar in" (5 Chor., lines 26-28). Brutus turns Caesar. There is a Roman fable in these swarming bees,

162

taking in the one that takes them in, offering participation, Caesar-like.

> Rome, here, includes England:
> As, by a lower but by loving likelihood,
> Were now the general of our gracious empress,
> As in good time he may, from Ireland coming,
> Bringing rebellion broached on his sword,
> How many would the peaceful city quit
> To welcome him! (5 Chor., lines 29–34)

When Essex returned, Elizabeth thought of herself as Richard II, as we noted when we began our examination of the player king. This moment of royal reference in *Henry V*, "a lower but ... loving likelihood," is unique in Shakespeare; in this play not only is history onstage, and the stage history (the final Chorus, after all, places Henry's future in the plays that Shakespeare has already written and put onstage), but England turns toward Rome, representing itself. This moment, when Shakespeare misreads the present in the past, and represents that parallel, Fluellenlike, is one of Roman representation, imperial doubling. Henry, who contains both Brutus and Caesar,[52] is most often paralleled to Alexander; his god, like Bussy's, was Hercules. And it was that part, Heywood tells us, Caesar played first: "*Julius Caesar* himselfe for his pleasure became an Actor . . . in his owne Theater he played *Hercules Furens* . . . yet was *Caesar* so extremely carried away with the violence of his practiced fury, and by the perfect shape of the madnesse of *Hercules*" ($E3_v$) that, to cut a long story short, he committed an actual murder onstage. Thus, Caesar played himself, a perfect act of representation committed onstage. "Like himself" Henry aspires to deity, to the godlike acts possible to a Roman actor.

4. THE ROMAN ACTOR: *Julius Caesar, Sejanus, Coriolanus, Catiline,* and *The Roman Actor*

Some Parallel'd him to *Tiberius* for Dissimulation, yet Peace was maintained by him as in the Time of *Augustus:* And Peace begot Plenty, and Plenty begot Ease and Wantonness, and Ease and Wantonness begot Poetry, and Poetry swelled to that Bulk in his time, that it begot strange Monstrous Satyrs against the King's own Person. —Arthur Wilson, *Life and Reign of James I*

D ISMISSING THE CONSPIRATORS, BRUTUS GIVES THEM this final piece of advice:
> Good gentlemen, look fresh and merrily.
> Let not our looks put on our purposes,
> But bear it as our Roman actors do,
> With untired spirits and formal constancy.
>
> *(Julius Caesar,* 2:1, lines 224-27)[1]

Brutus is instructing the conspirators in the acts of duplicity, yet there is a contradiction in the lines that surpasses those that we may suppose Brutus intends. Inviting the conspirators to disguise purposes in pleasant looks, Brutus calls for them to put on a "look" even as he asks them not to have their "looks put on our purposes." This contradiction is sustained in the attitude toward acting that underlies the passage. Assuming the "untired spirits and formal constancy" of Roman actors, the duplicity of the conspirators is invested in an imagined form of resplendent transcendence. The Roman actor, untired, formal, constant, has all the permanence of Roman representation, lively statues. The duplicitous form of the actor, masking purposes in a look that is not seen, a look that is not "looks," achieves the permanent form of a spirit. This is not only the form of an actor, it is also, quite simply, the form of power in the play. It is how Caesar sees himself:

> I could be well moved, if I were as you;
> If I could pray to move, prayers would move me:
> But I am constant as the Northern Star,
> Of whose true-fixed and resting quality
> There is no fellow in the firmament.   (3:1, lines 58-62)

This is what Caesar would be. A moment later hands speak, and the drama in Pompey's Theater issues in the savage spectacle of Caesar, bleeding beneath Pompey's statue.

We need to pause over that moment in a theater, and over Brutus's injunction to his fellow actors, for ideas fundamental to action on the stage of history (as fundamental as that metaphor)[2] seem at issue. Why does Brutus conceive of the action of the conspiracy as a theatrical event? Why does it occur in Pompey's Theater? To answer fully those questions, we will need to look beyond *Julius Caesar,* and the scope of this chapter includes a number of Roman plays of the Jacobean period. It is no accident that we can look there for representations that bear on the nature of history and the understanding of power in this time. James had placed a Roman stamp on his reign; that was the "style of gods" he claimed with imperial precedent, those were the laws he depended upon to assert his prerogative and mystery, that was the form of his entertainments, his Banqueting House, the ideology of his reign. John Chamberlain put the Roman comparison less kindly, but in a casual manner that suggests how pervasive it was. He wrote to Sir Dudley Carleton in 1614: "You may thincke there want no wooers for your place . . . when a knight whom you know well and whose name begins with R. Dru: would part with 2000[li] for the purchase, but yt were pitie things shold passe that way, for then we might well say *omnia Romae vaenalia,*" in Rome everything is for sale.[3] Comparisons of James with Tiberius were on the whole even less flattering.

The Roman plays that came to claim the stage in the Jacobean period reflect the style of the monarch and James's sense of himself as royal actor. They bear, as *romanitas* does in the Renaissance, a strong notion of public life, the continuities of history, the recreation of Rome as England's imperial ideal. In this Roman world, a particular kind of hero exists. In him, the absolutism that James espoused in his own self-division is tragically revealed. Absolute, measurable only by himself, he is described by himself. Cleopatra recognizes this in Antony: "none but Antony/Should conquer Antony" (4:15, line 16-17). Antony is—simply—Antony, even when he is not: "when he is not Antony/He comes too short of that great property/Which still should go with Antony" (1:1, lines 57-59). And he is never more himself than when he plays that particular Roman's part that Brutus plays in his final scene, suicide. "A Roman, by a Roman/Valiantly vanquished" (4:15, lines 57-58), Antony puts it. Absoluteness coincides with self-destruction: "There is left us/Ourselves to end ourselves" (4:14, lines 21-22).[4] Self-referentiality doubles back upon itself; the hero who is *sui generis* undoes himself. In the Roman heroes, the Jacobean stage offers the image of the tragedy implicit in the royal role of the actor replaying the spectral kingdom of Augustus on the stage of history.[5]

The king as actor: constant, unchanging, unique—a single star, unmoving; history as theater and history made in the theater; the purpose of this chapter is to pursue these connections in a group of Roman plays—*Julius Caesar, Sejanus, Coriolanus, Catiline,* and *The Roman Actor.* They will permit an investigation of the language of power that James expressed. The purpose of this inquiry is not to argue causality or to suggest influence in one direction or another; nor do I mean to identify characters in these plays with the monarch. Rather, I intend to suggest that the concerns that shaped James's conception of his role—and the fact that he conceived of it as a role—can also be found in these plays. Monarchs and dramatists speak the same language, pursue the same concerns: the nature of conscience, the relation between inner states and external ones, private lives and public persons, absolutist identity and recreative role playing. The staging of power and the powers of the stage are the central themes in this investigation, as they have been in earlier portions of this study. In the Roman plays, we may find a convenient place to examine closely the politics of literature.

After the bloodletting in Pompey's Theater, the theater of cruelty gives way to the ritual act by which the death of Caesar is inscribed in history. The history of liberty turns out to be the history of dramatic performance:

> *Brutus.*   Stoop, Romans, stoop,
>   And let us bathe our hands in Caesar's blood
>   Up to the elbows and besmear our swords.
>   Then walk we forth, even to the market place,
>   And waving our red weapons o'er our heads,
>   Let's cry "Peace, freedom, and liberty!"
> *Cassius.*   Stoop then and wash. How many ages hence
>   Shall this our lofty scene be acted over
>   In states unborn and accents yet unknown!
> *Brutus.*   How many times shall Caesar bleed in sport,
>   That now on Pompey's basis lies along
>   No worthier than the dust!
> *Cassius.*   So oft as that shall be,
>   So often shall the knot of us be called
>   The men that gave their country liberty.
>
>   (3:1, lines 105–8)

The "now" in this performance demands that it refer to the real event, not the staged one. Yet, in fact, the lines are about that performance, too, and the claims upon an audience that they can make.

166

They can make us believe that the staged event is real. The "acting over," the representation before our eyes, may be taken for the act itself; and perhaps what the perfect reciprocity of the metaphor hints is that history itself may be a series of representations. The acts on the stage of history in Brutus's formulation embody power in a form of transcendent constancy; events recur but do not change, unique events are acted over. We could say that the shape of these lines conveys something of that meaning: two voices speak, the brotherly co-conspirators Brutus and Cassius, two voices, and yet as one. Brutus's reiterated "stoop" is Cassius's first word, his initial "how many" echoed by Brutus; the passage demonstrates an "acting over" in its own cumulative repeating rhetorical patterns. There is one language here, although there are two voices. That language has many names. We might call it politics, or power, or theater, or impersonation, or action. Thomas Heywood provides a good gloss.[6] Actors, he says, are such powerful impersonators that they can bewitch us into thinking "the Personater were the man Personated" (B4r). That statement may carry a profound truth if all the world is a stage and all men are actors. And, as for Roman actors, Heywood says: "If wee present a forreigne History, the subject is so intended, that in the lives of *Romans, Grecians,* or others, either the vertues of our Countrymen are extolled, or their vices reproved" (F3v). Reversing Horatio, we might say that Hamlet discovers that to act at all one must be more Roman than Dane, especially if one is to play the king. It is in the closet, after all, that Polonius, once again, enacts the part of Julius Caesar; he falls to an actor who, having avoided the role of Nero, has become Brutus instead.

LET US begin by seeing how Brutus comes to be an actor.

The extraordinary scene occurs barely one hundred lines into *Julius Caesar.* Caesar and his entourage have passed across the stage briefly as they pursue the course for the celebration of the Lupercal, leaving Cassius and Brutus behind. Throughout the subsequent scene which Brutus and Cassius play together, another will occur offstage, the offer of a crown to Caesar thrice refused and the final swoon in the marketplace when Caesar falls before the crowd. These offstage events punctuate those onstage; this is the only moment in all of Shakespeare when the backstage area is conceived of as one on which the action onstage depends, one continuous with action onstage. Normally, the *frons scenae* defines a limit, occasionally pierced by the opening of the discovery space. In the tiring house behind, costumes (attire) are changed, and the actor retires. But, in this scene in which Brutus emerges into public life, the very deployment of the stage carries a parallel structure. Public life is pervasive. There is no privacy, no retirement, no place to shift a scene or change a costume. Even behind the scenes, the actors continue to impersonate. The very shape of the stage serves, then, to carry a meaning we have seen before, the continuity of inner life and outer life, private and public. What the stage conveys, the scene portrays: Brutus is born as an actor in this scene, ushered into his part; he emerges as a public figure.

The scene between Brutus and Cassius begins with a piece of observation, "Brutus, I do observe you now of late" (1:2, line 32), that alerts us to the fact that there is no way *not* to be observed, no retiring from view. Cassius's observation here is knotty, complex. He complains that Brutus does not appear to love him, and Brutus responds with assurances that he does. Yet this very private matter is hardly all that they are talking about. The opportunity for Cassius's observation is, after all, the fact that Brutus has markedly absented himself from Caesar's retinue; perhaps Brutus has even provoked Cassius's observation by his sour remarks about Antony. "Will you see the order of the course?" (line 25) was Cassius's first question to Brutus, and his refusal triggers Cassius's observation. The complaint about love, then, raises questions about taking sides; implicitly, Cassius questions where they stand in relation to Caesar—and Antony's "quick spirit" that Brutus confesses he lacks. (There are ironies in that confession: it is Antony who will run the race, it is upon Antony's touch that Caesar rests the hope of issue, and it is Antony who, in response to Caesar's commands, replies, "I shall remember./ When Caesar says 'Do this,' it is performed" [lines 9–10]. Antony's role is to be the echo of Caesar, the fulfillment of his word, embodied in performance. Antony takes upon himself to extend himself to represent Caesar. Antony's performance becomes history, as firmly as Cassius's lack of love for plays marks out his destiny.)

Cassius and Brutus raise a "quick spirit" of performance, not around the presence of Caesar and his imperial word, but around his absence—of which we are always reminded by the shouts of the crowd breaking through the scene, each time heightening its rhythms, lending urgency to the emergence of Brutus as conspirator—his absence, and Cassius's portrait of Caesar as no god but as the most mortal of men. The absent Caesar and the image of his diseased body, fallible, weak, frail: against these the conspiratorial, quick-spirited scene onstage is played. The Caesar offstage dominates what occurs onstage, a form of power we know James favored, withdrawing from view and into his absolute state. And we know, too, that state secrets sometimes masked the body. Here, Cassius's tale, Caesar's swoon, are private realms beneath the claims to deity and the crown offered—and, characteristically, denied—offstage.

Also backstage are correspondent segments of Brutus and Cassius, parts of themselves equally private, fallible and as unavailable as the scene not seen. Offstage and on, a crown is being offered; Caesar refuses it, yet Casca says his no means yes. Brutus will not even quite acknowledge that Cassius has made the offer. The scene will end in silence, just before Caesar returns from the Forum, Brutus having emerged so far into public life that he will cover his emergence with the very absences and denials that mark Caesar's performance and thus suggest his attainment of power. He says to Cassius:

> That you do love me I am nothing jealous.
> What you would work me to, I have some aim.
> How I have thought of this, and of these times,
> I shall recount hereafter. For this present,
> I would not so (with love I might entreat you)
> Be any further moved. What you have said
> I will consider; what you have to say
> I will with patience hear, and find a time
> Both meet to hear and answer such high things.
> Till then, my noble friend, chew upon this:
> Brutus had rather be a villager
> Than to repute himself a son of Rome
> Under these hard conditions as this time
> Is like to lay upon us.   (Lines 162–75)

The scene begun with a question of love ends with loving assurance. Love now has some explicit consequences, as explicit as Caesar's desire for issue, with which the scene opens, the imperious voice stopping the procession to proclaim his wife's barrenness. The scene is framed by this transformation of what might be thought of as the most private and intimate into matters of public concern. Caesar's imperious command serves as a precedent for making privacy public, and Shakespeare's art in this scene is to open to observation what might have been thought to be unobservable—or unspeakable. Love is politics. In his love, Brutus would make time stop, although his speech keeps glimpsing a past and a future bound to this present. He would not be further moved and would move no further. Yet, his denials carry hints of revelations, hints of actions. Brutus, not saying what he has thought, or what he will do, admits that he has thought and that he will act; he defers his recounting to hereafter; he posits a time in the future meet for action and for speech. Deferring himself to then, he extends himself into the future. Note the progression of tenses: from the assurance of the present love through the conditionals and on to an insistent futurity of "I will . . . I will." The speech to Cassius ends with a prophecy, couched as prophecies are, gnomically; what exactly does Brutus promise? As he says, it needs to be chewed. These obscure words, hinting at rebellion, yet declaring (in opposition, unvoiced, to Antony) proper sonship, true filial piety to Rome, bring Brutus into the sphere of politics. This saying and not saying at once has put onstage what is yet offstage. Brutus has entered the second body in which power is invested, the invisible body of power.

Here is how it emerges:

Brutus says that what Cassius has observed reading his face—a lack of love—is something else, absorption in himself so that he has "veiled" his look (line 37) forgetting "the shows of love to other men" (line 47). Between the initial "If I have veiled my look" and the final acknowledgment of forgetfulness, Brutus disowns and owns the perception that Cassius has brought to his countenance. He has seen that Brutus is out of love. The question is, with whom: himself? Caesar? Brutus answers himself and Cassius reads it as out of love with Caesar. (Later in the play, Portia will wonder if Brutus no longer loves her, and she will be sacrificed to the ghost of Caesar, and to Brutus's transformation of himself into the man of marble constancy, unfeeling.) The veiled face may be veiled even to its owner. "Tell me, good Brutus, can you see your face?" (line 51), Cassius asks; when Brutus admits that he can only see himself by reflection, Cassius offers (as Achilles does in *Troilus and Cressida*) to be the mirror in which Brutus may read himself. Cassius tells what Brutus believes hidden, what Brutus believes he hides in his self-absorption. Yet, plain to Cassius is what Brutus denies as "that which is not in me" (line 65), which Cassius emends to "that of yourself which you yet know not of" (line 70).

Brutus, self-absorbed, has retired into a private self, inarticulate, unrevealed, and unknown. To him, that self is nothing; "that which is not in me." Yet Cassius can read it in his face. To him it is public. This secreted self mirrors the offstage event, unacknowledged, denied. The hidden not-self that Brutus would deny is the public self clothed in the second body of power, a spiritual body, ghastly, ghostly, unchanging. Brutus, "with himself at war" (line 46), is about to issue into a monstrous birth. Conspiring together, Cassius offering, as he reads Brutus's face, declarations of "my love" (line 73), the not-self of Brutus is about to be acknowledged, to become the other self, conceptions "only proper to myself" (line 41) reconceived. For at this moment, there is a flourish and a shout. "What means this shouting?" Brutus asks, and answers himself, becoming two voices at once. "I do fear the people/Choose Caesar for their king" (lines 79-80).

The shout releases a fear, articulates "that which is not in me" (line 65), explains the "veil" and the "show" of forgetfulness. Brutus has been denying what he has been thinking, denying the fear that breaks out of him as the crowd roars and shouts. And, suddenly, he makes a declaration, couched in those abstractions that will mark Brutus's speech throughout the remainder of the play—words that will be resounded over the corpse of Caesar.

> What is it that you would impart to me?
> If it be aught toward the general good,
> Set honor in one eye and death i'th'other,
> And I will look on both indifferently;
> For let the gods so speed me as I love
> The name of honor more than I fear death.   (Lines 84-89)

Brutus reverses the direction of the scene; Cassius feeds him, does not draw him out. The co-conspirators begin to identify, imparting—Cassius will call this seduction as the scene closes (line 309). Imparting they join. And after the veiled looks, the tentative observation, the tortured reading in a mirror, Brutus finds what he can "look on . . . indifferently," a way of glossing himself that renames "that which is not in me" and calls it honor. Brutus is an honorable man—we know what will happen to the adjective he chooses to cover himself with, just as we know what to make of the cry of the conspirators, "Liberty! Freedom! Tyranny is dead!" (3:1, line 78). Every revolution has that rally. Without knowing it, with *honor* Brutus has arrived at the language of state, words housing contradictions that he will attempt to master and that will master him. The language of power, as James knew, cuts two ways. At this moment, Brutus chooses for himself *honor* and the *general good.* Cassius cements the connection between those names in the mirror he holds up for reflection: "I know that virtue to be in you, Brutus,/As well as I do know your outward favor" (lines 90-91). Transparent Brutus, seen through: Cassius reverses his words.

Hence, "honor is the subject of my story" (line 92) when Cassius proceeds to reveal that Caesar, the man that "is now become a god" (line 116), bears a dying body that cannot command the flood and that shakes with fever. Observant Cassius has "marked" him, has seen his eye lose its luster, has heard him groan. Good physician, Cassius scorns his feeble temper. Against the Caesar of his "story" another "general shout" (line 132) resounds, and Cassius is now ready to apply his tale of honor to the man of honor. He invites Brutus to substitute the names "'Brutus' and 'Caesar.' What should be in that 'Caesar'?/Why should that name be sounded more than yours" (lines 142–43). "Let him be Caesar" (3:2, line 50), the people will shout after Brutus has spoken over the corpse of Caesar. Cassius invites Brutus to compare the two names linked by honor, to weigh them, sound them, write them, conjure with them. He invites a double nomination and reminds Brutus of the history his name bears, for it is not his own but ancestral: "There was a Brutus once . . ." (line 159), he says, and there is a Brutus again. Brutus has two names, representing himself: Brutus and Caesar; Brutus in history—names to be inserted in a book, to be read, weighed, pondered.[7] Brutus's word, self-chosen, leads him to his name, chosen for him: his career is already written, his name already inscribed. The duplicities of language find Brutus out, James's spectral history of inescapable repetition, a Roman view, is Brutus's, too.

Later, replaying the scene alone, reading in his garden, stones with words attached to them will be flung in, destroying his privacy, violating himself.

> The exhalations, whizzing in the air,
> Give so much light that I may read by them.
> 'Brutus, thou sleep'st. Awake, and see thyself!
> Shall Rome, &c. Speak, strike, redress!'
> 'Brutus, thou sleep'st. Awake!'
> Such instigations have been often dropped
> Where I have took them up.
> 'Shall Rome, &c.' Thus must I piece it out:
> Shall Rome stand under one man's awe? What, Rome?
> My ancestors did from the streets of Rome
> The Tarquin drive when he was called a king.
>
> (2:1, lines 44–54)

Brutus "piece[s] out" the fragments and promises to act, binding himself to the example of his ancestors, acknowledging the not-self that Cassius gives him access to, the "hideous dream" that he shares with Calphurnia and that produces the savage spectacle of Caesar bleeding in Pompey's Theater:

> Since Cassius first did whet me against Caesar,
> I have not slept.

172

> Between the acting of a dreadful thing
> And the first motion, all the interim is
> Like a phantasma or a hideous dream.   (2:1, lines 61-65)

To Cassius's initial prompting, Brutus offers ambiguous promises, a prophetic riddle welcomed by Cassius as a "show" of something more (1:2, line 176). Another show follows immediately, Caesar's. For just as what was offstage in Brutus has come onstage in the concealed forms of political discourse, so Caesar returns. Now Brutus is all eye, knowing the force of observation: "But look you, Cassius,/ The angry spot doth glow on Caesar's brow" (lines 183-84). He has seen the need to observe, to read from the body to what it reveals. But despite all the signs of fear and anger, the blaze of eyes, the paleness of skin, all there before the eye, Caesar seems unfathomable. An interpreter is needed, and Casca will soon stay to tell. Caesar pauses to speak again, as he had done at first, to Antony; he speaks and unspeaks himself, talks of fear and fearlessness, of unchangingness, immovableness, "for always I am Caesar" (line 212), and, in the same breath, of the weakness of his hearing. Observant, Caesar pauses over Cassius's looks, over his powers of observation: "He is a great observer, and he looks/Quite through the deeds of men" (lines 202-3), and he closes by asking Antony to tell him what he thinks of Cassius. Nothing is revealed when two voices speak at once: Caesar's speech is the speech of power; there is more to him than can be observed.

And it is, according to Casca, with two voices that Caesar speaks. Each denial of the crown, he says, only showed how much he wanted it. Mere "foolery" is Casca's reiterated word for Caesar's show (lines 235, 284), a performance as he reports it. "He put it by with the back of his hand thus" (line 221), he gestures; claiming not to have "marked" the performance, Casca has observed all, seen through it. He can tell exactly what sort of crown it was, and how the breaths of the crowd stank, and the *coup de théâtre* when Caesar falls. Cassius tries to read the event symbolically; they, not Caesar have the falling sickness, he tells Brutus; but Casca dismisses that allegorization for a more complex reading. He sees Caesar's swound as a theatrical event:

> If the rag-tag people did not clap him and hiss him, according as he pleased and displeased them, as they use to do the players in the theatre, I am no true man. (Lines 256-59)

Casca is no true man; once he has gone, Cassius will say that his blunt manner is something he "puts on" (line 296), a piece of impersonation meant to add savor to his words. But, in Casca's account, Caesar is no true man either, but a consummate actor. Cassius had used a story about Caesar's infirm body as the theme of honor; Caesar uses his body itself to move the crowd. The body is transformed into an element of persuasion; it no longer bears a merely natural existence (did it ever?); through the body, we know, the royal actor is read.[8] In the public forum, before the roaring crowd, Caesar transforms his dying body into the body of power:

> Marry, before he fell down, when he perceived the common herd was glad he refused the crown, he plucked me ope his doublet and offered them his throat to cut. An I had been a man of any occupation, if I would not have taken him at a word I would I might go to hell among the rogues. And so he fell. When he came to himself again, he said, if he had done or said anything amiss, he desired their worships to think it was his infirmity. Three or four wenches where I stood cried "Alas, good soul!" and forgave him with all their hearts. But there's no heed to be taken of them. If Caesar had stabbed their mothers, they would have done no less. (Lines 261–72)

Between his infirm body and the crown he desires, Caesar constructs a performance in which his body can be owned or disowned, in which his deeds are countenanced and discountenanced, in which he is present and absent in his actions and his words. Caesar's openness, passion, honesty, and humility are all shows, yet not unreal, not simply to be translated into something else as if they were an allegory, or as if they were merely cynical. The language of state, we know, is not simply a cover. The show that Caesar puts on manifests power. "Well, Brutus, thou art noble," Cassius will say, alone, as the scene closes, "yet I see . . ." (line 305). "Thou art . . . ; yet. . . ." The syntax here holds two truths together as the basis for political action and political perception: two truths are essential to the imperial theme. As the scene closes Cassius appears to have power, but, in fact, his power is limited by his observations and his performance. He is never again so consummate an actor; nor is Brutus. Rather, as the opening of the scene suggested, the race belongs to Antony; his is the power to ride the tide and issue forth.

Antony inherits the mantle of Caesar. He takes it and invests that stage property with the savage spectacle. His function, he says, alone with the corpse, is to put a mouth in the wounds, to make them speak (3:2, lines 229–30). Once again, the hidden and the private are made public. With the crowd, the rent mantle of Caesar becomes the prop for the representation of Caesar's death. He puts his words in the holes of the mantle, and draws with them the blood of Caesar and the rage of the crowd. When he removes the mantle, the veil, he reveals the bleeding body, a body that has been clothed in the words he has threaded through the mantle's holes. Caesar's body becomes a prop behind the prop of the veil, and the veil serves as the vehicle of discourse, a place in which Antony is invested and yet not revealed, a place upon which the hidden springs of his action and the actions of the crowd and the actions of the conspirators can all be re-presented. The mantle is a figure for speech in the political domain.

"You all do know this mantle" (3:2, line 170), Antony begins, but in fact, only he knows it. To it he attaches a memory, Caesar first wearing it one summer night when he secured Rome against one of its enemies. The rhythms here are casual, private, intimate; yet the very domesticity carries a political meaning. Thus the great man invested himself when he made the world safe for you; his leisure was only possible when he had first secured the general good.

> I remember
> The first time ever Caesar put it on.
> 'Twas on a summer's evening in his tent,
> That day he overcame the Nervii.   (Lines 170-73)

"Caesar put it on": *put on* is the Elizabethan idiom for playing a part, and Antony's account of it is, in the modern idiom, a "put on"; indeed we have no way of knowing what is true in this story despite all its sense of observation, the evening, the season, the day, the very gown. "I remember" is a pure reconstruction, a remembering indeed. And then, a dismembering.

> Look, in this place ran Cassius's dagger through.
> See what a rent the envious Casca made.
> Through this the well-beloved Brutus stabbed.   (Lines 174-76)

Look, says Antony, look at the holes. He constructs his story in those tears and rents. Through them he works, threading his words. Antony makes the daggers speak.

> And as he plucked his cursed steel away,
> Mark how the blood of Caesar followed it,
> As rushing out of doors to be resolved
> If Brutus so unkindly knocked or no.   (Lines 177-80)

The eye is invited to follow the invisible flow of blood, to enter an

175

offstage area, the love of Brutus and Caesar violated, the bursting of a mighty heart, the mantling of his face in grief, falling beneath the bleeding statue of Pompey. The bleeding statue functions like the rent veil, for it, too, represents the double body of Caesar that falls and cannot die. This is the veil that Antony weaves, out of nothing, holes, wounds, a corpse. Over this body, he conjures that spectral one, to be seen, displayed, although it is invisible, the body of power, the king's spectral, spiritual body. "Look you here!/Here is himself, marred as you see with traitors" (lines 196–97). Here is himself. Yet what is to be seen when we look is not the "bleeding piece of earth" (3:1, line 254) Antony saw when alone with the corpse. In public, another body is to be seen, the invisible body Antony invites the crowd to see, the ghost that Brutus finally sees. "Didst thou see anything," Brutus asks, and "Nothing, my lord" is the reply (4:3, lines 297 ff.). As Cassius confesses finally, before he plays "a Roman's part" (5:3, line 89), "My sight was ever thick" (line 21).

> *Brutus.*　　　　　　　　Ha! who comes here?
> 　　I think it is the weakness of mine eyes
> 　　That shapes this monstrous apparition.
> 　　It comes upon me. Art thou any thing?
> 　　Art thou some god, some angel, or some devil,
> 　　That mak'st my blood cold and my hair to stare?
> 　　Speak to me what thou art.
> *Ghost.*　Thy evil spirit, Brutus.　　　　　　　(4:3, lines 275–82)

So, finally, Brutus sees "that which is not in me" (1:2, line 65), the specter that haunts him as his double, invisible before his eyes, the spirit of Caesar mighty yet.[9] At last, Brutus sees the very form of power before him.

INVISIBLE before his eyes: that is the formula for political power, for the mantle worn by the one who plays the king. We have seen it before in *Bussy d'Ambois* and in *Henry V*. It is regularly a feature of the Roman plays. And it is, we know, how James saw himself clothed on the stage of history, try as he might to retire or to disown what his spectacle suggested. It was also a spectacle of his power, as Ben Jonson reveals in his representation of Tiberius, the Roman emperor Arthur Wilson said James was perceived to be, dissimulating. Tiberius in *Sejanus* is no portrait of James, if by that we mean that the real king inspired the fiction; in all likelihood Jonson had written the play before James became England's king. Yet, the play spoke to present concerns; Jonson was called before the Star Chamber for possible treason. Actual history overtook staged history.[10] Causality is not the point. Were it not to reify language overmuch, we might say that history and staged history share the reality of language; or, following Foucault, we can point to shared epistemic limits conditioning discourse and actions, onstage and off. Actual power is invested in fictions, and fictions are potent. We know, and know it best in the theater, that the power of plays is that they convince us of their reality. Their reality may not be the same as everyday reality, but everyday reality is neither natural, neutral, nor simply given.[11] Political reality, ordinary events, and staged ones are all matters of representation; in the early seventeenth century, representation was governed by the notion of the king's two bodies; doubling himself and viewed doubly, his dissimulation described his state of being, *representing* himself. The spectral body dominates in absolutist representation. Because Jonson's royalism stopped short of James's absolutism, the picture of absolutism in *Sejanus* troubled James.[12] It is a fearful specter, and a specter of fear, that he offers.

In Jonson's *Sejanus,* all eyes are focused outward, everyone is busy observing others.[13] As in James's prefatory poem to the *Basilikon Doron,* all eyes are invited to double observation, "Observe the Statutes of your heavenly King" (line 6), and *observation* defines the crucial sphere of action, where the ruler—and the body of power—are to be glimpsed, obeyed, and imitated, represented. "And from his Law, make all your Lawes to spring" (line 7). In Jonson's play Tiberius, the emperor, observes most and is most observed. What he offers to sight is palpably a performance, and it puts in question exactly what is seen. Cordus comments on Tiberius's first manifestation in the play with the ironic, "Rarely dissembled" (1, line 395), and Arruntius concludes his line intending further irony, "Prince-like, to the life." Yet, Arruntius is more perspicacious than he imagines; rare dissembling is essential to rule. *Qui nescit dissimulare, nescit regnare.* Being prince*like,* Tiberius re-presents himself, doubles himself. He offers a lifelike show, not life in some simple, natural sense. The prince plays the prince, and the full wonder of his rare performance is, as even the opposing Germanicans admit, that if what he says could be believed, one could want nothing more.

> If this man
> Had but a minde allied unto his words,
> How blest a fate were it to us, and *Rome?*
> We could not thinke that state, for which to change,
> Although the ayme were our old liberty.   (1, lines 400–404)

177

So Silius comments, glimpsing "wish'd liberty" in Tiberius's show (1, line 408). Tiberius, as he says, aims "to be, what you desire" (3, line 151). Hence, in the central acts of the play, he advances the sons of Germanicus. At the same time he engineers the downfall of their supporters and the suicide of Silius. Republican pretenses serve absolutist ends, but in a baffling way. Arruntius, stunned by this set of events, confesses, "By Jove, I am not Oedipus inough,/To understand this Sphynx" (3, lines 64-65). The desires to which Tiberius matches himself have this paradoxical form, disarming desire at the same time as appearing to satisfy it. Like the monarch in the masque, Tiberius appears as the fulfillment of all wishes. Yet what he does really only serves his power. The question of Tiberius's believability is complicated in ways in which the credibility of any dramatic character is. He gives a performance; this means that something is performed. Although the relationship between what is said and done is obscure, things *are* done—or rather, appear to be done. In *Sejanus,* the obsessiveness of observation, the reading of looks, the complicated network of spies, is directed at finding what—if anything—is going on. When kings are onstage, for whom do they act? This is not easy to answer, for the entire substance of public life has that mixture of reality and unreality that characterizes life onstage, we know; the success of Tiberius in the play, the measure of his power, lies in the truth that Arruntius wishes to disallow when he comments, meaning it ironically, "Well acted, Caesar" (3, line 105). The realization that Caesar's actions in the play manifest power, that genuine power is represented in his acts, lies beyond the ironic perspective of Arruntius; that Caesar displays a kind of sphynxlike wisdom in his riddling behavior. We can see it from the first scene he plays.

Caesar enters the play by demanding that a man who has knelt before him rise. Kneeling is for the gods, he says, and he is only human. Like Shakespeare's Caesar, Jonson's makes no claims to divinity. The man, commanded by Caesar, presumably rises. An action has occurred, corresponding, no doubt, to the desires of those who espouse republican hopes, or still dream republican dreams. Yet, the action, which, reduced to Tiberius's words and the response of the kneeler to them, bears an apparent meaning, is not permitted to rest in that meaning. The action is observed; it is, indeed, a performance. It is observed, and commented upon, and one telling observation is that the act is a performance. Here is the action complete (or, rather, the complete text of the action; there is a difference):

178

Tiberius. (One kneeles to him.) Wee not endure these flatteries,
    let him stand;
    Our empire, ensignes, axes, roddes, and state
    Take not away our humane nature from us:
    Looke up, on us, and fall before the gods.
Sejanus.   How like a god, speakes Caesar!
Arruntius.   There, observe!
    He can indure that second, that's no flattery.
    O, what is it, proud slime will not beleeve
    Of his owne worth, to heare it equall prais'd
    Thus with the gods?
Cotta.   He did not heare it, sir.
Arruntius.   He did not? Tut, he must not, we think meanely.
    'Tis your most courtly, knowne confederacy,
    To have your private parasite redeeme
    What he, in publique subtilty, will lose
    To making him a name.   (1, lines 375–88)

At this point, a petitioner breaks in, and another action begins.

Refusing flattery, Tiberius speaks in the full voice of state, listing the symbols of authority—"ensigne, axes, roddes"—assuming the
royal "wee" for self-reference. Even as he disallows his divinity, he
extends his person to embrace "our empire . . . and state"; not putting off his humanity, he nonetheless reinvests himself in the full
panoply of royal insignia. In the voice in which he speaks, he is the
state. And even as he demands that his subject rise and stand face to
face, he expresses the demand in a way that keeps his petitioner sub-
servient: "Looke up, on us, and fall before the gods." Sejanus's
response is complex. We may "observe" what Arruntius observes,
flattery greeting the monarch who refuses flattery, and such simple
doubleness is not beneath Tiberius's arts. Sometimes he merely dis-
sembles. But if this first performance is "rarely dissembled," we must
pass beyond the limits of Arruntius's ironies. All doubling is not
merely dissimulation. So we may add to Sejanus's response the possibility of a genuine admiration for Tiberius; and since we know him
capable of this later in the play, total contempt for the emperor may
be in his words, too. Sejanus may mean his words or he may not. It
is likely, too, that the words are not his own, that he is saying what is
expected, conforming to a role and script. All these may be true
about these words. And what, exactly, has Sejanus said: "How like a
god, speakes Caesar!" He does not say that Caesar is a god. He points

179

at representation, and resemblance, and this is one explanation of the complexity of what he is saying. What, exactly, does he point to? How does a god speak? What are we to "observe"?

Arruntius's response to his words is reductive, lacking self-perception; blinded by his own "proud slime," his sour ironies are partial and partisan. He hears only one sort of "second" in Sejanus's response and assumes Caesar has heard it, too. Cotta, however, insists that Tiberius does not hear it at all. Presumably, as Cotta observes the scene, Caesar's performance with the kneeler is not violated by others. The structure of the scene seems to lend this view support, for it erects a shared space of perception and a sphere for speaking aside, unobserved. Correspondingly, Caesar's stage protects him from observing and hearing. Cotta's Caesar is untouched by flattery, denigration, or dissembling. Cotta keeps the Caesar he wants. Cotta, however, is a supporter of Sejanus. Denying Arruntius he may be equally partisan, but a flatterer—or he may believe Tiberius's godlike show, offering a deaf ear to demonstrate his remoteness, his unfathomable power. Or perhaps "He did not heare" merely means that like great Julius, this man suffers ordinary human limits. That is Tiberius's claim, too.[14]

Arruntius will not hear that. What, we may ask—which of these does he take Cotta to mean? "Tut, he must not," Arruntius says—correcting Cotta's naiveté, or caught in a trap Cotta has laid to draw Arruntius out so that he can spring upon him; in any case, Arruntius's comment is not neutral but a bid for supporters among those who speak in asides, judging the performance and attempting to stand outside of it, as if Caesar's powers could be limited by those asides, those voices presumed unheard, those faces presumed unfathomable. Arruntius insists on Caesar's performance, never on his own. "Tut, he must not." For Arruntius, Caesar cannot afford to show that he is performing. Yet that is not true. The performance can be seen; it cannot be seen through. Precisely because it is an act of representation, it invites interpretation, observation. The theatricality of Caesar carries a demand that the performance be attended to. But it does not promise that it will be transparent. It would hardly be rarely dissembled if it did. Indeed, in the consummateness of his art Tiberius can even overact, be caught in the act, and yet not be caught. Playing with the hopes of the Germanicans, he will finally "render all . . . suspected" (3, line 118) at the same time as he gives what they desire. As Arruntius only half guesses, there is a profound "confederacy" in the arts of Tiberius in which even he has a part. The emperor's acts maintain the state, preserving even the opposition.

180

Shall we murder Arruntius? Tiberius asks Sejanus. No, he responds, "preserve him. His franke tongue/Being lent the reines, will take away all thought/Of malice, in your course against the rest" (3, lines 498-500). Even Arruntius is part of the imperial performance, an allowed voice giving Tiberius scope for his acts. Politics makes all the world a stage.

Arruntius sees this "confederacy" in the sycophantic relation-ship of Tiberius and Sejanus, but not beyond. Yet it is everywhere a principle of political organization, like the all-embracing powers of the monarch celebrated in the masques. The play opens with the Ger-manicans congratulating themselves on their virtue and, especially, the nobility of their absences from court, that cesspool of vice and guilt. Yet their notion that simple physical absence and priggishness keeps them clear and free is one that the play destroys. (Donne's Idios, we might recall, was similarly disabused.) No place is free of spies, and the eyes of the court extend even into the secrets that never are allowed expression. A slip of the tongue does Sabinus in (4, line 216), a double entendre he may not intend; criminality lies in observation—to be taken, to be seen, and especially to be seen apart, are crimes in the reign of Tiberius, most criminal because they pre-sume on the royal prerogative. Only the king may not be caught, only he genuinely stands apart. As Arruntius says, Tiberius must cir-cumscribe himself, losing in "publique subtilty" what he gains in private: "'Tis your most courtly, knowne confederacy,/To have your private parasite redeeme/What he, in publique subtilty, will lose/To making him a name" (1, lines 385-88). Private gains cannot be seen. Tiberius has arranged for a public ventriloquism in which others voice what he cannot say; even the Germanicans wind up doing this. Conversely, the emperor says what others would hear, even voicing republican sentiments. The rewards are both private (a parasitic re-demption almost unmentionable) and public. There Tiberius gains a name. "Stile not us/Or lord, or mighty," he tells a petitioner urging a letter upon him, "who professe our selfe/The servant of the *Senate*" (1, lines 391-93). Tiberius takes upon himself the name that signals his fulfillment of the rhetoric of the republic. No tyrant he, no god.

And in his long harangue to the senate, it is the "stile, and note of gods" (1, line 471) that he refuses; assuring them that "there can be nothing in their thought/Shall want to please us" (lines 449-50), Caesar is then pleased to refuse them their request to deify him. This demonstrates Arruntius's perception about "confederacy." The senate has power to ask what Caesar desires and Caesar has the power to deny what they ask—precisely because they are asking for what he desires. So doing, he seems not to desire what he desires, and thereby gives what men desire—for they do not want to seem merely Caesar's instruments, mere mouthpieces. Tiberius gives them the illusion that they have autonomous desires by appearing to deny himself. Appearance is truth, however; he *does* refuse the style of gods; they do find their petition turned back. They find their fulfillment in that frustration, and Caesar finds his in his. This exchange keeps everyone happy—and mystified. And it keeps uncertain what has happened, except that Caesar remains Caesar, and power stays with him. In a flourish, this is displayed, displaced. Having refused the style of gods himself, Caesar allows it for Sejanus. His statue may be erected. Caesar gives no explanation for this arbitrary display; here, he makes arbitrary and absolutist claims: "Princes have still their grounds rear'd with themselves,/Above the poore low flats of common men,/And, who will search the reasons of their acts,/Must stand on equall bases" (1, lines 537-40). Tiberius invokes the reasons of state here and sounds like a Renaissance monarch—like James, perhaps, defending his prerogative. The kneeler raised to Caesar's eye does not stand on an equal basis, nor does Sejanus. For his statue is to be erected, as we might almost have expected after *Julius Caesar,* and knowing the theatricality of power, "in Pompey's theatre" (1, line 520). What Tiberius performs with the senators and to the Germanicans, disabling them by dissembling, he does to Sejanus; if the parasite thinks himself Caesar, Caesar has cast him in that part. "Some slave hath practis'd an imposture" (5, line 33), Sejanus will think, hearing that his statue breathes smoke. He recommends that its head be taken off, and a serpent is found inside. "Dearest head" (3, line 501) is Tiberius's term for Sejanus the last time in the play he appears to give him what he wants. Then Tiberius has his head; the serpent, rarely dissembling, remains unseen.[15]

Tiberius begins his acts in *Sejanus* with the public performance we have looked at in act 1. It is the only time he is in such full view. He subsequently appears onstage in two private conferences with Sejanus and one with Macro. In the last act of the play, he sends a letter. Like James, at last, he rules by the pen. Nearly invisible when seen, Tiberius remains as unseen as possible, retired even when present. The manifestations of power reside outside him, in the extension of his body into the body politic—to Sejanus his head, and then to Macro, his machine, fully obedient to his master's call, espousing the wisdom of the intelligencer, a "dumbe" instrumentality (3, line 718), an effacement modeled on Caesar's show. Caesar appears to reveal his arts at a stunning moment in act 2 when he claims that he has dropped all pretense, that having questioned Sejanus about the Germanicans, the attitudes Tiberius assumed were not those he meant. Rather, he meant to elicit from Sejanus what he would have said himself, and having done so, he says:

> We can no longer
> Keepe on our masque to thee, our deare Sejanus;
> Thy thoughts are ours, in all, and we but proov'd
> Their voice, in our designes, which by assenting
> Hath more confirm'd us, then if heartning Jove
> Had, from his hundred statues, bid us strike,
> And at the stroke clickt all his marble thumb's.
>
> (2, lines 278–84)

Even in private Tiberius accords the style and power of gods to Sejanus; Tiberius gives him potency, allowing him voice and thought by playing dumb. The reversal does give Sejanus power, but not the power to see that professing to unmask, Tiberius is impersonating again. Tiberius's revelation asserts that Sejanus has said what Tiberius wanted him to say, made him say. This does not keep Sejanus from continuing to do so, thinking he does not. Sejanus, contemplating his successful corruption of Livia (that invasion of the secrets behind her masked beauty, and the subornation of her body to his lust for power) before his first interview with Tiberius, prizes the actuality of his gains, and is quite willing, he says, to let Caesar have the "empty name" (2, line 157) as long as he reaps the benefits. But the empty name *is* the benefit. It is the actuality of power, for it preserves Caesar, keeping his hands clean. Caesar gives up his voice, gives it to Sejanus, and appears to give up his power to act and to plot. All plots seem in Sejanus's hands; he has "plots on all" (2, line 499). But Caesar, who appears not to plot, really does have all in his power. Such is his rare dissembling.

The action of *Sejanus* involves Caesar's withdrawal from view and his drawing out of Sejanus—drawing him out like the Germanicans, so that he can be drawn and quartered. Caesar withdraws to reinvest himself in others' bodies; hence, he may lop off his "dearest head" and still survive. His instruments suffer fully the mortality of the body. Caesar embodies his arts in them, but his arts survive and remain. He stays offstage, unseen (nor is he seen in what his surrogates do). And reports declare him absorbed in his body in its most private and most perverse pleasures, negligent of state. Arruntius imagines Caprae where Caesar retires to private theatricals, "acting his *tragedies* with a *comick* face" (4, line 379), erecting a theater of

183

cruelty and sexual depravity where murder and every manner of "strange, and new-commented lusts" (line 400) are practiced. This is, we must add, the picture that Caesar wishes believed, that historians report. The private invisibility matches the public one, and the connection between the two is manifested best in Sejanus (who apes his master in his corruption of Livia and in his murders), whose career covers this trajectory: from pathic to god (1, lines 216, 203), and this imagined one: "a stale *catamite*" (4, line 404) lording it over the one who made him lord. This comes close to Jacobean realities. The feeding of political desires in Sejanus begins in the body.

It ends there, too. The extensions of Tiberius make all others part of his body politic—he is married to his kingdom as is James—and the final dismemberment of Sejanus and his family occurs at the hands of the dismembered bodies of Rome, the instruments of Tiberius:

> A thousand heads,
> A thousand hands, ten thousand tongues, and voyces,
> Employ'd at once in serverall acts of malice!   (5, lines 811-13)

The power of Tiberius lies in the monstrous image of the hydra-headed beast, the multitude, the body politic, the furthest reach of the imagined "confederacy" of Arruntius. The emperor extends into these heads, tongues, voices; they represent the final working out of the empty name, the dead letter. At the conclusion of the play, Caesar has withdrawn, and sends in place of himself—to represent him—Macro, his hand, and his letter, a masterpiece of riddles, written in a "doubling line" (4, line 465).

"If you, Conscript Fathers, with your children, bee in health, it is aboundantly well" (4, lines 546-47), the letter begins, knowing the actor's dictum about the virtue of an *if;* for as he proceeds, Tiberius's words are sheer hypothesis, antithetical statements played off against each other as if they were not contradictory. We are retired, he says, yet present; we dismiss all the rumors we have heard, yet attend to them. We do not desire to punish any—"in a free state (as ours) all men ought to enjoy their mindes" (lines 562-63)—"yet, in things, which shall worthily, and more neere concerne the maiestie of a prince, we shall feare to be so unnaturally cruell to our owne fame, as to neglect them" (lines 565-67). Tiberius's words swerve back and forth, totally unpredictable. Like the poet, he nothing affirmeth. Like the actor, he stages a possibility; in his power anything is possible. And what follows these poised counterstatements is an apparent nonsequitur. "True it is, Conscript Fathers, that we have raysed Se-

184

janus, from obscure, and almost unknown gentrie, . . . yet, not without danger" (lines 567-71). "True it is . . . yet": thus Tiberius says
two things at once. At first it appears that he means to save Sejanus
from danger; but, as the letter weaves its way, it becomes increasingly
clear—although it is never definitely said—that the emperor himself is
the danger, and that Sejanus is in his net. The senators and Arruntius
interrupt the letter repeatedly, swayed one way and another. "But
the space, the space/Betweene the brest, and lips" (3, lines 96-97),
Arruntius had earlier lamented. In that space between, the empty
letter, like the act itself, stands. That is the space of observation, the
public arena into which all are drawn and revealed, where

> Our lookes are call'd to question, and our wordes,
> How innocent soever, are made crimes;
> We shall not shortly dare to tell our dreames,
> Or thinke, but 'twill be treason.   (1, lines 67-70)

For all but Tiberius this is true or, rather, it is true for all, but in
opposite and reciprocal senses. Almost at the close of his letter to the
Senate, Tiberius seals the death of Sejanus in a typical locution:
"What wee should say, or rather what we should not say, Lords of
the Senate, if this bee true, our gods, and goddesses confound us if
we know!" (5, lines 604-6). What he should say and what he should
not are said together, bound on either side with an *if*. Where is Tiberius in these words? What is this, if not godlike speech? "How like a
god, speakes Caesar" (1, line 378). What is it he dares not tell, what
word will he not say? What crime, what treason, what unspeakable
dream? What guilt?

AS THE century opened, Shakespeare and Jonson offered in *Julius
Caesar* and *Sejanus* images of the nature of political power, its inherent theatricalization, displaying a sphere in which the body of the
ruler, opaque and transparent, extends to the body politic. This is
the body and the office that James occupied in his divine lieutenancy,
haunted by specters of borrowed robes, desiring retirement, and
withdrawing into the mystery of his own privilege. The rhetoric of
power, onstage and off, is the same in the language of these Roman
plays, or in James's discourse. When Jonson and Shakespeare turned
again to Rome, Jonson for his sole other venture into tragedy, *Catiline,* Shakespeare for his last exclusively Roman play, *Coriolanus,* the
terms for tragedy have changed, although the absolutist conception
has not. In *Sejanus* and *Julius Caesar* the tragic experience lies in the
failure of the hero to become Caesar. The heroes of these plays aim

185

at Caesar's head; Brutus gets it and it does him in; it eludes Sejanus. In both plays, Caesar triumphs, whether dead or alive. The heroes insofar as they are attractive (and Brutus is, of course) are so precisely because they fail to become what they aspire to be (and Brutus, only at the very end, with the ghost, even sees what it was he wanted when he allowed Cassius's words to find out his spirit). In both plays, power remains in a Caesar who is mighty yet, though in one case he has become a ghost and in the other is represented by a letter. But in *Coriolanus* and *Catiline,* there is no Caesar. The hero attempts (or is supposed to attempt) to become Caesar, to fill a vacuum in power; the tragedy in each case is that the heroes triumph so fully that they manage to enter into the form of Caesar, the second body of invisible power, and are destroyed in that body without actually becoming Caesar—except to themselves. Coriolanus and Catiline are absolutists who outdo even the Caesars of the earlier Roman plays. They so fully enter the paradoxical form of power that they are victimized by the very transcendence they achieve. One easy way to see this is to recognize that Catiline's conspiracy, unlike Brutus's, has no clear aim—there is no Caesar to kill; similarly, Coriolanus's enmity to the people is concomitant with his return to Rome in triumph for having secured Rome against its enemy. These heroes turn on Rome; the power that they are intent upon manifests itself in the lure of total destruction. In these plays, the paradox of absolute power draws the heroes to a privacy that would so totally engulf the public world as to destroy it utterly. The logic of the royal retreat is carried so far that if the hero is not killed, nothing will survive. This is an even more radical version of political power than the earlier Roman efforts of Shakespeare and Jonson, for Coriolanus and Catiline represent what it would be really to inhabit the invisible body of power, to *be* fully what Caesar acts, to play his part for keeps.[16] In these plays, the self-divisions of James's rhetoric arrive at their tragic consequences.

CORIOLANUS is, among other things, a study in the relationship between power and language. The career of Coriolanus, and with it the trajectory of absolutism, is revealed in his names;[17] at first he has his family name, Caius Marcus. He is a Roman. But, victorious at Corioles, he acquires the name of the enemy camp. The name represents an extension of Rome to a world elsewhere, the incorporation of that inimical otherness into the hero. By this principle he can change sides and yet not change himself, remaining absolute to himself, the reversal in power that allows him to turn the words of Rome back

186

upon the Romans: "I banish you" (3:3, line 124). In his words, Coriolanus contains all the world. Finally, having encompassed his own negation, Coriolanus has no name at all:

> Coriolanus
> He would not answer to; forbade all names.
> He was a kind of nothing, titleless,
> Till he had forged himself a name o'th'fire
> Of burning Rome.   (5:1, lines 11-15)

Cominius describes a Coriolanus wrapped in the mystery of his own absolute selfhood, cut off from communication, self-banished, beyond any verbal formulation. The man who finally refuses words from others denies himself words. The incommunicability and incomprehensibility of what Coriolanus has become makes him "a kind of nothing," the most radical definition of the absolute hero—what Caesar would be if he really were what he is to all appearances, the actor lost in his act, the self thoroughly consumed. At the furthest verge of this "kind of nothing, titleless," Coriolanus is glimpsed in an even more refined "name" to be "forged" in the flames of Rome. Cominius imagines him as the phoenix. This is, too, how he sees himself, a "lonely dragon" (4:1, line 30), solitary and alone, absolutely singular, blazing anew in total, absolute destruction. Glimpsed is a body beyond the mortal body, an immortal body that would replace the body politic. Although it may look to our eyes as if *Coriolanus* plays the individual against society, nothing could be further from the truth. Coriolanus aims at devouring the world in order to become it. He is the most public of men, unself-reflective; at his most private moment, banished, deprived, standing outside the walls of Antium, he offers a soliloquy, what we may suppose to be his private reflections, that is couched in the most general terms, a banal set of understandings about how friends so easily become enemies. Coriolanus's mystery makes him as absolute as the state, private only in his own privation. Named as the enemy, banished, become "a kind of nothing," Coriolanus imagines his return to Rome—Rome destroyed, and Coriolanus rising from its ashes, remade—as Rome, himself a state.[18] The private sphere of inaccessibility that James claimed as his own is, in this absolutist hero, the excuse for consuming all the world.

Privacy, fully understood, leads to the central action of the play, privation, a crucial lack: "I shall be loved when I am lacked" (4:1, line 15), Coriolanus tells his mother, a line she is bound to understand, for as she tells Virgilia early in the play, "If my son were my husband, I should freelier rejoice in that absence wherein he won honor than in the embracements of his bed where he would show most love" (1:3, lines 2-5). Finding love in rejection is Volumnia's guiding ideal, and rather than keep her son at home, she deprived herself of the pleasures of his "beholding" for the greater pleasure of his "absence," exposing him to danger, to a victorious and bloody return. And if, Virgilia asks, he had come home a corpse? So much the better, Volumnia replies, so long as his name survived. She is devoted to a name for which the body may be sacrificed; by deprivation, absence, thrusting him out, the name is made. "The wounds become him," Menenius, his surrogate-father says (2:1, line 115), and Volumnia imagines his bloody wound as the very life she gave him at her breast:

> The breasts of Hecuba,
> When she did suckle Hector, looked not lovelier
> Than Hector's forehead when it spit forth blood
> At Grecian sword, contemning. (1:3, lines 38-41)

In this, her most exalted imaginative moment, she sees her son as Hector—as a failed, doomed hero—to whom she gives life by offering him a breast spitting forth blood. She gives food as deprivation, life as death. That life Coriolanus embraces to become nothing, that he devours. On this model of self-deprivation he turns against the world, denying it, railing at it, refusing it. What he will not allow others he denies himself. The most ungenerous of men, he aims at ungenerating himself. Nothing short of a universal cataclysm will fill the gulf of deprivation in which he enacts his own absoluteness. He withholds himself beyond the imagining of a real monarch, beyond James's retirement or announcements of a secret, unapproachable self.

What Coriolanus learned at the breast he directs at Rome. "My birthplace hate I," he says outside Antium, "and my love's upon/This enemy town" (4:4, lines 23-24). The hatred leads him to curse the citizens and to wish to deny them food, just as he would deny them voices and votes. Like James, he finds them greedy, sucking nourishment from him. Everything that comes from the mouth is suspect, as is everything that goes into it.[19] To seal himself off utterly he needs to deflect everything and to deny himself utterance, embracing only what will destroy him: "When blows have made me stay," he tells his Roman welcomers, "I fled from words." Although he follows this immediately with the assurance, "You soothed not, therefore hurt not" (2:2, lines 70-71), he absents himself within three lines rather than hear "my nothings monstered" (line 75). Even his mother,

188

"Who has a charter to extol her blood,/When she does praise me grieves me" (1:9, lines 14-15). He wants hate, loves his enemy, indeed, as noted earlier, identifies with the enemy. The enemy of the people, the tribunes call him, failing to see that enmity rests in identification. The process of displacement creates the plebians as alter egos, binding him to those he would cut off.

The plebians cry out for food. They demand their voices. They want to put words in his wounds. "For if he show us his wounds and tell us his deeds, we are to put our tongues into those wounds and speak for them" (2:3, lines 5-7). Just such a show—the show Antony brilliantly performed—Coriolanus refuses. Rather than the theatricality of power, Coriolanus will play for keeps, showing nothing, saying nothing, withdrawing totally into total deprivation, playing "the man I am" (3:2, line 16) or nothing at all. Like James, he has a horror of being a king in a play. "You are too absolute" (3:2, line 39), Volumnia tells Coriolanus, when he wishes to pluck out the tongues of the people rather than feed them or take their words. "This viper," the viper Sicinius says,"would depopulate the city and/Be every man himself" (3:1, lines 263-65). In fact, he would be no man, "a kind of nothing." His denials are also self-denials. Volumnia urges him to "perform a part/Thou hast not done before" (3:2, lines 109-10). But the part does not suit; he wears a borrowed robe of humility, hides himself behind words that cut two ways, promises of revelations deferred. He plays himself attired in the robes of the enemy, lacking a name, thoroughly dishonored, saying nothing at all, but simply extending his hands to his mother kneeling before him. That gesture of contact, connection, is his undoing. Connecting, participating, betrays the absoluteness of self-referentiality. Only then does Coriolanus falter in his project of being "too absolute." Before, Herculean and godded, he rises out of nature into an apotheosis beyond the merely natural, standing, "As if a man were author of himself/And knew no other kin" (5:3, lines 36-37). This dream of autochthonosis denies generation and makes him *sui generis*. But then, the silence he has married as a wife stands before him, the mother who has made him fit for sacrifice voices her demand, playing Juno to his Hercules, and "like a dull actor" (5:3, line 40), Coriolanus forgets his self-authored part and falls for the "best of my flesh" and bends his knee in the earth before his mother. As devoted to the absolutist project as Bussy d'Ambois, Coriolanus is done in by his own humanity.

In *Coriolanus*, Shakespeare invests the absolutist strategies of Caesarism—the assumption of the mystical body as the only one—with

189

tragic implications. His hero fails only by being unable to cut himself off as completely as necessary; rather than absolutely destroying himself, he is implicated in a world of destruction. The Rome against which he turns, that city of "kites and crows" (4:5, line 42), is bent on devouring, and Coriolanus turns that impulse back. A city of factions—patricians, tribunes, plebes—Coriolanus acts to "please his mother and to be partly proud" (1:1, line 36); the factions writ large in the body politic are rewritten in his family circle—in Menenius, spokesman for the patricians and his surrogate father, in the infantile behavior of the crowd which matches his own infantilism (reproduced in the boy who kills butterflies whom Coriolanus fathers in imitation of himself), and in his failed consulship which echoes the tribunes' betrayal of public voices. The primary identification is between Volumnia and the city; she is the "patronness, the life of Rome" (5:5, line 1), never less so than when Rome turns upon Coriolanus, "like an unnatural dam" (3:1, line 292), cannibalizing her issue.[20] Volumnia's maternal appeal to Coriolanus's nature produces this "unnatural" (5:3, line 84) event; she preserves Rome with his life. Finally he is murdered in a city without a name and as a man with a name he refuses to acknowledge, so far degenerated that the enemy he loves names him with a mother's name for him. He calls him *boy:*

> Cut me to pieces, Volsces. Men and lads,
> Stain all your edges on me. Boy? False hound!
> If you have writ your annals true, 'tis there
> That, like an eagle in a dovecote, I
> Fluttered your Volscians in Corioles.
> Alone I did it. Boy?   (5:6, lines 110–15)

He recoils at the name that links him to natural generation, binding him to his mother ("There's no man in the world/More bound to's mother" Volumnia says [5:3, lines 158–59]), remembering himself as the one who "alone" penetrated the walls of Corioles to emerge bloody and renamed, he desires that birth again, at their swords, so that he can be "alone" at last, dismembered—cut to pieces, ungenerated, can have transcendent solitude like an imperial eagle. The true rewriting that Coriolanus demands will occur on his broken body.

   In short, that image of himself dominates the play's political discourse, from Menenius's initial fable of the rebellion of the belly on. Rome is in parts, engaged in a deadly struggle in which each part would be all. Coriolanus, who would give nothing, would also not take. "He pays himself" (1:1, line 30) and devours himself as well;

190

his would be an absolute self-absorption were he able to break all bonds. But he is joined to the people in hate, attached to the silence of his wife, drawn to Rome to devour it as his way of loving it and to devour it as his way of having it. His first thought in exile, viewing Antium, conveys this: "A goodly city is this Antium. City / 'Tis I that made thy widows" (4:4, lines 1-2), creation by deprivation. So has he made himself alone and solitary, silent, self-banished, sealed up in himself.

The fearful negations of Coriolanus belong to the tragic actor who takes upon himself a power so large that it leaves the world empty. Coriolanus is last remembered by "the man of my soul's hate, Aufidius" (1:5, line 10) as the man who has "widowed and unchilded many a one" (5:6, line 150), a tribute fitting to the monstrous powers that Coriolanus has assumed in the name of playing "the man that I am" (3:2, line 16). Tiberius's debaucheries and murders are nothing to the undoing that Coriolanus engages and is, ultimately, engaged in; the constancy of Julius Caesar is pure sham next to his unwavering self-destruction and self-undoing. What they did offstage to maintain themselves in power, what they denied themselves onstage to be able to play off, Coriolanus enacts upon himself. There is no world elsewhere for him, and ultimately, no world. It is all or nothing, and all is nothing.

> My mother, you wot well
> My hazards still have been your solace; and
> Believe't not lightly—though I go alone,
> Like to a lonely dragon, that his fen
> Makes feared and talked of more than seen—your son
> Will or exceed the common or be caught
> With cautelous baits and practice.   (4:1, lines 27-33)

"Or exceed . . . or be caught" becomes exceed *and* be caught. "He mocked us when he begged our voices . . . No, 'tis his kind of speech; he did not mock us" (2:3, lines 154-56). His kind of speech exceeds the possibilities of speech, passing over into an excess of vituperation, into . . . silence. To inscribe him truly in the annals would require a soaring speech that leaps the walls and limits and that would found the city in ruins and conflagration, making it the den of the dragon, "feared and talked of more than seen." In that empty space, unseen, would Coriolanus be alone, absolute, a world unto himself. Instead, he takes his mother's hand and sees that he has failed to play his part fully, has not achieved the style of gods.

> Behold, the heavens do ope,
> The gods look down, and this unnatural scene
> They laugh at. (5:3, lines 183–85)

The gods witness "this unnatural scene." As James knew, too, there is no way not to be onstage. Even the inner theater of absolutism has a divine witness.

Theatricality is ultimately inescapable.[21] Before this moment on his knees, Coriolanus had attempted to avoid the stage. His heroic capture of Corioles occurred behind closed gates. His display of himself to the people hid behind double language and deferred promises, the wounds not shown but cloaked. Onstage he railed or ran away; if he stayed, he said nothing, heard nothing said to him. Although others call him the enemy of the people, their plots match his; "we may deny him yet," the tribunes assure the people, when they have lent him their voice, and then the voice is withdrawn, and Coriolanus is banished. But as he says, quintessentially, "I banish you"; whatever Coriolanus does to others, he does to himself. Although from the first scene of the play forward, the people try to figure out who deprives them of food—and, thus, what Coriolanus wants of them—he wants nothing. This is so unimaginable that they think that he wants everything. There is truth in this, too, for Coriolanus's absolute negations meet such aspirations. His is the dream of power formed in ultimate annihilation. Coriolanus is an ultimate solipsist who, turning upon himself, makes his identity in undoing, so deprived of a self that he never once expresses a private desire—or, indeed, a public one. He has a sense of what others owe him—nothing; and that he owes them the same thing. These nothings bind him politically to his mother and to the state. For Rome projects its desires onto him and reads in his empty behavior what would devour them. And devouring him, Rome devours itself, and the gods look down at the spectacle of this internecine war, this body eating up itself, this family engulfed by a cannibalistic mother, and laugh at the spectacle of cruelty, "this unnatural scene."

Coriolanus is no exact replication of Jacobean politics, of course, but a study couched in and extending the absolutist language that can be found in James's writing, or in *Julius Caesar* or *Sejanus*. The model upon which Coriolanus builds his self-destructive identity is the contradictory stance of the absolute hero in which sustaining antitheses have become devouring ones, and in which the divided theater of conscience splits the actor. Coriolanus lives in his flesh as if it were spirit, as if the realm of privacy and privation could encompass all the world. Like James, he depends on invisible and un-represented confirmation; like James, he suffers by being all too visible, and by being seen as a representation. It is on such absolutist models as the king—or a Caesar from an earlier play—that Coriolanus is imagined. And it is in the inherent theatricality of power that he falls.

IN DEFEAT, Catiline, too, recognizes his own theatricality; rallying his supporters for the final confrontation, he can only imagine the gods as witnesses to the cataclysm he wishes to unleash: "Me thinkes, I see *Death,* and the *Furies,* waiting/What we will doe; and all the heav'n at leisure/For the great spectacle" (5, lines 412-14).[22] What occupies Catiline's mind occurs onstage; Petreius, the captain who defeats him, witnesses the death of Catiline by setting the scene this way: "The *Furies* stood still, on hills,/Circling the place, and trembled to see men/Doe more, then they" (5, lines 655-57). Petreius dae-monizes the deities and reduces them so that they stand trembling in men's view, not scorning, as the gods do at the "unnatural scene" in *Coriolanus,* not withdrawn, as in *Sejanus,* where the gods, if they operate at all, are present in the godlike words of Caesar; or, as in *Julius Caesar,* where Julius's might beyond death is that play's version of deity. All these are, nonetheless, versions of that supernatural force in history that makes the monarch—in James's eyes— spectral. These heroes are haunted by the past and by the observation of deity as the king was.

The end of *Catiline* suits its opening, one of the most remark-able scenes ever written, the apparition of the past in the form of Sylla's Ghost, breathing life into Catiline's conspiracy. Quite literally, this evil spirit invents the play, giving life and mind to its hero. As it opens, he alone is onstage, speaking: "Do'st thou not feele me, *Rome?*" (line 1). Addressing the audience, Sylla begins to work his impressive talents, evoking the darkness in which he stands and in which Rome sleeps, summoning it to awake, and to be destroyed. He catches one sleeper; he *"discovers Catiline in his study"* (s.d., line 15), the private man called onto the stage of history. This is a conspiratorial moment, Catiline conspiring with the evil spirit, having his life breathed into him. In his mind, he is alone, plotting revolu-tion; the presence of the ghost of the past intimates how occupied privacy is, however. Sylla speaks Catiline's thought, listing his singular qualifications; a private life of unparalleled monstrosity, including all kinds of debauchery, serves as preparation for public deeds, "new acts" to piece out the old "incests, murders, rapes" (lines 28, 30).

The "act of thy incestuous life" (line 35) provides a basis for political action: "The ruine of thy countrey: thou wert built/For such a worke, and borne for no lesse guilt. . . . That is thy act, or none" (lines 45-46, 48). As in *Julius Caesar*, private life and public acts are one, and internal conscience is present as external agent.

What is "thy act" in this formulation? We can ask this question of Catiline, as we asked it earlier of James, for Catiline opens with a demonic version of that spiritual inhabitation that made the realm of power spectral, that robbed actions of individual agency and made them the working of some supernuminous force outside the grasp of the power of any person. Such power Caesar seizes and may be seized by. In *Catiline*, the hero, imagining himself to awaken to work ruin, is, instead, being awakened by a spirit, a ghost of the past, who also recognizes Catiline as the one who bears the ruinous destiny as his "act." The mind that speaks through Sylla is both individual and spiritual, internal and external; a theater of conscience is presented.

Thus, Catiline comes to think that if his acts require spectators, only the heavens—the trembling heavens—will do. He has some reason, too, to believe that his acts are his own. For, like Coriolanus, he scorns mere theatricality, mere instrumentality; like Coriolanus, his theatricality is so total that he rejects any playing in which his entire self has not been invested. Like Coriolanus, he combines monstrous egotism with complete self-abandonment. Built out of his crimes, launched into that continuous space that extends from private monstrosity to public ruin, Catiline is urged by Sylla to remember his past even as he expunges it to be himself: "Make all past, present, future ill thine owne;/And conquer all example, in thy one" (1, lines 53-54); Sylla tells him to destroy time to make his own, to have "conscience" (line 29) of his misdeeds, and to propagate them—at the expense of conscience: "Conscience, and care die in thee" (line 59). In this annihilative space of awareness and oblivion, remembrance and destruction, Catiline is born onstage, divided in conscience. His first words take Sylla's words as his own, and impose upon them the permanence of writing; he says, "It is decree'd" (line 73). He has become inscribed in a text.

Out of a sense of inevitability, Catiline assembles his co-conspirators; corruption begins at home, in private debauchery, and Aurelia, Catiline's wife, who appears to complain about domestic privations, is fed, through Catiline's sexual appeals, the greater lure of power. "You court me, now" (line 111), she confesses, and he, in turn, reveals the hopes and promises with which he has fed his conspiratorial crew, reveals it with utmost contempt for their pettiness,

194

folly, and crudity. He imagines a genuine masque to answer their antic one:

> For us, Aurelia, we must hazard honors
> A little. Get thee store, and change of women,
> As I have boyes; and give 'hem time, and place,
> And all connivence; be thy selfe, too, courtly;
> And entertayne, and feast, sit up, and revell;
> Call all the great, the faire, and spirited *Dames*
> Of *Rome* about thee; and beginne a fashion
> Of freedome, and community. Some will thanke thee,
> Though the sowre *Senate* frowne, whose heads must ake
> In feare, and feeling too. We must not spare
> Or cost, or modestie. It can but shew
> Like one of Juno's, or of Jove's disguises,
> In either thee, or mee: and will as soone,
> When things succeed, be throwne by, or let fall,
> As is a vaile put off, a visor chang'd,
> Or the *scene* shifted, in our *theaters*.   (Lines 170–85)

"Court" here, as in *Bussy d'Ambois,* is a prolifigate place for court-ing, and Catiline imagines his house filled with catamites and whores (a version of that house is realized in the course of the play through the figure of Fulvia.) It is a house of pleasure, the private "freedome, and community" that answers the call for liberty that Catiline makes on the few occasions when his language encompasses explicitly polit-ical terms.[23] Precisely because this image of debauchery carries polit-ical meanings Catiline's conspiracy finds expression in a masque celebrating pleasure. Catiline defends theatricality here in just those terms that made its puritanical opponents shudder; and even as he describes what he would do, it is clear that his masque, like any court masque, is a passing fancy—to be replaced by the real thing. Masque scenes may glide by, but the power they display will remain, not sub-ject to succession, nor to be "throwne by," "let fall" or "shifted"—rather, as permanent as writing, as the "decree" to which Catiline remains committed.

To him, then, theatricalizing revolution, the conspiracy is a matter of ventriloquism, giving roles and words to others, masking himself. He can lie, and say to Cethegus, "I love these voices in thee" (1, line 229), although, alone, he sees the conspirators for what they are, "the dregs of mankind" (3, line 716) whom he merely uses. "I am your creature" (1, line 283), Lentulus tells him, but he claims to be their instrument and demurs: "I am shaddow/To honor'd Lentulus" (lines 286–87), ambiguously, to be sure. Nonetheless he wishes to own his power: "The cruelty, I meane to act, I wish/Should be call'd mine, and tarry in my name" (3, lines 746–47). This formulation conveys something of the entirely spectral nature of power. Catiline's conspiracy—what he means "to act"—is little more than a matter of whispers and innuendos, private debaucheries hinting at public ones. As Sylla's spirit breathes life into his act, he inspires his fellow actors, only to recoil, disgusted and disheartened by the reduction of his power involved in such instrumentality. Hence, although he means to act, he does not do so. Instead, he catches himself—acting:

> Did I appeare so tame, as this man thinkes me?
> Look'd I so poore? so dead? So like that nothing,
> Which he calls vertuous? O my breast, breake quickly;
> And shew my friends my in-parts, lest they thinke
> I have betraid 'hem.   (3, lines 149–53)

But as he surmises overhearing them, he has, by acting, become in their eyes "a shaddow" (3, line 165), what he had pretended to be with Lentulus. But what would Catiline reveal as a true act were he to show his fellows his "in-parts"? Inhabitation by Sylla? Whether he acts, or fails to act, or plays himself, he is doomed to be a shadow. This defines Catiline's dilemma and the spectral nature of power. To succeed and really act, Catiline would need to be "so like that nothing" as to be it indeed, a spirit without a body. Like Coriolanus, then, his power entails undoing, self-denial. Cicero, Catline's opponent, reveals the "nothing" of Catiline's conspiracy and allows him his self-destructive, distinctive act of self-banishment, the only deed that is his own and bears his name. Cicero can penetrate Catiline's schemes because his spy system encompasses the entire world of the play. He is Catiline's alter ego.[24]

A self-proclaimed new man, a man without origins, Cicero floats even freer of the past than Catiline with his demonic ties; his power is so great that he thoroughly ingratiates himself into Rome to become its spokesman in the expulsion of Catiline. Cicero's ascendancy does not represent, as some have supposed, a scene of the tirumph of virtue over vice, political stability over political ruin. Rather, one power drives out another. Cicero's is a familiar form, the mask of republicanism covering absolutism. He is the spirit of consultation in the play and is fittingly made Consul—Jonson invites the point by sometimes writing Counsel; but to demonstrate that despite appearances his consulship bears no genuine republican mean-

196

ing, we might note the way the word and title are used in the play, for instance the "saving counsaile" (3, line 406) that Fulvia offers Curius at Cicero's explicit prompting. She counsels him to betray the conspiracy, but not to betray the betrayal—in a word, to become a counterspy. Or, here is how Cicero prompts Curius: "Keepe still your former face" (3, line 414). The "former face" to be kept hid conspiracy until Cicero saw through it; he counsels Curius to appear the same, but to wear his face at the Consul's bidding. Caesar, who will soon be converted to Cicero's party, offers this advice to Catiline: "Mind but your friends counsells" (3, line 528), and Catiline agrees, "Or, I will beare no mind" (line 529). "Counsells" here are no different from conspiratorial unity, and Catiline recoils, vowing that he will "make Caesar/Repent his ventring counsells, to a spirit,/So much his lord in mischiefe" (3, lines 733-35). The determination to show his spirit replaces one shadow, one shade, with another. It demonstrates that republican consultation is another form of absolute subversion.

On the basis of his own conspiratorial consultation, Cicero attempts to reveal Catiline's conspiracy to the Senate. Like Catiline, he scorns mere acting and those "worthlesse to be nam'd" whom he must nonetheless "use" (3, lines 451, 453). In Catiline, he finds a genuine opponent, however, just as Catiline sees finally what he is up against in Cicero (his scorn for this social nobody prevents him from realizing how much they resemble each other). "Were I that enemie,/ That he would make me," Catiline says of Cicero, denying what he has ascribed to him, but recognizing that men are made in such ascriptions, "I'ld not wish the state/More wretched, then to need his preservation" (4, lines 476-77). Even as the Senate thrusts Catiline out, Rome takes to itself another version of him in Cicero. Banishment for Catiline as for Coriolanus indicts Rome. Catiline virtually banishes himself, and sacrificing himself to the guilt Cicero projects upon him, he leaves Rome in the Consul's hands:

> *Quintus.* Butcher, traytor, leave the *Senate.*
> *Catiline.* I'am gone, to banishment, to please you, *Fathers.*
>   Thrust head-long forth!
> *Cato.*   Still, do'st thou murmure, monster?
> *Catiline.* Since, I am thus put out, and made a—
> *Cicero.*   What?
> *Catulus.* Not guiltier then thou art.
> *Catiline.*   I will not burne
>   Without my funerall pile.   (4, lines 502-7)

Catulus completes Catiline's thought and makes this identification with Cicero explicit; but the thought remains unexpressed. From what he has been made, Catiline leaps to what he will do; like Coriolanus, he would burn Rome to ashes and be consumed in that final conflagration, his own doing and undoing at once, the work he was born to do, his act.

Cicero brings Catiline to this point by showing up the insubstantiality of the conspiracy through his own invisible powers of observation, one form of nothing answers another; demons of power face each other. The spy system is a version of the whispering plotters. Cicero's opening words to the Senate echo Sylla's; again, Rome is in darkness and sleeps, and he, Cicero, will waken it. Yet he renders even this awakening silent and shadowy, for his speech is hypothetical; like Tiberius, he operates in the realm of an "if":

> If I were silent, and that all the dangers
> Threatning the state, and you, were yet so hid
> In night, or darkenesse thicker in their brests,
> That are the blacke contrivers; so, that no
> Beame of the light could pierce 'hem: yet the voyce
> Of heav'n, this morning, hath spoke loud inough,
> T'instruct you with a feeling of the horror;
> And wake you from a sleepe, as starke, as death.
>
> (4, lines 66-73)

Speaking, Cicero pretends to be silent, merely to point the senators to a voice from heaven that has spoken; he claims that voice speaks, not him, and that it reveals, or has revealed already what he would say. And, of course, he does not say what the voice has said or shown—*that* is presumed known (if Cicero's words refer to anything at all they allude to a compromising scene in his garden in which Cicero's spies trap the conspirators into revealing themselves to him, not a very edifying spectacle). With this powerful strategy of double speech, he confronts Catiline: "Do'st thou not blush" (line 171), Cicero asks, precisely because Catiline does *not*. Do not the "nightly guards" (line 178) and the "cities watches" (line 179) mean that there is something to watch, something to fear in the riot and excess that Catiline displays? Do "the present lookes upon thee, strike thee nothing?" (line 182). Are his spies insubstantial, do they not have an object? To these nothings, Cicero points:

> Do'st thou not feele thy counsells all laid open?
> And see thy wild conspiracie bound in
> With each mans knowledge?   (Lines 183-85)

The Consul opens nothing laying it all open this way; rather, he invites Catiline to make the revelation. He assures him that everything is known, but nothing is said; it all remains hidden, bound in each man's mind.

> Which of all this order
> Canst thou thinke ignorant (if they'll but utter
> Their conscience to the right) of what thou didst
> Last night, what on the former, where thou wert,
> Whom thou didst call together, what your plots were?
> O age, and manners! This the *Consul* sees,
> The *Senate* understands, yet this man lives!   (Lines 185-91)

"Yet this man lives" becomes Cicero's refrain, yet what "the *Consul* sees" and "the *Senate* understands" he never says: "If they'll but utter." For all the prolixity of *his* utterance, Cicero never goes beyond the "if." So he lays his plot, as subtly dissimulating as Tiberius.

Cicero declares the absolute visibility of two invisibilities: Catiline's conspiracy and men's knowledge of it, Catiline's conscience (guilty thoughts) and men's conscious knowledge, unuttered. He forbears from saying enough to put Catiline to death; he makes veiled accusations, half threats, asks Catiline to remember what he has said or done. But nothing is said, neither banishment nor death, toward which all this tends, is uttered; opening the door for Catiline, he wonders at his inaction, his silence.

> Yet thou dar'st tarry here? Goe forth, at last;
> Condemne thy selfe to flight, and solitude.
> Discharge the common-wealth, of her deepe feare.
> Goe; into banishment, if thou wait'st the word.
> Why do'st thou looke? They all consent unto it.
> Do'st thou expect th'authoritie of their voyces,
> Whose silent wills condemne thee? While they sit,
> They approve it; while they suffer it, they decree it;
> And while they'are silent to it, they proclaime it.
> (4, lines 366-74)

They banish him by doing nothing; Catiline is invited to banish himself, to realize the word by enacting what has not exactly been said, to give them voice by removing himself from the stage. Catiline is asked to conspire against himself to make his act his own.

Cicero proclaims his power, claiming invisible knowledge of the Senate and of Catiline. The invisible deeds, the invisible heart, these he says his spies have penetrated. Against "my watches" (line 258), he tells Catiline, nothing can be done:

> Thou do'st nothing, Sergius,
> Thou canst endeavour nothing, nay not thinke,
> But I both see, and heare it; and am with thee,
> By, and before, about, and in thee, too.   (Lines 259–62)

Demonic possession, spiritual inhabitation, can go no further. This "watch" Cicero erects in the Senate; at this moment, the spirit of Sylla passes from Catiline to Cicero. Caesar, who will soon change sides, marks the departure: "He's lost, and gone. His spirits have forsooke him" (4, line 300). Yet Cicero drives out what he fears, and what he would banish, he declares will only be seen when banished. He knows that there is more to Catiline than even he can see.

> I would now send him, where they all should see
> Cleere, as the light, his heart shine; where no man
> Could be so wickedly, or fondly stupide,
> But should cry out, he saw, touch'd, felt, and grasp't it.
>   (Lines 407–10)

Making Catiline visible, Cicero sends him away, banished, just short of dead. He grants him a life-in-death, and a life-out-of-sight so that he can be seen, felt, touched. Catiline is made palpable when no longer present in Rome, made himself in his absence, a "publike" man and a public spectacle (line 435). Offstage, Catiline is last seen in the words of his enemy, Petreius. His speech grants Catiline even more than the conspirators who named him "God-like Catiline!" (1, line 530), for Petreius lends him the representational form of constancy, the "lively statue" beneath which great Julius bled, and in which Sejanus first suffered dismemberment. Reformed as a statue, Catiline stands finally as the essence of state.

The furies watch, Petreius affirms (5, lines 655 ff.), trembling, and the sun stands still; indeed, the noise of battle drives the sun backward. That initial prospect upon time which Sylla offered is now made manifest; time withdraws before Catiline's devouring flames. Catiline falls upon his enemies as Coriolanus had turned upon Corioles, running into the midst to be surrounded, "circled in himselfe with death" (line 675), as the ambiguous line so accurately records. And so, when suicidally slain, the Romans turn their countenance upon him, like "Minerva holding forth Medusa's head" (line 678). The Medusa's head produced "killing sight" (line 680). It turned one of the rebel giants to stone, making him the very embodiment of his fear, astonished at that sight. And so, too, Rome transforms Catiline:

> So Catiline, at the sight of *Rome* in us,
> Became his tombe: yet did his looke retayne
> Some of his fiercenesse, and his hands still mov'd,
> As if he labour'd, yet, to graspe the state,
> With those rebellious parts.　　　　(Lines 684–88)

Dead and moving, transfixed by a gaze that he nonetheless returns, whole and constant and yet composed of rebellious parts, Catiline at this moment is captured forever in an essential form of state, and is yet, at the same time, as fully private as anyone can be, dead, a grave of himself, consuming himself, totally retired into himself, thoroughly withdrawn. Such interiority is the only privacy, pure privation; but there, too, it touches the very spirit of Rome. His "looke" answers the "sight of *Rome* in us," and he withdraws into the space that erects that eternal monument.

In the last act of the play, Catiline's death becomes Cicero's power. Cicero makes living death and deathly life the act of state. He congratulates himself for "my watchings, and my dangers" (5, line 695), claiming Catiline's death as *his* doing; in repayment he asks that the Romans erect within their thoughts the eternal memory of that final tragic scene:

> 　　　　　　only the memorie
> Of this glad day, if I may know it live
> Within your thoughts, shall much affect my conscience,
> Which I must alwayes studie before fame.
> Though both be good, the latter yet is worst,
> And ever is ill got, without the first.　　　　(Lines 697–702)

These final words erect Cicero's theater of conscience. In it, his virtuous self arises from the consciousness with which he has constructed his audience. Public thought in this formulation is that shared spirit that produces their thoughts and his conscience; the conscience he proclaims is the divided one that Sylla drew from Catiline, in which the past is remembered and destroyed to suit the present. This, too, occurs onstage in the audience for the drama that Jonson provided in the play, the chorus. They began by distancing themselves from the ills of Rome lamented at the end of act 1, claiming that the city's "excesse" and "disease" (line 550) were some foreign strain, an Asiatic influence from which they are immune. But, finally, the chorus sees that it has seen nothing; although it comes to know its ignorance of Catiline, it does not see through Cicero, and so still sees nothing, and it praises "the Counsel" asking for the "evill seede" to be plucked "out of our spirits" (4, lines 887-88). At the end, the Consul plants just such seeds and calls them conscience. With the disappearance of Catiline, Cicero has not secured Rome against the enemy; rather, he has managed a mastery of the political sphere, and has secured an audience ready to receive its speculative instruments and its mind from him. "The onely father of his countrey" (5, line 313), as Cato, his mouthpiece, calls him, he answers Catiline's "spectacle" with his own.

"I," says Cethegus, assenting to the image of the horrors Cicero builds from his watchings and his dangers, but if the conspiracy had that shape, it would have been another drama; "your part," he says, "Had not then beene so long, as now it is:/I should have quite defeated your oration;/And slit that fine rhetoricall pipe of yours,/I'the first *Scene*" (5, line 272-77). Instead, what Cethegus would have done to Cicero, Cicero has done to Catiline, and the "fine rhetoricall pipe" that sounded in the first scene becomes his voice at the end. Cicero is a demonic version of republican sentiment in the play, fearful to absolutism because of the masquerade of being a man-of-the-people (in fact, as we have seen, he is the man without origins, as autochthonic in his way as Coriolanus would have been), fearful because he is so fully disguised an absolutist, so totally possessed by Sylla's ghost as to be unrecognized by his countrymen as a version of the conspiracy he expelled, but also made, from his fears and watchings. The spectacle he has made he proposes as the instruments of vision for the audience. He wishes to take their consciences and twine them with his, co-conspirators, breathing one life, seeing with the same eyes the visions he constructs.

It would be an illusion to claim for Cicero more power in the theater of cruelty than this. He remains where he earlier located himself, part of the action, in the show. The "unbated strengths/Of a firme conscience" (3, lines 783-84), he says, are produced by the "great powers" of vigilance, by spies, ever watching, monstering nothings, making everything; "O brother! now,/The engine[r]s I told you of, are working;/The machine 'gins to move" (3, lines 759-61). Cicero is in the machine, an engine of destruction, a theatrical device. And here is a definition of Coriolanus: "When he walks, he moves like an engine. . . . He sits in his state, as a thing made for Alexander" (5:4, lines 18 ff.). The "thing" is a statue, moving and unmoving at once. "He wants nothing of a god but eternity and a heaven to throne in," Menenius concludes. Catiline, too, ends at that absolute verge of state, confined at last by the theater of the gods and the theater of conscience.

AT THE END of the Jacobean period, the confluence of power, theater, and impersonation constructed in Pompey's theater—the high Roman style of Jacobean absolutism—recurs in Philip Massinger's *The Roman Actor* (1626).[25] This play fulfills conflicting versions of the concerns that run through Shakespeare's and Jonson's Roman plays and, like many late Jacobean plays, it reads at times as if it were an anthology of best-loved moments of Jacobean drama. It is, on as many counts as one can imagine, highly theatrical. Yet its stuff is not mere theater, and, indeed, it has no notion of the *merely* theatrical. Instead, throughout it voices the absolute continuity, whatever it may mean, however it may be disclaimed, between politics and theater. The central situation, constantly refigured, is of being at a play, and the inevitability of that situation, whether one is aware of it or not. Such inevitability closes *Catiline,* too, for having erected the theater of conscience, it absorbs even the onstage audience so that no final chorus speaks; Cicero addresses the real audience, as Sylla's ghost had done at first. *Catiline* speaks to present concerns, however glancingly, simply by leaving the play to the audience's response to it. Cicero, at the end, constructs a theater, acts as a dramatist, and casts the audience in his play. This elementary situation of power we know from *Hamlet:* "The play's the thing/Wherein I'll catch the conscience of the king" (2:2, lines 590-91).[26] Hamlet's play in the play will double the death of old Hamlet, as he imagines it—as the ghost told it—and the death of Claudius, as he imagines it. Two ghostly representations here; and Hamlet, taking his father's part, occupies a spectral domain of malign shadows. This may be an elementary strategy for power, yet it is manifestly obfuscatory: genuine action meets false representation, the playwright, the actor, and the represented join to be caught and tangled. To "catch the conscience" is to be taken with the disease. *The Roman Actor,* indebted to that play of Roman turned Dane, knows with Hamlet that "he that plays the king shall be welcome" (2:2, line 314). In Massinger's play, the king onstage—the emperor Domitian—comes to occupy the royal position of being an actor onstage.

In every act, *The Roman Actor* stages a play within the play. In the opening act, the play merges with state power. The scene opens with actors in a law court; Paris, the Roman actor, and his fellow actors are charged with the crime of Cordus in *Sejanus,* implicit sedition. Paris argues that the actor bears no responsibility for the effect of the play; if it happens to find a guilty conscience that does not necessarily mean it sought it: "If there be/Among the auditors one whose conscience tells him,/He is of the same mould, we cannot helpe it" (1:3, lines 112-14). Since representation inevitably represents the audience, the actor cannot be charged with intentionality. Aretinus, whose business as a spy is to read from observation to intention, cannot accept Paris's view of representation; to him, as to most instruments of state, the actors "search into the secrets of the time,/And under fain'd names on the Stage present/Actions not to be toucht at" (1:3, line 37-39), like the "queasy" actions spied in Cordus's histories. Cordus and Paris make precisely the same defense that Jonson offered in a letter about *Eastward Ho,* the play that got him and Chapman into trouble with the crown.[27] He insists that what he represents does not represent himself; he uses, that is, a ploy of power, a royal assertion against royal power.

Paris's claim is undercut by his defense of the theater as a pervasive principle of reality. In the law court, pleading passionately for the rights of theater in society, and although claiming its harmlessness, he seems offensively brash to Aretinus, mouthpiece of absolutist observation and intelligence. "Are you on the Stage/You talke so boldly?" (1:3, lines 49-50), he taunts, and Paris answers, not surprisingly, with the motto of the Globe: "The whole world being one/This place is not exempted" (lines 50-51). The law court becomes a theater; Paris's impassioned speech has a double appeal—"I have said, my Lord, and now as you finde cause/Or censure us, or free us with applause" (1:3, line 141-42)—give me liberty and give me applause (the end of *The Tempest*)—and Latinus responds, admiringly, "Well pleaded on my life! I never saw him/Act an Orators part before" (lines 143-44). This tribute makes the speech into a set of lines played convincingly by an actor. Although Latinus's response would seem to deny the totalism of the world as theater by setting off this speech as a performance, it is one—and it has a "real" effect in the court of law. At the end of the scene, the emperor exonerates the players.

That the absolutism of playing should be first manifest in a law court makes complete sense. Absolutism, after all, grounds itself in a Roman theory of law; Domitian voices it in *The Roman Actor,* and thereby the actor's law court is joined to the royal court. Having carried off Lamia's wife to make her his empress, the emperor claims for himself "unlimited power" of "possession" (2:1, lines 136, 140) of Domitia. What he wills is absolute, as Parthenius explains to the abducted Domitia, "When power puts in its Plea the lawes are silenc'd" (1:2, line 44); and Caesar reveals even more to Aretinus, claiming that the whole point about power is that it can be openly criminal. It is Jove's prerogative to do what a private man cannot. "You should else take from/The dignitie of *Caesar*" (2:1, lines 149–50), Aretinus admiringly murmurs. Not surprisingly, then, the emperor who thinks "the stile/Of Lord, and God" deserved (1:4, lines 35–36) immediately exonerates Paris. The arguments in the law court and the arguments at court are both for the absolute power of the royal actor. "*Paris* my hand" (1:4, line 74) is Caesar's first word to the actor; at the end of act 4, having slain Paris for supposedly repeating the royal crime—seducing Domitia—Caesar again offers "our imperiall hand" (4:2, line 300) in applause for that final performance. But then Caesar has become the Roman actor.

The death of Paris is a complex moment. Caesar has seen Paris making love to Domitia—rather, he thinks that is what he has seen; actually, Domitia pursues the actor. Alone with Caesar, Paris, good servant that he is, accepts his condemnation; Caesar, however, suggests a reenactment of the scene with Domitia, for he has recognized its theatricality, claiming to have seen it performed before in a play called *The False Servant*. So the actors double themselves, a boy playing Domitia (a nice touch), Caesar and Paris continuing to represent thenselves. Here, to recall Heywood's terms, "Personator" and "Personated" meet in what is and is not identification and identity. Just such doubling was Paris's rally to the actors when they were called before the court of law:

> *Paris.* Nay droope not fellowes, innocence should be bould.
>   We that have personated in the Scæne
>   The ancient Heroes, and the falles of Princes
>   With loude applause, being to act our selves,
>   Must doe it with undaunted confidence.
>   What ere our sentence be thinke 'tis in sport.
>   And though condemn'd lets heare it without sorrow,
>   As if we were to live againe to morrow.
> *1 Lictor.* 'Tis spoken like your selfe.   (1:1, lines 50–58)

"To act our selves," to speak "like your selfe," formulas for identity as representation. From that position Paris turns theatricality on its head; it is real, and the judgments of law courts are not. He affirms the Caesarean constancy of the Roman actor in a theater where no one ever dies.

So Caesar reenacts *The False Servant;* in his part as injured husband killing the titular hero Paris onstage, he aspires to the eternal dignity of the actor. The play he performs would not stand up in a court of law except, as in this play where the courts of law—like the theater—are the instruments of the will of the monarch. Calling for the actor who had presented the injured lord in the earlier performance of *The False Servant,* Domitian dismisses him:

> Thou didst not
> Doe it to the life. We can performe it better.
> Off with my Robe, and wreath; since *Nero* scorn'd not
> The publike *Theater,* we in private may
> Disport our selves. (4:2, lines 222-26)

"To the life" here is like Paris's "act our selves." The "life" is the scene we have just seen between Paris and Domitia: life is always a scene in a play, a play within a play. Thus Caesar pretends to erect a private theater; yet his private sport is not the same as the actual performance, which the title page announces for *The Roman Actor,* a play that "hath divers times beene, with good allowance Acted, at the private Play-house in the *Black-Friers,* by the Kings Majesties Servants." These servants play *The False Servant:* how plays represent power is glimpsed. The actor claims an imperial precedent—Nero is invoked—an allusion that Heywood explicates:

> It was the manner of their Emperours, in those days, in their
> publicke Tragedies to choose out the fittest amongst such, as
> for capital offences were condemned to dye, and imploy them
> in such parts as were to be kil'd in Tragedy, who of themselves
> would make suit rather to dye with resolution, and by the
> hands of such princely *Actors,* then otherwise to suffer a
> shamefull & most detestable end. And these were Tragedies
> naturally performed. And such *Caius, Caligula, Claudius Nero,
> Domitianus, Comodus,* & other Emperours of *Rome* . . . used
> to act. (E³v)

A tragedy performed, acted to the life, is what Caesar gives.

Caesar overhears the scene of betrayal again. Is that my cue? he asks; "Yes Sir, be but perfect" (4:2, line 280), Aesop, Paris's fellow actor, and now his, advises. And perfect, in his way, he is.

> *Dom.* O villaine! thankelesse villaine! I should talke now;
>   But I have forgot my part. But I can doe,
>   Thus, thus, and thus. [*Kils Paris.*]
> *Par.*   O, I am slaine in earnest.
>   (Lines 281-83)

He drops his Hamlet-like railing, reflecting upon his own quoted line. Forgetting his lines in one play, he still has lines in another. Even the inarticulate string of thuses has its point; the hand that clasped Paris now stabs him; he acts in earnest in this play. And then, to make his act complete, Domitian claims that his forgetting was itself part of his play, not someone else's script. "'Twas my purpose" (line 284) he tells Paris, his "plot that thou/Shouldst dye in action, and to crowne it dye/With an applause induring to all times,/By our imperiall hand" (lines 297-300). "Action" is theatrical; Domitian claims power asserting his authorship, his acting, and, at last, his audition. Inside and outside the action at once, occupying all places in the theater, power coincides with a total theatricality.

The power of plays is affirmed throughout *The Roman Actor,* in each of its plays. A son has an avaricious father; how is his avarice to be cured?—show it to him in a play. This is done in act 2. *The Cure of Avarice* fails to work—the father, watching the play, turns to Caesar, begging him to defend the man onstage—and Caesar simply has the old man killed. It may seem that Caesar's power undercuts what the show meant to accomplish, but the old man's response, appealing to Caesar, and Caesar's sponsorship of the play, connect theatrical power to royal power. Caesar makes sure that *The Cure of Avarice* works. The play also touches another member of the audience, the Empress Domitia. She falls in love with the actor who plays the physician, Paris; we know to what play that ultimately leads. But before *The False Servant,* Domitia produces *Iphis and Anaxerete,* ostensibly for Domitian's pleasure, but in fact for her own, to see Paris play a lover. Domitia is "transported" by this play (3:2, line 283); she becomes enraged when her lover is scorned, and is so afraid that Paris's suicide is in earnest that he stops the play to assure her he lives. She is, as she says, "carried . . . beyond my selfe" (line 289), so much so that her performance is viewed. To the trained eyes of Aretinus, Domitia has revealed her passions in her response to the play. Her spectatorship places her onstage, her rapt observation draws out a self she would keep hid. Unconsciously, conscience is revealed. There is no way not to be onstage. This is the truth that finds Hamlet out. "Your majesty, and we that have free souls, it touches us not" (3:2, lines 232 ff.), he says to Claudius about that play that doubles upon itself his act and his uncle's. To be touched, to be caught: theater engages the guilty conscience, and none is free.

Hence, when Domitian stands aside to watch his wife betray him with Paris, he assumes a theatrical stance we have seen before, the style of gods; he is one of the "sad spectators" of "the *Theater of the Gods*" (4:2, line 115), and he descends upon them like Vulcan with his net. Finally, Vulcan's net finds Domitian out, however, and all those whom he has violated to serve his prerogative join hands with political opponents and murder him. Their triumph is short-lived; they are immediately apprehended, for killing Caesar remains unjustifiable, and these assassins have no political principles for their actions that would replace Caesar's. Before he dies, Domitian knows this: "*Caesar,*" he says "by *Caesar's,* sentenc'd" (5:1, line 197), and by Caesarism killed—in the theater of the gods: "The offended Gods/ . . . now sit judges on me" (5:1, lines 282-83). He is made their spectacle. In the scene before his death, the emperor sleeps on-stage, and his most privy thoughts, what lies on his conscience, are represented, in a dumb show, before our eyes: it is, literally, the theater of conscience, and it is viewed by multiple audiences—by the gods, Domitian imagines, by the spectators, us, unimagined—and on-stage, by Domitia and Parthenius, the onetime procurer and injured son, co-conspirators, plotting the emperor's death.

Tiberius-like, Domitian had had spies that made even dreams fearful of betrayal: "we hardly sleepe/Nay cannot dreame with safe-tie" (1:1, lines 71-72), one subject confesses. "To be vertuous/Is to bee guilty. They are onely safe/That know to sooth the Princes appe-tite,/And serve his lusts" (lines 78-81), he continues. The emperor's pleasures, unspeakable lusts and unspeakable cruelty, meet in the death of Paris: "We remember/A Tragedie, we oft have seen with pleasure" (4:2, lines 205-6). In such a show, caught in his pleasures, in his dreams, Domitian is ultimately cast. "Insensible of all my actions" (5:1, line 143), Caesar thinks he has "sear'd up" (line 142) his conscience and that he is exempt, that his privacy remains private. It is instead made public, onstage. The dumb show presents two of his victims, not of private crimes, but of public ones. These are two who whispered against Caesar and whom he tortured before his eyes, making them a spectacle of state. The two stood silent in torture. Caesar had threatened them;

> I'll afflict your soules.
> And force them groaning to the *Stigian* lake
> Prepar'd for such to howle in, that blaspheame
> The power of Princes, that are Gods on earth;
> Tremble to thinke how terrible the dreame is
> After this sleepe of death.   (3:2, lines 54-59)

But their silence answered Caesar: "Securely,/(As t'were a gentle slumber,) we indure/Thy hangmens studied tortures" (3:2, lines 96–98). At last, the emperor's slumber is afflicted by the terrible dream that they have become, and he awakens aghast at these ghosts that have claimed his spirit and submits to their sentence: "'twas no dreame, but a most reall truth" (5:1, line 200). Real and royal. When the ghosts appear, it is hard to know who has triumphed, for they manifest the horrors Domitian had promised, his power now turned upon himself. In the theater, everything is representation, doubling itself, replaying itself.

In that mirroring theater of conscience, the king and the king's conscience were caught—whether offstage or on, for there is, as James knew, no off. The actors need not worry; they will never lack support. There will always be a performance in "our *Amphitheater,*/ Great *Pompies* worke" (1:1, lines 8–9), and there will always be an audience, ready to be taken in. "We that have free souls, it touches us not." But who has a free soul? The conspirator who cries "Liberty! Freedom! Tyranny is dead"? The poet who writes "To the Ghost of Martial"?

> Martial, thou gav'st farre nobler *Epigrammes*
>   To thy DOMITIAN, than I can my JAMES:
> But in my royall subiect I passe thee,
>   Thou flattered'st thine, mine cannot flatter'd bee.
>
> (*Epigrammes:* 36)

5. SOCIAL TEXTS, ROYAL MEASURES:
Donne, Jonson, and *Measure for Measure*

And then, as he had formerly asked God with Moses, "Who am I?" so now,
being inspired with an apprehension of God's particular mercy to him, in the
King's and others solicitations of him, he came to ask King David's thankful
question, "Lord, who am I, that thou art so mindful of me?" —Izaak Walton,
The Life of John Donne

O N 27 MARCH 1625, TWENTY-TWO YEARS AFTER
ascending to the throne of England, and almost to the day,
King James died. A month later, some few days before the body was
to be interred, John Donne preached over the corpse. It was the last
time the king and the Dean of St. Paul's were to face each other, the
ultimate episode in the story of Donne's making and coming to have
a place in the world. Reviewing it, we can further our understanding
of the role of the king in the realm of the word; reading Donne's last
words over the body of the king, we can sum up some of the crucial
features in the relation between the royal word, the royal body, and
the language that constitutes the social body-as-text.

TOWARD the end of his life, in the middle of a flap with King
Charles about possible disloyalty to the Laudian position, Donne
wrote a letter to his friend Sir Robert Carr, defending himself: "My
Tenets are always, for the preservation of the Religion I was born in,
and the peace of the State, and the rectifying of the Conscience."[1]
Perhaps by 1627 Donne no longer remembered that "the Religion I
was born in" was Roman Catholicism. More likely, however, is the
possibility that Donne did not consider he had been born as himself
until he entered the Church of England. Years before he had written
to his close friend and familiar correspondent, Sir Henry Goodyer,
that "I would fain do something; but that I cannot tell what, is no
wonder. For to chuse, is to do: but to be no part of any body, is to
be nothing" (*Letters*, p. 44). It was Donne's recurrent sense in the
years during which he sought to regain a position in the world after
having lost all for love that he was "nothing." "No man is lesse of
himself then I," he tells Goodyer (*Letters*, p. 39); for when he married and fell from favor, "I dyed at a blow then when my courses
were diverted" (*Letters*, p. 105). Correspondingly, when the king
preferred him and advanced him in "the Religion I was born in," he
claimed to be reborn. In the dedicatory epistle to the *Devotions
Upon Emergent Occasions* addressed to Prince Charles, Donne testi-

fies to James's role in his life: "I *have had three* Births; *One,* Naturall, *when I came into the* World; *One* Supernatural, *when I entred into the* Ministery; *and now, a* preternaturall Birth, *in returning to* Life, *from this* Sicknes. *In my* second Birth, *your* Highnesse Royall Father *vouchsafed mee his Hand, not onely to sustaine mee* in it, *but to lead mee* to it" (*Devotions,* p. 3).[2] And in the first Paul's Cross sermon that he preached at royal command, Donne exhorted his audience to take an active part in the world: "In a word, he that will be *nothing* in this world, shall be nothing in the next."[3] His second birth made him an apt spokesman for this message.

Running through the *Letters to Severall Persons of Honour* is the recurrent motif of Donne's need to have a place in the world if he is to be anything and his complete dependence upon others if this is to happen. Although his manner of expression of this belief may sometimes seem to be hyperbolic, the extremity of his discourse fits the facts. The precipitous anger of Sir George More and the instantaneous dismissal by Sir Thomas Egerton could not readily be undone. For some ten years Donne lived off others and was dependent upon them. "Your favour keeps me alive" (*Letters,* p. 2) is practically the opening sentence in the collection of letters; it is a sentiment echoed repeatedly. "My best degree of understanding is to bee governed by you" is almost a closing sentence (*Letters,* p. 255). Donne's dependence is self-constitutive. He virtually admits this in a letter to Goodyer: "I love to give you advantages upon me, therefore I put my self in need of another pardon from you" (*Letters,* p. 129). "I wish my self whatsoever you wish me," he continues; soon Lady Bedford is involved in these designs: "I have made her opinion of me, the ballance by which I weigh my self" (*Letters,* p. 130).

This mode of self-creation through self-abandonment, placing oneself entirely in the hands of another, registers Donne's response to his sense that being a part of the world means allowing the world to work its will upon the self. Donne's letters function as testaments to his "impotencie" and nothingness;[4] their role is to keep his name in circulation. He solicits favor: "I must intreat you to continue that wherein you have most expressed your love to me, which is, to maintain me in the same room in my Lady *Bedfords* opinion, in the which you placed me" (*Letters,* p. 82). Donne offers gratitude to his correspondent in exchange for his actions on Donne's behalf. Letters function as intermediaries in the complex of exchanges in which the various parts of the social system are held together. Donne writes on the margins of the court and as an outsider. "You mocke us when you ask news from hence. All is created there, or relates thither

211

where you are," he writes in 1614 to George Gerrard at court (*Letters,* p. 242). "Sir," he tells him, "you do me double honour when my name passes through you to that Noble Lady in whose presence you are" (*Letters,* p. 223). Gerrard exists, has his life, literally and figuratively, by being at court and in the presence of Lucy. As in the poem on the Somerset wedding, the court is the center of existence. Donne sends his name there through a letter; another takes his name and presents it. Through these acts of intervention and mediation, his nothing is converted into something and he comes to be in the world. The brief letter below displays, in its perfect lack of content, the elementary structures by which Donne attempts to insert himself into the world by presenting himself in his letters:

> Sir,
>
> If I shall never be able to do you any reall service, yet you may make this profit of me, that you be hereafter more cautelous in receiving into your knowledge, persons so uselesse, and importune. But before you come to so perfect a knowledge of me, as to abandon me, go forward in your favours to me, so farre, as to deliver this Letter according to the addresse. I think I should not come nearer his presence then by a Letter: and I am sure, I would come no other way, but by you. Be you therefore pleased, by these noble favours to me, to continue in me the comfort which I have in being
>
> Your very humble and thankfull servant
>
> Drury house, 23 Sept. J. Donne
>
> (Letters, p. 258)

Walton's picture of Donne being solicited by noble friends, aided by the royal favorites,[5] needs to be balanced by the total self-abandonment that Donne professes. To Gerrard, he can at least offer himself as an admonitory example of the folly of helping those who are nothing in themselves. To Somerset, he says, however, that he has sold himself entirely: "After I was grown to be your Lordships, by all the titles that I could thinke upon, it hath pleased your Lordship to make another title to me, by buying me" (*Letters,* p. 247). In this transaction, Donne's letters serve as evidence of Somerset's "hold" upon him. That hold is his life, however, for the favorite's favors are to Donne a resurrection, or so he claims at the close of this letter.

The metaphor, we have seen, Donne used more particularly to describe the king's role in his life: "*Your* Highnesse Royall Father *vouchsafed mee his Hand, not onely to sustaine mee . . . but to lead mee*" (*Dev.,* p. 3). As he told his audience in the opening of that first

Paul's Cross sermon, the text that he offered them, "He that loveth pureness of heart, for the grace of his lips, the king shall be his friend" (Prov. 22:11), contained two "pictures" at once: "You have a good picture of a good King, and of a good subject" (*Sermons*, 1: 183); "King and subject come at once and together into consideration" (1:184). Mutually constitutive, yet, as Donne also urged upon his hearers, "equality . . . cannot stand between *King* and *Subject*" (1:212). To gain what the king can give—love—the subject must offer the service of his lips, lip service; he must show "a duty of *utterance*" (1:209). This, of course, the speaker of these words does, preaching at the royal command. Donne found a voice in the royal favor; there he found his words.

Not surprisingly, then, that sermon proclaims James as "God's Lieutenant" (1:210). As John Carey suggests, Donne's royalism frequently echoes James's words.[6] So, in this sermon, James is as insistently the light as he was in the celebrations of his entrance into London. Indeed, remembering the death of Elizabeth and the accession of James (the Paul's Cross sermon was preached on the fourteenth anniversary of that event), the metaphor appears: "In her death we were all under one common flood, and depth of tears. But the *Spirit of God moved upon the face of that depth;* and God said, *Let there be light.*" (1:217). James here has, as well, the style of gods, if not of God. In him, sweetness comes from strength, peace is his blessed gift. Herculean, Solomonic, imperial: such is the king's nature declared to Donne's audience, "you *Senators* of *London*" (1:208). That Donne found a voice in the king's words was his first discovery in his reconstitution and rebirth. In Walton's account, Donne's calling began with the royal command that resulted in the writing of *Pseudo-Martyr*. As Donne tells it, however, it was not the king's command, but the exemplary force of the king's word that moved him: "The influence of those your Maiesties Bookes, as the Sunne, which penetrates all corners, hath wrought uppon me, and drawen up, and exhaled from my poore Meditations, these discourses."[7]

A single metaphor—the metaphor of the hand, sustaining, leading—describes James's role in Donne's life and works, recreating him, giving him words to write. Walton expresses it when he points to the destiny in the ministry that Donne did not choose for himself (indeed, in Walton's account, Donne explicitly rejected it; if he did, it was because Donne thought that others would not admit that he was a suitable prelate—this was Chamberlain's opinion at first;[8] if Walton's story is untrue, it nonetheless conveys a truth, as does Walton's

213

account throughout, the truth of discourse, of what is said about how lives are constituted by the actions of others).[9] Walton affirms that Donne could not make his life—he could only undo it: "He was destined to this sacred service by an higher hand; a hand so powerful, as at last forced him to a compliance" (p. 20). It is a metaphor that Walton reports Donne voicing toward the end of his life: "It was his hand that prevented me from all temporal employment" (p. 76). In Walton's usage, the hand presumably belongs to the king; in Donne's, to the king of kings. But the ambiguity resides already in Walton's sentence. And its source might well have been Donne himself. "Thy hand supports that hand, that supports us," Donne says in a prayer to God at the end of the section of the *Devotions* in which he pays tribute to James for his role in his life (8 Prayer, p. 45). The preternatural hand offered in his disease is, he tells God, "but the twi-light, of that day, wherin thou, thorow him, hast shind upon mee before; but the *Eccho* of that voice, whereby thou, through him, hast spoke to mee before; Then, when he, first of any man conceiv'd a hope, that I might be of some use in thy *Church,* and descended to an intimation, to a perswasion, almost to a solicitation, that I would embrace that calling" (8 Expo., pp. 43-44). James represents hand, light, and word; in him, Donne is made.

Reclaimed by James, Donne found himself and came to the essential position figured in the transactions that the letters reveal as the shape of his life. Writing to Goodyer, he had described his letters as "conveyances and deliverers of me to you" (*Letters,* p. 94), and had gone on to consider and compare prayers and letters. Their natures are parallel, as this description of prayers shows: "Our accesses to his [God's] presence are but his descents into us; and when we get any thing by prayer, he gave us before hand the thing and the petition" (pp. 95-96). In a parallel fashion, Donne had been commanded to write *Pseudo-Martyr,* and the king's words had been his model; he rose to the descending words: "Having observed, how much your Maiestie had vouchsafed to descend to a conversation with your Subiects, by way of your Bookes, I also conceiv'd an ambition, of ascending to your presence, by the same way" (sig. A³r-v). In the *Devotions,* his conception remains the same when he describes the king's behavior to his subjects: "When abounding and overflowing, as *God,* to a communication of their abundances with men, according to their necessities, then they are *Gods*" (8 Med., p. 41). The king's descent shows his deity as much as God's did. Donne's transactions in the world are based in this interlocking, mirroring paradigm of descent and ascent in which God and the world are linked.

214

I who was sicke before, of a vertiginous giddiness, and irresolution, and almost spent all my time in consulting how I should spend it, was by this *man of God,* and *God of men,* put into the poole, and recovered: when I asked, perchance, a *stone,* he gave me *bread,* when I asked, perchance, a *Scorpion,* he gave me a *fish;* when I asked a temporall *office,* hee denied not, refused not that, but let mee see, that hee had rather I took this. (*Dev.* 8 Expo., p. 44)

In the *Devotions,* Donne celebrated James as God's instrument, "that royall Instrument, my *Soveraigne*" (p. 42), and as God's image in descending to him. As the image of God, the king is a royal gift, a royal "*Coyne*": "I look upon the *King,* and I aske whose *image,* & whose *inscription* hee hath; and he hath *thine*" (p. 42). When Donne viewed the king's corpse, he still saw the same thing, and drew out the same meaning for himself and his audience, about the king, his relation to God and to his subjects. Preaching on a text from the Song of Songs, "Goe forth ye daughters of Sion, and behold King Solomon, with the crown, wherewith his mother crowned him, in the day of his espousals, and in the day of the gladnesse of his heart," Donne arrives at the word *Solomon* and has this to say: "Here, at your coming hither now, you have *two glasses,* wherein you may see your selves from head to foot; One in the Text, your *Head, Christ Jesus,* represented unto you, in the name and person of *Solomon, Behold King Solomon crowned, &c.* And another, under your feet, in the dissolution of this great *Monarch,* our *Royall Master,* now layd lower by death then any of us, his Subjects and servants" (*Sermons,* 6:286). The dead body of the king is an equal authority to the text in which the name of Solomon represents Christ. The authority of the corpse is the authority of the text; both illuminate and represent God, equally instruments and mirrors. Donne, preacher of the word, preaching over the body of the king, gains his authority by looking in these "*two glasses.*"

For the text he preaches is part of a chain of authority in which he is placed. The echo of voice can be heard here, as it had been before, when Donne heard the voice of God in the king's near solicitation, "the *Eccho* of that voice, whereby thou, through him, hast spoke to mee" (*Dev.* 8 Expo., p. 44). In the sermon, the echo embraces God, the king, the texts that have come before the speaker, and the institution in which and through which he speaks, the church in which James placed him and gave him life: "That which the *Scripture* says, *God* sayes, (says St. *Augustine*) for the Scripture is his word; and that which the *Church* says, the *Scriptures* say, for she is their word, they speak *in her;* they authorize her, and she explicates them" (*Sermons,* 6:282). In the same manner, Donne is "authorized" to "explicate" his text, and his opening words justify him to "enlarge, and spread, and paraphrase that one word" (6:280) so that the immediate sense of *"Solomon crowned"* is "Christ invested with the royall dignity of being *Head of the Church"* (280-81). Christ's crown is the crown of humiliation, the very same one we saw James wear when he descended to Donne's care, and one that allowed Donne, as he says in a letter to Sir Robert Carr, to implicate the royal family in his *Devotions:* "I whisper into your earre this question, whether there be any uncomlinesse, or unseasonablenesse, in presenting matter of Devotion, or Mortification, to that Prince, whom I pray God nothing may ever Mortifie, but Holinesse" (*Letters,* p. 215). Christ and the king, those twin mirrors, are united in mortification, humbly descending, equally royal and godlike; they are joined in the name of Solomon. "For, *Solomon,* in this text, is not a *proper* Name, but an *Appellative;* a significative word: *Solomon* is *pacificus,* the *Peacemaker"* (*Sermons,* 6:286), and the name covers both Christ and the king.

The text, composed of sliding signifiers, has its authority from something absent from it, the unmentioned Christ, the dead king. Christ is not Solomon, nor is the king. Neither Christ nor the king is present in the text, yet the word and Donne's words take their meaning and power from them. The text, written in "significative" words, exists as the representation of and replacement for an absent voice. Of Christ, Donne says that "as long as he was to stay with them, it was not likely that they should need provocation, to hear him" (6:281); present, he needed no voice; dead and absent, Christ can only be heard, not seen, heard in the text in which another word serves as his representation. The dead king is similarly present and absent in the Solomonic text: "Heare him" (*Sermons,* 6:290), Donne insists. God's "second *Image"* (to use the language of the *Devotions*), "imprinted indelibly in their [kings'] *power"* (*Dev.* 8 Expo., p. 42) is irresistible. Hence, although the king may err in his conscience toward God, although he may sin like any man, this is of no concern to others: he is always God's image. Conscience remains hidden, a matter for the king and God. But the visible power of the king is the image of deity, an image "imprinted indelibly." The text bears that imprint and Donne reads and hears it in his authorized acts of explication. As God speaks through his son—and particularly through his absent son, mortified—so he speaks in the royal corpse. Donne transcribes these inscriptions, opens these words to find the voice of deity, and to find his voice. What he pursues in the text are traces, footsteps of those who come before him in the chain of signification. "And truly the best way to discerne footsteps, is *Daniels way, Daniels* way was to *straw ashes*" (*Sermons,* 6:285). Donne pursues the authority in ashes, those marks strewn before on his path. These take him beyond himself to find voice in his text and in the corpse of the king.

As in his first Paul's Cross sermon preached at the royal command, here, too, activity in the world is measured by the service of the lips. Life resides in the voice, and the voice is given by another. In Christ's baptism, God pronounces him his son; and in his transfiguration, God repeats himself, and adds, *"Hear him"* (6:281). *"No man hath seen God,* and lives; but no man lives till he have *heard God;* for God spake to him, in his *Baptisme,* and called him by his name,* then" (ibid). The name is itself an appellative, not a proper name, a name that signifies being called and being taken into God's text by being named by him. To be such a text and to be heard one must be dead. This is the meaning of the transfiguration. The invisible, dead Christ God renames as the one who must be heard: "When he was gone out of this world, men needed a more particular solicitation to heare him" (6:282). This is as true of Christ as of the king, and it justifies Donne's speech, and gives him voice. God does not speak *"mouth to mouth"* (6:281) but through representatives: his son, the king, the church, the apostles—and the king's preacher.

Those to whom he preaches are named in his text as well, as the daughters of Sion. For "in your *baptisme,* your *soules* became daughters of the Church" (6:283). The text is spoken in the voice of the Church, *"imperatively,* authoritatively" (ibid). The voice of power reduces all hearers to the status of subjects and subjection (the text can no more be resisted than can the state, Donne says). Obedience and submission are registered best in the gender of those addressed and named as female, the undifferentiated sex of powerlessness. Parents or churches may disinherit their children, Donne says; but children cannot renounce their parents. Named by another and given identity—and robbed of self-determination at once; this is like the condition Donne imagines for himself in the letters, totally submissive so that he may gain a place in the world. In the sermon, pursuing the traces of ashes to the beyond—to the corpse of the king, the mortified Christ—Donne pursues the self beyond itself: "Consider thy selfe at thine end" (6:285), he enjoins his hearers. He pursues the subject-in-subjection, the subject under the chain of signifiers, the subject under the imposition of death. Only from the vantage point of the beyond can the self be constituted. "Go forth" is the injunction to the daughters of Sion. As Donne reads this, it means to go beyond the self by pursuing the self that has gone beyond (pursuing the corpse, the dusty path). The king is a mirror in which the dead self may be viewed, the self through which the voice of another speaks, authoritatively, constituting the subject in subjection to an absent voice. And so, too, is Donne made.

The voice speaking, Donne's voice, echoes royal commands. The royal household functions, Donne remarks, even if the king is gone; so, too, does the house of God (6:281). And thus does the preacher have words. "Hearken to the voyce of God, in the Church" (6:282); "that which Christ says to the Church it selfe, the Church says to every soule in the Church" (6:284). It is an everlasting echo chamber. And by it, community, society in this life, is made by the absent power (Christ, James, *Deus absconditus*):

> Let none of us, goe so farre from him [James], or from one
> another, in any of our wayes, but that all we that have served
> him, may meet once a day, the first time we see the Sunne,
> in the eares of almighty God, with humble and hearty prayer,
> that he will be pleased to hasten that day, in which it shall
> be *an addition,* even to the joy of that place, as perfect as it is,
> and as infinite as it is, to see that face againe, and to see those
> eyes open there, which we have seen closed here. (6:291)

God continues to make his voice heard in the king; the king continues to exert his authority in the world, to make the human community those joined through him, speaking, directing their prayers in just that manner Donne had said that letters and prayers both worked, to make a place for oneself in the world.

"That royall Instrument, my *Soveraigne*" (*Dev.* 8 Expo., p. 42) continues to function "by his owne hands" (p. 43)—God's hands—"thy hand supports that hand" in its faithful "*Stewardship*" (8 Prayer, p. 45). Over the corpse, Donne meditates upon the dead hand, "that Hand, which was the *hand of Destinie, of Christian Destinie,* of the *Almighty God*" (*Sermons,* 6:290), and such it remains. James is a speaking corpse—"heare him," Donne enjoins; signed and sealed, the king is delivered "as a beame of that Sunne, as an abridgement of that *Solomon* in the Text . . . , and an abridgement of *Christ* himselfe" (6:290). James is written as a text, read as a text, the royal instrument, the all-powerful hand.

His last inscription in Donne's life is also his first. On Donne's tomb, the first date—it might as well be his date of birth—is the date of his ordination. The hand behind this event is a double one, the king's and God's.

Instinctu et Impulsu Sp. Sancti, Monitu
et Hortatu
Regis Jacobi, Ordines Sacros Amplexus,
Anno Sui Jesu, MDCXIV. Et Suae AEtatis XLII.
(Walton, p. 79)

In those last words, speaking beyond himself, Donne inscribes himself in an eternal text, the one he preached over the corpse of the king: "All this life is but a *Preface,* or but an *Index* and *Repertory* to the book of *life;* There, at that book beginnes thy Study; To grow perfect in that book, to be dayly conversant in that book, to find what be the marks of them, whose names are written in that book, and to finde those marks, ingenuously, and in a rectified conscience, in thy selfe" (*Sermons,* 6:286). To do so, one must "see thy self, beyond thy self" (ibid); see oneself in the mirror of the beyond, the royal glass and representation. In him, Donne found "the Religion I was born in, and the peace of the State" (*Letters,* p. 260).

DONNE's self-constitution is absolutist; like Lear, his concern is who's in and who's out, and there seems to be no alternative to that either/or situation. He is fully made—or unmade—in relation to the powers of society. This, however, is not the only social position possible in Jacobean culture. One could be both in and out at once. In Donne's terms, the court is the center and the only reality of society; not to be there is to be nowhere. To be out is not to exist; life at Mitcham is living death; there is no realm save His Majesty's. A broader social view is possible. It extends to embrace what Donne would label as "out"; hence, it can be in and out at once because "in" has absorbed "out." In this view, there is no outside society for there is no realm that is not the king's. This way of thinking is as absolutist as Donne's if not as absolute in its divisions. James, we know, could think both ways, as his double theatrical metaphor in the *Basilikon Doron* shows. If he wished to deny parts of himself, he also wished to affirm them and to allow with the same breath with which he disallowed. This greater inclusiveness, in short, is not that of democractic society, nor is it an egalitarian gesture. It takes in more only to absorb it, not to permit it its own terms. It allows and contains contradictions.[10]

This is the form of Ben Jonson's mature masques, as we have seen, and the shape of his life as well. It defines his relationship to the king and the king's role in his writing. We may, reviewing the life, glancing at a few of his preeminently social texts as well, see this paradigmatic mode of life in action and summarize anew another facet of the relationship of authority to the texts that constitute the reality of social life.

The career began auspiciously, with charges of scandal and sedition for *The Isle of Dogs*. [11] The ability to write soon proved to be his salvation, however; it saved him from the gallows for the murder of his fellow actor, Gabriel Spencer. But at the same time, a war of words was being waged, the War of the Theaters; his main opponent was his sometime collaborator, John Marston. If there is not quite a pattern in these events with their poised antagonisms, there almost is, and it comes clearer with the arrival of the new monarch. Jonson was there, writing, we know, for the king's entrance into London; yet he was, at virtually the same time, called before the Star Chamber to answer charges of sedition in *Sejanus*. In the same year as the royal entrance, Jonson was once again in trouble with the authorities, for his satire of the Scots—and royal favoritism—in *Eastward Ho*. That very year his upstart behavior in court caused him to be thrust out for disorderly conduct; he was that same year asked to provide the first of the Christmas season masques with which he entertained James's court almost every year following. Once in, he was employed by the government to investigate the Gunpowder Plot; yet this insider was also a Catholic (he had converted just when he was taken back into society after he escaped execution for murder), and so in 1606 he was called for nonattendance at Anglican communion. His answer to this was to practice an outer conformity at odds with his Catholicism. These events begin to define what C. H. Herford calls his "chequered" relations with the court (*H&S* 1:57). They continued into the next reign, for Charles extended favor to the poet just after he had been arrested on the charge of having written a poem praising Buckingham's assassin.

These are acts in a career of contained rebellion. Jonson's characteristic mode of explanation of this behavior can perhaps be caught best in the letters he wrote during his imprisonment for *Eastward Ho*. He appeals to Salisbury to consider "whether it be possible, I should speake of his Maiestie as I have done, without the affection of a most zealous and good subiect" (1:194). That sentence admits and denies the charges against him at the same time, claiming to be a "good subiect" but not retracting a word. Jonson's mode of being a "good subiect" allows him to speak out. As he explains in another letter, his innocence gives him the security to do so. Just as

Jonson was later willing to practice an outer conformity that failed to match his inner state, keeping his conscience clear, in this case the integrity of his conscience argues against his appearance of rebellion. Hence, what he is "most Inwardlie sorie" (1:197) for is "his Maiesties high displeasure," not what he has done, and he hopes to be restored to favor, not that he needs it for his own belief in his innocence, but because he would as soon "stand iustified in sight of his Soveraignes mercy" (ibid.). What Jonson affirms here is not quite individual integrity; the interiority he claims for himself has been overseen by zeal and good subjection. His need for the king's outward approbation of his inner state lies in the fact that "no subiect hath so safe an Innocence" not to need such outer signs. Jonson does not quite claim that he can stand on his own (how could he? No matter how innocent he was he needed the king's release from imprisonment), nor that his own conscience is enough. He is asking for an outward sign to confirm his inner state. James, we recall, had similarly demanded that signs of dissolution be reunderstood. So, too, Jonson simply acts as if there were no cause for his imprisonment. Similarly, he told Pembroke in the epistle dedicatory to the *Epigrammes* that he was unjustly taxed for censuring the great; the faults were theirs, not his own, and (like the actors in *The Roman Actor*) he named no names (8:25-26). Walton summarizes acutely the relationship to society that Jonson's stance entails when he reports that "he got in time to have a 100^{li} a yeare, from the king, also a pention from the Cittie, and the like from many of the nobilitie, and som of the gentry. Wch was well pay'd for love or fere of his ralings in verse, or prose, or both" (1:181). Paid for love or fear: Jonson's success—pensioned by the king, patronized by his courtiers, the city, and the gentry—exhibits how well he fit within his society, how fully he contained it. His is so entirely a voice constituted by and representative of his society that he could speak out against it and yet speak within it. The fantasy of power that he spun for William Drummond catches this nicely: "He heth a minde to be a churchman, & so he might have fevour to make one Sermon to the King, he careth not what yr after sould befall him, for he would not flatter though he saw Death" (1:141). Protected by the institution of the church, granted royal favor to speak out, Jonson imagines himself then free to speak his mind in a sermon to the king. His fantasy of rebellion is licensed by the king. And throughout his career, that fantasy was very close to the facts. His rebellions were royally countenanced.

The poet who declared his identity with the king in a favorite tag—*Solus Rex, & Poeta non quotannis nascitur,* The king alone, and the poet, is not born everyday"[12]—extended their kinship tellingly in the poem spoken to Bacchus as "The Dedication of the Kings new Cellar" (*UW*:48). In it the design intimated in *Oberon* comes true; the inebriate god is a type of the king—and of the poet as well. He is invoked as ringleader of the muses (lines 25 ff.), chief entertainer at the king's feasts (lines 37 ff.) and, since the Banqueting House also served as the center of the serious business of the court, Bacchus is hailed as the underlying support in all royal activity, too. The poem emblematizes the double life of the court: the Banqueting House above, the wine cellar below. One realm extends into the other, and Bacchus is asked to be present whether James "feast it" (line 38) or

> Be it he hold Communion
> In great Saint *Georges* Union;
> Or gratulates the passage
> Of some wel-wrought Embassage:
> Whereby he may knit sure up
> The wished Peace of *Europe:*
> Or else a health advances,
> To put his Court in dances,
> And set us all on skipping,
> When with his royall shipping
> The narrow Seas are shadie,
> And *Charles* brings home the Ladie.   (lines 43–54)

This vision of the court tipsily draws no lines between the serious and the playful. All is allowed in James's realm, and even the proprieties of place—the hierarchical division into an above and a below—give way, as they did in the jostling of business and festivity in Whitehall. The mixtures here parallel those in that charming grace that exists in several versions (*UV*:47). In them, blessing is asked for the king and queen and their children, and for "Buckingham the fortunate"; then, at the end, Jonson includes himself, "God blesse me, and God blesse Raph." That final line, drawing Jonson and his boy (or serving man) into the realm of the blessed, represents no democratic gesture. Rather, as in the poem on the wine cellar, decorum is momentarily violated when he invades the royal circle, but only because the royal circle allows such admissions and countenances them—Buckingham's position serves as a warrant for this extension. Jonson participates in the court as he audaciously proclaims himself outside and equal. The concluding moment of the grace takes us to the center of Jonson's relationship to the king and to the role of the king in his writing.

There is no better place to examine this than in two of his greatest poems, "To Penshurst" (*For:* 2) and "To Sir Robert Wroth" (*For:*
3). In the first, King James enters the poem as soon as the poet has
found his place in the Sidney mansion, lodged and fed there "As if
thou, then, wert mine, or I raign'd here:"

> There's nothing I can wish, for which I stay.
>> That found King JAMES, when hunting late, this way,
> With his brave sonne, the Prince, they saw thy fires
>> Shine bright on every harth as the desires
> Of thy *Penates* had beene set on flame,
>> To entertayne them. (Lines 74–80)

In "To Penshurst," James finds what the poet found; in the poem to
Wroth, the king replicates the master of the estate and "makes thy
house his court" (line 24). These poems, in which the king finds a
place, a place defined by the royal entrance into the text, mirror the
relationship of Jonson's texts to society.

James's entrance in "To Penshurst" has been understood in a
variety of ways.[13] His entertainment has been seen as the final example of the old value of housekeeping that the Sidney estate displays. The king has been read as the last in the great hierarchical chain
of society that leads up from the peasant and clown of earlier lines
and which the house contains. In the juxtaposition of the king and
the poet, an incipient egalitarianism has been found. Yet the meeting
is complementary, not an identification. James appears when the "I"
declares that all his wishes have been fulfilled. The king finds out the
poet's wish. The poet's wish claims the king, for he hypothesizes the
longings of the house and mythologizes them ("as the desires/Of thy
Penates") and the king and the prince are drawn into his designs. The
governing condition here is an "as if"—"As if thou, then, wert mine,
or I raign'd here"—for it is the poet's fancied reign that meets the
fact of the king's visit. Penshurst is the poet's, not because it fulfills
his desires, but because it allows him to extend them, to project
them, in short, to invent desires that go beyond himself to meet the
king. The house literally houses the poet; it gives his fancy a local
habitation and a name.[14] "That found King James": the king discovers what the poet has invented, found out, made of Penshurst.
The poet's sovereign imagination meets the king: it is a single shape,
and the king's entrance into the poem makes the poem true. The visit
confirms the activity of the poet's mind. Together, poet and king
present a picture of the mutually constitutive nature of society. As in
the fantasy declared to William Drummond, the poet's imagination

fulfills itself under the aegis of constituted authority. This is the answer to the condition Drummond reports as Jonson's prevailing state of mind, "oppressed with fantasie, which hath ever mastered his reason" (1:151). The oppression is lightened when subjected to the king. When the king enters the poem, he duplicates the poet's experience of wish fulfillment and provides a model for it. The king who declared his will to be law and affirmed the innate propriety of all his desires gives the pattern for the poet.

This is a point Jonson makes in celebrating those whom the king chose to counsel and serve him. For example, Jonson celebrates Bacon's birthday as if his only begetter were the king, for after pointing to Bacon's lineage, he concludes by calling for the royal drink: "Give me a deepe-crown'd-Bowle, that I may sing/In raysing him the wisdome of my King" (*UW:* 51, lines 19–20). Bacon is not simply his father's son; he is the king's creation—and the poet's, too. The poet's occasion for "raysing him" comes from the king. Similarly, when Jonson praises Salisbury, it is to see "the judgement of the king so shine in thee" (*Ep:* 63, line 4); and, likewise, Lord Ellesmere shows in his judgments the king's: "So, may the King proclaime your Conscience is/Law, to his Law" (*UW:* 31, lines 3–4). In a poem praising Thomas Howard, Earl of Suffolk (*Ep:* 67), the king enters the poem, much as he does in "To Penshurst," as a valorization of desires. Howard is praised as the end of "mens wishes" (line 7), as the living confirmation of what before existed "in each good mans heart" (line 10). Yet the fulfilled desire gains authority from the king's act: "Which, by no lesse confirm'd, then thy kings choice,/ Proves, that is gods, which was the peoples voice" (lines 11–12). *Vox populi, vox dei:* because both voices meet in the king, and what men desire imitates the king's desires. Salisbury, Suffolk, and their ilk are representative men because they represent the king.

Jonson celebrated James as a king "that rules by'example, more than sway" (*Ep:* 35, line 2), "Whose manners draw, more than thy powers constraine" (line 3). Jonson had recommended imitation as a necessity for the true poet: "To make choise of one excellent man above the rest, and so to follow him, till he grow very *Hee*" (*Disc:* 638). This dictum applies to the making of proper men as well. In Jacobean society, there could be no doubt about whom to choose. Elsewhere in *Discoveries,* Jonson finds in royal representation the perfect analogy for self-representation (pp. 628–29). Words, he says, represent a man, and improper language reflects upon the speaker much as the "Image of a *King,* in his Seale ill-represented, is not so much a blemish to the waxe, or the Signet that seal'd it, as to the

Prince it representeth." The image represents the king as language represents man; yet the king is not the maker of his image, or even its material substance. So, too, language is not the user's creation, nor is it material to his existence. A bit later, Jonson likens speech to a royal ambassador. That second analogy furthers the first. Self-representation has a royal model on two counts, for the language men use bears a royal stamp. Hence, Jonson's words find out the king in "To Penshurst," for his desires are royal.

There is abundant evidence in *Discoveries* that Jonson subscribed to the basic tenets of absolutism, for he transcribed its founding principles. Jonson's prince stands only a bit below God (p. 594), and he is accountable to him alone: "Let no man therefore murmure at the Actions of the Prince, who is plac'd so farre above him. If hee offend, he hath his Discoverer. *God* hath a height beyond him. But where the *Prince* is good, *Euripides* saith: *God is a Guest in a humane body*" (p. 600). We have seen already that Jonson found self-justification in this royalist position. Even his declaration that "a *good King* is a publike Servant" (p. 601), directed against the exemplary tyranny of a Tiberius, does not make Jonson a democrat. The good king's service involves extending himself to society as an exemplar and as the embodiment of desire. He is the fact that words find out, making them true, making the people's voice God's. The chain of command is one of re-presentation. Royalist tenets become the principles of Jonson's poetics. Hence, in "To Penshurst," the king and the poet present matching fantasies and desires that the poem and the place enclose. As closer examination will show, the text is a representative vehicle for such enclosure, and its final image of dwelling is a controlling one. Not only does the poem take in the king; his inclusion is itself inclusive, a model for all that the poem represents. In the poem the poet exercises royal powers. What he exacts from the waiter at dinner epitomizes them; the waiter "gives me what I call" (line 69). Demands and desires are fulfilled in the very act of nomination.[15]

In "To Penshurst" the act of naming and renaming occurs throughout. From its opening dismissal of what the estate is not, the poet passes to what it is. He builds it from the ground up, having first called it "an ancient pile" (line 5). The poem is not simply the discovery of the "better markes" (line 7) of the place; it is their creation. Hence, the survey of the mount issues in the Sidneian tree, genealogical and poetic at once, flourishing amidst a mythological crew. The lower land is also "nam'd" (line 19) by the Sidney family. As the poem ranges over high and low grounds, it catalogs what "thou hast" (line 9), a series of names supplied as much by texts as by nature, and a topographical distribution endlessly rhetorical in organization. High feasts occur below trees, walks serve for health and sport; such juxtapositions dispose the elements of the verse, and these keep joining "where all the *Muses* met" (line 14). The poem contains these patterns of opposition seemingly effortlessly. And what it places on the grounds, as the soil yields gods and goddesses, is the very image of an endlessly fertile and yielding estate. What it gives to be devoured become the words on the page which give back to the estate as much as it yields. The poem repeats again and again this poetic economy, exchanging word and food, a paradigm of sustenance and the concrete valorization of the poet's play. "All come in" (line 48): this is crucial to the inclusive art of this poem. Penshurst presents an image of an absolute totality, an inclusive fantasy of containment. And the poem in its royal largesse manages to contain rebellion as well.

For, from the first, dismissing negative exemplars and reducing Penshurst so that it momentarily seems to be an uncreated pile rather than an edifice, the poem takes in what it negates. As the poem continues, it embraces the reality of exploited workers, encroached-upon landowners, mean-spirited lords, unchaste wives, servile servants, and begging suitors. Such inclusions are not attacks on society, but a register of its sustaining conditions. And these, as we know from Jonson's masques, could be presented before the monarch. Indeed, "To Penshurst" is masquelike in its construction.[16] Its antimasque, dismissed at the opening, is the proud pretension of overwrought estates; its main masque features the "free provisions" (line 58) that permit the productivity of the poem and the house, complementary and inclusive images that manage to include even what the house excludes. The model for such inclusive exclusiveness is the last to enter the house, the king. After him, what occurs as the consummation of society is repeated familiarly, in the procreative Sidney line.[17]

One could say that the poem takes, throughout, the Sidney line, marrying verse and family estate into a sustained image of the royal bounty. Jonson's edifying poem reproduces the sustaining terms of his society. Raymond Williams is, thus, perfectly correct in seeing this poem as a piece of official, ideological discourse; he errs by not seeing how broad a compass this allows, and what knowledge may be represented.

Most succinctly, Jonson's poems are both in and of society, part of social production and contributions to it. Unlike Donne, Jonson does not claim to be constituted solely by society; rather, he is a constituent of it, engaged in it, inseparable from it. Hence, he could always argue for his own innocence and find a place for his own rebelliousness. Thus, his poems remain in the great and central tradition of English Renaissance literary theory in which writing poetry is inevitably a political act.[18] Sidney had proclaimed in his *Defense* that poets founded society, and he had ended his treatise appealing to patrons and stressing the powers of poets to make or break reputations. Jonson also viewed his poems as dangerous. "Beware the Poet," he writes before the *Epigrammes,* and he claimed to be "given out dangerous" (*For:* 13, line 11) in times when "'tis growne almost a danger to speake true/Of any good minde" (lines 1-2)—almost a danger, perhaps, but not entirely one, since "speake true" he did, and get away with it. Indeed, at least during James's reign, he reaped rewards and royal protection. James, after all, did not think the times were perfect, even if he thought he was, and his lectures to Parliament, his urging courtiers to return to the country, his regulation of sports, dueling, even tobacco, indicate attempts at social reform. The point is that Jonson was able to speak against society because he was so much of society, and his opposing voice was yet within the framework of his culture.

The social ideal for Jonson of constituent membership, what he strove for himself, saw in others, and found a model for in the king, recurs again and again in his poems, for example, in his praise of Lucy, Countess of Bedford, as one who lived at court free of its vices, remaining responsive to the satirist's attacks upon the corruption of the place she occupies untainted: "living where the matter is bred,/Dare for these poemes, yet, both aske, and read" (*Ep:* 94, lines 11-12). "Rare poemes aske rare friends" (line 6), Jonson writes, for the community of letters serves an aristocracy of the word, not a counterculture but a community within the larger community, socially placed and productive, exclusive in taste, but not excluded from social exchanges. Hence, Salisbury is praised as a worthy patron precisely because he has no need of Jonson's pen; to reverse the statement that Jonson makes in the epistle before *Volpone,* Salisbury is, being a good man, himself a good poem. "Thou stand'st cleere," Jonson concludes (*Ep:* 43, line 12), defining an essential stance;[19] Cecil is in and out of society just as he is in and out of the poem.

Not surprisingly, Jonson casts this social situation in theatrical terms: "I *have* considered, our whole life is like a *Play:* wherein every man, forgetfull of himselfe, is in travaile with expression of another. ... *Good men* ... plac'd high on the top of all vertue, look'd downe

227

on the Stage of the world, and contemned the Play of *Fortune*. For though the most be Players, some must be *Spectators*" (*Disc:* 597). All of life, Jonson meditates, is a play. At first, this seems to be a totalistic statement—all men play parts, all men are actors. But then Jonson's theater divides, and good men are not onstage but off, looking down like gods—or stoics. Yet, as spectators, they still play a role; there remains something compulsory in their activity ("some must be *Spectators*"); they may even be imagined on the gallery on-stage. In any case, the image of the theater continues to express an inescapable totality that encompasses onstage and off. The image of life-as-a-play recasts the contradictory stance of a Countess of Bed-ford or Lord Salisbury, which Jonson embodied, idealized, and ex-pressed. The *Epigrammes,* like Martial's book of spectacles, he entitled his "Theater"; but unlike his predecessor's work, all might come in, even "Cato, *If he liv'd, might enter without scandall*" (*H&S* 8:26).

Hence, when King James enters Wroth's house, as he does in line 24 of "To Sir Robert Wroth" (*For:* 3), he arrives at a realm of contained contradiction. The poem opens dividing court and country, praising Wroth for standing clear of the corruption of the town by residing away. But when the king arrives, the poem ceases to be divi-sive and celebrates country pleasures that were also royal ones. The shift in attitude occurs first in the language of the poem. The open-ing opposition, in which Wroth is praised for being

> no ambitious guest
> Of Sheriffes dinner, or Maiors feast.
> Nor com'st to view the better cloth of state;
> The richer hangings, or crowne-plate;
> Nor throng'st (when masquing is) to have a sight
> Of the short braverie of the night   (Lines 5-10)

is reversed in the language in which home life is contemplated. The lowing cattle and heavy-footed herds are placed in "curled woods, and painted meades" (line 17). Masquing, having been renounced, is relocated. The country backdrop is artificial, masquelike, too. If there is no court, there is, punningly, "courteous shade" (line 19), and Wroth has these more lasting pleasures than "the short braverie of the night" by a proprietary act of nomination that is inherently poetic: "he calls" the land "his,/And makes sleepe softer then it is" (lines 19-20), an act like the poet's in "To Penshurst." It is into this landscape of civilized, courtly desires that James arrives. Then the fleeting pleasures of the court become the permanent joys of the countryside, seasonal repetition replacing the short sport of an evening's entertainment. The country proves to be a better court, more lasting and permanent.

There is, admittedly, something delusive in all this, as Wroth's proprietary act and its magical sleep suggest. These pleasures cannot be owned: they are mind-made, and Wroth is enjoined finally to "thinke life, a thing but lent" (line 106). The permanence, unchangingness, and containedness of the country represents nature as a social, moral, and conceptual ideal, in short, nature as an ideological image. Wroth offers one more version of Salisbury's standing clear, for he can, securely, "Live, with un-bought provision blest" (line 14). His relation to the country presents an economy of endless appropriation without depletion; days are worn out (line 35), game is hunted beyond any need and for sheer sport (line 30), trees are sacrificed to make warming fires (lines 45–46). Yet there is no grasping here, no maintenance of privilege or place. "Freedome doth with degree dispense" (line 58), not because Wroth's world is democratic, but because Wroth has all, receiving the provision of the court and the country at once. The only evil and temptation for Wroth would be to try to hold onto what he has and to make claims upon it. Rather, he must "Strive . . . to live long innocent" (line 66), in this situation to be out of this situation. The estate represents a mirror for Wroth, an image of his own containedness and separation, an innocence that reincorporates what had been banished by taking in those pleasures without being taken in by them. Possessiveness would put an end to this life—literally, it would be an ownership of death. It would set limits upon life and treat it as a commodity. Instead, the poem celebrates an endless round of country activities in which Wroth partakes and contributes but which he cannot claim to own.

There Wroth reigns; his activity of naming is a poet's act and a royal one as well. "When the civil and literary hierarchies met in one person," Richard Helgerson comments, "as Puttenham claimed they did in Elizabeth, or Jonson in James, the Renaissance man felt a particular *O altitudo.*"[20] Heights and depths meet in this confluence, in the royal paradigm. In Jonson's eyes, James's exemplary rule illuminated the nature of society and the role of poetry. The poet's position can be exemplified by a poem written to celebrate Cecil's appointment to the position of lord treasurer (*Ep:* 64); Jonson excludes base motives from his praise—of course, by mentioning the base motives all too often seen in the world in poems to those with power, he includes them in his poem; he commends "so wise a king/ [who] Contends t'have worth enioy, from his regard,/As her owne conscience, still, the same reward" (lines 12-14). The king's action, in advancing Cecil, externalizes and enacts an internal and unchanging truth of conscience. He is the poet's model, advancing Cecil's name (line 16). Yet, as the poem concludes, this no isolated act. Advancing Cecil demonstrates "the greater fortunes of our state" (line 18); "our" here includes the poet as well, for he, too, raises Cecil. Poets and kings alone are not born everyday. And the true poet, like the historian Jonson praises elsewhere, must "speake of the intents,/The councells, actions, orders, and events/Of state, and censure them" (*Ep:* 95, lines 31-33).

The poet's speech constitutes the truth of society. His words are not simply the founding stones of civility; they maintain the state. Poets mirror kings in their universal learning, Jonson affirms in *Discoveries;* the advancement of learning maintains rule, and by "the consent of the Learned" (*Dis:* p. 622), custom is established, "*Custome* . . . the most certaine Mistresse of Language." Not an ideologue like Donne, Jonson is nonetheless a representative voice—perhaps the representative voice—of Jacobean culture, creating its language and being created by it, the voice that most fully reproduces his society. As he affirms in *Discoveries,* speech "is the Instrument of *Society*" (p. 621). Instrumentality, unlike Donne's submission, points to the nature of Jonson's engagement and activity in society, produced and reproduced in his language.

WITH Shakespeare, instrumentality, or, as Stephen Greenblatt calls it, improvisation, is everything.[21] Shakespeare's relation to his culture remains difficult to summarize, not because he is apart from it, but because he assumes no fixed relationship to it. This has often made it possible to act as if Shakespeare was some timeless figure, a man for all times and yet of none. This is, palpably, erroneous. Yet, opposing attempts, for instance E.M.W. Tillyard's,[22] to moor his political and historical attitudes in a morass of Elizabethan commonplaces, have foundered. As Greenblatt says, it seems untrue to characterize Shakespeare as a Tudor propagandist, but equally unconvincing to speak of him as a Marlovian rebel; it is false, too, to locate him (with Jonson) on some *via media.* The space of Shakespearean representation is, Greenblatt concludes, radically unstable, a place of improvisation where all the beliefs of the culture are trotted out, tried on, but where none is ultimately adopted. This is not Keatsian negative capability exactly; rather, Shakespeare occupies a thoroughly theatrical space. But, we must add, his theatrical space is inscribed in a cultural theater. James, we need hardly recall, viewed himself as an exemplary performer onstage. Shakespearean improvi-

230

sation partakes of the royal mode; it achieves the show of transparency, the heart of inscrutability, to which the king's double language aspired.

Unlike Jonson or Donne, Shakespeare appears to have had no firsthand dealings with the king. Yet their paths crossed significantly. When James came to the throne, his first act in the literary realm was to take the theaters under his patronage. Shakespeare's company, as we all know, became the King's Men. As part of his entertainment, James demanded court performances of plays; the King's Men were favored, and many plays by their leading playwright were performed at court. This is about as far as one can faithfully state the relationship between Shakespeare and the king. Many critics have gone further and have supposed that royal patronage circumscribed the subject matter and attitudes expressed in plays, or involved commissioning plays for court performance. This does not seem to have been the case. Plays performed by the King's Men, like *Sejanus,* could be suspected of sedition and atheism. Plays performed at court were always drawn from the public repertory, and there is no example of a play written for court. Even the plays chosen for court performance need not have been overtly adulatory or even topically suitable, *Othello,* for instance, being one play chosen for the marriage celebrations of Princess Elizabeth, nor were the companies performing always in good standing with the court. To take one example, Marston's *The Dutch Courtesan,* performed several times before the king, derives some of its humor from dialects, and the Scots—and thus James and his favorites—are not immune.[23] Cocledemoy, the witty knave and parodist, determining that he "must dissemble, must disguise" takes first the identity of "a Northerne Barbar" (2:1, lines 205-7) named Andrew Sharke (2:2, line 3). The name combines the patron saint of Scotland with Scottish rapacity. Yet, presumably, the play pleased the king for much the same reasons that Jonson's antimasques succeeded. James countenanced what he would not have tolerated behind his back.

In the canon of Shakespeare's works, one play that has induced frequent speculation about the relationship of playwright and king is *Measure for Measure.*[24] We have been assured that it was written for court performance in 1604 (it seems clear that it was performed before the king on Christmas that year), or, at the very least, that the text we have is one revised for that performance.[25] And we have been told that the Duke mouths James's opinions and apes his actions. These claims are as easily answered: no plays were written for court performance; we know too little about the status of Shake-

231

speare's texts to be able to determine that the one we have is a court revision; the opinions that the Duke and James share can be found readily in many political treatises of the time; much as some of the Duke's acts may recall James's, more do not—for instance, his crucial disguise as a monk has no literal counterpart in James's career. Yet criticism is no doubt correct in feeling that *Measure for Measure* has some special relationship to the king. In the pages that follow, that relationship, and with it, Shakespeare's relationship to his culture, are explored through the crucial notion that links theater and culture in James's time: representation. Perhaps one hardly need say more than this, that *Measure for Measure* is a play about substitution, re-placement—and thus, re-presentation.[26] In it, the power of theater bears a royal stamp. Hence, it is not surprising to find Josephine Waters Bennett spinning out this fantasy about the play:

> If the author himself acted the part of the Duke, then there could be no suggestion that the Duke was, or represented, King James. He *is* Shakespeare, acting a play which exemplifies what King James had written about kingcraft (that is, he is the King's puppet), and, in the last act, producing a play he has created (as the Duke) to resolve all difficulties and make everything come out right in the end. Shakespeare as actor and playwright is the "God on earth" of his play, manipulating the other characters like puppets, and creating Lucio, the puppet who talks back to his creator. He is the God-Ruler in his world of make-believe, as King James thought himself to be in the real world.[27]

Se non è vero (and there is not a shred of evidence for any of the suppositions here) *è ben trovato*.

Not even the vagaries of stage tradition support Bennett's sup-position that Shakespeare took the Duke's part. Yet her literalistic fantasy is based on an inchoate insight. The Duke plays two roles that overlap: as a monarch he has powers so extensive that Angelo can say that "your grace, like power divine,/Hath looked upon my passes" (5:1, lines 365-66)—like James he rules by Divine Right. Hence, he is also responsible for Angelo's "passes" as well as those of other characters in the play. He authorizes and authors their actions, and Angelo's career, in the seat of government and in bed with Mariana, is entirely scripted by the Duke. In the Duke, Shakespeare has written a role that represents his powers as playwright as coinci-dent with the powers of the sovereign. This is more than the ana-logical statement that dramatist and king rule their realms, for the

Duke reigns in both; dramatist and monarch represent each other, a doubleness housed in his single person. In her study of *Measure for Measure,* Bennett wavers in identifying the Duke with James; without realizing why, she is nonetheless correct; the play of representation does not invite exact identification. The Duke plays his part in two costumes, as ruler and as friar. [28] He is split, and he casts the characters into doubling, substitutive roles as well. In these re-presentational procedures, the play offers an image of its relation to sovereign power.

The play opens in a manner that characterizes its proceedings throughout. The Duke starts a disquisition on the nature of rule, "Of government the properties to unfold" (1:1, line 3), but gets no further than this opening clause. Instead of words, the Duke points to Escalus, to whom he speaks, as the embodiment of the words about government he would have spoken. Although the dramatic procedure is not absolutely clear, its representational force is: as exemplar, Escalus doubles and embodies the Duke's learning and knowledge of government, and the Duke has "unfolded" himself in Escalus. Since Escalus embodies the words, an audience might presume that the Duke is resigning his powers to him, since his "commission" (line 13) embraces "our city's institutions, and the terms/ For common justice" (lines 10-11). This supposition proves false immediately. Instead, the reins of power are handed to Angelo. The Duke thus puts two commissioners in his place as his representatives. Escalus seconds the Duke's choice of Angelo, but Angelo does not. The doubling thus produces division, too. "Let there be some more test made of my mettle/Before so noble and so great a figure/Be stamped upon it" (lines 48-50), Angelo asks. "No more evasion" is the Duke's evasive reply.

The Duke has "unfolded" himself in Angelo, who wishes, like the Duke, to refuse to play his part. Yet we cannot know how far Angelo represents the Duke, for we do not know why the Duke has chosen Angelo, or even if he knows why. When, later, it seems that Angelo's refusal to play his part stems from an incipient awareness of his unworthiness to administer a law he himself would violate, we do not know whether this is the Duke's case as well, although Lucio suggests that it is. Lucio exists to suggest that such analogies are identities and that the "Duke of dark corners" (4:3, lines 154-55) "had some feeling of the sport" (3:2, line 112). "The Duke yet would have dark deeds darkly answered" (3:2, lines 165-66). Yet there is no reason to believe Lucio. What we can know is that the exercise of sovereign power and dramatic power as the play opens depends upon the enactment of substitutions whose analogical force remains mysterious. "Do you call, sir, your occupation a mystery?" (4:2, line 30), Pompey the bawd turned executioner asks the hangman Abhorson, whose name at least suggests that he is an alter ego. His avowal of the mystery of his occupation echoes in a play where "though you change your place, you need not change your trade" (1:2, lines 104-5), as Pompey counsels Mistress Overdone, Madam Mitigation as he also calls her. The same places are forever reoccupied. Hence the whorehouse becomes a prison, a bawd an executioner, men's heads pay for maidenheads. Substitution is the law of the play and inherent in justice, the law of society as well. The "mystery" in these multiple replacements and substitutions centers on the Duke, sovereign in both realms.

"What figure of us think you he will bear" (1:1, line 16), the Duke asks Escalus about Angelo, a central question throughout the play. How does Angelo represent the Duke and how far does such representation go? Angelo's pun on *mettle* in the first scene suggests that he is a coin stamped with the Duke's figure. Sovereign power, real and stamped, sustains the exchange system of society, the endless refiguration of the king in representative acts of substitution. At the end of *Measure for Measure,* the Duke replays the opening scene anew, departing and reinvesting himself in Angelo and Escalus. "The Duke's in us" (5:1, line 293), Escalus says. Interior inhabitation there matches Angelo's condition; the Duke has "lent him our terror, dressed him with our love" (1:1, line 19). Similarly, the absent Duke dons a friar's habit and is dressed with love. Thus, the Duke's language of figuration, supplementation ("Elected him our absence to supply" [line 18]), and investiture for his deputy predicts his own form in the play that follows. Angelo may well be called the Duke's "motion generative" (3:2, line 104), his puppet. The substitute occupies the seat of power. But if "the body politic be/A horse whereon the governor doth ride" (1:2, lines 154-55), then public rule has private—and sexual—implications. The law of Vienna connects these two spheres, enforcing the fact that the private sphere is realized in public. The properties of government unfolded from the opening line of the play onward continually catch individual desire within the web of the body politic. This is "the state, whereon [Angelo] . . . studied" (2:4, line 7).[29]

Thus the substitutions within the play are not exactly duplicative, but a series of analogies in which differences are crucial though unfathomable. Hence, at the end of the play, Angelo is in Claudio's position, having repeated his crime (so, too, have Lucio and Elbow, both virgin violators), and the Duke appears to be in Angelo's place, offering redemption to Isabella in exchange for sexual favors. Yet Angelo's crime seems monstrous whereas Claudio's seemed no crime at all, and the Duke's wooing of Isabella, even though he offers marriage, seems at least as much an assault upon her integrity as Angelo's proposition.

The final unsettling refigurations of *Measure for Measure* return the play to its initial premise, the unfolding of individual and communal government, and provide a mirror for the cultural situation of the play. No exact replay of James at all, the play yet manages to catch at central concerns: in the disguised Duke, the king's divided self; in the relations between privacy and the public, the play between internal and external theaters of conscience; in the Duke's actions, the combination of absence and presence through which James claimed authority. More specifically, commentators have felt that the Duke's initial decision to sneak away from Vienna reflects upon James and his aversion to crowds.

> I'll privily away; I love the people,
> But do not like to stage me to their eyes;
> Though it do well, I do not relish well
> Their loud applause and aves vehement,
> Nor do I think the man of safe discretion
> That does affect it.   (1:1, lines 67–72)

What genuinely seems to reflect James's government in this decision is the function of the Duke's retirement. Although, like James, the Duke could be accused (and is, by Lucio) of having little interest in running the government, delegating all responsibility to others, he does not retire to country pleasures; rather, he rules in absence, through others and in disguise. His presence-in-absence figures a mode of power. James claimed it; Tiberius exemplifies it. Power-in-absence is the central stance of absolutism necessary to maintain prerogatives and the secrets of state. The complexity of the relationship of *Measure for Measure* to this absolutist mode, and to its cultural situation, lies in the fact that the Duke, who professes complete power and control, is not in fact all-powerful. Lucio's accusations have force; the Duke's plots cause us discomfort and strain our credulity, too. Yet the Duke even asserts control over what he cannot control. His withdrawal figures his inability and his disinclination to enact his powers; yet his power lies in withdrawing.

The two Dukes—absolute and absent—meet in act 5 when the two Dukes of the play—Vincentio and Friar Lodowick—confront each other. The Duke, having returned, disappears once again to return disguised anew. He faces his delegates, Escalus and Angelo, dispensing the Duke's justice ("The Duke's in us" [5:1, line 293]). They unfold him. Responding to their attempt to send him to prison—the place where virtually everyone in the play arrives so that it reconstitutes the world and erases the margin between the world outside the prison walls and that within—he protests that the Duke has no power over him:

> The Duke
> Dare no more stretch this finger of mine than he
> Dare rack his own: his subject am I not,
> Nor here provincial. My business in this state
> Made me a looker-on here in Vienna.   (5:1, lines 311–15)

The Duke's double entendres stem from a doubleness that runs throughout the play (notably present in Angelo's second scene with Isabella where his *sense* fails to meet hers).[30] Self-referentiality is self-divisive: "His subject am I not." More crucially, these double entendres point to the nature of the absolutist ruler—"nor here provincial"—his separateness from the state he rules. Only he is not subject in such a state, and it is his special status—his aloneness, the fact that he is *sui generis*—that makes him no "provincial" even at home, and always a "looker-on," observing, a divine status. The Duke assumes this stance repeatedly, as did James, modeling himself on God in his lieutenancy, standing in place of God. The Duke represents James's Divine Right claims; as a divine—a friar—he claims the right not to be subject to the Duke.

From this stance, the Duke enacts his power, dispensing grace. The return of "royal grace" (5:1, line 3) in the final act recasts the Duke's divine actions throughout; but the point about grace is made best by Lucio: "Grace is grace, despite of all controversy: as, for example, thou thyself art a wicked villain, despite of all grace" (1:2, lines 24–26). As he explains, grace is and is not grace. The wit of Lucio's statement lies in the way a tautology and identification ("grace is grace") becomes exclusionary and self-divisive. That which refers to itself cannot be contained. This explains the Duke's inexplicable behavior. Grace is grace despite the law; it lies beyond the boundaries. Just as Pompey can rename Mistress Overdone and call her Madame Mitigation, so bawdry—the Duke's bed trick, for instance—becomes grace in this play. In the exchanges that lead up to Lucio's definition of grace, this situation is epitomized by the pirate who stole the commandment "thou shalt not steal" and thus re-

236

mained pious, breaking no commandment, yet remained a pirate, too. These equivocations are suspended in the figure of the Duke and in his various deputies in the play—in Angelo, of course, and even in Elbow, the elbow of the law if not its right hand.

> *El.* Bless you, good father friar.
>
> *Du.* And you, good brother father. What offense hath this man made you, sir?
>
> *El.* Marry, sir, he hath offended the law; and sir, we take him to be a thief too, sir.   (3:2, lines 10–14)

The Duke's parodic greeting scores a reflective point, as does Elbow's bumbling doubling of Pompey's offenses—for in the play one could offend the law and yet be innocent. The Duke does—and his extension of grace makes it true for Angelo as well as Claudio. They are measured by his own measure. The pirate's loophole is extended to them, in the form of Ragozin the pirate's head. Even Barnardine, who resists the Duke's attempts to manipulate the plot through representative, substitutive acts, is also reprieved at the end. Nothing and nobody escapes the Duke's grasp. He makes the strongest opposing themes of the play, restraint and liberty, one. By a principle like the allophanic extension of Donne's poem on the Somerset wedding, all the characters reflect the Duke and become engaged in his schemes. "The doubleness of the benefit defends the deceit from reproof" (3:1, lines 250–51), the Duke-as-friar tells Isabella, recommending her lying to Angelo and Mariana's lying in her place. The benefit may be double, yet it also leads Isabella to experience the reported death of Claudio, her accusation of unchastity, and imprisonment. All this, the Duke affirms, is for her good, as is, presumably, his final grace—wooing her, and presenting—re-presenting—Claudio as a double of himself, "as like almost to Claudio as himself" (5:1, line 485). In the play, tautology is the Duke's truth, and with it all's good, all's one, reflecting him, serving his ends.

We know that we will never know his ends, that the Duke's motives, unrepresented, can never be known. We see a play of representation in which the rule of doubleness is, from the Duke's perspective, endlessly to his credit, representing multiple mirrors of his powers. Yet representation maintains, from the start, its opacity precisely because the principle of substitution opens up unfathomable differences, making it unclear whether we should read grace-as-grace or grace-despite-grace. We see this when Isabella cannot hear what Angelo says to her, and he assumes that she either is ignorant or pretending to be (2:4, lines 74–75). And we see it uproariously when

Escalus attempts to determine what was done to Elbow's wife (2:1). This, of course, will be a vital question later in the play, when it turns out that Angelo has done nothing more than sleep with his betrothed. "Do you hear how he misplaces?" (2:1, line 84), Escalus's question about Elbow's speech—the speech of a constable of the Duke's, an administrator of his justice—applies to all who are replaced in the play— from the Duke in his habit, to Angelo in his. "O place, O form,/How often dost thou with thy case, thy habit,/Wrench awe from fools, and tie the wiser souls/To thy false seeming" (2:4, lines 12-15).

The enactment of justice is always a scene of representation, putting into language what has occurred, doubling an event in words. In *Measure for Measure,* both events and words share a doubleness, and language when it is most accurate unspeaks itself. Thus, Angelo speaks "empty words" (2:4, line 2) and would have "good Angel" inscribed on the devil's horn (2:4, line 16), a duplicitous autonomy that follows from a tautology—"Blood, thou art blood" (line 15). Such is the language of things and the nature of events. Claudio's deed "with character too gross is writ on Juliet" (1:2, line 150), and Angelo tells Isabella, "I do arrest your words" (2:4, line 134), demanding that she put her body where her mouth was. Instead, she repeats herself. The play operates within language, Claudio apprehended "for a name . . . 'tis surely for a name" (1:2, lines 164, 166). He knows the double nature of "the demigod Authority": "on whom it will, it will;/On whom it will not, so: yet still 'tis just" (1:2, lines 116, 118-19). Authority speaks a language—the Duke's— in which what is and what is not remain the same, always just. The power of authority takes root in language itself, endlessly reduplicative, endlessly re-presenting. "I hope here be truths," Pompey affirms in his first dealing with the law (2:1, line 120); and this character, who has more names than any other character in the play—Thomas Tapster, bawd, caitiff, varlet, Hannibal, Pompey Bum—and whose change in "mysteries" mirrors the Duke's transformation, tells a central truth no matter how much he lies.

> *Es.* How would you live, Pompey? By being a bawd? What do
> you think of the trade, Pompey? Is it a lawful trade?
> *Po.* If the law would allow it, sir.   (2:1, lines 211-14)

The law to which Pompey refers is the law of Vienna: the law of representation. Representation includes acts of restatement and of interpretation as well as the dramatic act of renaming.

Shakespeare's Vienna is a curious locale, a landscape of Italianate vice (and with a cast of characters whose names are largely Italian)

238

with its leader, the Duke, bearing an Italian title. It is a dramatic domain as another mirror for princes suggests: "This play is the image of a murder done in Vienna. Gonzago is the duke's name; his wife, Baptista" (*Ham.* 3:2, lines 30–31).[31] The dominant trope of *Measure for Measure* is the unfolding of government, the revelation of the politicization of the body, of the single cloth that links public and private spheres. No one is free from another's construction, everyone does himself wrong "whether thou art tainted or free" (1:2, lines 40–41), for "every true man's apparel fits your thief" (4:2, line 42). All men are clothed similarly, free or restrained, innocent or criminal. All are subject to the Duke and his endless scheming and mysterious plotting. All: even the Duke; he, too, is caught within the web, part of the vice he wishes to separate himself from, and, in the last act, caught in his own dramatic manipulations. It is not merely that Lucio "makes" the Duke (5:1, lines 352, 511); his act of revelation and unmasking suggests the contained subversion that deconstructs what the Duke constructs. Lucio's claims that he "spoke . . . according to the trick" (5:1, lines 499–500) deny autonomy in his act; his lie tells a truth. For, although he pretends that his words were given him by the Duke and form part of his play, they do form part of the play, one in which he and the Duke have parts, actuating each other, operating as bound antagonists, linked as firmly as main masque and antimasque in a courtly entertainment. These are the measures of *Measure for Measure,* the principle of representation that prescribes a single law for the state and the theater. In this elusive relationship, the king, the author, and the text of the play all have a part.

Measure for Measure suggests that the essential question that links politics and literature in the Jacobean period is representation. By representing representation, Shakespeare contributes to the discourse of his society and to its most pressing questions about prerogative, power, and authority. These questions also affect him, and his meditation on the nature of rule is inevitably self-scrutinizing as well. Although neither the dramatist nor the king is onstage, the Duke in *Measure for Measure* represents them both, the clearest emblem for the relationship of literature and politics in the Jacobean period. As the careers of Jonson and Donne, and their more explicit confrontation with royal power, suggest, the dilemma of representation that Shakespeare takes as his subject is at the heart of the relationship of literature to royal power, of the words of the poet to the king's language. For Donne, words came from the king directly; for Jonson, double language provided a reflecting glass; for Shakespeare, re-presenting assured autonomy. It was his law, and the king's.

239

TAILPIECE

C HARLES I SOUGHT A PROGRAM THAT WOULD AT ONCE
summarize his father's reign and provide a justification for his
own; he thus commissioned Rubens to provide the paintings that
grace the ceilings of Inigo Jones's Banqueting House in Whitehall.
We know, thanks to D. J. Gordon and Roy Strong, what a powerful
ideological conjunction resulted: vast baroque canvases, Venetian in
layout and style, in an imposing Palladian, classical building. The
paintings themselves, topical, allegorical, and heroical, bring together
classical motifs of triumph, Christian celebrations of apotheosis,
antique Britons, Roman gods and goddesses. An Augustan and Christian peace is celebrated, and the Solomonic reign of James joins
justice, peace, unity, and plenty into an overwhelming image of
reconciliation. Nothing on the ceiling fails to have its counterpart in
James's own self-proclaimed style: the "style of gods" embraces
what the ceiling imagines. These images of rule are the ruling images
of James's reign.

If one sought a literary text that combined these elements—without, let me hasten to add, thereby having the same aim as the Whitehall paintings—*Cymbeline* might leap to mind.[1] The last word of that
play is *peace,* the result of the union of "imperial Caesar," Caesar
Augustus, with Britain's king, Cymbeline; along the way, the Italianate machinations of Iachimo and the primitivistic retreat of the
king's sons in Wales are encountered and subsumed in the figure of
Imogen, who bears the name of Brute's wife. In the play, her husband is Posthumus Leonatus, who, living beyond himself, manages
to be visited with a lasting dream and the descent of Jupiter. At the
end of the play, those who have lived beyond themselves—surpassing
their deaths, their identities as Britons, Romans, primitives, corpses,
and their identities as male or female, brothers, friends, lovers,
spouses, servants, children, or parents—meet in the king who asks,
"O, what am I?/A mother to the birth of three? Ne'er mother/Re-
joiced deliverance more" (5:5, lines 368–70). Finally, like another
loving "nourish-father" to his kingdom, he proclaims his peace:

> Laud we the gods,
> And let our crooked smokes climb to their nostrils
> From our blest altars. Publish we this peace
> To all our subjects. Set we forward; let
> A Roman and a British ensign wave
> Friendly together. So through Lud's town march,

240

And in the temple of great Jupiter
Our peace we'll ratify, seal it with feasts.
Set on there! Never was a war did cease,
Ere bloody hands were washed, with such a peace.

(5:5, lines 475–84)

NOTES

1. Authorities

1. *Calendar of State Papers Scottish,* 2:723; reprinted in Frederic Ives Carpenter, *A Reference Guide to Edmund Spenser* (Chicago: University of Chicago Press, 1923), pp. 41-42. Two years later, a reply to Spenser by Walter Quin was refused publication; see pp. 42 and 21. On the queen's sponsorship of Spenser, see p. 21. On Spenser's poetic pretensions, see Richard Helgerson, "The New Poet Presents Himself: Spenser and the Idea of a Literary Career," *PMLA* 93 (1978): 893-911.

2. All citations from *The Poetical Works of Edmund Spenser,* ed. J. C. Smith and E. De Selincourt (London: Oxford University Press, 1912).

3. Hugh Singleton's fate remains unclear; the book that got him into trouble was John Stubbs, *The discoverie of a gaping gulf.* Stubbs lost his hand for this anti-Alençon treatise; his speech before dismemberment is in John Harington, *Nugae Antiquae,* ed. Henry Harington and Thomas Park, 2 vols. (London: J. Wright, 1804), 1:154 ff.

4. Spenser's imagined punishment of Bonfont is not more savage than actual punishments. These are often presented in excruciating detail, e.g., by James Howell in his *Epistolae Ho-Elianae. The Familiar Letters,* ed. Joseph Jacobs, 2 vols. (London: David Nutt, 1892), 1:48 (Book 1:18), a description of the dismemberment of Ravillac, the murderer of Henry IV, who was drawn and boiled in oil; or 1:52 (Book 1:19), a description of the torture, after death, of the body of the Duke d'Ancre, which was dragged through the streets of Paris; "They then sclic'd off his Ears, and nail'd them upon the Gates of the City; they cut off his Genitories (and they say he was hung like an Ass) and sent them for a Present to the Duke of *Main;* the rest of his Body they carry'd to the New-bridge, and hung him his Heels upwards and Head downwards upon a new Gibbet, that had been set up a little before, to punish them who should speak ill of the present government."

On punishment, see Michel Foucault, *Discipline and Punishment,* trans. Alan Sheridan (1975; New York: Vintage Books, 1979): "The body of the condemned man became the king's property, on which the sovereign left his mark and brought down the effects of his power" (p. 109).

On violence in Spenser and its paradoxical relations to power—political and poetic—see Stephen Greenblatt, *Renaissance Self-Fashioning: From More to Shakespeare* (Chicago: University of Chicago Press, 1980), pp. 157-92, esp. pp. 187-88, on "regenerative violence," a concept akin to the contained subversion discussed by Greenblatt in "Invisible Bullets: Renaissance Authority and Its Subversion," *Glyph 8: Johns Hopkins Textual Studies* (Baltimore: Johns Hopkins University Press, 1981), pp. 40-61. Greenblatt's work informs the present inquiry.

5. *The Prophetic Moment* (Chicago: University of Chicago Press, 1971), p. 237. I am deeply indebted to Fletcher's analysis of book V; some of the matters discussed here are also treated, from a somewhat different angle, in my *Endlesse Worke: Spenser and the Structures of Discourse* (Baltimore: Johns Hopkins University Press, 1981), pp. 166-68.

6. Sir John Harington expresses this contradiction wittily: "Treason

dothe never prosper;—What's the reason?/Why;—if it prosper, none dare call it Treason" (*Nugae Antiquae,* 1:385). A particularly curious example of sovereign contradiction can be found in a letter of James to Northampton (BL, Cot. Titus C.vi, fol. 178). The letter begins by praising Northampton's service, but then turns to attack his "greate hipocrisie" (about the union of England and Scotland) and his "often crewall & malicious speachis against babie charles, & his honest father." The close of the letter fails to resolve its two impulses, "so praying you to beleeve the contraire, ather the first or last pairte of this lettir."

7. *The Political Works of James I,* ed. Charles H. McIlwain (Cambridge, Mass: Harvard University Press, 1918), p. 326. He repeats the point on page 327. On the trope of Jove's judgment seat, see Jane Aptekar, *Icons of Justice* (New York: Columbia University Press, 1969), pp. 13 ff. As the proem to book V makes clear, to sit in this divine seat is to occupy the "state of present time" (pro. 1.1), a present without a future or past, an unchanging state.

8. *Power/Knowledge,* ed. Colin Gordon (New York: Pantheon Books, 1980), pp. 93-94. Foucault argues that the sovereign's right has been clothed in legalism, particularly once Roman law was revived in the Middle Ages; law defines the legitimate rights of the sovereign and the obligations of subjects. As Foucault goes on to argue (see p. 103), this discourse is a shared language, and revolutionaries still cling to it, even when the king is deposed or decapitated. The discourse of law affirms a universal level outside of the individual participant. Yet it also disguises power.

9. The tendency of criticism to read Spenser as a Christian humanist has blinded readers to the Machiavellianism of book V; the terms of the poem are those of the *Prince:* force and fraud (equity turns out to be a version of guile), fortune, and the like. Further, the poem is Machiavellian in another sense: it exposes the reality of power that lurks beneath the justification of it in such myths as chivalric rescue, the dispensation of mercy, the enactment of equity. Rescue—of Irena, for instance—is imposition (English peace forced upon Ireland); Mercilla's mercy does not save Duessa; Britomart's vision of equity does not save her from submission to bestial sexuality or to her effacement before Arthegall. Throughout book V, what is said and what is done are two different things, and the exposure of this gap makes the poem a piece of Machiavellian discourse.

10. State derives from *stare* (Latin), to stand or stay. In a poem attributed to Henry VI, a pun makes this etymological point: "State ys devoyd of staie" (Harington, *Nugae Antiquae,* 1:386). A similar connection is made in Shakespeare's *Henry VIII:* "We should take root here where we sit,/Or sit state-statues only," Wolsey says (1:2, lines 87-88), ed. F. David Hoeniger (Baltimore: Penguin, 1969). In book V, Arthegallian imposition often involves staying others, or opening a way for himself that involves the removal of the hindrances of others intent upon imposing impediments (this is enacted with Pollente in canto ii; his name conveniently combines head and power and insemination).

11. *A View of the Present State of Ireland,* ed. W. L. Renwick (Oxford: At the Clarendon Press, 1970). Page references are to this edition. There is a remarkable congruence between Spenser's treatise and book V that extends to the language, making it clear that, for instance, the imagery of planting and of decapitation that runs through book V is political. Reformation in *A View* always is spoken of in terms of "cutting off" (see, e.g., pp. 9, 14, 17, 75, 90), a necessary event before "planting" (i.e., of colonies). Heads in book V are heads

of state, crowns—or heads to be polled, or put on poles. For a cogent analysis of *A View*, see Greenblatt, *Renaissance Self-Fashioning*, pp. 184–88.

12. In a 1603 letter to Sir John Harington, Sir Robert Cecil characterized the queen as "more than a man, and (in troth) sometyme less than a woman" (*Nugae Antiquae*, 1:345).

13. Fulke Greville (?; the work has also been assigned to Arthur Wilson), *The Five Yeares of King James* (London, 1643), p. 2.

14. A wonderful anecdote that may be true reveals Spenser's knowledge of the strategy of power; it occurs in Lodowick Bryskett's *A Discourse of Civill Life*, ed. Thomas E. Wright (Northridge, Calif.: San Fernando Valley State College, 1970), p. 22. Spenser has just been asked to discuss the virtues needed to live a good life; he gets out of the request by referring his fellow dialogists to read *The Faerie Queene*, which, he says, covers the same ground. At the end of the treatise, Bryskett says his is a book that should have been written by Spenser; he has been, he "will not say" (yet does) "betrayed" or, at least "cunningly thrust in" (p. 205). The book is indeed Spenserian; it represents itself as a translation of another's words; it praises Lord Grey for having "plowed and harrowed through ground" (p. 118); and Bryskett is aware from the first that what he writes has already been written, so that he "write[s] thereof againe" (p. 2); yet his repetition constantly finds out differences. From retirement he writes of civil life—and attempts to turn retreat into public life; he writes of how a gentleman must live, yet his work is constantly on the verge of being an education-of-princes treatise. Public and private, subject and sovereign, are joined in this text, which repeats the unwritten poem of Spenser that it replaces.

15. Bodl. Ms. Ash. 836, fol. 277. For James's relationship to his mother, see Antonia Fraser, *Mary Queen of Scots* (London: Weidenfeld & Nicolson, 1969), pp. 455 ff. James's final acts on Mary's behalf are detailed on pp. 552 ff. For James's actions in the final years of his mother's life, see Robert S. Rait and Annie I. Cameron, *King James's Secret* (London: Nisbet & Co., 1927); the secret of the title is that despite James's official protestations, he sacrificed Mary for the English crown. Letters between James and Elizabeth appear on pp. 98–99, 179–82, and 188–210 passim. Even in his official threats, Rait and Cameron argue, James never suggested breaking league with England (p. 116), and in a letter of 26 January 1587 he let the queen know that "though he would deeply resent his mother's execution, he was not prepared to take offensive action to avenge it" (p. 178). To Leicester, he was more open, writing "how fonde and inconstant I were if I shulde preferre my mother to the title" (p. 102). For a summary treatment of James's relation to his mother, see the standard biography by David Harris Willson, *King James VI and I* (New York: Oxford University Press, 1956), pp. 52, 54 ff., 73 ff., 79.

16. Cited from *Letters of Queen Elizabeth and King James VI of Scotland*, ed. John Bruce (London: Camden Society, 1849), p. 15. Letters in the months following this one tend to be addressed to "madame and mother"; Elizabeth did not fully subscribe to this mode; she called James brother and cousin—brother monarch and cousin by blood. By the time of the Armada threat, James was on such good terms with Elizabeth as to offer her aid "as zour [sic] natural sone [sic] and conpatriot" (see Rait and Cameron, *King James's Secret*, p. 207).

17. *Letters*, p. 41 for Elizabeth's letter; p. 45 for James's. The exchange can also be followed in *King James's Secret*, pp. 194–202.

18. That these meet in her death Samuel Y. Edgerton, Jr., reveals in "*Maniera* and the *Mannaia:* Decorum and Decapitation in the Sixteenth Century," pp. 67-103 in *The Meaning of Mannerism,* ed. Franklin W. Robinson and Stephen G. Nichols, Jr. (Hanover, N.H.: University Press of New England, 1972). Mary's scaffold was an altar, her block a communion table, the rail a chancel rail, her robes those of a martyr (p. 80), and such costuming and staging, Edgerton argues, reflect pictures of martyrdom, including Christ's crucifixion, which were regularly shown to criminals. Further, beheading was regarded as an aristocratic, noble death, a saint's death (p. 87).

19. Jonson's poems are cited from vol. 8 of *Ben Jonson,* ed. C. H. Herford and Percy and Evelyn Simpson, 11 vols. (Oxford: At the Clarendon Press, 1925-52).

20. James's poems are available in *The Poems of James VI of Scotland,* ed. James Craigie, 2 vols. (Edinburgh and London: William Blackwood & Sons, 1955, 1958). The first volume contains the printed poems, the second those in manuscript. All references are to this edition; volume, page, poem, and line numbers cited as needed.

For some positive evaluations of James's literary efforts, see G.P.V. Akrigg, "The Literary Achievement of King James I," *University of Toronto Quarterly* 44 (1975): 115-29, and C. J. Sisson, "King James the First of England as Poet and Political Writer," pp. 47-63 in *Seventeenth Century Studies Presented to Sir Herbert Grierson* (Oxford: At the Clarendon Press, 1938). Akrigg wishes to judge James's literary merits without considering his politics, and generally praises James for vividness, pungency, and the like. He concludes by suggesting that language was so important to James that he counted on it too much in trying to handle Parliament or foreign powers (p. 128). Sisson defends James's mind as well as his art. Willson treats James's poetry in chapter 4 of his biography.

21. Citations from the nonpoetic works are drawn from *The Political Works of James I.* Page references appear in the text.

22. Harington, *Nugae Antiquae,* 1:395.

23. James's rewriting of the most authoritative text in his culture to make it conform to his principles is matched by the heretical reading of scripture that Carlo Ginzburg describes in *The Cheese and the Worms,* trans. John and Anne Tedeschi (Baltimore: Johns Hopkins University Press, 1980). Ginzburg notes "the connection that has always indissolubly bound writing and power" (p. 59) and finds a source for it in the heretic Menocchio's "aggressive originality of . . . reading" (p. 33). What is noteworthy is that Menocchio could find his heresies in the Bible and similar books. No text has a stable or single meaning; Menocchio's "misreadings" are capable of being so labeled only because they fly in the face of orthodoxy, of prescribed modes of reading. Not surprisingly, the vernacular Bible was on the index—because it was readable by those most likely to "misread" it.

24. For the context of this belief, see Christopher Hill, "The Norman Yoke," pp. 50-122 in *Puritanism and Revolution* (New York: Schocken Books, 1958).

25. Cited in *James I by His Contemporaries,* ed. Robert Ashton (London: Hutchinson, 1969), p. 1.

26. All citations of *A Counterblast* are from James's *Workes* (London, 1616).

27. *Letters of Queen Elizabeth and King James*, p. 106.

28. Harington, *Nugae Antiquae*, 1: 395.

29. Greenblatt, *Renaissance Self-Fashioning*, pp. 168-69.

30. Harington, *Nugae Antiquae*, 1: 354 ff. Page references appear in the text.

31. In several essays on Elizabethan literature and society, Louis Adrian Montrose has written about the nexus of courting and courtship; see, for example, "Celebration and Insinuation: Sir Philip Sidney and the Motives of Elizabethan Courtship," *Renaissance Drama*, n.s. 8 (1977): 3-35; "'Eliza, Queene of shepheardes,' and the Pastoral of Power," *English Literary Renaissance* 10 (1980): 153-82.

32. *The Progresses and Public Processions of Queen Elizabeth*, ed. John Nichols, 3 vols. (London: John Nichols, 1823), 1:38. The phrase cited below appears on the following page.

33. Clifford Geertz, "Centers, Kings, and Charisma: Reflections on the Symbolics of Power," in *Culture and Its Creators: Essays in Honor of Edward Shils*, ed. Joseph Ben-David and Terry Clark (Chicago: University of Chicago Press, 1977), p. 160; David M. Bergeron, *English Civic Pageantry, 1558-1642* (Columbia: University of South Carolina Press, 1971), p. 15. Bergeron sees Elizabeth's entrance as the kind of drama presented by medieval theater; he finds James's 1604 entrance "more dramatic" (p. 66), although James's role, he admits, is "more passive" (p. 75). The entrances are further compared on pp. 88-89. The entrance is also recounted by Graham Parry in *The Golden Age restor'd: The culture of the Stuart Court, 1603-42* (New York: St. Martin's Press, 1981), pp. 1-21. Parry stresses the classical iconography of the spectacle.

Bergeron's recent research appears in "Elizabeth's Coronation Entry (1559): New Manuscript Evidence," *English Literary Renaissance* 8 (1978): 3-8.

34. Summaries of the pageants and explanations of their connections are offered at the last two shows, at Little Conduit (see Nichols, *Progresses of Elizabeth*, 1:51) and Fleet Street (1:56). The queen's progress matches the progress of the pageants as they display their interconnected and supportive meanings about the nature of good rule, all summed up in the queen's response, "Be ye well assured I will stande your good Quene" (1:57). The passage cited below appears in 1:39.

35. *Spectacle, Pageantry, and Early Tudor Policy* (Oxford: At the Clarendon Press, 1969), pp. 354, 358. Anglo also regards the pageant as somewhat contractual (e.g., "Advice was . . . being given; or, rather a plea was being made" [p. 352]).

36. Contemporaries drew many comparisons between Elizabeth and James. Early in his reign, they tend to tip in the king's favor; Sir Roger Wilbraham in 1603, for instance, praises both monarchs, but finds Elizabeth less forthright and more ceremonious (see Ashton, ed., *James I by His Contemporaries*, pp. 6-7); Arthur Wilson, however, takes James to task for his scorn of the populace in his entrance (see Ashton, p. 64). Harington finds James's court degenerate compared to Elizabeth's (*Nugae Antiquae*, 1:352-53). The king's prodigality, at first the subject of rejoicing, especially in comparison to Elizabeth's tight-fistedness,

soon became the object of invidious comparisons, as did his progresses to the countryside that tended to deplete forests of game and houses of their resources.

37. Dekker's account appears in *The Progresses, Processions, and Magnificent Festivities of King James the First*, ed. John Nichols, 4 vols. (London: J. B. Nichols, 1828), 1:337 ff. Citations appear in the text.

38. Geertz, "Centers, Kings, and Charisma," p. 160.

39. *Negara: The Theatre State in Nineteenth-Century Bali* (Princeton: Princeton University Press, 1980). Page references appear in the text.

40. This contrast is drawn by Bergeron, *English Civic Pageantry*, pp. 75, 88.

41. On the arch as an element of classical style, see John Summerson, *The Classical Language of Architecture* (Cambridge, Mass: MIT Press, 1963), p. 15 and passim. Summerson stresses the importance of the five orders, and the Old Schools Tower discussed below functions as a kind of textbook example of classical style; it presents what might well be an illustration of the orders in an architectural text (e.g., Serlio), rather than a genuine classical usage of the orders. It is important to remember, however, that classicism, especially in England, was in the Renaissance always something of a hybrid. D. J. Gordon's essay on *Hero and Leander*, "The Renaissance Poet as Classicist," in *The Renaissance Imagination*, ed. Stephen Orgel (Berkeley and Los Angeles: University of California Press, 1975), makes this point admirably. The connection between classicism and absolutism is stressed in James S. Ackerman, *Palladio* (Baltimore: Penguin, 1966), pp. 75 ff., and by Parry, *Golden Age*, pp. 20, 51.

42. Andrew Martindale, *The Triumphs of Caesar by Andrea Mantegna* (London: Henry Miller, 1979), pp. 32, 68. It is of course important that Mantegna's panels, now in Windsor Castle, entered the collection of Charles I in 1629-30. The style of gods that James claimed continued into the Caroline period. The taste for antiquities is best shown in the collection of the Earl of Arundel. Arundel traveled on the Continent with Inigo Jones in 1612, and it was then that he began the first important collection of antiquities and European art. See D.E.L. Haynes, *The Arundel Marbles* (Oxford: Ashmolean Museum, 1975), for further details, as well as William Gaunt, *Court Painting in England* (London: Constable, 1980), pp. 65 ff., and Parry, *Golden Age*, chap. 5. As Kevin Sharpe argues in *Sir Robert Cotton, 1586-1631: History and Politics in Early Modern England* (Oxford: Oxford University Press, 1979), Arundel's attachment to Romanitas bears a political meaning (see pp. 243-44), and Roman values were central to Cotton and his circle (which included Jonson, Camden, and the Society of Antiquaries).

One further classical revival that James may have instigated is argued by Frank Livingstone Huntley in *Essays in Persuasion* (Chicago: University of Chicago Press, 1981), the revival of classical "characters" as a genre; see "King James as Solomon, the Book of Proverbs, and Hall's *Characters*," esp. pp. 48 and 56.

43. *The Elements of Architecture* (1624), ed. Frederick Hard (Charlottesville: University Press of Virginia, 1968), pp. 106-7.

44. This point is emphasized by Paula Johnson in "Jacobean Ephemera and the Immortal Word," *Renaissance Drama*, n.s. 8 (1977): 151-71, esp. pp. 156-58, 167-71.

45. Citations in the text from Jonson's entertainment are drawn from vol.

7 of Herford and Simpson, *Ben Jonson,* abbreviated H&S; page, and where necessary line numbers, are cited in the text.

46. For further examples and for a discussion of the use of architectural motifs in books, see Margery Corbett and R. W. Lightbown, *The Comely Frontispiece: The Emblematic Title-page in England, 1560-1660* (London: Routledge & Kegan Paul, 1979), pp. 6-9, and the frontispieces for DuBartas, Chapman, Chyrsostom, Ralegh, Jonson, Drayton, and others. Drayton's explanatory verse describes the page as a *"Triumphant Arch"* (cited p. 154).

47. The history of the tower is hard to come by. It may have been designed by Thomas Holt, who is named as a carpenter in Bodley's project. Anthony à Wood tells a story of James visiting Oxford and being dazzled by the tower, but the story is undated and may be apocryphal. What little is known about the tower, its architect, and James's connection to the project can be found in Charles E. Mallet, *A History of the University of Oxford,* 2 vols. (New York: Longmans, Green & Co., 1924), 2:227. I am grateful to Lindsay Kaplan for tracking down the history of the tower, and to Stephen Orgel for transcribing the inscription beneath James; it reads: "Regnante D. Jacobo Regem Doctissimo / Munificentissimo Optimo Hae Musis / Extructae Moles Congesta Biblioteca / Et Quacumque Adhuc Deerant Ad Splen/dorem Academiae Feliciter Tentata/Coepta Absoluta. Soli Deo Gloria." James presented his works to both universities in 1619 (see Willson, *King James VI and I,* p. 292), and a 1620 oration of thanks can be found in Bodl. Ms. Ash. 1153, fol. 68.

On the classicism of the Banqueting House, see D. J. Gordon, "Rubens and the Whitehall Ceiling," in Orgel, ed., *The Renaissance Imagination,* and Roy Strong, *Britannia Triumphans: Inigo Jones, Rubens and Whitehall Palace* (London: Thames & Hudson, 1980). Strong notes the strong Roman elements in the ceiling, identifying one figure in Roman costume as Brute, founder of Britain (p. 28), thus linking British antiquity to classicism.

48. On the relationship of architectural fantasies to power, see Erik H. Erikson, *Young Man Luther* (New York: W. W. Norton & Co., 1962), pp. 105-10.

49. All citations from Jonson's masques are from *The Complete Masques,* ed. Stephen Orgel (New Haven: Yale University Press, 1969). Here, and throughout, I depend on Orgel's work: *The Jonsonian Masque* (Cambridge, Mass.: Harvard University Press, 1965); with Roy Strong, *Inigo Jones: The Theatre of the Stuart Court,* 2 vols. (London: Sotheby Parke Bernet and Berkeley and Los Angeles: University of California Press, 1973); *The Illusion of Power* (Berkeley and Los Angeles: University of California Press, 1975). The classicism of *Prince Henry's Barriers* and its connection to political realities are stressed in Norman Council, "Ben Jonson, Inigo Jones, and the Transformation of Tudor Chivalry," *ELH* 47 (1980): 259-75, although Council perhaps overstates his thesis that the masque repudiates a chivalric revival. A mixture of classical, contemporary, and medieval elements marks the masque and is characteristic of classicism in the English Renaissance. And in Italy, too, as Ackerman notes in *Palladio,* the architect's patrons fostered classicism and a chivalric tradition that met in the tournaments and court festivals they sponsored (p. 32). In *Britannia Triumphans,* Strong notes that the Pantheon was Jones's model for the circular temple in the *Masque of Augurs,* and that the first panel in the Whitehall ceiling has a similar

model (p. 22). On the classicizing that surrounded Prince Henry, see Parry, *Golden Age*, chap. 3, esp. pp. 68-76.

50. *Great Britains Salomon* (London, 1625), p. 36. Further citations appear in the text. It should be stressed that Solomonic justice is central to book V of *The Faerie Queene* and to the program of the Banqueting House ceiling. Indeed, the scene of Solomon and the baby stands behind one of Rubens's panels as well as canto i of book V. Strong stresses Solomonic parallels in *Britannia Triumphans*, pp. 19, 34, 59 ff. If the Banqueting House was meant to recall the Temple of Solomon, as Strong claims, it might be compared with another utopic space of James's reign, Solomon's House in Bacon's *New Atlantis*.

51. The allegorical paintings referred to are *The Horrors of War* and *War and Peace*, both now in the National Gallery, London. The central meaning of the ceiling for Gordon is that "the blessings or gifts of the divine king to his people are peace and the fruits of peace" ("Rubens and the Whitehall Ceiling," p. 35). This program suited James and Charles, as Gordon says; it is also important that Rubens and James had negotiated about the decoration of the Banqueting House, although we do not know whether the final program followed these earlier plans of 1621; see Gordon, p. 31, and Huntley, *Essays in Persuasion*, pp. 50-52. Strong believes that the Solomonic program may well have been laid out in these earlier discussions; see *Britannia Triumphans*, pp. 10, 59 ff. On James as Augustus on the ceiling, see Gordon, p. 37.

52. Petowe's Caesar is Julius, of course; Jonson undoes this reference in his entertainment. It is a far more problematic identity than Augustus.

53. On the emblem of the pillars, see Frances Yates, *Astraea: The Imperial Theme in the Sixteenth Century* (Harmondsworth: Penguin, 1975), pp. 22 ff., and pp. 54-58; see also Roy Strong, *The Cult of Elizabeth* (London: Thames & Hudson, 1977). On the use of the statue of Marcus Aurelius as a model for royal representation, and specifically for Van Dyck's portrait of Charles I on horseback, see Roy Strong, *Van Dyck: Charles I on Horseback* (London: Allen Lane, The Penguin Press, 1972).

54. Herbert A. Grueber, *Handbook of the Coins of Great Britain and Ireland in the British Museum* (London: British Museum, 1899), p. 103. In Rubens's apotheosis in Whitehall Palace, a crown of laurel awaits the king. For an early medal naming James *Caesar Caesarum* see Willson, *King James, VI and I*, p. 168.

55. All citations from *The Elegies and the Songs and Sonnets of John Donne*, ed. Helen Gardner (Oxford: At the Clarendon Press, 1965). For other uses, see John Carey, "Donne and Coins," pp. 151-63, in *English Renaissance Studies Presented to Dame Helen Gardner*, ed. John Carey (Oxford: At the Clarendon Press, 1980).

56. See "Masquing Occasions and Masque Structure," *Research Opportunities in Renaissance Drama* 24 (1981): 7-16. The paper was first presented at the MLA convention in Houston in 1980, and I am grateful to Professor Marcus for supplying me with an advance copy. On James's attachment to Roman law and his clashes with Parliament, see Willson, *King James VI and I*, pp. 257 ff.

57. Latin was used in Elizabeth's entrance, but in a wholly different manner. It was almost always translated; it signified humanistic ideals of learning, not Roman style but school style. Thus, pointedly, Elizabeth kissed the English Bible; Latin was suspect on religious grounds.

58. Wilson and Bacon are cited from Ashton, *James I by His Contemporaries*, pp. 18, 147.

59. The connection between authoritarian imposition and time is also a major idea in Richard Sennett's *Authority* (New York: Vintage Books, 1981). Authoritarian interpretation solidifies itself into a thing, a "defiance of history, a defiance of time" (p. 19); it is "deceptions about the timelessness of authority" (p. 191) that most tyrannize subjects. See also J.G.A. Pocock, *Politics, Language and Time* (New York: Atheneum, 1973), discussed in detail in "The Theater of Conscience."

2. State Secrets

1. All citations of James's prose are drawn unless otherwise noted from *The Political Works of James I*, ed. Charles H. McIlwain (Cambridge, Mass.: Harvard University Press, 1918); page numbers are provided in the text. On the reception of the *Basilikon Doron* in London, see David Harris Willson, *King James VI and I* (New York: Oxford University Press, 1956), p. 166.

For some further discussion of James's rhetoric of state secrets, see J. W. Allen, *English Political Thought, 1603-1660* (London: Methuen, 1938), pp. 4 ff.; G. L. Mosse, *The Struggle for Sovereignty in England* (New York: Octagon Books, 1968), pp. 50-53 and 71; W. H. Greenleaf, *Order, Empiricism and Politics* (London: Oxford University Press, 1964), with its emphasis that Divine Right arguments are based on analogies of order—see pp. 8-9 and, for James, pp. 59 ff. The language of mysteries continued to the end of James's reign, and in a 1621 letter to Parliament, James tells them not to "presume . . . to meddle with any thing concerning our Government, or deep matters of State" (he has in mind both the Spanish match and the law courts); in a second letter, James glosses this sentence as alluding to "mysteries of State" (John Rushworth, *Historical Collections of Private Passages of State* [London: 1721], 8 vols., 1:43, 51).

Writing to James from Spain, Prince Charles added a postscript to his joint letter with Buckingham on 17 March 1623: "I beseech your M^tie advyse as littell with your Counsell in thease businesses as you can," and James agreed, writing, on 1 April, that their secrets were safe with him (BL, Harl. Ms. 6987, fols. 33, 50).

As John Chamberlain reports, Coke ran into difficulties with the king about the Overbury scandal; he "dived farther into secrets than there was need, and so perhaps might see *nudam sine veste Dianam*," an odd way to describe Lady Somerset (*The Letters of John Chamberlain*, ed. Norman McClure, 2 vols. [Philadelphia: American Philosophical Society, 1939], 2:14). He, too, reports the Spanish negotiations as "a misterie of state beyond common capacities" (2:40).

2. Cited by Maurice Lee, Jr., *Government by Pen: Scotland under James VI and I* (Urbana: University of Illinois Press, 1980), p. vii; Lee studies the accuracy of James's claim.

3. He does continue the sentence by saying, "till you consult with the King or his Councell, or both: for they are transcendent matters." Still, this allowance does not lower the boundaries by much and, as I indicate below, shows of council often mask absolutism.

4. All citations are drawn from Ben Jonson, *The Complete Masques*, ed.

Stephen Orgel (New Haven: Yale University Press, 1969); line numbers are provided in the text.

I do not mean to suggest, of course, that *all* mysteries or that all uses of the word and its synonyms—secret, arcana—are political, nor do I mean to flatten out distinctions between political beliefs of poets and king. D. J. Gordon, for instance, reads the phrase from *Hymenaei* neoplationically in his essay "The Imagery of Ben Jonson's *Masques of Blacknesse and Beautie,*" in *The Renaissance Imagination,* ed. Stephen Orgel (Berkeley and Los Angeles: University of California Press, 1975), pp. 136, 155. Nonetheless it is important to restore the vocabulary of the Jacobean period to its historical situation, and to recognize the shared language of the age. I am encouraged to do this by some recent revisionist history: Kevin Sharpe in the introduction to *Faction and Parliament: Essays on Early Stuart History* (Oxford: At the Clarendon Press, 1978) stresses the shared "language of law, history, and religion, of order and tradition" (p. 3) that characterizes both court and parliamentary spokesmen; it is a parliamentarian who affirms that royal prerogative imitates paternalism (see pp. 15 ff.) and who writes that members of Parliament "ought not to draw the veyles that princes are pleased to sett between theyr secret ends and comon eyes" (p. 16). In *Sir Robert Cotton, 1586–1631: History and Politics in Early Modern England* (Oxford: Oxford University Press, 1979), Sharpe makes similar points, insisting that Cotton knew no party and served *both* the House of Commons and the king (pp. 160, 171, 190, for example), that he shared the king's notion that Parliament served for counsel. For Sharpe, policy and personality, not principles, caused divisions in Stuart government (see, for example, p. 223). Conrad Russell demonstrates in *Parliament and English Politics, 1621–1629* (Oxford: At the Clarendon Press, 1979) the need for historians to rethink such oppositions as court vs. country by showing the *shared* ideology of supposedly opposing groups and the factions within presumed hegemonies. The more familiar understanding of the relationship of king and Parliament and their opposition is offered in Francis D. Wormuth, *The Royal Prerogative, 1603–1649* (Ithaca: Cornell University Press, 1939); the standard treatment of the court/country opposition is Perez Zagorin's, *The Court and the Country* (New York: Atheneum, 1971).

5. "Roles and Mysteries," in *The Renaissance Imagination,* p. 18.

6. The final phrase is indebted to Stephen Orgel, *The Illusion of Power* (Berkeley and Los Angeles: University of California Press, 1975), p. 77. I am indebted to Orgel's study as well as to his earlier book, *The Jonsonian Masque* (Cambridge, Mass.: Harvard University Press, 1965), for the description of the form that follows. Graham Parry is similarly indebted in his account of the masque in chapter 2 of *The Golden Age restor'd: The culture of the Stuart Court, 1603–42* (New York: St. Martin's Press, 1981).

7. Jonson's concern to print his works and establish them as texts is brilliantly studied by Richard C. Newton in "Ben Jonson and the (Re-)Invention of the Book," in *Classic and Cavalier: Essays on Jonson and the Sons of Ben,* ed. Claude J. Summers and Ted-Larry Pebworth (Pittsburgh: University of Pittsburgh Press, 1982). I am grateful to have had the opportunity to read this essay before it appeared.

8. That Mercury was on Jonson's mind can be seen in the other masque provided for festivities in 1617, *Lovers Made Men,* the entertainment written for Lord Hay's reception of the French ambassador a month after *The Vision of De-*

light. Mercury plays a central part in the masque, leading the lovers out of Elysium. Here, as in the Argus story underlying *The Vision,* the transformation involves a passage through death. In *Lovers Made Men,* "death" is a metaphor— the lovers have been reduced to shadows by Cupid. The resolution of the masque returns them to humanity—they become men again—and to love; finally, Mercury's opposition to Cupid is overcome in witty reconciliation. The second life given the lovers is a doubling of Mercury and Cupid.

9. This meeting is rooted in the occasion of the masque, as Leah Sinanoglou Marcus describes it in "'Present Occasions' and the Shaping of Ben Jonson's Masques," *ELH* 45 (1978): 201–25, for *The Vision* celebrates the publication of James's *Workes* (p. 203): "The king is exalted as author and as center of creative political energy for the kingdom." Its pastoral movement reflects James's repeated commands to repopulate the countryside, Marcus claims (pp. 203–12). Parry, *Golden Age,* shares my emphasis; see pp. 51–52.

10. The "setting" of the king opens *Love Freed from Ignorance and Folly* (1611), *The Irish Masque at Court* (1613), *Neptune's Triumph for the Return of Albion* (1624), and *The Fortunate Isles, and Their Union* (1625). James's presence is noted at the opening of *For the Honor of Wales* (1618) in lines that replace the bellygod of *Pleasure Reconciled to Virtue.*

11. *Britannia Triumphans: Inigo Jones, Rubens and Whitehall Palace* (London: Thames & Hudson, 1980), p. 44. Strong goes on to say (p. 45) that the main source of Rubens's iconography was James's *Basilikon Doron.*

12. All citations of Donne's poems are drawn from *The Elegies and the Songs and Sonnets of John Donne,* ed. Helen Gardner (Oxford: At the Clarendon Press, 1965); line numbers are provided in the text. On Donne's preoccupation with patronage, and the inherently social nature of his literary production, see Arthur Marotti, "John Donne and the Rewards of Patronage," in *Patronage in the Renaissance,* ed. Guy F. Lytle and Stephen Orgel (Princeton: Princeton University Press, 1981). Marotti remarks of a poem like *The Canonization* that it joins the language of the court to Petrarchan courting.

13. That is the heading addressed to the reader of *Love's Triumph through Callipolis.*

14. "Haud dubium erat eam sententiam altius penetrare et arcana imperii temptari" (*Annales* II.36); the translation, *On Imperial Rome* (Harmondsworth: Penguin, 1956), p. 92. For Tacitus in the Renaissance, see Kenneth C. Schellhase, *Tacitus in Renaissance Political Thought* (Chicago: University of Chicago Press, 1976), esp. pp. 109 ff. on the adaptation of Tacitean *arcana imperii* to "reason of state" in Bodin, Machiavelli, and their followers. Schellhase notes that England was unique in the seventeenth century in its continued belief in the applicability of Tacitus to politics (p. 157), as well as James's, Bacon's, and Jonson's familiarity with Tacitus (pp. 147 ff.).

15. The contemporary is Arthur Wilson; the remark is reprinted in *James I by His Contemporaries,* ed. Robert Ashton (London: Hutchinson, 1969), p. 18. It can also be found in Rushworth, *Historical Collections,* 1:159–60. Weldon's remark appears in *The Court and Character of King James* (London, 1817), p. 32, in the context of a discussion of the king's behavior toward Somerset at the time of his disgrace.

16. *The Arte of English Poesie* (Kent, Ohio: Kent State University Press facsimile, 1970), III. xviii, pp. 196–97). The emperor is identified as Louis XI

by Gladys D. Willcock and Alice Walker in their edition of Puttenham (Cambridge: Cambridge University Press, 1936), p. 333.

17. Cited from Ralegh, *The Works*, 8 (Oxford: Oxford University Press, 1829), p. 67; a definition of state secrets appears in the *Maxims of State*: "Mysteries, or sophisms of state, are certain secret practices, either for the avoiding of danger, or averting such effects as tend not to the preservation of the present state" (p. 8), and in *The Cabinet-Council,* the Tacitean line is taken mainly in terms of preserving power (see, e.g., pp. 59–60). *The Prerogatives of Parliaments in England* voices views that revisionist historians are coming to see as central to the seventeenth-century political scene; the king's will is law (see p. 153), and king and Parliament share prerogatives; what is done in privy council "is done by the king's absolute power. . . . And by whose power is it done in parliament, but by the king's absolute power?" (p. 213). The dangers underscored in the treatise are those of false counsel, not of false power in the king.

18. All citations of verse and drama are from *Ben Jonson*, ed. C. H. Herford, Percy and Evelyn Simpson, 11 vols. (Oxford: At the Clarendon Press, 1925–52); line numbers are provided in the text.

19. Letters are cited from *Correspondence of King James VI of Scotland with Sir Robert Cecil and Others in England during the Reign of Queen Elizabeth*, ed. John Bruce (London: Camden Society, 1861).

20. Notably by Jonas A. Barish, "The Double Plot in *Volpone*," *Modern Philology* 51 (1953): 83–92. My understanding of the role of Sir Pol is also supported by Peggy Knapp in "Ben Jonson and the Publike Riot," *ELH* 46 (1979): 577–94, particularly the following remark offered in passing: "Sir Politic Would-Be is new and bad at the disguise game, but he explains the theory of it to Peregrine very well, and he links the less demonic version of it to some topical abuses of King James's reign: projecting, bribery, and buying knighthoods. As the wholly comic embodiment of the new way, and a loser at its stratagems, Would-Be diverts the horror we might feel at Volpone's success to laughter at Sir Politic's would-be success" (p. 583).

21. The equations of food and word are central to Jonson, as Don K. Hedrick argues in "Cooking for the Anthropopagi: Jonson and His Audience," *Studies in English Literature* 17 (1977): 233–45, and form one side of the Ben Jonson presented by Arthur F. Marotti in "All About Jonson's Poetry," *ELH* 39 (1972): 208–37, esp. pp. 214–19. They are vital to the economy of *Neptune's Triumph* and help to explain the identifications between the Poet and Cook there.

22. Venice's role in republican thought is detailed in William J. Bouwsma, *Venice and the Defense of Republican Liberty* (Berkeley and Los Angeles: University of California Press, 1968). Its value for English thought, especially in the mid-seventeenth century, is discussed by Bouwsma in "Venice and the Political Education of Europe," pp. 445–66 in *Renaissance Venice*, ed. J. R. Hale (Totowa, N.J.: Rowman & Littlefield, 1973); by Zera S. Fink, *The Classical Republicans* (Evanston: Northwestern University Press, 1945), esp. pp. 28 ff., who stresses that Venice was a countercurrent to Italianate vice in English minds (see p. 44); by J.G.A. Pocock, *The Machiavellian Moment: Florentine Political Thought and the Atlantic Republican Tradition* (Princeton: Princeton University Press, 1975), which has a long chapter on the myth of Venice (pp. 272 ff.) and the importation of civic humanism into England. Harington is the

fulfillment of the Venetian legacy to England: "He that understands *Venice* right, shall go nearest to judge (not withstanding the difference that is in every Policy) right of any Government in the World" (cited in Greenleaf, *Order, Empiricism and Politics,* pp. 236-37).

23. Jonson's knowledge of Venetian justice is studied in Richard H. Perkinson, "'Volpone' and the Reputation of Venetian Justice," *Modern Language Review* 35 (1940): 11-18. Perkinson also sees a mixed Venice—"Venice at this time was singly notable not only for its 'sinister repute,' but also for the integrity and severity of its republican courts" (p. 12). He also notes that Sir Pol has read Contarini (4:1, line 40).

24. Citations from Logan Pearsall Smith, *The Life and Letters of Sir Henry Wotton,* 2 vols. (Oxford: At the Clarendon Press, 1907).

25. *The Crisis of the Early Italian Renaissance* (Princeton: Princeton University Press, 1966). Citations appear in the text. The historical account depends upon pp. 387 ff., and also draws upon Bouwsma. On the creation of the myth after the events of 1509, see Lester J. Libby, "Venetian History and Political Thought after 1509," *Studies in the Renaissance* 20 (1973): 7-45. Libby suggests that the myth was a humanist invention, sponsored in part by the Aldine Press, and involving such figures as Andrea Navagero, Gasparo Contarini, Gian-Battista Egnazio, and Andrea Mocenigo.

26. Citations from the Lewkenor translation, *The Commonwealth and Government of Venice* (New York: Da Capo Press, 1969), appear in the text. English readers could also peruse Thomas de Fougasses, *The generall historie of the magnificent state of Venice,* trans. W. Shute (London, 1612).

27. *The Machiavellian Moment,* pp. 324-25. Pocock considers Contarini more mythical (see p. 320) than Donato Giannotti, who is closer to what Pocock defines as the essence of politics: "the erection of conditions under which men might freely exercise active virtue" (p. 317); this is a definition of politics rooted in the tradition of civic humanism that Pocock traces to the English and American revolutionary situations; Pocock's bias is to equate consult, and constitutionalism, with politics (see p. 74, e.g.).

28. These tend to be recorded in *Calendar of State Papers Venetian.* The letters more rarely touch it. Yet Wotton seems to have felt that Venetian liberty, and Venetian isolation, were features that resembled his native land.

29. All citations from *Coryat's Crudities* (Glasgow: James MacLehose, 1905), vol. 1. Fynes Moryson's 1617 account was also available; it includes (in the edition printed in Glasgow: University Press, 1907) in his *Itinerary,* some thirty pages on Venice, concluding (1:196) with praise for the city's freedom, "preserved from the first foundation." Englishmen were especially drawn to Paolo Sarpi's defiance of the pope; see John Lievsay, *Venetian Phoenix: Paolo Sarpi and Some of His English Friends* (Lawrence: University Press of Kansas, 1973), pp. 22-24 on English knowledge of Sarpi, chap. 6 on the availability of Sarpi's works in English, pp. 39 ff. on the reception of his *History of the Council of Trent,* and pp. 44 ff. on James's role in the publication of the English translation of that work.

30. See Ernst H. Kantorowicz, "Mysteries of State: An Absolutist Concept and Its Late Mediaeval Origins," *Harvard Theological Review* 48 (1955): 65-91. Kantorowicz provides further Jacobean examples and mentions the possible Tacitean origin of the phrase; nevertheless, for him, the trope is mainly to be

associated with the mystical body of state which, like the phoenix (see p. 88), can never die.

For further consideration of the relationship of the human body to the commonwealth see chapter 3 of Leonard Barkan's *Nature's Work of Art* (New Haven: Yale University Press, 1975), particularly pp. 69 ff. on *res publica* and *corpus mysticum*. Barkan tends to read the English uses of the metaphor in a Whiggish manner ("the head is primary but not absolute," p. 75), which is how Henry VIII spoke (to Parliament: "We as head and you as members are conjoined and knit together in one body politic," cited p. 76), but not, as Barkan says, acted. Hence, the Elizabethan usages express, as Barkan says, an official conservatism. Barkan does not discuss the absolutist subversion of the body for the body politic, which is my subject here.

31. All citations from the Anthony Raspa edition (Montreal: McGill-Queen's University Press, 1975); section and page numbers are provided in the text.

32. Note on page 152. On the relations of *arcana imperii* to sudden action, see Pocock, *The Machiavellian Moment*, p. 28. Some years earlier (in 1610), Chamberlain had similar worries: "To see our monarchicall powre and regall prerogative strained so high and made so transcendent every way, that yf the practise should follow the positions, we are not like to leave our successors that freedome we receved from our forefathers, nor make account of any thing we have longer then they list that govern" (*Letters*, 1:310).

33. The report is by de Fontenay and is printed in S. J. Houston, *James I* (London: Longman, 1973), p. 111. In Ashton, *James I by His Contemporaries*, the passage is translated as follows: "He is too idle and too little concerned about business, too addicted to his pleasure, principally that of the chase, leaving the conduct of business to the Earl of Arran, Montrose and the Secretary" (p. 3). The versions differ because the report was written in cipher. For a seventeenth-century decipherment, see Bodl. Ms. Sancroft 76, fols. 25–27.

Chamberlain frequently reports James as a *roi fainéant;* see *Letters*, 1:201, 493; 2:317–18. For James's predisposition to retirement, see Willson, *King James VI and I*, pp. 39, 48, 53–54, 73, 174, 178–85, 232.

34. Molin, in Luigi Firpo, ed. *Relazioni di Ambasciatori al Senato* (Torino: Bottega d'Erasmo: 1965), vol. 1, Inghilterra, p. 528. A similar account is given by Marcantonio Correr (1611), see pp. 582 ff. Molin's account of the king's negligence is echoed in later *relazioni:* Francesco Contarini, in 1609, comments on the King's propensity to let others rule and to do nothing himself: "Stima il re buona ragione di stato il lasciare il governo nelle mani de' grandi, ed egli pigliarsense poca parte" (Firpo, p. 632). Still, for Contarini, James's high praise for the republic (see p. 634) seems to outweigh these negative qualities. In the account of Foscarini (1618, describing James in 1611–15), the balance seems to turn; James's need for constant flattery, his ready words and little action are noted (pp. 661–62); there is also a very full picture of his retirement, surrounded by his favorites, whose constant familiarity and strong influence on decision making are noted (see pp. 643 ff.). In Pietro Contarini's account (1617–18), James's parliamentary troubles begin to come to the front (see p. 676), and the growing unpopularity of the king, along with a yearning for the reign of Elizabeth, is also described (pp. 680 ff.). Here, a specific contrast is drawn between the queen's love of popular display and James's undisguised loathing. By the

NOTES TO PAGES 83-85

1622 account of Girolamo Lando, there is scarcely a word said in James's defense—largely because of his pro-Spanish policies, his hesitancy in Palatine affairs, and his subservience to Buckingham—and he counsels the republic not to trust James. A final jotting of Alvise Contarini, the last ambassador under James, returns to the first point, the king disinclined to conduct any hard business: "Il re d'Inghilterra fugge per natura tutt'i negozi ardui e difficili" (p. 761).

35. Sarpi's attitudes are discussed in John L. Lievsay, "Paolo Sarpi's Appraisal of James I," pp. 109-17 in *Essays in History and Literature*, ed. Heinz Bluhm (Chicago: Newberry Library, 1965).

36. The remark at *Pleasure Reconciled to Virtue* was recorded by Orazio Busino, and I cite the translation prepared with the assistance of David Kalstone in Stephen Orgel and Roy Strong, *Inigo Jones: The Theatre of the Stuart Court*, 2 vols. (London: Sotheby Parke Bernet and Berkeley and Los Angeles: University of California Press, 1973) 1:283. D'Ewes is cited from *The Diary of Sir Simonds D'Ewes*, ed. Elizabeth Bourcier (Paris: Didier, 1974), pp. 57, 87.

37. Cited by Lawrence Stone, *The Causes of the English Revolution, 1592-1642* (New York: Harper & Row, 1972), p. 89. It is printed in Godfrey Goodman, *The Court of King James the First*, ed. John S. Brewer, 2 vols. (London: Richard Bentley, 1839), 2:379. Cf. Willson, *King James VI and I*, p. 445. In the letters written to Charles and Buckingham in Spain, they are, repeatedly, his "sweete boyes" and in one written on the last day of February 1622 he confesses: "I weare steenies picture in a blew ribben under my wastcoate nexte my hairte" (BL, Harl. Ms. 6987, fol. 16; Goodman, 2:257; Willson, p. 433).

38. James added to Divine Right theory "the identification of indefeasibility with hereditary succession by primogeniture in the legitimate line," Elton claims in "The Divine Right of Kings," *Studies in Tudor and Stuart Politics and Government*, 2 vols. (Cambridge: Cambridge University Press, 1974), 2:203. On the importance of genealogies to absolutist monarchs, see Werner L. Gundersheimer, *Ferrara: The Style of Renaissance Despotism* (Princeton: Princeton University Press, 1973), pp. 280-83, and Stephen Orgel, "The Royal Theatre and the Role of King," in Lytle and Orgel, eds., *Patronage in the Renaissance*.

39. All citations are drawn from *Patriarcha and Other Political Works*, ed. Peter Laslett (Oxford: Basil Blackwell, 1949); page numbers are provided in the text. Besides Laslett's introductory essay, the fullest study of Filmer's thought is provided by Gordon J. Schochet, *Patriarchalism in Political Thought* (New York: Basic Books, 1975).

In *Childhood and Cultural Despair* (Pittsburgh: University of Pittsburgh Press, 1978), Leah Sinanoglou Marcus stresses the political status of children in the patriarchal family; they displayed deference to their parents (p. 29) and tended to spend most of their time in the company of servants (p. 31). Marcus goes on to show that attitudes toward childhood in the seventeenth century were ideological. Anglicans and Puritans divided in their attitudes toward childhood and in the uses they put it to, Anglican conservatism linked to the obedience of children, Puritan revolution linked to childhood innocence and reformative capacities (see pp. 42 ff.).

A particularly stimulating study is offered by R.W.K. Hinton, "Husbands, Fathers and Conquerors," *Political Studies* 15 (1967): 291-300. Hinton's point is that the family is an ideological construct marshaled in defense of theories of government as various as Sir Thomas Smith's case for a commonwealth in *De*

Republica Anglorum or Bodin's absolutist state. "It would be absurd to argue that Bodin's vitriolic patriarchalism and Smith's happy partnership represented an actual difference between French and English families" (p. 294). As I suggest below, the images of the family, then, are constructed on political lines, just as Hinton argues that politics reshaped the natural family to support its argument (see pp. 291-93). Hinton goes on to show that Filmer's patriarchal argument is an extreme one, powerful as a "metaphor for the naturalness and inescapability of government" (p. 298), but less cogent logically in determining the relationships between patriarchal families and the power of kings: "On Filmer's premises every father ought to have been a king, and there ought to have been no sovereign outside the household at all. . . . He could not magnify fathers without diminishing kings, his kings could not be sovereign without making fathers impotent" (p. 299). In a continuation of his essay in *Political Studies* 16 (1968): 55-67, Hinton argues that Hobbes overcomes this logical impasse by having fathers agree to the powers of despotism, and that this weds as well the traditions of Bodin and Smith.

40. For typical and provocative statements of this point of view, see Georg Lukács, "Reification and the Consciousness of the Proletariat," pp. 83-222 in *History and Class Consciousness,* trans. Rodney Livingstone (Cambridge, Mass.: MIT Press, 1971), and Pierre Bourdieu, *Outline of a Theory of Practice,* trans. Richard Nice (Cambridge: At the University Press, 1977), esp. pp. 183 ff., "Modes of Domination." In *Marxism and Literature* (Oxford: Oxford University Press, 1977), Raymond Williams offers a useful summary of perspectives on ideology (pp. 55 ff.).

41. *The Family, Sex and Marriage in England, 1500-1800* (New York: Harper & Row, 1977), p. 152. A definition of the "restricted Patriarchal Nuclear Family" and its relationship to other family configurations is discussed in the opening pages of the book. Although Stone's work has come in for criticism, mainly on methodological grounds, his description of patriarchalism echoes many standard studies. Stone's remark is supported directly by Jean-Louis Flandrin, *Families in Former Times: Kinship, Household and Sexuality,* trans. Richard Southern (Cambridge: At the University Press, 1979), p. 130: "It seems that the authority of parents and their powers of coercion of their children increased from the sixteenth century onwards. This development is generally attributed to the interest of the absolute monarch in supporting the authority of fathers of families, as well as to the vogue of the principles of Roman Law and of the ideas of antiquity." Or, cf. Randolph Trumbach, *The Rise of the Egalitarian Family* (New York: Academic Press, 1978), which presents the movement from medieval cognatic kinship, to post-1000 patriarchalism, to post-1700 egalitarianism. Patriarchalism basically presumes "that at the head of each household stood a man who in his roles as master, father, and husband owned his wife, his children, his slaves, his animals, and his land" (p. 3). "Patriarchy presumed that there was property not only in things but in persons and that ownership lay with the heads of households" (p. 119). As Polonius says, "I have a daughter (have while she is mine)" (*Hamlet,* 2:2, line 106, ed. Willard Farnham [Baltimore: Penguin, 1957]), and Lear measures filial love in terms of property divisions.

42. Philippe Ariès, *Centuries of Childhood: A Social History of Family Life,* trans. Robert Baldick (New York: Vintage Books, 1962). Ariès's work has

been the guiding influence in the field; it established the notion of the family as a social rather than a biological unit; it pointed out the cultural factors that lead to the perception and demarcations in the biological development of people; the lack of sexual differentiation between children as manifested in their dress (female clothes for both sexes; see chapter 3); the emergence of the idea of the innocent and educable child from the notion of the child as savage and immodest; the child's importance as the continuer of the family line and the emergence of the *paterfamilias* as a domestic monarch; the sociability and publicness of family life. In the discussion that follows I draw upon these ideas freely because I believe that the images of the family I discuss reflect these concepts.

43. The disputes are about matters of demography, about how to read records, about which families to look at, about whether distinctions between parts of the same nation or from country to country are wide. Peter Laslett's work, beginning with *The World We Have Lost* (New York: Scribners, 1965; rev. ed., 1971), has continued to shape and provoke English investigators; in France, the work of the Annales school (see, for example, the collection *Family and Society*, ed. Robert Forster and Orest Ranum [Baltimore: Johns Hopkins University Press, 1976]) and the study by Flandrin cited above, have performed a similar function. The multiple view espoused by Stone finds its French counterpart in the work of Foucault and Donzelot (for the latter, see n. 46 below).

44. The liberal notion can be represented by Barbara Laslett, "The Family as a Public and Private Institution: An Historical Perspective," *Journal of Marriage and the Family* 35 (1973); 480–92, which argues that the private family, free of public control and intrusion, is a modern development of postindustrial society. This thesis underlies much modern sociological inquiry into the family as it emerges in modern times, such as Edward Shorter, *The Making of the Modern Family* (New York: Basic Books, 1975), which traces a movement from the extended to the nuclear family, from the household to the private home, from love dominated by family interests to free choice and intimacy, or the Parsonian study by Fred Weinstein and Gerald M. Platt, *The Wish to Be Free* (Berkeley and Los Angeles: University of California Press, 1969).

45. Two studies support these ideas of the family as reproducer of society. One is John Demos, *A Little Commonwealth: Family Life in Plymouth Colony* (London: Oxford University Press, 1970), which although overly influenced by modern psychological and sociological models, does, as its title suggests, see the early modern family as a replica of its society. Summarizing his study, Demos says, "The family was joined to other institutions and other purposes in an intricate web of interconnections. It did not stand out in any special way from adjacent parts of the social backdrop" (p. 186). The description implies the opposite conditions as prevailing in the modern family situation. The other study is Eli Zaretsky's *Capitalism, The Family, and Personal Life* (New York: Harper & Row, 1976). Zaretsky's study, which sees that the rise of a private sphere is part of the development of capitalism, and rooted in an ideological revaluation of the family (see p. 35 for a summary), which led to the oppression of women and to the subordination of the family to class distinctions, contrasts this modern situation with that before the seventeenth century, when society was composed of families, not individuals (see p. 42). The major consequence was the rise of the bourgeois notion of the individual vs. society, the family vs. society, in the

nineteenth century (see pp. 56 ff.). As Zaretsky argues, these notions mystify the personal and embed individuality in unrecognized social constructs which belie the sphere of freedom they pretend to proclaim.

46. Christopher Lasch, *Haven in a Heartless World: The Family Besieged* (New York: Basic Books, 1977); Jacques Donzelot, *The Policing of Families*, trans. Robert Hurley (New York: Pantheon Books, 1979). Under the *ancien régime*, Donzelot argues, the family directly reproduced society, both homologously and as part of a continuity (see pp. xx, 48-49); the essential change is described on pp. 91-92: the family woven into a complex web of alliances and dependencies was separated from society and yet connected by intervening social mechanisms; the "freedom" of the family from the state was granted by the state apparatuses that granted that freedom; in short there was a "transition from a government of families to a government through the family" (p. 92). The family ceased to reproduce society and became instead a social mechanism. Donzelot's work is indebted to Foucault with his insistence on the emergence of the modern idea of man in the nineteenth century. The ills of the family, taken up by Donzelot in his final chapter, and as the inevitable consequence of the situation of the family in modern society is also the burden of such studies as David Cooper's *The Death of the Family* (New York: Vintage Books, 1971).

47. For R. D. Laing, see *The Politics of the Family* (New York: Vintage Books, 1972); the "relays" of Donzelot have their correspondences in the unconscious maps and charts that Laing describes, ways in which the family-in-the-head determines what is done in life. Laing's work seems crucially revisionary of Freud because it posits a psychology that is rooted in social and political practices, including the politicization of psychiatry. A rather reductive, but insistent, study of the family and its ideological functions, which also reviews much of the literature on the subject is Mark Poster's *Critical Theory of the Family* (New York: Seabury, 1980).

48. David Hunt, *Parents and Children in History: The Psychology of Family Life in Early Modern France* (New York: Basic Books, 1970). Hunt attempts to wed Ariès and Erik Erikson, a mistaken notion, because Eriksonian psychology is not universal but historically determined. Nonetheless, focusing as he does on the extraordinary upbringing of Louis XIII and its recording by Jean Heroard, Hunt's study is full of documentation of striking differences in family life. Because adults were so fully socially circumscribed, he says, their children, too, were severely limited (see p. 153); yet the rigidities of authoritarianism also produced homologies; for example, precisely because children were seen as uncontrollable savages no differences were admitted between adult and child sexuality (see chapter 8). Hunt locates autonomy as the central issue in the seventeenth-century family. Although he brings an Eriksonian perspective to this problem, it seems nonetheless accurate to recognize that the child in the seventeenth century was less separate than the modern counterpart, just as the family was perceptibly bound into social nexuses.

49. "Rubens and the Whitehall Ceiling," *The Renaissance Imagination*, p. 50; cf. Gordon's discussion of the apotheosis as combined classical and Christian image on pp. 35-38. On the adaptation of religious formulas to rulers, see Marianna Jenkins, "The State Portrait, Its Origin and Evolution," *Monographs on Archaeology and Fine Arts* 3 (1947). On Elizabeth, see Frances Yates, *Astraea: The Imperial Theme in the Sixteenth Century* (Harmondsworth: Pen-

guin, 1975), and Roy Strong, *The Cult of Elizabeth* (London: Thames & Hudson, 1977).

50. Terisio Pignatti, "The Relationship between German and Venetian Painting in the Late Quattrocento and Early Cinquecento," in Hale, ed. *Renaissance Venice*, pp. 244-73; in a discussion of Dürer's borrowing from Bellini's San Zaccaria altarpiece for his *Feast of the Rose Garlands* (p. 258), Pignatti argues that the motif of the minstrel angels is peculiarly Venetian.

51. Webster's verses are printed in Arthur M. Hind, *Engraving in England in the Sixteenth and Seventeenth Centuries*, 3 vols. (Cambridge: At the University Press, 1955), 2:311-12.

52. *Van Dyck: Charles I on Horseback* (London: Allen Lane, The Penguin Press, 1972), p. 70.

53. The female-landscape, male-architecture formula can be seen in numerous family pictures of the period; for examples, Jacob Jordaens, *A Man and his Wife* (Museum of Fine Arts, Boston); Van Dyck, *Jan Wildens and his Wife* (Detroit). It is a formula that Van Dyck works out, as can be seen in two early family portraits (reproduced in Alan McNairn, *The Young Van Dyck* [Ottawa: National Gallery of Canada, 1980]). In one (#72 Hermitage), the father's hand rests on a chair adorned with the family coat; lineage is declared by that gesture; the mother's hand is on a child, who holds a vase; this may suggest that the child is not male (a female vessel), or that, undifferentiated as an infant, the child is a fragile vessel. The actuality of the line, conveyed by the husband's gaze and his hand on the chair, is answered by the tilted head of the child, looking at the father, and the mother's gaze, forward, but oblique; her hand touches the child's lap; the father's almost hidden left hand supports the child. In this case landscape and curtain function in reverse; nature is behind the father, the curtain behind the mother. The entire canvas is thus supported by the binding of nature and art, reproduction and re-production, that centers on the child. #73 (London) is similarly constructed, but with some further tension, for here there are two children, an older female and a younger child who is probably male, for he, like the father, looks forward, while the daughter and mother each look sideways. Hands in this picture support a circle of interrelationships; yet both the baby and the father raise a hand that is unsupported, while both mother and daughter take hold of the child (the father also rests a hand on his wife). The unsupported hands may point to autonomy; McNairn sees sibling rivalry in the embrace of the infant; this seems to me too modern a reading; but the situation can be explained in terms of male and female inheritances. Once again, backgrounds serve to unify cross-purposes, although the husband's hat almost totally dominates the landscape behind him.

54. For an account of some pictures bought for Buckingham (including works by Titian, Tintoretto, and Bassano) see Bodl. Tanner Ms. 7311 fols. 122-23. Arundel's collection is tabulated in the appendix to Mary F.S. Hervey's *The Life of Thomas Howard, Earl of Arundel* (Cambridge: At the University Press, 1921). As she remarks (p. 131), Venetian paintings were central to Arundel's collection. Cf. Parry, *Golden Age*, pp. 116-18.

55. Carlo Ginzburg, "High and Low: The Theme of Forbidden Knowledge in the Sixteenth and Seventeenth Centuries," *Past and Present* 73 (1976): 28-41. Ginzburg aruges that the penetration of *arcana naturae* had consequences for *arcana Dei* and *arcana imperii* (p. 32), and, of course, the case of Galileo is one

clear sign. He presents at some length the emblem book of Florentius Schoon-hovius (printed in Gouda in 1618) in which artistic self-assertion and Icarus re-figured as a picture of intellectual daring (see pp. 38–39) can be found, along with the fact that Schoonhovius was eventually forced by religious and political circumstances to retreat from such assertions. Like the Van Dyck painting, there are present in both instances the uneasy tensions surrounding the emergence of an intellectual community in the early seventeenth century. As Ginzburg says, the chain from nature (cosmos)/religion/politics, was part of a system of under-standing which could render a figure like Icarus subversive, and at the beginning of the seventeenth century, these links were in place and yet separations were also beginning to be made, so that spheres of activity need not automatically trigger responses in other spheres (see pp. 35–37).

56. One other painting by Van Dyck should be mentioned here, the self-portrait of 1633 in which he fingers a golden chain and points to a large sun-flower (reproduced in Hugh Honour, *The New Golden Land*, [New York: Pantheon Books, 1975]). The flower emblematizes the *roi soleil*, and natural gold has become the golden chain that binds artist to patron. The sunflower is presented as a kind of mirror, and the artist facing it, faces us; fingering the flower and his chain, he tells his connection to the world of nature, the transfor-mation of nature under his gaze, but the control of both nature and art by sover-eign power. As Honour notes, the imported flower is a sign of imperialistic ventures in the New World, and it is such imperialism that is also the support and link that the golden chain adorning the artist conveys.

57. *King James VI and I*, p. 286. Chamberlain reports it this way: "The next morning the King went to visit these young turtles that were coupled on St. Valentines day, and did strictly examine him whether he were his true sonne in law, and was sufficiently assured" (*Letters*, 1:424).

58. In "Beaumont and Fletcher: Jacobean Absolutists," in *Elizabethan and Jacobean Poets* (London: Faber & Faber, 1952), John Danby discusses the poem (on pp. 158–59) as a premonition of Jacobean absolutism.

59. It would be tempting to label this the secret of the emperor's new clothes were it not for the fact that even the naked body is clothed in the lan-guage of power. On this vertiginous situation of representation, one acute guide is Stephen Greenblatt, "More, Role-Playing, and *Utopia*," *Yale Review* (Sum-mer 1978): 517–36, esp. p. 520: "Strip off the layer of theatrical delusion and you reach nothing at all," and the following discussion of More's profoundly dis-quieting ability to play roles that confound our sense of ever locating, or of there ever being, a real More. This essay is incorporated into the chapter on More in Greenblatt's *Renaissance Self-Fashioning: From More to Shakespeare* (Chi-cago: University of Chicago Press, 1980).

3. The Theater of Conscience

1. The metaphor, voiced by Elizabeth I, runs through Shakespeare's plays as Anne Righter [Barton] demonstrates in *Shakespeare and the Idea of the Play* (London: Chatto & Windus, 1962; reprint, Harmondsworth: Penguin, 1967), pp. 102 ff. A fairly extensive recent bibliography on the topic of the player king can be found in Eileen Jorge Allman, *Player-King and Adversary* (Baton Rouge: Louisiana State University Press, 1980). The metaphor derives

from the world-as-stage trope, the history of which Righter treats in a brief but excellent discussion in *Shakespeare and the Idea of the Play*, pp. 59 ff. and 150 ff., and which may be supplemented by Ernst Robert Curtius, *European Literature and the Latin Middle Ages*, trans. Willard R. Trask (New York: Harper & Row, 1953), pp. 138–44. James is most like Richard II, and it is not impossible to imagine that he learned to express his part from the monarchs who trod the stage (and history) before him. Elizabeth's self-theatricalization is briefly but cogently explored by Stephen Greenblatt in *Renaissance Self-Fashioning: From More to Shakespeare* (Chicago: University of Chicago Press, 1980), pp. 165–69. Elizabeth had also seen herself as Richard II, but from a different vantage point; referring to the Essex conspiracy, which had involved mounting a production of *Richard II*, she said, "I am Richard II; know ye not that?" (see J. E. Neale, *Queen Elizabeth* [Garden City, New York: Doubleday Anchor Books, 1934], p. 398). The classic study of *Richard II* in relationship to Renaissance uses of the world-as-stage as a political trope is by Leonard Dean, "*Richard II*: The State and the Image of the Theater," *PMLA* 67 (1952): 211–18.

The sources of James's commonplace include Cicero and Plutarch as well as earlier sixteenth-century authors, including his teacher Buchanan. See *Basilikon Doron*, ed. James Craigie, 2 vols. (Edinburgh: William Blackwood & Sons, 1950), 2:193, note, p. 12, lines 20–23; 254, note, p. 163.

Whether the trope was reversible was questioned by Elizabeth; rulers were onstage, but the stage ought not show rulers—such representation was potentially revolutionary, or demeaning. Chamberlain reports the same of James: "The tragedie of Gowrie with all the action and actors hath ben twise represented by the Kings players, with exceeding concourse of all sortes of people, but whether the matter or manner be not well handled, or that yt be thought unfit that princes should be plaide on the stage in theyre life time, I heare that some great counsaillors are much displeased with yt: and so is thought shalbe forbidden" (*The Letters of John Chamberlain*, ed. Norman McClure, 2 vols. [Philadelphia: American Philosophical Society, 1939], 1:199).

2. All citations from the *Basilikon Doron* are drawn from the 1603 and 1616 editions reproduced in *The Political Works of James I*, ed. Charles H. McIlwain (Cambridge, Mass.: Harvard University Press, 1918). James rephrases this point and refers his audience to the *Basilikon Doron* in his 1609 speech to Parliament (p. 310).

3. My categories are indebted to Ernst Cassirer, *The Myth of the State* (New Haven: Yale University Press, 1946), esp. chap. 8, "The Theory of the Legal State in Medieval Philosophy." See also chap. 14, on the relationship of stoic thought to democratic political ideas. The literature on political theory in the seventeenth century is extensive. The standard treatment of absolutist thought remains J. N. Figgis, *The Divine Right of Kings*, as G. R. Elton affirms in his introductory essay to Figgis in his *Studies in Tudor and Stuart Politics and Government*, 2 vols. (Cambridge: At the University Press, 1974).

4. "Languages and Their Implications: The Transformations of the Study of Political Thought," the stimulating introduction to *Politics, Language and Time* (New York: Atheneum, 1973), p. 15. Pocock presents his views largely through Kuhn's idea of the paradigm, and this leads, as he admits, especially in his final essay, "On the Non-Revolutionary Character of Paradigms: A Self-Criticism and Afterpiece," to conservative historiography. Yet Pocock is wrest-

ling with the essential question here, and it is one that has engaged thinkers from a remarkable number of perspectives. Put simply, it is the question of limits and exclusions, of how the unthinkable ever gets thought, of how the inexpressible finds expression; and also, how those negatives (the unthinkable, the inexpressible) are nonetheless substantive, even if inarticulate. This is a pressing problem for marxists, for to imagine the overthrow of the present state of things and to make a revolution would seem to involve the destruction of the very limits in which thoughts and actions occur, and there would seem to be no way to express this—and perhaps therefore no way for revolution to occur. Pocock does not quite address this issue, but let it be noted that his view of the paradigm is not of a *closed* system, simply of the inevitability of a systemic. In a stimulating essay, "The Politics of Representation," in *Allegory and Representation*, ed. Stephen J. Greenblatt (Baltimore: Johns Hopkins University Press, 1981), Michael Holquist uses the example of Bakhtin to argue for the inevitably heteroglossic nature of language, language neither wholly the property of the utterer nor entirely subject to its limits. In Bakhtin, Holquist locates an inevitable ventriloquism that necessitates the indirectness of all representation (see pp. 181-82) and therefore allows for subversion, even (or especially) knowing subversion.

5. Lawrence Stone makes a similar point in *The Causes of the English Revolution, 1529-1642* (New York: Harper & Row, 1972), when he writes that "historians are increasingly realizing that the psychological responses to changes in wealth and power are not only not precisely related to, but are politically more significant than, the material changes themselves" (p. 17). Response—and articulation in language of that response—is thus a more significant reality than material fact. Indeed, the facts of politics are linguistic events, and for Stone, such representations are never simple, single reproductions of material events. For him, as for Pocock, pluralism is essential to all interpretive acts. This is, for both of them, an article of political faith and one, as I suggest below, quite at variance with the political model James advanced.

6. On such ideological dilemmas, see Karl Mannheim's *Ideology and Utopia*, trans. Louis Wirth and Edward Shils (New York: Harcourt, Brace & World, 1936). Mannheim argues for the social determination of knowledge, and presents absolutist epistemology as a closed and imposed system of distortions that promote concealment (see, for example, p. 96), a description of state secrets suggestive of James's Divine Right aims, or the obscurities of a poet such as Chapman.

7. In an extraordinarily stimulating essay, "Lying Like Truth: Riddle, Representation and Treason in Renaissance England," *ELH* 47 (1980): 32-47, Steven Mullaney presents through the notion of amphibology, this most radical instance of ambiguity, "an aspect of language that neither treason nor authority can control" (p. 41), "an interplay of likeness and difference . . . less readily ruled than are the antitheses of authority" (p. 42). Mullaney is attempting to capture through amphibology that which is in and yet beyond language, what gives James power and what circumscribes him, too, for the limits—the exclusions—are somehow within what power means to include *and to rule out*.

8. The authoritative treatment remains Sir Henry Maine's, *Ancient Law* (1864; reprint, New York: Henry Holt & Co., 1887); see, e.g., the discussion of *Patria Potesta*, chap. 5, esp. pp. 136 ff.; of testamentary succession, chap. 6, esp. pp. 182 ff. As J.G.A. Pocock argues in *The Ancient Constitution and the Feudal*

Law (1957; reprint, New York: W. W. Norton & Co., 1967), the connections be-tween monarchical authority and Roman law, which were once commonplace, are now increasingly questioned (see, e.g., p. 16). The thrust of Pocock's argu-ment is that legal theorists, intent upon affirming the immemorial nature of cus-tom as expressed by the common law, erected the basic terms of political and historical thought in the seventeenth century in England. He argues that these terms are remarkably parochial, and that, at the time of James I and Coke, op-posing arguments for parliamentary power and royal prerogative were couched in the same terms of an "ancient law" (see the fine summary on pp. 233-34). Again, then, we are dealing with a question of what is "included" and what is "excluded," and with a radical multivalence within a single vocabulary. So far, so good. Yet, James also invokes the language of Roman law, which is other than the language of the common lawyers; and invokes the ascendancy of his will, which is other than the immemorial nature of custom which would justify royal prerogative. Pocock sees that royalist thought after James made use of these be-liefs (see p. 123), but finds the transformation to be in terms of the discovery of the implications of feudalism in its relationship to the common law. There is no disputing that point, but there is also, it seems to me, no point in denying that James often sounds like those continental absolutists who habitually rooted their powers in Roman law. That tradition is studied in Myron P. Gilmore, *Argu-ment from Roman Law in Political Thought, 1200-1600* (Cambridge, Mass.: Harvard University Press, 1941), where the evidence is largely French. To sum-marize a complex argument baldly, Gilmore is intent on tracing a debate on whether there is a power that the sovereign alone has, which is not delegated or shared, and how that power came to be viewed as the one that inheres in the office of the sovereign. James, in the text cited above, refers to the king as a "publike person" on the basis of "office and authority" (*BD*, p. 5), and that locution seems to me to fit within the tradition of Bodin derived from Roman thought about *merum imperium*. Pocock summarizes the differences between France and England in *Politics, Language and Time*, pp. 240-41, which certainly are generally true, but which, I believe, too far underplay the ways in which James's language was founded on continental precedents; the multiplicity of the French model has to be extended across the channel, even if it remains in large measure true that the English tradition of the common law is the major matrix for political discussion of the time. W. H. Greenleaf, in *Order, Empiricism and Politics* (London: Oxford University Press, 1964), argues at length that the royal-ist case for order was immensely supported by the revival of Roman law with its claims for "*imperium* or supreme power inhering in the ruler whose will had the force of law" (pp. 42-43), and he sees James's claims for absolute obedience founded in such concepts. One further Roman connection is suggested by Kevin Sharpe in *Sir Robert Cotton, 1586-1631: History and Politics in Early Modern England* (Oxford: Oxford University Press, 1979). Rome was an ideal for the Jacobeans, Sharpe stresses (see, e.g., pp. 210, 233, 243), and the Society of Antiquaries founded by Camden had a political point in an era in which his-torical precedent served as the basis for governmental practice. The Society had been concerned to argue for James's succession (pp. 199 ff.), and Cotton's library continued to serve as a storehouse for historians, like Speed (p. 67n.), providers of masques, like Jonson, and parliamentarians, which explains why it was disbanded by the court.

265

9. See *The Trew Law of Free Monarchies, Political Works*, pp. 61–62. On the tendency of English royalist thought to avoid such justifying myths, see Pocock, *Ancient Constitution*, pp. 149–50. Pocock suggests (p. 189) that *beginnings* are always arguments for absolute power, whereas the English tradition has been more concerned with the immemorial; see "Time, Institutions and Action: An Essay on Traditions and Their Understanding," pp. 233–72 in *Politics, Language and Time*, a complex meditation on the relationships between time and timelessness, genuine historical knowledge and mythologization of the immemorial.

10. The crucial issue here is whether the self can be said to be owned at all. As I haved argued in *Endlesse Worke: Spenser and the Structures of Discourse* (Baltimore: Johns Hopkins University Press, 1981), pp. 92n–93n, the term *self* can, by the end of the sixteenth century, have a modern meaning, although this is not usual. By the end of the seventeenth century, however, it is. In C. B. Mac-Pherson, *The Political Theory of Possessive Individualism* (London: Oxford University Press, 1962), the idea of the self as property—as one's own possession—is seen as an invention of Hobbes and as a product of his material situation. Individualism, MacPherson argues, is rooted in the notion of the proprietary; the self, in this view, is what one does not owe to society (see pp. 3 and 270 for summations), although, paradoxically, this view of the self owes everything to the market economy (see pp. 4, 90, 106, for acute summary statements). This idea of the individual is not James's; the difficulty of self-possession is his central theme; the need to escape from a personhood which is *public property* into a privacy which is nonproprietary—that is, which cannot be claimed, viewed, or shared, is markedly different from the individualism that MacPherson describes. Yet we should note that the claims for privacy that James makes, the claims for what is *not included*, are the negative version of the Hobbesian appeal. Again, to use MacPherson's terms, we might point to the economics of the court, its conspicuous consumption, to the king's claims of absolute ownership which are acted out in displays of total prodigality and emptying, and contrast that with the market economy which is behind Hobbes. As Christopher Hill points out in *The Century of Revolution* (New York: W. W. Norton & Co., 1961), liberty and property are twin—if not synonymous—terms in the period (see, for example, pp. 45, 106); the king's claims of ownership, and the extension of those claims, so that he was also owned, point to the problematic nature of the "publike person" James represented.

Questions of conscience are crucial to James's polemical presentation of the oath of allegiance. Thus, in *Triplici Nodo*, he allows "conscience," but in the same breath, demands "obedience," the "naturall obedience" due to the sovereign (*Political Works*, p. 72; "naturall" here is, we know, a piece of ideological mystification) and his "fatherly care" (p. 73). Fittingly, what James attempts to control with his oath is *"Equivocation"* (p. 88; cf. 74, 91).

11. James's predicament reflects the experience of the king's two bodies, authoritatively treated by Ernst Kantorowicz, *The King's Two Bodies* (Princeton: Princeton University Press, 1957).

12. Citations drawn from *Ben Jonson*, ed. C. H. Herford, Percy and Evelyn Simpson, 11 vols. (Oxford: At the Clarendon Press, 1925–52), vol. 7.

13. The point is even more explicit in Samuel Daniel's *A Panegyrike Congratulatorie* (1603) when Daniel constantly demands that James be what his

writings have promised; James is "subject to thy Pen" (st. 22). Daniel's poem, in fact, reminds James of the numerous constraints, of ideals, of history, of audience, that limit him, telling him finally, "The pedestall whereon thy greatnesse stands,/Is built of all our hearts, and all our hands" (st. 73).

14. Orgel's remarks about *Oberon* are found in the Introduction to *The Complete Masques* (New Haven: Yale University Press, 1969), pp. 13-14, and more fully in *The Jonsonian Masque* (Cambridge, Mass.: Harvard University Press, 1965), pp. 82 ff.

15. I borrow Stephen Orgel's admirable description in *The Illusion of Power* (Berkeley and Los Angeles: University of California Press, 1975): "The mirror of the king's mind allows him to know only himself" (p. 77).

16. For the word *shape*, see lines 82, 92, 175; Robin also uses *figure* (lines 86, 108). Self-described as an "honest plain country spirit" (lines 52-53), he is, of course, a quintessential trickster, "fain to be myself" (line 121). Citations from *Complete Masques*, ed. Orgel.

17. Leah Sinanoglou Marcus remarks in "The Occasion of Ben Jonson's *Pleasure Reconciled to Virtue*," *Studies in English Literature* 19 (1979): 271-93, that among the masquers were the very licentious revelers under attack, among them the king's favorite, Buckingham, and that the king's behavior—his drinking and his favoritism—were implicitly in question (p. 290). She, too, believes that *For the Honor of Wales* was designed to erase such notions (pp. 291-93).

18. In *Jonson's Gypsies Unmasked* (Durham: Duke University Press, 1975). Angus Fletcher has also suggested that Jonson's ordering structures in the masque can be read satirically in *The Transcendental Masque* (Ithaca: Cornell University Press, 1971), e.g., p. 114.

19. Citations from John Donne, *The Epithalamions, Anniversaries and Epicedes*, ed. W. Milgate (Oxford: At the Clarendon Press, 1978).

On Donne's relation to patrons, see John Danby, "Fortune's Hill and the Poets," in *Elizabethan and Jacobean Poets* (London: Faber & Faber, 1965), and Richard Hughes, *The Progress of the Soul* (New York: William Morrow & Co., 1968), pp. 230 ff.

For the social context of Donne's poems, see Margaret M. McGowan, "'As Through a Looking-Glass': Donne's Epithalamia and Their Courtly Context," pp. 175-218 in *John Donne: Essays in Celebration*, ed. A. J. Smith (London: Methuen, 1972). McGowan finds the 1613 poem a strained performance (p. 214) and believes that Donne uses the persona of Idios to distance himself (p. 216). Still, in general she argues that poets reproduced the language of king and court (see pp. 193, 217), and that Donne's court aspirations and connections familiarized him with this rhetoric (p. 202). Hence, although Idios and Allophanes debate in the *Ecclogue* they do not question the primacy of the king or his familiar image as *roi soleil* (pp. 211-12).

Jonson may have something like Donne's conceit in mind when he resolved *A Challenge at Tilt, At a Marriage* (1613), the first part of his celebration for the Somerset wedding, by joining the opposed cupids of the tilt as Eros and Anteros, love and love returned—"the lover transforms himself into the person of his beloved" (202-3) is Hymen's final piece of wisdom in a speech whose message is make love, not war. The hope is extended in a piece of wishful thinking, *The Irish Masque at Court*, that followed the tilt, a celebration of the marriage of James and his country, including the loyal Irish who are allowed to pay obeisance and to be booted out until, under James's warming rays, they metamorphose into court gallants by being "looked on by his light" (line 177).

20. "The Real Presence of Lucy Russell, Countess of Bedford, and the Terms of John Donne's 'Honour is so Sublime Perfection,'" *ELH* 47 (1980): 210. As Maurer argues, Donne's courtship aped the royal style (p. 212), and both he and Lucy participated in a court in which contradictory extremes had to be negotiated.

21. All citations from *Poems*, ed. Phyllis Brooks Bartlett (1941; reprint, New York: Russell & Russell, 1962).

22. Jonson chose to conclude the first folio with *The Golden Age Restored* (1615). Crassly put, the masque concerns James's largesse, for the simplest terms that translate the restoral of the golden age are monetary ones. The repeated burden of the masque is that the inhabitants of the earth live in the iron age and are not deserving of the bounty of Jove. Divine dispensations thereby reflect "what heav'n should do,/And not what earth deserveth" (lines 21–22), and the descending spirits of Astraea and the Golden Age are made to agree that grace is theirs to give even if they receive no gratitude:

> *Golden Age.* But do they know
> How much they owe
> Below?
> *Astraea.* And will of grace receive it, not as due?
> *Pallas.* If not, they harm themselves, not you.
> *Astraea.* True.
> *Golden Age.* True.
> *Chorus.* Let narrow natures, how they will, mistake;
> The great should still be good for their own sake. (Lines 96–104)

Whether James in fact learned this charming lesson is questionable; he went on giving and grudging, and although Jonson revised the printed version of *The Golden Age Restored* to leave the kingdom of Jove quite firmly "present here" (line 215), the poet's power in that instance remained something he could only exhibit in his text and not with the monarch he tried to imprint. It might be argued that Shakespeare's *Timon of Athens* presents a malign version of the dangers of prodigality, fitting a time when the monarch lived on credit and depended on others to manage his finances.

23. *Reliquiae Wottonianae* (London, 1651), p. 77.

24. *James I* (University, Ala.: University of Alabama Press, 1967), p. 26.

25. Marcus Aurelius, *Meditations*, X:27, trans. Maxwell Staniforth (Baltimore: Penguin, 1964).

26. Citations from vol. 2 of *The Poems of King James VI of Scotland*, 2 vols., ed. James Craigie (Edinburgh: William Blackwood & Sons, 1955, 1958).

27. The standard account is in David Harris Willson, *King James VI and I* (New York: Oxford University Press, 1956), pp. 161–64, to be supplemented by G.P.V. Akrigg, *Jacobean Pageant* (Cambridge, Mass.: Harvard University Press, 1962). The Arcadian longings are summarily expressed in James's poem *Off Jacke, and Tom*, e.g., lines 17–18: "And Tom was, to our Royall Pan/his truest Swayne and cheiffest Man."

28. On the ideal king as hermaphrodite, see Edgar Wind, *Pagan Mysteries in the Renaissance* (New York: W. W. Norton & Co., 1968), p. 214. The image also concludes Donne's "To Mr. Tilman"; for further discussion, cf. A. R. Cirillo,

"The Fair Hermaphrodite: Love Union in the Poetry of Donne and Spenser," *Studies in English Literature* 9 (1969): 81-96.

29. James's homosexual orientation seems indisputable, although some historians try to underplay it. Lawrence Stone, however, is forthright on the subject in *The Causes of the English Revolution, 1529-1642* (New York: Harper & Row, 1972), e.g., p. 89. Most telling is the evidence provided by James himself, poems such as *The Phoenix*, the letters to Buckingham in Spain (a phrase from which is cited below), or the unfinished poem on his marriage, broken off when the king tries to explain his dilemma of division between public duty and private desire.

30. Citations from the Penguin edition, ed. H. Levin (Baltimore, 1956). Fuller discussion of this play occurs in the next chapter.

31. *The Diary of Sir Simonds D'Ewes, 1622-1624*, ed. Elizabeth Bourcier (Paris: Didier, 1974), pp. 92-93. *The Traditionall Memoyres*, from vol. 1 of *Secret History of the Court of James I*, 2 vols. (Edinburgh: James Ballantyne & Co., 1811), p. 275. Osborne goes on to tell how the Earl of Holland failed to gain James's favor by spurning his advances, "turning aside and spitting after the king had slabered his mouth" (1:276). The editor of *The Court and Times of James the First*, 2 vols. (London: Henry Colburn, 1848), repeats Osborne: "To a handsome countenance and well-shaped limbs he was as sensitive as a schoolgirl" (1:372). For a modern evaluation, see Willson, *King James VI and I*, pp. 337-38, 350-52, 383-84. Some further evidence of attitudes toward the promiscuity of James's favoritism can be found in a set of scurrilous verses on Buckingham and his family in BL, Add. Ms. 5832, fols. 206-8.

32. The rereading of eros implicit in *Hymenaei* is more explicit in the *Haddington Masque* (1608), celebrating the marriage of James's rescuer in the Gowrie Conspiracy. The antimasque appears to be about Moschus's runaway Cupid and Venus's search for him. But, in fact, Venus errs and antic Cupid is in the right, responsible for the forthcoming union (just as he has been for previous ones, as an allusion to *Hymenaei* [line 51] declares), as Hymen lectures Venus (lines 74 ff.), putting her roughly in her place—why has she abandoned her starry position on this night, he asks; does she know where she is? She is shown the king's majesty and, when Vulcan presents the major device of the masque, a sphere adorned with the heavenly virtues of marriage, Venus agrees to return to her husband's bed (lines 270 ff.). At that point, it seems that she, not Cupid, has stood in need of correction. As D. J. Gordon points out, in "Ben Jonson's *Haddington Masque*: The Story and the Fable," the burden of the masque is squarely focused on the physicality of marriage, the heat of copulation represented in the marriage of Venus and Vulcan (*The Renaissance Imagination*, ed. Stephen Orgel [Berkeley and Los Angeles: University of California Press, 1975], p. 190). Perhaps it was these meanings, and not the abstruseness of the masque, that got Jonson into trouble with its original audience. He is, at any rate, at great pains to declare, in the initial words, the honorable intentions expressed by the masque. Still, perhaps, more can be read than he allows; what is one to make of an epithalamium that declares at one point that "Love's common-wealth consists of toys;/His council are those antic boys" (lines 345-46)? This may have come too close to truths not apt for honorable celebration.

33. I cite the Penguin edition, ed. Virgil K. Whitaker (Baltimore, 1958), except for the emended reading of "mirror'd" for married. "Married" is the

reading in both F and Q; however, the Cambridge edition, ed. W. A. Neilson and C. J. Hill (Cambridge, Mass.: Houghton Mifflin, 1942), emends the line on the basis of "Coll. MS." I have been unable to determine exactly what this represents, but assume that it is a seventeenth-century manuscript copy of the play in which this reading is found; it would not have any authority, of course; but it does represent a perfectly logical reading, which keeps the metaphor of speculation. In the case of "married," the gaze returns to the gazer; in the case of "mirror'd," it does not, that is, the mirror retains its difference and otherness, whereas, in the first case, the gazer finds himself in the other. The distinction between mirror and marry is a fine one, difficult to maintain.

34. Cf. Jean Starobinski, "The Inside and the Outside," trans. Frederick Brown, *Hudson Review* 28 (1975): 333–51. Starobinski examines the distinction between inside and outside through some classic texts, *The Iliad*, *The Odyssey*, and *Proverbs*. His main point is that interiority is not absolute, but is both made by and revealed externally. What we are within comes from "our relationship with the *outside*" (p. 335); the revelation of interiority is perilous; but so, too, is the refusal; Ulysses is the model for the wisdom, recommended in *Proverbs* as well, of "discriminating at every turn what one must store (inside, in the secret of the heart, the breast) and what it is meet to surrender" (p. 346), and his final reunion with Penelope, Starobinski suggests, in a reading whose brilliance I cannot duplicate here, produces "a kind of vertigo [that] blurs the edge between outside and inside" (p. 351). Starobinski's essay, beyond its penetrating reading of the texts at hand, bears on the question of the royal gaze, and James's attempts to hold onto himself. This, as Starobinski suggests (p. 337), means a refusal to give, specifically the refusal to give each man his due, and it involves dissimulation, since it hides what is refused; however, Ulysses' model behavior also involves dissimulation, since it suits what is given to the receiver; the refusal to give assaults in its refusal, openness dissimulates what is not being given. Hence, for James, the strategy of power—which involves holding back—is what terrifies him most; in Starobinski, this secret withheld is death; for James, too, it is the possibility that he is a specter.

35. Richard Sennett, *The Fall of Public Man* (New York: Vintage Books, 1978). Sennett focuses on the eighteenth century as the period when public man—and specifically, public man as actor—was a term of central importance. Then, the equation of the world as stage held neither its older sense of the illusory nature of material existence as compared to spiritual truths, nor did it see a conflict between nature and culture, individual and society, which was to dominate the nineteenth century. As Sennett points out, what is crucial in the history he presents is the fact that the terms public and private have shifted meaning over the centuries, and that public life, which has almost invariably been seen in theatrical terms, has been understood in different ways through that metaphor. As Karen Hermassi points out in the introduction to *Polity and Theater in Historical Perspective* (Berkeley and Los Angeles: University of California Press, 1977), it is commonplace to find contemporary social theorists using theatrical language; Erving Goffman is the most striking example. Hermassi says that this may be "generic to the study of political theory itself" (p. x) because politics and theater coincide in defining public life, and theater—as Kernodle might remind us—began in the streets (p. 137).

Conversely, as Erich Auerbach demonstrates in "La Cour et la Ville," in

Scenes from the Drama of European Literature (New York: Meridian Books, 1959), in seventeenth-century France "le public" came to mean the literary/dramatic audience; rather than meaning the political community, "le public" came to mean polite society. In England, we can see the same shift in the movement from public theaters to private theaters that occured in the time of James I.

There was also a Puritan theory of the public person; see Christopher Hill, "Covenant Theology and the Concept of 'A Public Person'," in *Powers, Possessions and Freedom*, ed. Alkis Kontos (Toronto: University of Toronto Press, 1979), pp. 3-22.

36. *Discipline and Punishment*, trans. Alan Sheridan (1975; New York: Vintage, 1979). To summarize in a phrase, Foucault's history of the techniques of power traces "the reversal of the political axis of individualization" (p. 192; page numbers are provided in the text). The term the *gaze* also figures strongly in Foucault's study of medical perception, another modern phenomenon, where a particular way of seeing the body is born; see *The Birth of The Clinic*, trans. A. M. Sheridan Smith (1963; New York: Vintage Books, 1975), esp. chaps. 7 and 9. The term, and its connection to the mirror of the self that is made in the glance of the other, is the burden of the discussion "Of the Gaze as *Objet Petit a*," pp. 67 ff. in Jacques Lacan, *The Four Fundamental Concepts of Psycho-Analysis*, trans. Alan Sheridan (1973; New York: W. W. Norton & Co., 1978).

37. Franco Moretti makes a similar point in "La grande eclissi: Forma tragica e sconsacrazione della sovranita," *Calibano* 4 (1979): 9-52. It is the sovereign who is the sole actor, Moretti claims (p. 12), and the drama presents the ideology of absolutism in order to show its weakness (see pp. 17 ff.) and the inherent opposition of the will of the sovereign to the desires of the people, an opposition acted out in the self-division of the monarch, which leads to an inevitable downfall (see pp. 31, 50): "La tragedia giacomiana ... [segue] la traiettoria dell'inautenticita fino alla sua inevitabile autodissoluzione." This is similar to the view of Jean Duvignaud in *Sociologie du théâtre: Essai sur les ombres collectives* (Paris: Presses Universitaires de France, 1965), pp. 184-92. For Moretti, stage history leads to Charles's tragic scaffold. Moretti's argument has some validity for James. He does think of himself as sole actor, at least in that internal theater where God alone is his witness; on the stage where he is viewed by the populace, however, he stands not as actor but as spectacle—he stands there to be seen, and, crucially, to manifest what cannot be seen, that is, what is reflected in the consciences of his audience. The king is distinguished by his view, by his gaze, by his penetrating glance, and by his invisibility and his obscurity. The king is distinguished by where he is placed—in state—standing, unmovingly fixed in the perfect vantage point. Moretti's inevitable self-destruction is what James sustains in his *onus/honos*, in his two bodies, body mortal, body politic—the latter including the invisible body of power.

38. These matters are discussed by Stephen Greenblatt in "Invisible Bullets: Renaissance Authority and Its Subversion," pp. 40-61 in *Glyph 8: Johns Hopkins Textual Studies* (Baltimore: Johns Hopkins University Press, 1981). They are also considered by Louis Adrian Montrose in a provocative exploratory study, "The Purpose of Playing: Reflections on a Shakespearean Anthropology," *Helios* n.s. 7 (1980): 51-74. Montrose's point is that the theater was a far more accurate mirror of society than the texts that preached social order, and that the theater contained the anomalous, the marginal, the ideologically suspect (see p.

66 for a summary). Thus, the theater is the public form, the institution that genuinely mirrors the fullness of society, including its sustaining contradictions. Cf. Duvignaud, *Sociologie du théâtre,* pp. 4-5, 10, for similar arguments about the social responsiveness of theater. For an argument about the English Renaissance theater as centrally involved with political aims, see Philip Edwards, *Threshold of a Nation* (Cambridge: Cambridge University Press, 1979).

39. I depend upon Sennett here; similar questions are raised in an essay on "Ruthlessness in Public Life," in Thomas Nagel, *Mortal Questions* (Cambridge: At the University Press, 1979). The troubling separation of public and private morality is Nagel's concern; how does an office get between a person and his public acts? Why do we want our public figures to have impeccable private lives, and then allow them latitude to do in office what we would deny them at home? In Nagel's account, these questions raise the larger issue of the relationship of subjectivity and objectivity. And, I believe, they help illuminate the fact that those opposing terms are also meant significantly differently in the Renaissance than now as the double meaning of consciousness shows. That just then these become real questions is of course clear from Machiavelli.

40. *Speech and Phenomena,* trans. David B. Allison (1967; Evanston, Ill.: Northwestern University Press, 1973). Page numbers appear in the text.

41. *Ursprung des deutschen Trauerspiels* in *Gesammelte Schriften,* ed. Rolf Tiedemann and Hermann Schweppenhauser (Frankfurt am Main: Suhrkamp, 1974) 1:1:245: "Der Souverän repräsentiert die Geschichte. Er hält das historische Geschehen in der Hand wie ein Szepter." (The sovereign represents history. He holds historical events in his hands as if it were a scepter.) In *Speech and Phenomena,* Jacques Derrida offers a useful summation of the various meanings of representation and their German equivalents on pp. 49 ff. "Repräsentiern" has, usually, a strong substitutive sense, something standing for something else, *occupying the place* of something else, as James represents the deity by standing in his place.

42. I cite the Penguin edition, ed. Ralph M. Sargent (Baltimore, 1959). That pastoral and power go together, we have seen earlier, examining Jonson's late Jacobean masques. But it is equally true of pastoral from its beginnings; retirement has always provided a mirror for the larger world of affairs; pastoral retreats are not places of silence, cut off from the world; they return to the world, just as Raphael Hythlodaye returns to the world, to court, to tell about the no-place that exists only when it is told about, and when it is finally inscribed. Utopia is a topos, a literary trope, it has always existed as a place—on a page, and it is connected from the first with role-playing; see the final note to "State Secrets."

43. *The Theater and its Double,* trans. Mary C. Richards (New York: Grove Press, 1958); page citations are in the text. My understanding of Artaud has been aided by Jacques Derrida's essay, "The Theater of Cruelty and the Closure of Representation," in *Writing and Difference,* trans. Alan Bass (1967; Chicago: University of Chicago Press, 1978); see esp. 237, on how Artaud's theater attempts to stage primary representation, which we know for Derrida means language representing itself; that is, writing (cf. the essay "Freud and the Scene of Writing" in the same volume, where writing as mise-en-scène is everywhere Derrida's concern, what he calls "the *sociality* of writing as *drama*" [p. 227]).

44. As Charles Dempsey remarked in a recent unpublished paper, "Gentile

Bellini and Renaissance Hieroglyphic Lore," the Renaissance rediscovery of hieroglyphics developed in two directions: one, neoplatonic, treated the hieroglyphic as an intuitive symbolic statement, nontranslatable; another tradition used hieroglyphics as an alternate mode of inscription (literally, based on the hieroglyphics inscribed on obelisks) in which the symbols were to be assembled by a grammar which the viewer was to provide. In one case, the hieroglyphic speaks immediately, nondiscursively; in the other, the viewer brings his discursive powers to bear to assemble this other language and make it his. Artaud's (and Derrida's) emphasis on writing as rebus thus seems to have a genuine Renaissance tradition; indeed, Dempsey emphasizes that hieroglyphic lore is not on the fringes of Renaissance thought but central to the recovery of antiquity.

45. *Sade, Fourier, Loyola,* trans. Richard Miller (New York: Hill & Wang, 1976); page citations are provided in the text. Loyola's text is, of course, the one located in the historical period of concern; and it is a remarkable text precisely because it asks its reader to construct an imaginary scene which supplements the biblical text, and then to experience that scene on his body. So, for example, in the second week, the beginning of the exercises involves creating "a mental picture" (all citations from *The Spiritual Exercises of St. Ignatius,* trans. Anthony Mottola [Garden City, N.Y.: Image Books, 1964] p. 67), which is then filled out, by providing speeches for the imagined figures, or the entirety of the place in which the scene occurs: "I will see, in imagination, the great extent and space of the world" (p. 69). But then, this imagined scene is transferred from the mind to the flesh: "to smell and taste in imagination" (p. 72), to pray, speak, desire amends; to put oneself in the imagined scene and to act it out. The *Exercises* repeat this process, over and again; representation is repetition here and is the act of coming to occupy the place that the mind makes, and putting the flesh into that space. Inside and outside are thus violated as boundary terms, and the very conditions of re-presentation here are self-contained and yet repeatable.

46. This use of language is, for those who write within the liberal tradition, and for those to whom the tradition of civic humanism is the only genuine politics, antipolitical because anticommunal. It is such a usage of language that J.G.A. Pocock regards with displeasure: "In the context of a political system, to send me a message in terms such that I cannot reply to it is an assertion of pure power over me" (*Politics, Language and Time,* p. 282). Speech is the realm of political reality for Pocock, and speech should therefore be responsible, even as it remains endlessly open to decipherment. But there are, he recognizes, other alternatives: "To speak at all is to give some other power over us [because we then become their object of interpretation], and some assert their own power by refusing to speak at all, to speak intelligibly or (so far as this is possible) within any frame of reference they cannot unilaterally prescribe" (p. 24). These are all absolutist strategies, and they are part of politics in the Renaissance, even in England.

47. Citations from *The Plays and Poems of George Chapman: The Tragedies,* ed. Thomas M. Parrott (London: George Routledge & Sons, 1910). The textual situation of this play is complex, and I have consulted as well the New Mermaid text, ed. Maurice Evans (London: Ernest Benn, 1965), which draws more heavily upon the 1607 quarto than Parrott does, and which is also more fully annotated.

273

48. This is the interpretation offered by J. W. Lever in *The Tragedy of State* (London: Methuen, 1971); Lever's book offers a valuable corrective to those studies of Jacobean drama that have seen it as voicing commonplaces of Tudor homilies about order, hierarchy, and the like. He sees that Jacobean drama is dominated by absolutism (see pp. 4 ff.). But, for him, this means that these plays regularly display individuals who are attempting to oppose such states. That is, Lever imposes upon these plays liberal and democratic values and modern ideas about the individual. Thus, although he often describes Jacobean plays with a great deal of acuity, he rarely interprets them convincingly. Bussy is not an individualist; the term is meaningless. Rather, he is an absolutist, and that is why he is on Henry's side in the play. His "individualism" is the selfhood that absolute monarchy claims for itself. Lever comes close to seeing this in his discussion of *The Revenge of Bussy* when he is made uncomfortable by the fact that Clermont, the supposed hero of the play, advances what sound like absolutist arguments (see p. 52). Clermont's suicide, like Bussy's death, is the inevitable end for heroes whose self-referentiality is also a principle of self-destruction. Those who are *sui generis* can also be those who hold their own deaths in their hands. "I am Duchess of Malfi still" is an absolutist assertion; even that Jacobean hero, who would seem to be making very private demands—to have a husband— claims herself finally through her title (she has no Christian, personal name in the play); and we might recall that in response to the obsessive court observation that plagues her, the Duchess finds that she must speak her own language; Antonio, wooed by her, asks her to explain her conceit to him. So she is neither private, nor as Lever claims, innocent; she, like Bussy, is an absolutist; and her language is the language of state.

49. The quarto reads "full creature" (5:3, line 46, Evans ed.) at this point, an echo of an earlier usage, "full men" (2:1, line 166), which also appears only in the 1607 quarto. "Full" does seem to me to be the right word for Bussy, and Evans keeps the word in his edition. Both Parrott and Evans note the borrowings from Seneca's *Hercules Oetaeus* that I allude to below.

50. Citations from the Penguin edition of *Henry V*, ed. Alfred Harbage (Baltimore, 1966).

51. Thomas Heywood, *An Apology for Actors* (1612; facsimile ed. Arthur Freeman [New York: Garland Publishing, Inc., 1973]); sigla citations in the text.

52. In the Roman play exactly contemporary with *Henry V*, the figure who manages this doubling is Antony, who becomes Caesar, and who moves the mob. In *Henry V*, Pistol is mistaken by Fluellen for Antony (3:6, line 13). The error is not without its point; Pistol is the most disturbing reflection of Henry in the play, the echo that most fully mirrors and yet must be most disowned. Only Pistol survives from the tavern world of Hal's past; and he returns a robber and a bawd, as Henry returns owning France and her princess, that final breach filled. On the relation of this "arrant counterfeit" to the real thing, see Righter [Barton], *Shakespeare and the Idea of the Play*, pp. 125-29. I have also drawn upon Righter's persuasive discussion of Shakespeare's double attitude toward theatricality; her final remark on Shakespeare's movement toward the masque is one that I find illuminating, but believe applicable from 1599 on. The theater imagined by the Chorus at the opening of *Henry V* is at once the private Roman theater and the court theater where kings did both perform and watch the spectacle in which they were repesented.

4. The Roman Actor

1. Citations from the Penguin edition of *Julius Caesar*, ed. S. F. Johnson (Baltimore, 1960). The pervasiveness of acting imagery has been noted, for example, by J. L. Simmons, *Shakespeare's Pagan World: The Roman Tragedies* (Charlottesville: University Press of Virginia, 1973), pp. 87 ff.; Maurice Charney, *Shakespeare's Roman Plays: The Function of Imagery in the Drama* (Cambridge, Mass.: Harvard University Press, 1959). Yet the commonplace that acting is simply opposed to "reality" seems mistaken. Rather, acting touches that absolute spirit that G. Wilson Knight so stunningly describes in two essays on *Julius Caesar* in *The Imperial Theme* (London: Methuen, 1931), "the spirit of empire and order" (p. 51). Knight's reading of *Julius Caesar* and of *Coriolanus* heavily influences mine in the pages that follow. In *Shakespeare and the Idea of the Play* (London: Chatto & Windus, 1962; Harmondsworth: Penguin, 1967), Anne Righter [Barton] correctly notes that the lines I discuss in *Julius Caesar* glorify the stage; see pp. 140 ff. On p. 169, she contrasts this to the antitheatricalism of *Coriolanus*. Both plays, I believe, share attitudes toward the theater that they have in common with the Jonsonian masque; Righter makes a similar point in the final pages of her book.

2. In a brilliant essay on *King Lear*, "The Avoidance of Love," in *Must We Mean What We Say?* (New York: Scribner's, 1969), Stanely Cavell questions this fundamental idea, suspecting the theatricalization of history; see esp. pp. 331 ff. Admittedly, the phrase can be empty; in common parlance, surely, *tragedy* is used far too loosely to describe any number of unfortunate events. Yet, as the work of Michael Fried suggests, particularly *Absorption and Theatricality* (Berkeley and Los Angeles: University of California Press, 1980), theatricalism and antitheatricalism are mutually supportive, mirrors of each other, not necessarily exclusive, and often on a continuum (one age's antitheater is the next one's staged tableau). Theater seems inescapable as a mode of seeing and organizing the visible world; it is an institutionalized form of seeing in a social setting—public seeing, and being seen in public. That social experience cannot be divorced from society at large. As Cavell points out, we cannot respond in the theater as if we were on the street—we cannot stop Cornwall from blinding Gloucester, or shout out to Othello that he is being duped—but we cannot deny that we want to do these things. As Cavell argues, those onstage are caught in our position, too; they cannot avert tragedy. Hence, there is a continuity from stage to audience. In the Elizabethan theater, these continuities would have been, if anything, stronger, for the stage was open, thrusting out into the audience. As Stephen Orgel reminds us in *The Illusion of Power* (Berkeley and Los Angeles: University of California Press, 1975), there was no dividing curtain, no dimming of the house lights; the audience, composed of the middle reaches of society (no kings or peasants) was complemented by the figures onstage, so that the entire society met in the playhouse, as it did nowhere else in Elizabethan society. On this last point, see Louis Adrian Montrose, "The Purpose of Playing: Reflections on a Shakespearean Anthropology," *Helios* n.s. 7 (1980): 51–74, for a stimulating argument on the overcoming of social contradictions in the theater.

3. *The Letters of John Chamberlain*, ed. Norman McClure, 2 vols. (Philadelphia: American Philosophical Society, 1939), 1:548.

4. As Reuben A. Brower notes in *Hero and Saint: Shakespeare and the Graeco-Roman Tradition* (New York: Oxford University Press, 1971), self-

referentiality translates *sui similia* or *par sibi* (p. 121); applied to Achilles in Ovid (*Meta.* 12:619), it is also used by Shakespeare for Henry V (see p. 221), Brutus (p. 233), Coriolanus (p. 237): "I play/The man I am." Brower summarizes the classical theme: "The passion for glory in Plutarch is an expression of the hero's high sense of self, of the battle to be 'worthy of himself,' a recurrent theme in Virgil, Ovid, and—to the point of caricature—in Seneca" (p. 213). To this must be added the problematic nature of self-referentiality when the self is not so readily separable as a category; self is a social category, and the individual is not realizable outside society.

A most poignant instance of self-referentiality occurs in Cleopatra's parting from Antony, when her distraction—for once, even she is at a loss—can only be called an Antony: "O, my oblivion is a very Antony,/And I am all forgotten" (1:3, lines 90–91). "A very Antony" here anticipates the ultimate negations that Antony's absoluteness entails. Citations from the Penguin text, ed. Maynard Mack (Baltimore, 1960).

5. In *Shakespeare's Rome: Republic and Empire* (Ithaca: Cornell University Press, 1976), Paul A. Cantor argues a point that challenges much Shakespeare criticism, that *Coriolanus, Antony and Cleopatra,* and *Julius Caesar* display genuine knowledge about Rome (see pp. 10 ff.). This is usually only granted to Ben Jonson's Roman plays. For Shakespeare, Cantor argues, Romanness, as a value, means republican Rome (see p. 27); hence, the Rome of *Antony and Cleopatra,* the Roman Empire, lacks Romanness. In that play, the imperial ideal claims both the public and private spheres—love is a form of tyranny (p. 127), Antony and Cleopatra make each other absolutes (p. 194), and they want the rest of the world to conform to their desires (p. 202). What Cantor describes tallies with the pages that follow, but with one crucial difference: the ideal in the republic is itself imperial—Coriolanus shows this, as Cantor indeed makes clear; and "the Republican regime can function only as long as the people realize their unfitness for rule and are willing to defer to the Senate's government" (p. 75). The republic, as Cantor says, is not a democracy, but a mixed government, and it requires strong leadership. In *Antony and Cleopatra,* this sovereign principle is cut off from participation and the lovers turn in on each other; but such a movement is perhaps the end point of the mirroring of Brutus and Cassius or the self-reflexiveness of Coriolanus. Cantor's desire to take Shakespeare's Rome seriously is anticipated by T. J. B. Spencer in "Shakespeare and the Elizabethan Romans," *Shakespeare Survey* 10 (1957): 27–38. For Spencer, Rome's meaning is exemplary, particularly for monarchs, and hence it is imperial Rome and the question of tyranny that is central. Spencer reverses some commonplace views about Jonson's classicism and Shakespeare's by ending his essay denigrating Jonsonian bookishness in favor of Shakespeare's broader historical imagination.

6. Citations in the text from *An Apology for Actors* (1612; facsimile ed. Arthur Freeman [New York: Garland Publishing, Inc., 1973]).

7. Simmons, *Shakespeare's Pagan World,* notes that in the play the people wish to deny Caesar the name of king, although not in fact the kingly prerequisites (p. 78). As he suggests, an Elizabethan would have regarded the name Caesar as the equivalent of the title; Thomas Platter, for instance, records his visit to the Globe in 1599 to see "the tragedy of the first Emperor Julius Caesar" (cited p. 5), and Bacon, in *The Advancement of Learning,* notes that when Caesar, who yearned to be king, said *"Non Rex sum sed Caesar,"* as if Rex were some lesser

family name, "he presumed Caesar was the greater title; as by his worthiness it is come to pass till this day" (cited p. 78). As Simmons notes (p. 79), the name *Caesar* occurs frequently in *Julius Caesar* and it comes to be divorced from the man and to be a title.

8. G. Wilson Knight discusses images of the body—especially of the diseased body—in *The Imperial Theme*, pp. 40 ff. In *Illness as Metaphor* (New York: Vintage Books, 1977, 1978), Susan Sontag provocatively treats the history of the meanings of consumption and cancer; in her occasional forays into the meanings of disease before the modern period, she lights on the profound idea that disease in the Elizabethan period is invariably social (see pp. 37 and 72 ff.), rather than individualizing or stigmatizing; further, whereas modern disease is inevitably linked to some notion of sexual repression, disease in the Elizabethan period seems linked to sexual excess—this is clearer in Jonsonian drama than in Shakespeare (in *Catiline*, the private side of revolution is the libertinage of Fulvia; in *Sejanus* it is Livia's overindulgence in cosmetics provided by her doctor—there disease and sexuality meet clearly).

9. Knight puts it this way: "He has 'dismembered' Caesar, but has not 'come by' his 'spirit', partly because he himself from the first made that unreal mental division of Caesar the man and Caesar the imperial force in Rome. So Caesar's disembodied 'spirit', his ghost, Brutus' own creation, pursues Brutus to his death" (*The Imperial Theme*, p. 79).

10. As Herbert Lindenberger suggests in *Historical Drama: The Relation of Literature and Reality* (Chicago: University of Chicago Press, 1975), "the continuity between past and present is a central assertion in history plays" (p. 6), and since plays were read for such continuities, and with an eye to the exemplary function of history, the continuing relevance of plays to present times was readily assumed. Those suppositions get Cordus into trouble in *Sejanus*, and Jonson, too. In *The Moral Vision of Jacobean Tragedy* (Madison: University of Wisconsin Press, 1965), Robert Ornstein accurately notes the political concerns of *Sejanus* that brought it under royal scrutiny: the picture of a state in which aristocrats are limiting freedoms, and a court where favoritism promotes new men at the expense of those with traditional claims for preferment (p. 87). The comparison of James to Tiberius was not only Arthur Wilson's; it appears in character writers, too, as Geoffrey Hill notes in "The World's Proportion," in *Jacobean Theatre*, ed. J. R. Brown, and B. Harris (New York: Capricorn Books, 1960). As W. G. Zeeveld shows in "*Coriolanus* and Jacobean Politics," *Modern Language Review* 57 (1962): 321–34, James himself viewed encroachments upon his prerogative as arising from the overzealous claims of "some Tribunes of the people" (p. 327), as he announced to Parliament in 1605, attacking the republican institution that gave the people a voice. Zeeveld comments that James was a "self-conscious phrasemaker" and that the Roman allusion was not lost or forgotten in subsequent discussions of the royal prerogative.

11. Everyday reality is about as ordinary as ordinary language, which, Stanley Fish reminds us in the final essays in *Is There a Text in This Class?* (Cambridge, Mass.: Harvard University Press, 1980), is only ordinary in the sense it is made institutionally and sanctioned as ordinary by them: "Categories like 'the natural' and 'the everyday' are not essential but conventional" (p. 271).

12. Jonson's politics are complex, and not easily summarized in a phrase. If they had to be, Coleridge's remark, recorded by Hill in "The World's Propor-

tion," seems valuable: "The anachronic mixture in this Arruntius, of the Roman republican, to whom Tiberius must have appeared as much a tyrant as Sejanus, with his James-and-Charles the First zeal for legitimacy" (p. 126); or, as Hill puts it: "Jonson's two most powerful social attitudes—disgust at corruption; and reverence for consecrated power" (p. 124). Of course, the problem lay in the fact that those conflicting attitudes met in the single person of James, and Jonson's ability to survive in the world as a poet depended upon the king as well.

The complexities in Jonson's attitudes are flattened out in K. W. Evans, "*Sejanus* and the Ideal Prince Tradition," *Studies in English Literature* 11 (1971): 249–64, where Jonson's conservatism becomes a rigid medieval reverence for the prince and a loathing for all things modern; Evans does admit and is good at describing the "brutal realities that lie behind . . . [the] pretentious facade of government for the public good" (p. 264) in the play, and argues, in a general way, that these reflect on contemporary trends in the direction of despotism.

13. The obsessiveness and uncertainties of observation are well described by John J. Enck in *Jonson and the Comic Truth* (Madison: University of Wisconsin Press, 1966), pp. 102–3. Ornstein contributes the important, and often overlooked, point that the central power in the play, however out of sight, is Tiberius's; see pp. 88–89 ("Tiberius, who even *in absentia* controls the situation") and p. 96. This view counters Matthew H. Wikander's in "'Queasy to be Touched': The World of Ben Jonson's *Sejanus*," *Journal of English and Germanic Philology* 78 (1979): 345–57; although Wikander correctly sees that the play has contemporary relevance without being a one-to-one allegory, he makes narrow equations (with the Essex uprising), concluding that Jonson, who favored a strong monarch, presented in Tiberius an image of Elizabeth in her dotage (p. 357). This misreads the nature of power in the play and could be corrected by Philip Edwards, *Threshold of a Nation* (Cambridge: Cambridge University Press, 1979), which finds Tiberius an image of authority (p. 173).

The intense theatricality of *Sejanus* is demonstrated by Arthur F. Marotti in "The Self-Reflexive Art of Ben Jonson's *Sejanus*," *Texas Studies in Literature and Language* 12 (1970): 197–220: esp. pp. 207 ff. on "the themes of play acting and playmaking," their relationship to "observation scenes," and the association of villainy with dramaturgy. Of Tiberius, Marotti remarks: "He stands behind the action of the play's final two acts like the playwright hidden behind his creation, and more and more the characters onstage look like his creatures" (p. 214), a fine point, as is his conclusion that we are to remember that even Tiberius fell in "the falling of the theater at *Fidenae*" (p. 219), in which the illusion that his power is all-encompassing is overcome in the theater of the gods. The way Tiberius comes to seem godlike in his powers is noted by Marotti on p. 215 and argued further in Gary D. Hamilton, "Irony and Fortune in *Sejanus*," *Studies in English Literature* 11 (1971): 265–81, esp. pp. 271–72.

Citations from *Sejanus* are drawn from vol. 4 of *Ben Jonson*, ed. C. H. Herford and Percy and Evelyn Simpson, 11 vols. (Oxford: At the Clarendon Press, 1925–52); I have also consulted the Yale edition, ed. Jonas Barish (New Haven: Yale University Press, 1965), with profit.

14. The text as printed by Herford and Simpson assigns this line to Cordus. In a note, however, they remark that since the line seems inconsistent with Cordus, Cor. in the text must be a misprint for Cot. Barish supports this emenda-

tion, and I follow it. However, I think it is perfectly possible that the line is said ironically by Cordus. In the reading I offer, it is not crucial who says the line; either way, it cannot be penetrated. The textual crux about the speaker—is it a Germanican or a supporter of Sejanus?—supports the interpretive problem discussed.

15. The classic study of images of the body in *Sejanus* is by Christopher Ricks, "*Sejanus* and Dismemberment," *Modern Language Notes* 76 (1961): 301-8. Ricks demonstrates the imagery of the body dismembered in a play where persons are always being imagined as parts of the body. Besides the dramatic effect toward which this tends—the final scene of dismemberment—it is, of course, a political image of the king's second body, the state. Tiberius preserves himself by totally investing himself in the body politic and by withdrawing into the invisible body reported and conveyed in his final letter to the senate. Cf. the discussion of *Sejanus* in Leonard Barkan's *Nature's Work of Art* (New Haven: Yale University Press, 1975), pp. 90-95. Barkan uses the play to demonstrate the most complex of his body/politic categories, where the actual bodies of persons (usually rulers, in this case, Sejanus) overlap with the body politic to produce complex body-within-body images. This notion is also applied by Barkan to Coriolanus (pp. 95-109), which is seen as the conflict of the plebian organic social theory with Coriolanus's solipsism "in which each man, and particularly the emperor, is a whole social world within himself" (p. 100). As I suggest, both plays are informed by a double body image, and the emperor is the quintessential embodiment of this doubleness.

16. In his Roman play of about the same period, *Caesar and Pompey* (1611-12?), Chapman presents a drama that has perplexed criticism. Three figures dominate it: Pompey, finally defeated by Caesar and, in defeat, becoming the spokesman for inner values that hold the world up to scorn; Cato, initially Pompey's supporter, but absent for most of the play, and a suicide at the end (a final speech combines stoicism and Christianity and also seems to bid farewell to the republican values usually associated with Cato); and Caesar, who is picked out by Fortune in the play and who ends in a victory that Chapman renders paradoxical by labeling it in the argument to the play as a victory without victory. That paradox Pompey also embodies in defeat, Cato in suicide.

The play's protagonists claim their partisans. Millar MacLaure, in *George Chapman: A Critical Study* (Toronto: University of Toronto Press, 1966), argues for Cato; Peter Bement, in *George Chapman: Action and Contemplation in His Tragedies,* Salzburg Studies in English Literature (Salzburg: Institut für Anglistik und Amerikanistik, Universität Salzburg, 1974), claims Pompey; Suzanne F. Kistler, in "The Significance of the Missing Hero in Chapman's *Caesar and Pompey*," *Modern Language Quarterly* 40 (1979): 339-57, makes a case for Caesar as hero.

I believe, however, that the three protagonists are versions of each other. Each offers the paradox of power; all are subject to the irony of victorious defeat; each is a kind of self-destructive absolutist. Caesar in power at the end is literally in power, contained by its shattering force (throughout the play he is buoyed by Fortune—a sign of his Machiavellian power; a sign, too, that he is gripped by larger forces than he controls); his status is mirrored by the invisibility embraced by Cato when he plunges a sword in his breast or by Pompey who arrives in his wife's arms disguised and eschewing "observation" (5:1, line 184) in preference to an inner kingdom. In this light, Cato is a genuine "mirror of men" (5:2, line 178) because his suicidal specter holds up a mirror for power.

Citations from *The Plays and Poems of George Chapman: The Tragedies*, ed. Thomas M. Parrott (London: George Routledge & Sons, 1910).

17. In beginning with his name, I wish to acknowledge the brilliant essay of D. J. Gordon, "Name and Fame: Shakespeare's *Coriolanus*," in *The Renaissance Imagination*, ed. Stephen Orgel (Berkeley and Los Angeles: University of California Press, 1975), pp. 203-19. The essay is a meditation on the meaning of naming in the play; how names are what endures, what make deeds permanent (pp. 203-5). As Gordon says, *voice* is the central word in the play (p. 206), catching in it utterer and utterance. Coriolanus wants the voices in the play to pronounce his name; and such pronouncing is profoundly social; it is by voices that the community is linked (p. 213) in *conversation* (a word that means the social bond, p. 218). But running counter to this in the play is Coriolanus's opposition of his deeds to these voices, his belief in the fame/name in what he himself has done. Here are Gordon's final words: "But within the walls absolutes turn out to be instrumental; the words that identify and bind become words that debase and destroy: whoops, or hoots, curses, lies, flatteries, voices, stinking breath. Words are torn from what they signify. They pass into their antonyms. Deeds are not-deeds. Names are not-names. The absoluteness of the self, the I, cannot be maintained; but the necessary relationship of the I with name or fame destroys. In this city to speak is to be guilty" (p. 219). To reduce this to a structuralist point: voices in the play are turned into the text.

An essay that builds on D. J. Gordon's is the first part of Stanley Fish's "How to Do Things with Austin and Searle: Speech-Act Theory and Literary Criticism," in *Is There a Text in This Class?*, pp. 197-245. Fish is acute in seeing that the state constituted in the play is formulated by utterance, and that Coriolanus aims at making himself an opposing state (see pp. 213, 216), although he errs, I believe, when he makes Coriolanus apolitical in his absolutism (p. 217).

Further essays on language in *Coriolanus* include: James L. Calderwood, "*Coriolanus*: Wordless Meanings and Meaningless Words," *Studies in English Literature* 6 (1966): 211-24; Lawrence N. Danson, "Metonymy and *Coriolanus*," *Philological Quarterly* 62 (1973): 30-42; Carol M. Sicherman, "*Coriolanus*: The Failure of Words," *ELH* 39 (1972): 189-207; Leonard Tennenhouse, "*Coriolanus*: History and the Crisis of Semantic Order," *Comparative Drama* 10 (1976): 328-46.

Coriolanus is cited in the Penguin edition, ed. H. Levin (Baltimore, 1956).

18. As Paul Cantor says in *Shakespeare's Rome*, the crucial question the plays leave about Rome is this one: "What must one say of Rome if it can achieve domestic tranquility only at the expense of expelling the most great-souled man in its midst, the man who is in some sense the fullest embodiment of the city's own ideals?" (p. 123). In "'There is a world elsewhere': Tragedy and History in *Coriolanus*," *Studies in English Literature* 16 (1976): 273-85, Patricia K. Meszaros also argues for this opposition, but in her terms, Rome is the Renaissance state (embodied as well in Jacobean England)—a function of history—and Coriolanus is the tragic human subject. My argument runs counter to this latter claim, but I find the treatment of the state (pp. 274-79) suggestive.

19. The psychoanalytic implications of these patterns have been noted before, by none so ably as Janet Adelman in "'Anger's My Meat': Feeding, Depen-

dency and Aggression in *Coriolanus*," in *Shakespeare: Pattern of Excelling Nature*, ed. David Bevington and Jay Helio (Newark: University of Delaware Press, 1978). Adelman presents the fundamental wound/mouth equation (p. 110), suggesting that the central premise of the play is that to take any food (or words, see p. 112) is to display vulnerability, whereas Coriolanus wishes to display himself *sui generis* (p. 112), godlike in his aggression (p. 116). This, as Adelman notes, he learned at the breast, and Volumnia is Rome (pp. 111, 115, 117–18). The effect of the play, as she cogently concludes, is to alienate and draw the audience (pp. 119–20). Just as Coriolanus will not display himself to the crowd, he denies us, his audience in the theater (only the gods are admitted as spectators); we admire his attempt at self-sufficiency since it is a human fantasy, but we are horrified at its consequences, the refusal of human dependency and community which we tend to think makes life valuable. Adelman's essay is also remarkable for its extensive bibliography.

20. The identification of Rome and Volumnia is a critical commonplace; see Brower, *Hero and Saint*, p. 369; Cantor, *Shakespeare's Rome*, p. 105. It has led to such insights as Janet Adelman's provocative reading (see n. 19 above). Through the family matrix, private, bodily images are attached to politics in the play. G. Wilson Knight discusses body images in *The Imperial Theme*, pp. 176 ff. Judah Stampfer, in *The Tragic Engagement: A Study of Shakespeare's Classical Tragedies* (New York: Funk & Wagnalls, 1968), closes his provocative reading of the Roman plays with the speculation that the path from *Julius Caesar* to *Coriolanus* is circumscribed by the deaths of Shakespeare's father and mother (see summary, p. 335).

21. The image of the theater of the gods is a commonplace. Heywood opens *An Apology for Actors* with a prefatory poem that moves from the trope "The world's a Theater, the earth a stage" (line 1) to Jehovah who "doth as spectator sit" (line 24). The totalization and reversibility of the world/stage metaphor provides Heywood with his closing couplet: "He that denyes then Theaters should be,/He may as well denye a world to me" (lines 29–30).

22. Citations from *Catiline* are drawn from Herford and Simpson, *Ben Jonson*, vol. 5; I have consulted the edition of W. F. Bolton and Jane R. Gardner, Regents Renaissance Drama Series (Lincoln: University of Nebraska Press, 1973), as well.

23. In "The World's Proportion," Hill comments cogently on how the political rhetoric of liberty becomes the language of license (p. 116). "Liberty" becomes the codeword for irresponsible power, or for the claims of absolute prerogative. As Hill says, the sphere in which that transformation is most frequently displayed is the private sphere (precisely because, as I have been arguing, the two spheres are continuous), most notably in sexual relations (p. 118). This accounts for the scene of attempted homosexual seduction in *Catiline* (1, lines 506–11), for the scenes with Livia and Fulvia in Jonson's plays. Fulvia is the full picture of the feminine side of conspiracy; her sexual masquerades, her plays at power, her acting make her a sheer exteriority, a voice without substance, ready to take any side. Femininity in these plays seems to be for Jonson a root image of betrayal of the body; beneath female counsel and female political argument lurks the hidden form of passion, the ghost that moves inside these corrupt and painted bodies. Jonson sees in Livia the condition that underlies all political behavior. Women are seen as more fully and entirely sexual and passional than men; what moves

their bodies is what moves men's spirits. There is thus a male-female continuity here as vital as the link between Brutus and Portia or Coriolanus and Volumnia. Sexual politics, family politics, and the body politic form a series of interconnected meanings.

24. As I argue below, I think it is a misreading to view Cicero as the embodiment of an ideal republicanism. This replaces the humanists' Cicero with the one in the play, as Ornstein, for one, notes in *The Moral Vision of Jacobean Tragedy*, pp. 97 ff., esp. 102-3, where the Machiavellianism of Cicero is appreciated. Ornstein echoes Joseph Allen Bryant, who also finds Cicero the central machiavel in the play, in "*Catiline* and the Nature of Jonson's Tragic Fable," *PMLA* 69 (1954): 265-77. Whereas Bryant finds Cicero to be unaware of Caesar's powers, Ornstein justly sees the confrontation of two masters of duplicity. Like Sejanus, then, Catiline is undone by those who play at being what he would really be. Contemning mere acting, Catiline is less active and less articulate than Cicero, doing nothing, which marks the fullness of the power he aspires to. It is for this reason, because of the nature of power that he embodies, that the play is as static and lethargic as critics complain it is.

Perhaps the most vigorous attempt to argue that the mirroring of Catiline and Cicero is meant to suggest differences is Garbriele Bernhard Jackson's in *Vision and Judgment in Ben Jonson's Drama* (New Haven: Yale University Press, 1968), pp. 159-68; she offers as well a brief and telling account of the imagery of masking in the play on pp. 128-30. Although I do not agree that "Cicero brings together the roles of prince, judge, and artist" (p. 37, see the entire discussion pp. 31 ff.), Jackson remains a valuable guide to the language of the play, if not to its ultimate moral complexity.

25. All citations from *The Roman Actor* are from the *The Plays and Poems of Philip Massinger*, ed. Philip Edwards and Colin Ginson, 5 vols. (Oxford: At the Clarendon Press, 1976), vol. 3.

In *The Tragedy of Nero* (1624), ed. Elliot M. Hill (New York: Garland Publishing Inc., 1979), there is a similar, although far less fully developed, confluence of theatricality and *Romanitas*. Nero opens the play celebrating his peaceful victories, triumphs that take the form of "Singing, Dancing, Horse-rase, Stage-playing" (1:2, line 9), and the conspirators find a continuity between his murderousness, his lasciviousness, and his theatricality: "Is he not a Parracide, a Player" (1:4, line 107), they ask; almost their last complaint about him is that "Caesar has now become/A Player on the stage" (4:5, lines 7-8). Although Caesar dies by his own hand, and not by the conspirators', they plot to kill him in the essential public place, "on the Stage/And so too truely make't a Tragedy" (2:3, lines 120-21). The most theatrical events occur in act 3 where there is a report of Nero playing Orestes "To the life" (3:2, line 4;), and keeping his audience (literally) captive, then killing those spectators less than pleased with his performance (every actor's dream). He claims that this is "the sceane that I would have" (3:4, line 22), confirming what others had wished earlier (3:3), that Caesar might be confined to being a stage tyrant. Finally, when Caesar discovers that his enemies have overwhelmed his forces, he is left alone to strip off the "vizard, shadow, nothing (Maiestie)" (4:3, line 25), but not so entirely as to fail to theatricalize his suicide: "O *Rome*, farewell, farewell you Theaters,/Where oft, with popular applause/In song; action—" (5:3, lines 135-37); these are his dying words.

Nero's connection with ancient theater was well known; Heywood and *Hamlet* afford ample evidence. As David Scott Kastan notes in *"Nero* and the Politics of Nathaniel Lee," *Papers on Language and Literature* 13 (1977): 125-35, Nero continued to have strong political meaning into the Restoration as the crystallized image of royal prerogative and absolutism. The Nero of the 1624 play also delivers political speeches with those implications. These are theatricalized, too; absolutism expresses the royal pleasure (2:2) and prerogative (see line 75); tyranny is placed as a scene.

26. All citations from the Penguin edition of *Hamlet,* ed. Willard Farnham (Baltimore, 1957).

27. Jonson's letter to Salisbury is printed in vol. 1 of Herford and Simpson, *Ben Jonson,* and on p. 221 of the edition of *Eastward Ho,* ed. R. W. Van Fossen (Baltimore: Johns Hopkins University Press, 1979). Equally typical is Chapman's letter to James (p. 218), in which the monarch is asked to show "Caesar-like Bountie." For Chapman, this involves the typical paradoxical display of power that the Caesar in his *Pompey and Caesar* displayed; James is to be like Caesar "who Conquerd still to spare the Conquerd: and was glad of offences that he might forgive." Power is displayed in self-defeat.

5. Social Texts, Royal Measures

1. *Letters to Severall Persons of Honour,* ed. Charles Edmund Merrill, Jr. (New York: Sturgis & Walton Co., 1910), p. 260. Subsequent references to *Letters* in the text are to this edition.

2. All references cited from John Donne, *Devotions Upon Emergent Occasions,* ed. Anthony Raspa (Montreal: McGill-Queen's University Press, 1975).

3. *The Sermons of John Donne,* ed. George R. Potter and Evelyn M. Simpson, 10 vols. (Berkeley and Los Angeles: University of California Press, 1953-62), 1:209. Subsequent references to *Sermons* in the text are to this edition.

4. To Mrs. Martha Garet he says, "I am willing to confesse my impotencie" (*Letters,* p. 35); he is "nothing" (*Letters,* pp. 57, 240) and frequently reports himself dead or moribund (*Letters,* pp. 77, 105, 120, 132, 202). In "John Donne and the Rewards of Patronage," in *Patronage in the Renaissance,* ed. Guy F. Lytle and Stephen Orgel (Princeton: Princeton University Press, 1981), Arthur Marotti emphasizes Donne's continuous engagement with the court, so that even anticourtly statements reflect this preoccupation.

5. See Walton, *The Lives* (London: Henry Washbourne, 1847), pp. 31, 33-34, 38. Subsequent references in the text are to this edition.

6. *John Donne: Life, Mind, and Art* (New York: Oxford University Press, 1981), pp. 113 ff. He is lieutenant again in *Sermons,* 4:209. He is repeatedly *rex pacificus.*

7. *Pseudo-Martyr,* intro. Francis J. Sypher (Delmar: N.Y.: Scholars Facsimiles & Reprints, 1974), sig. A3r. Further citations are to this edition.

8. See *The Letters of John Chamberlain,* ed. Norman McClure, 2 vols. (Philadelphia: American Philosophical Society, 1939), 1:591.

9. R. C. Bald, in *John Donne: A Life* (Oxford: At the Clarendon Press, 1970), remarks of the story of James calling Donne to dinner to give him St.

Paul's that "the story is suspect, for Aubrey tells a very similar anecdote about Bishop Andrewes . . . and it looks very much as if the same basic tale was told and retold of different participants" (p. 374).

10. The position articulated here is supported, I believe, by Don E. Wayne's essay, "Poetry and Power in Ben Jonson's *Epigrammes:* The Naming of 'Facts' or the Figuring of Social Relations?," *Renaissance and Modern Studies* 23 (1979): 79–103. For Wayne, Jonson's poems "concretize and thereby criticize a historical and existential situation" (p. 101); both satiric and epideitic impulses stem from a single source, metacommunicative, "the expression of a contradiction" (p. 102).

Isabel Rivers, in *The Poetry of Conservatism, 1600–1745: A Study of Poets and Public Affairs from Jonson to Pope* (Cambridge: Rivers Press, 1973), claims that public poetry re-creates society (p. ix) and that Jonson "combined a deliberate self-distancing . . . with a conviction that traditional forms of society were valid and, with his collaboration, could be made to work" (p. 21). Hence, Jonson was the voice of both court and country, of individual self-sufficiency and inevitable social engagement (see pp. 70–71 for a summary of Jonson's "amphibiousness").

My terms are indebted, too, to Stephen Greenblatt's provocative essay, "Invisible Bullets: Renaissance Authority and Its Subversion," *Glyph 8: Johns Hopkins Textual Studies* (Baltimore: Johns Hopkins University Press, 1981), pp. 40–61.

11. For Jonson's biography I depended upon the account in vol. 1 of *Ben Jonson*, ed. C. H. Herford and Percy and Evelyn Simpson, 11 vols. (Oxford: At the Clarendon Press, 1925–52). All citations from Jonson's works, unless otherwise noted, are drawn from this edition. *Epigrammes (Ep), The Forrest (For), The Under-Wood (UW), Ungathered Verse (UV),* and *Discoveries (Disc)* are in volume 8.

12. The tag appears at the end of the *Panegyre*, in *Discoveries* (8:637), and is the animating force behind the fourth epigram.

13. William Alexander McClung, *The Country House in English Renaissance Poetry* (Berkeley and Los Angeles: University of California Press, 1977), emphasizes the nature of the country house and its moral meanings; his account depends upon such treatments as G. A. Hibbard's, "The Country House Poem of the Seventeenth Century," *Journal of the Warburg and Courtauld Institutes* 19 (1956): 159–74, reprinted in *Essential Articles for the Study of Alexander Pope,* ed. Maynard Mack (Hamden, Conn.: Archon Books, 1964). Hibbard finds that the poem represents a slightly idealized social norm (p. 403); he stresses the role of the house as the nexus of social and natural relationships (pp. 412–13), a vital center. Similar views about the poem are expressed by George Parfitt in *Ben Jonson: Public Poet and Private Man* (New York: Barnes & Noble, 1976); "Jonson's social ethic is basically simple and traditional" (p. 147), he claims, and the ideal in "To Penshurst" "is not impossibly distant from the conceivable reality" (p. 152), which embraces such notions as hierarchy and social decorum. These views can also be found in Hugh Maclean's "Ben Jonson's Poems: Notes on the Ordered Society," in *Essays in English Literature from the Renaissance to the Victorian Age Presented to A.S.P. Woodhouse,* ed. Millar MacLure and F. Watt (Toronto: University of Toronto Press, 1964), pp. 43–68. Isabel Rivers, in *The Poetry of Conservatism,* reads "To Penshurst" as a microcosm of society (p. 40) which,

nonetheless, shows Jonson's sense of the breakdown between the country and the court (p. 50); hence, for Rivers "To Sir Robert Wroth" exhibits more fully the anticourt side of Jonson; as Rivers goes on to argue, however, the masques exhibit a double attitude toward the court, pro in the figure of James, anti in the antimasques (pp. 52 ff.).

Jonson has been attacked for unthinkingly espousing Jacobean ideology (mystifying nature as an image of society, failing to recognize the oppression upon which Penshurst was reared) by Raymond Williams in *The Country and the City* (New York: Oxford University Press, 1973), pp. 27-34; he has been answered by William E. Cain in "The Place of the Poet in Jonson's 'To Penshurst' and 'To My Muse,'" *Criticism* 21 (1979): 34-48; Cain argues that Jonson knows what Williams insists he ignores.

14. On the role of fantasy in Jonson's poems, see the crucially important treatment by Arthur Marotti, "All About Jonson's Poetry," *ELH* 39 (1972): 208-37. Marotti's Jonson is divided between Apollonian and Dionysian impulses, restraint and release. Food fantasies are Jonson's characteristic expressions of oral prodigality, and "To Penshurst," for all its neoclassic restraints, portrays nature as essentially edible (p. 217), so that even the country girls are ripe for plucking.

15. Naming is vitally important in Jonson's poetry as Eric Partridge points out in "Jonson's *Epigrammes:* The Named and the Nameless," *Studies in the Literary Imagination* 6 (1973): 153-98; the relation of names and facts is considered by Wayne, "Poetry and Power," 85-87, where Wayne argues that names point beyond facts and persons to the structures of social relations. The discussion of negation and dismissals in Jonson that follows depends upon Richard C. Newton's illuminating essay, "'Ben./Jonson': The Poet in the Poems," in *Two Renaissance Mythmakers*, ed. Alvin Kernan (Baltimore: Johns Hopkins University Press, 1977), pp. 165-95, esp. pp. 166 ff. Newton's Jonson like Marotti's balances oppositions; his are Sidneian and Baconian, lyrical and empirical impulses. On Jonson's materialism and empiricism see also Wayne, pp. 94 ff.

16. Stephen Orgel suggests the masquelike nature of Jonson's poems, particularly "To Sir Robert Wroth," on pp. 190-94 of *The Jonsonian Masque* (Cambridge, Mass.: Harvard University Press, 1965).

17. The most explicit statement about the meaning of Sidney occurs in *Ep.* 79, where the poet is a progenitor in the flesh and of the word; see also Newton, "'Ben./Jonson': The Poet in the Poems," pp. 184-89.

18. On this, see Richard Helgerson, "The Elizabethan Laureate: Self-Presentation and the Literary System," *ELH* 46 (1979): 193-220, esp. pp. 213 ff. on the humanistic tradition and Jonson's self-proclaimed laureateship; Helgerson concludes by seeing the laureates as testing the values of their society and, ultimately, finding them to come up short—hence his laureates, like my presentation of Jonson, re-present the contradictions of society. For the argument that Renaissance poetic theory always involves social engagement, see Jane P. Tompkins, "The Reader in History: The Changing Shape of Literary Response," in *Reader-Response Criticism: From Formalism to Post-Structuralism*, ed. Jane P. Tompkins (Baltimore: Johns Hopkins University Press, 1980), pp. 206-11.

19. This is what Thomas M. Greene points to in "Ben Jonson and the Centered Self," *Studies in English Literature* 10 (1970): 325-48; his thesis about the

tension between the centered self within the circles of society and cosmos and the isolated self turned in upon itself is taken up by Don E. Wayne. Wayne argues that this difference is ultimately no difference at all, that in either case—whether treating isolates or ideal selves—Jonson presents a world of fragmentation and enclosure ("Poetry and Power," 90–92). Such isolation affects Jonson's verse, or so George A.E. Parfitt argues in "Compromise Classicism: Language and Rhythm in Ben Jonson's Poetry," *Studies in English Literature* 11 (1971): 109–23, esp. pp. 119–21. The essays of Newton and Marotti alluded to earlier end in search of the Jonsonian center.

20. Helgerson, "Elizabethan Laureate," p. 215.

21. *Renaissance Self-Fashioning: From More to Shakespeare* (Chicago: University of Chicago Press, 1980), pp. 222 ff., esp. pp. 227–28, 252–54.

22. In, for example, *Shakespeare's History Plays* (1944; reprint, New York: Collier Books, 1962). Perhaps the most useful account of Shakespeare's relation to the political and social beliefs of his time is W. Gordon Zeeveld's *The Temper of Shakespeare's Thought* (New Haven: Yale University Press, 1974).

23. Citations from Marston's *The Dutch Courtesan*, ed. Peter Davison (Berkeley and Los Angeles: University of California Press, 1968).

24. Citations from the Penguin edition, ed. R. C. Bald (Baltimore, 1956). The topicality of *Measure for Measure* is the burden of Josephine Waters Bennet's *Measure for Measure as Royal Entertainment* (New York: Columbia University Press, 1966) and an appendix to David Lloyd Stevenson, *The Achievement of Shakespeare's Measure for Measure* (Ithaca: Cornell University Press, 1966). Occasional arguments are the subject of Richard Levin's attack, "The King James Version of *Measure for Measure*," *Clio* 3 (1974): 129–96 (reprinted in his *New Readings vs. Old Plays* [Chicago: University of Chicago Press, 1979]) and his debate over Roy Battenhouse's "*Measure for Measure* and King James," *Clio* 7 (1977): 193–215, in *Clio* 7 (1977): 217–26. Levin characteristically attacks straw men; Battenhouse's predictably theological reading (in which James is lectured by Shakespeare for not being a Catholic) is easily answered, as are the literalisms of much topical criticism. Still, as Battenhouse says ("*Measure for Measure* and King James," p. 221), Levin is merely a skeptic, and he sidesteps any real confrontation with the play. It is surely incontrovertible that Shakespeare is of his time; the question is how to describe that relation accurately, not to dismiss it out of hand.

25. This point is made by J. Dover Wilson in the New Cambridge edition, and by John Wasson in "*Measure for Measure*: A Text for Court Performance?," *Shakespeare Quarterly* 21 (1970): 17–24. J. W. Lever in the Arden edition points to many of the limits in this argument about the text.

26. The most cogent treatment of this point is Nancy S. Leonard's, "Substitution in Shakespeare's Problem Comedies," *English Literary Renaissance* 9 (1979): 281–301.

27. *Measure for Measure as Royal Entertainment*, p. 137.

28. The Duke's double form leads to a particularly breathtaking display of power when he consigns Mariana to Angelo: "I have confessed her and I know her virtue" (5:1, line 522). This seems to be an ultimate violation of privacy, and a demonstration of the confluence of sovereign power with the confessional. It is comprehended in the argument of Michel Foucault's *The History of Sexuality*, trans. Robert Hurley (New York: Pantheon Books, 1978). Foucault argues that

the law that maintains sovereignty is entangled with the law that constitutes desire (see e.g., pp. 81, 113); the confession is the form of discourse in which sex is made to speak, and the history of sexuality is the history of its being put into discourse. Sexuality is not, for Foucault, a natural phenomenon but "a historical construct" (p. 105, cf. pp. 155–57), and in sexuality one has a "dense transfer point for relations of power" (p. 103). In *Measure for Measure*, the Duke's two forms—as Angelo and as friar—are forms of the virtues upon which government rests, justice and religion. Both meet in sexuality in the play, the underlying privacy dragged into public.

29. In *Shakespeare and Society* (New York: Schocken Books, 1967), Terence Eagleton sees the crime of Claudio and Julietta as their attempt to keep sexual union private; "Personal action, to be real, must be available for social verification" (p. 67).

30. On the meanings of *sense* and for a reading of the play that emphasizes much that is unsettling in it, see William Empson's "Sense in *Measure for Measure*" in *The Structure of Complex Words* (Ann Arbor: University of Michigan Press, 1967). For a reading of the play in which theatricality casts doubt upon the Duke's powers and virtues, see Ann Righter [Barton], *Shakespeare and the Idea of the Play* (London: Chatto & Windus, 1962; Harmondsworth: Penguin, 1967), pp. 158–62.

31. *Hamlet,* ed. Willard Farnham (Baltimore: Penguin, 1957).

Tailpiece

1. All citations from the Penguin edition, ed. Robert B. Heilman, (Baltimore, 1964). I can find nothing of value in the topical reading of the play provided by Frances A. Yates in *Majesty and Magic in Shakespeare's Last Plays* (Boulder: Shambhala, 1978). The identification she suggests (the three royal children as James's; Posthumus as the Elector Palatine; the Welsh scene as derivative from the celebrations of Prince Henry's investiture as Prince of Wales)—some of which have been suggested by other Shakespeare critics, as she notes—fly in the face of the evidence that the play presents. Like Josephine Waters Bennett, Yates is guilty of the most limited notion of how a text may reflect its historical period, literalistic reproduction. Yet, to produce such reflections, Yates is forced to ignore most of the play and to rewrite the parts that suit her. This is not to restore the play to history as she claims, but to fit it to her mystical belief that all of Renaissance history was building to some grand love feast at the beginning of the seventeenth century.

INDEX

References to illustrations are in italics.

Adelman, Janet, 280–81n.19
Arcana imperii: absolutist trope, xiv, 68–69, 85, 116; Donne's, 82; political, 68, 177; religious, 80; sources, 68, 243n.14; uses of, artistic, 106–7, 116
Ariès, Philippe, 86, 89, 259n.42
Artaud, Antonin, 154
Arundel, Earl of, 248n.42

Bacon, Sir Francis, 21, 50, 68, 87, 224, 276–77n.7
Barkan, Leonard, 256n.30, 279n.15
Baron, Hans, 75
Barthes, Roland, 154
Bedford, Lucy, Countess of, 211, 212, 227, 228
Benjamin, Walter, 152
Bennett, Josephine Waters, 232–33
Bergeron, David, 29, 247n.33
Bodleian, Old Schools Quadrangle, 35, *38–39, 39*
Bowes, Robert, 1, 2, 3
Bryskett, Lodowick, 245n.14
Buckingham, Duke of (George Villiers), 24, 71, 76, 84, 105, 129, 130, 137–39, 142, 143–46, 220, 222

Cabinet-Council, 69. *See also* Ralegh, Sir Walter
Carey, John, 213
Carr, Robert. *See* Somerset, Earl of
Carr, Sir Robert, 132, 210, 216
Cavell, Stanley, 275n.2
Cecil, Robert. *See* Salisbury, Earl of
Chamberlain, John, 165, 213, 251 n.1, 256nn.32, 33, 262n.57, 263 n.1
Chapman, George: career, 134, 204, 283n.27; Works: *Andromeda Liberata,* 133–34; *Bussy d'Ambois,* 155–61, 163, 176, 189, 195; language and power in, 155–57, 158; privacy and absolutism in, 157, 159–60; Roman style in, 157, 160–61; *Caesar and Pompey,* 279–80n.16, 283n.27; *Hymns of Homer,* dedication, 134; *Iliads,* epistle dedicatory, 134; *Revenge of Bussy, The,* 274n.48

Charles I, 91, 94, 97, *98,* 143, 144, 210, 220, 240, 251n.1
Coins, 43, *45,* 46
Contarino, Gasparo, 76–77
Coryat, Thomas, 77–78, 255n.29

Daniel, Samuel, 58, 266–67n.13
De Fontenay, 25–26, 82, 83, 256n.33
Dekker, Thomas, 30, 31, 43, 51
Demos, John, 259n.45
Dempsey, Charles, 272–73n.44
Derrida, Jacques, 151, 154, 272nn.41, 43
Des Granges, David, 97, 99, *104*
D'Ewes, Sir Simonds, 84, 143
Divine Right, 84, 94, 117, 119, 135, 232, 236
Dobson, William, 99–100, *106*
Donne, John: career, 87, 210–13, 218–19. Works: *Anniversarie, The,* 66; *Canonization, The,* 46, 65–67, 81, 84, 87, 253n.12; dedicatory poem to *Coryat's Crudities,* 77; *Devotions Upon Emergent Occasions,* 81–82, 210–11, 212, 214, 215, 216, 218; *Ecclogue* and *Epithalamium,* 131–33, 136, 212, 237, 267n.19; *Letters to Severall Persons of Honour,* 210–12, 214, 216, 219, 283n.4; *Pseudo-Martyr,* 213, 214; sermon: at Paul's Cross, 211, 213, 217; —over corpse of James I, 210, 215–18; *Sunne Rising, The,* 107, 111–12
Donzelot, Jacques, 89–90, 260n.46
Drummond, William, 221, 223–24
Dugdale, Gilbert, 33

Elizabeth I: and James I, 2, 11, 27–28, 113; letters to, 16; London entrance (1558/9) of, 29–30, 31, 33, 247n.34, 250n.57; and Mary Queen of Scots, 11, 16, 116; representations of, 43, 45, *48,* 90, 159, 163, 262–63n.1; and Spenser, 1, 3, 10–11, 28
Elizabeth of Bohemia: marriage of, 81, 91, 94, 97, *99,* 107, 231
Elton, G. R., 84
Essex, Earl of (Robert Devereux), 29, 163

289

54; "Lord Bacons Birth-day" (*UW:* 51), 224; *Love Restored*, 126, 267 n.16; *Lovers Made Men*, 252-53n.8; *Love's Triumph through Callipolis*, 67, 97; *Masque of Augurs*, 84, 249 n.49; *Masque of Beauty*, 59-60, 64; *Masque of Blackness*, 57, 59; *Masque of Queens*, 57-58, 64, 87-88, 99; *Mercury Vindicated from the Alchemists at Court*, 60-61, 62, 64, 69, 88, 128; *Neptune's Triumph*, 71-72, 73, 131; "New Crie, The" (*Ep:* 92), 69-70, 72, 74, 80; *News from the New World*, 64-65, 70, 72, 127-28; *Oberon*, 123-26; "Panegyre, on the Happie Entrance of James, A," 120-24; *Pan's Anniversary, or the Shepherd's Holiday*, 130-31; *Pleasure Reconciled to Virtue*, 62-64, 67, 83-84, 126-27; *Prince Henry's Barriers*, 40, 42; *Sejanus*, 142, 176-85, 192, 193, 203-4, 220, 231; and *Julius Caesar*, 178, 182, 185-86; observation in, 177, 178, 179-81; style of gods in, 179, 181, 183; theatricality and power in, 177-80, 182-85; "To Elizabeth Countesse of Rutland" (*Ep:*79), 285n.17; "To King James" (*Ep:* 4), 17-18; "To King James" (*Ep:* 35), 224; "To Lucy, Countesse of Bedford, with Mr. Donnes Satyres" (*Ep:* 94), 227; "To Penshurst" (*For:* 2), 223-24, 225-26, 228; king and poet in, 224, 228; King James in, 223, 226, 228; language in, 225-26; society in, 226; "To Robert Earle of Salisburie" (*Ep:* 43), 227, 229; "To Robert Earle of Salisburie" (*Ep:* 63), 224; "To Robert Earle of Salisburie. Upon the accession of the Treasure-ship to him" (*Ep:* 64), 229-30; "To Sir Henrie Savile" (*Ep:* 95), 230; "To Sir Robert Wroth" (*For:* 3), 223, 228-29; "To the Ghost of Martial" (*Ep:* 36), 209; "To Thomas Earle of Suffolke" (*Ep:* 67), 224; "To Thomas Lo: Elsmere" (*UW:* 31), 224; *Vision of Delight, The*, 61-62, 64, 67, 88; *Volpone*, 72-74, 77, 79-80, 81, 91, 94, 104, 107, 227

Laing, R. D., 89
Lever, J. W., 274n.48

Lewkenor, Lewes. *See* Contarini, Gasparo
Lindenberger, Herbert, 277n.10

Machiavelli, 75, 78-79; and Chapman, 155; and Shakespeare, 161; and Spenser, 6, 9, 244n.9
MacPherson, C. B., 266n.10
Marcelline, George, 34-35
Marcus, Leah Sinanoglou, 47, 253n.9, 257n.39
Marston, John, 220, 231
Mary Queen of Scots, xiv; and James I, 15; trial and death of, 12-14, 17, 246n.18. *See also* James I; Spenser, Edmund
Massinger, Philip: Works: *Roman Actor, The*, 203-9, 221; observation and spying in, 207, 208; public and private in, 207-8; style of gods in, 205, 206; theatricality and power in, 203-7, 208, 209
Mathew, David, 139
Matthew, Sir Tobie, 145
Molin, Nicolo, 83, 256n.34. *See also* Venice
Montrose, Louis Adrian, 271-72n.38
Moretti, Franco, 271n.37
Mountin, Gerrit, 94, *96*
Mullaney, Steven, 264n.7
Mytens, Daniel, 97, *102*

Nagel, Thomas, 272n.39

Orgel, Stephen, 71, 123, 249n.49, 252n.6, 267nn.14, 15, 272n.2, 285 n.16
Osborne, Francis, 143, 269n.31

Petowe, Henry, 43
Player King: and political representation, 113-15, 116, 118, 140; and royal representation, 134, 136, 147-50, 176, 192-93, 209, 263n.1; and theatrical representation, 152-55, 165, 168, 263n.1
Pocock, J.G.A., 76, 78, 115-16, 255 n.27, 263-64n.4, 164-65n.8, 273 n.46
Pot, Henrick Gerritsz, 97, 99, *103*
Puttenham, George, 69

Ralegh, Sir Walter, 91, *95*, 254n.17
Randall, Dale, 128